REDPRINT

REDPRINT

OVERCOMING MANCHESTER UNITED'S IDENTITY CRISIS

Wayne Barton

First published by Pitch Publishing, 2019

Pitch Publishing
A2 Yeoman Gate
Yeoman Way
Worthing
Sussex
BN13 3QZ
www.pitchpublishing.co.uk
info@pitchpublishing.co.uk

A CIP catalogue record is available for this book
from the British Library.

ISBN 978 1 78531 554 1

Typesetting and origination by Pitch Publishing
Printed and bound by TJ International Ltd, Padstow, UK

Contents

Introduction

Identity matters. Of course it does. In May 2012 a global survey revealed that Manchester United had a reported 659 million supporters. Theoretically that means one in every 11 people on planet Earth is a fan of the Old Trafford club. If such a figure seems ridiculous then the statistic must be counter-balanced by evidence, and much of the evidence does at least suggest that Manchester United are the most popular sports franchise in the world.

The team Harry Gregg has dubbed 'the Hollywood of football' receive the superstar treatment wherever they are in the world; their global appeal never more apparent than in a 2014 pre-season friendly in Michigan, USA, where 109,318 fans packed into the Michigan Stadium to watch United face Real Madrid. Red shirts clearly outnumbered white shirts in the crowd. In 2017 Forbes listed Manchester United as the most valuable soccer franchise in the world, even after a four-year spell since winning their last Premier League title. The commercial appeal of having the likes of Wayne Rooney and Cristiano Ronaldo represent the 'brand' has also been an important factor, while the club have additionally transitioned into an era where it seems important to make statement signings. United have broken their own transfer record three times since Sir

Alex Ferguson retired in 2013, as opposed to the three times in the previous 12 years (and the July 2001 signing of Juan Sebastian Veron from Lazio for £28.1m came a few weeks after Ruud van Nistelrooy's own record £18m move which broke the record for the first time in three years). The glamour of breaking the club transfer record for Angel Di Maria, and then the world transfer record for Paul Pogba compensated — at least as far as their worldwide platform was concerned — for the lack of top-level trophies.

However, it was United's popularity that caused the commercial interest in the club. So, what caused the popularity? Of course, there is the notion that many started following the club due to their success. But even if we accept that has to be somewhat true, it cannot be entirely so. There is also the suggestion — and again, it is a suggestion that can't be completely dismissed — that after the Munich Air Disaster Manchester United attracted people who were sympathetic to their cause and keen to see how they would recover.

If the primary suggestion is to do with success, then maybe it's a good place to start. Manchester United are the most successful English club and have been for a while, even though busy revisionists down the M62 have continuously attempted to redefine what constitutes a 'major' trophy in order to preserve Liverpool's stake to that particular claim (for example, for a while, their European Super Cup trophies were cited, and United's 1999 Intercontinental Cup and 2008 Club World Cup were dismissed as minor trophies, presumably because the Anfield club have never won either incarnation of that trophy). Plenty of teams win trophies, however, and the reason most often given by those who are not of the locale of the club for their support is because of their enjoyment of that particular team's style of football.

It is altogether more satisfying from a purist's perspective if that style of football is synonymous with the club's history — Real Madrid supporters have long enjoyed their club's unapologetic approach to buying the best players in the world, Barcelona have the 'Cruyff' model, and Manchester United have, at the risk of paraphrasing something which is going to take a few thousand words more to elaborate upon, the reputation of counter-attacking football played by a majority of home-grown players, as well as a reputation for never giving in. What makes it even better for those clubs? Their greatest successes are drenched in the hallmark of their traditional brilliance. Whether it's Real Madrid's world-record signings scoring spectacular goals, Barcelona's tiki-taka being at its most imperious, or Manchester United's last gasp turnaround (or their George Best-inspired audacity), all three of the world's biggest clubs have their finest hours defined by their most noteworthy characteristics.

The purpose of this book is to examine what has happened to that identity of Manchester United since Sir Alex Ferguson retired, but, as the club's greatest-ever manager once said, to know your future as a United player, you must first know your history. There are a number of books and records that have the time to go into Sir Matt Busby's philosophies in much more detail, but his objective upon taking over the reins at Old Trafford was a relatively straightforward one — to provide a footballing team which would entertain the hard-working locals at the end of the week, and to do so with a team comprised of locally sourced and developed players. The latter part of that was also the shared vision of Walter Crickmer, Louis Rocca and James Gibson; though, considering the financial difficulties the club was suffering due to the bombing of Old Trafford in the Second World War, it is not exactly clear whether this was a proposal of necessity rather than one as visionary as it seems. However, given the qualities of the three gentlemen, it would be wise to give them the benefit of the doubt.

Certainly as far as Matt Busby was concerned, one can comfortably describe him as a visionary. Before the European Cup was even conceived, Busby was taking his Manchester United team on world tours — a glamorous 12-date tour of Canada and North America took in the bright lights of Los Angeles after the 1949/50 season concluded — to increase the profile of his club. They played against Atlas Club Mexico in LA where their presence in the city was acknowledged by a number of top Hollywood film stars and even the president of Mexico.

Still, even Matt Busby himself could not have comprehended the amount of work Jimmy Murphy would do for him after he spotted him training some soldiers in a camp in Bari towards the end of the war. Busby was enamoured by Murphy's passionate team talks, taken in by how determined he was for his team to win even though these games were effectively meaningless. He offered him a job looking after everything but the first team back in Manchester, and Murphy took those words literally and very seriously indeed. Helped by coaches Bert Whalley and Tom Curry, as well as chief scout Joe Armstrong, Murphy created a youth set-up that was the envy of the footballing universe. When United triumphed 10-0 against Anderlecht in September 1956, many sections of the British media declared that the Manchester team were the best in the world. This was a team which, faithful to the wish of Gibson and Rocca, was comprised of the best home-grown players. It was a team that won back-to-back league titles. However, more than that, it was the personality of the team and the way they played that won so many admirers throughout the country and continent. Aggressive, confident and with an insatiable appetite to have the football, the Manchester United young players were in the mould of their mentor, Jimmy Murphy.

Then Munich happened. Jimmy Murphy, and Matt Busby, did remarkable work to remain true to their shared philosophy, and even more remarkably, ten years later, after the disaster, they won a European Cup with all of their four goals in the final coming from home-grown players.

When Matt Busby retired, the club struggled in transition. Wilf McGuinness knew as much about the identity of Manchester United as anyone else. Frank O'Farrell was a gamble which didn't work out, and while it took him some time, Tommy Docherty restored the club to its Cup-winning glory in 1977. Docherty was sacked the same year and was replaced by an antithesis in the form of Dave Sexton. Sexton would be quiet and uncontroversial off the pitch — just what the directors wanted. He would also be defensive and conservative on it — just what the supporters *didn't* want.

Despite a second-place finish in 1980 and winning the last seven league games in 1981, the dissatisfaction from the United fans was not exactly restrained to a vocal minority, and so the flamboyant and quotable Ron Atkinson was hired in an attempt to recapture some of the flair of the Docherty era.

Atkinson's arrival was a significant one in the history of Manchester United, even if it was a reluctant appointment from the board. 'Big' Ron was an outstanding candidate, of that there is no doubt, and his time at the club won many admirers. But the directors braced themselves for the potential of more controversy — controversy that never really came, it should be added — and in doing so, sent out something of a message to the football world. The personality of the Manchester United manager was an important factor, as was the style of the football played by the team. After the stunning run of form at the start of the 1985/86 season fell apart, Atkinson's view of a solution was to make short-term signings which a) appeared to be a gamble and b) only served to disillusion the senior professionals at the club. The short-term approach didn't work, and Atkinson was on his way.

The 1989 protests came against a backdrop of a failed takeover bid and unfulfilled promises; when United lost four games out of five in December, the speculation that Alex Ferguson would be sacked was mounting. We all know how that turned out, but for the sake of completion, the board gave Ferguson the time to see his masterplan bear the fruit it promised to. And the plan was good, very good. An FA Cup, European Cup Winners' Cup, European Super Cup, League Cup, a Premier League and a League and FA Cup double had already been delivered before the mass influx of youth-team players into the first team.

In 1977 United had four youth products starting the FA Cup Final (David McCreery, the substitute, made it five in the team on the day). Two started the 1985 Cup Final, with Mike Duxbury from the bench making it three. A decent number — favourably comparable with any other trophy-winning side — but United's hopes were greater. In the 1996 FA Cup Final, four youth products started, and two came off the bench. Sir Alex Ferguson's 1999 Champions League Final squad also featured six players. Whilst it wasn't quite the number of the 1950s, it was nonetheless a staggering achievement in the modern age; when senior players were injured, chances were given to young players instead of hastily bought foreign imports.

The main strength of the 'Class of 1992' was undoubtedly in midfield. David Beckham, Nicky Butt, Paul Scholes and Ryan Giggs formed an imposing foursome even without the driving force of Roy Keane. The other mainstays, Gary and Phil Neville, played the majority of their careers at full-back, working in tandem with Beckham or Giggs. Forget the talismanic leadership of Eric Cantona, forget the stellar roll-call of talent who played alongside them, Manchester United would not have enjoyed the success they did without the benefit of the natural chemistry that developed through playing six young players who had come through the same system and knew each other inside and out.

Under Busby, and particularly Murphy, training routines were centred around repetition of simple things. Pass and move. Always keep the ball, and yourself, moving. Never allow an opponent a second's peace. Straightforward principles which should be the basics of any good game plan, and, drummed as they were into the mind of gifted young players, principles which became their natural instinct when playing on a Saturday. Of course, it helped that the player playing next to them was also schooled on the same methods. It meant that they could depend upon them. The repetition of the drills meant that each player understood the movement of those around them. The importance of working hard on self-improvement was constantly driven into the players, and this was passed down as an example through the ranks. Imagine being a youngster watching Bobby Charlton being told to work repeatedly on his left foot? Or a young academy hopeful watching David Beckham stay behind in training to relentlessly work on his crossing, even after he has risen to fame by scoring a goal from the half-way line? The message: skill is all well and good, but there is no substitute for hard work. Add into the melting pot the fact that many were local lads — and if not they were United fans anyway — and they not only had an added determination for their team not to lose, but they were working for each other. Suddenly, their repeated comebacks and late victories begin to make perfect sense.

Paul McGuinness, former United youth-team coach and son of Wilf, spoke about a game in the 2011 FA Youth Cup run. Chelsea were 2-0 up in the first leg of the semi-final and their coach told Paul that he was going to tell his team to be wary because United never give up. That was music to the ears of McGuinness, who went and repeated the conversation to his own team. 'So make sure you do keep going, because they will get tired.' United scored two crucial away goals and won in the second leg en route to winning the trophy. Their reputation for recovery, earned through the ages going back to the physical recovery after Munich and then relegation in 1974, the

1968 semi-final fightback against Real Madrid, the 1984 turnaround against Barcelona, and of course 1999, a year which had so many late turnarounds and yet one is remembered more than any other, had almost become a player of its own.

There are moments for the sporting romantics to positively coo over in United's history, the heartbreaking, bittersweet Wembley triumph of 1968 being possibly the most noteworthy. How about winning the treble with a last-minute goal on Sir Matt Busby's birthday? Or how about Ryan Giggs breaking the club's appearance record and scoring the decisive penalty to help win United their third European Cup?

Most of all, though, football supporters are generally attracted to a certain style of football, and, generally, even if forced into it by family heritage (one of those wonderful oddities sport throws at us), we find ourselves strangely defensive of the brand of football our club has a reputation for playing. You never hear, for example, of a fourth-generation United fan who just loves watching the way Liverpool play. And why would you? That is *sacrilege* in football parlance. You would never find a Tottenham Hotspur supporter who admired 'Boring, Boring Arsenal' and just can't get enough of the reinvention of the Gunners' style into a possession-based game Arsene Wenger has favoured on the expansive Emirates Stadium pitch. We like what we like, even if we were forced to like it. On the same train of thought, you're unlikely to find a supporter who is apologetic for the way their team plays if it is successful. Chelsea's late 1990s team were just as influential in leading the foreign invasion as Arsenal were — in fact, on Boxing Day 1999 Chelsea became the first team to field a complete team without a single British player in it. Instead of being panned for setting a dangerous trend, Chelsea were heralded as pioneers of the new post-Bosman era of football, and their cosmopolitan brand of football was a reasonable argument. Throughout the decade, the Stamford Bridge club had fielded the likes of Ruud Gullit, Gianfranco Zola and Gianluca Vialli, three indisputable legends of the European game. None of them were present for that December '99 game against Southampton, and even though high-standard players such as Frank Leboeuf, Dan Petrescu, Didier Deschamps and Roberto Di Matteo played, it's hard not to think that Emerson Thome and Gabrielle Ambrosetti were not pioneers of a different kind — fairly average squad players blocking the way for a young British player. In December 2014 *The Express* journalist Niall Hickman wrote a retrospective feature on the game, quoting the poet WB Yeats — '*All changed, changed utterly, a terrible beauty is born*'.

Vialli was unapologetic; and when Roman Abramovich took over, and it became less about the football and more about the winning, the entire philosophy of Chelsea as a football club was unapologetic as Jose Mourinho arrived and implemented a defensive strategy that won the Premier League at a canter. That 2004/05 season included 11 1-0 wins and a staggering 25 clean sheets.

On the other end of the scale, Arsenal supporters have long claimed their side to be the best footballing side in the country, endorsed by a section of the media faithful to Wenger even if the proof hasn't exactly been forthcoming. Arsenal were presented as the neutral's team of choice because of how they played football, but their side from 2006 to the present day was never as convincing in possession as Chelsea, never as devastating on the counter-attack as Manchester United, and never as stylish as either when it came to the crunch. And as soon as they had been declared to be a wonderful footballing outfit, Barcelona came along and did everything Arsenal professed to do, only better, and much more successfully. It's easier for us to confess to admiring a foreign team — it's more neutral, less treasonable. And still, as is their right, Arsenal supporters defend their claim to being the 'purist's' choice, although the older, more time-served supporters are appreciative of the difference between football that looks good and football that is good and effective.

Manchester City's modern identity has never settled due to the repeated hiring and firing of their managers during their post-2007 boom; it could be said that they instead hired a manager in Pep Guardiola to finally install his own personality and philosophy on the club.

Meanwhile, at Liverpool the same sort of idea is being followed. Tribal bias aside, their successful defensive strategy of the 1980s was outdated as soon as the back-pass was outlawed, and so their transition was happening in more ways than one. Whether that should theoretically make things easier for incoming managers is a matter for other writers to consider, but what is true is that beyond the 'pass-and-move' idea, which is essentially applicable to any style of football, Liverpool supporters have been more obsessed with the idea of winning than they are precious about their 'identity'. In recent years, the following men have been hero-worshipped — Rafa Benitez, who, as a successful cup manager, was essentially a Mourinho-lite; Kenny Dalglish, whose legendary status at Anfield meant that the majority of the club's support sided with him during an incredibly ugly episode where he publicly defended Luis Suarez after he had been found guilty of racially abusing then-Manchester United player Patrice Evra; Brendan Rodgers, whose mannerisms drew comparisons to Ricky Gervais's character David Brent; and, most recently, at the time of writing, German Jurgen Klopp. Klopp was certainly a coup for Liverpool; his work at German club Borussia Dortmund made him one of the most desirable names in management alongside Pep Guardiola in the time before both came to England. His 'gegenpressing' style of football, lovingly dubbed 'heavy metal football', is a style that the Liverpool faithful are more than happy to not only watch on a weekly basis but also subscribe to as a superior brand. As, of course, they would. Consistent questions about the defensive deficiencies in Klopp's game plans did not deter fans from believing his way is the right way. Klopp was backed financially, and made the record signing of Virgil van Dijk. The Dutchman made a significant difference as Liverpool challenged for the Premier League, and won the Champions League, in 2019.

What makes Liverpool's plight so fascinating is that Manchester United have been tipped to suffer through the same sort of prolonged heartache in the league. Three years after United decided to hire David Moyes when Jose Mourinho was available, Mourinho finally arrived at Old Trafford. On one hand he was armed with a blank chequebook to strengthen the squad; on the other, it would only have been on undertaking the job and working at the club that he would have experienced the depth of the malaise. In some respects, United had to do what City and Liverpool had to — hire a manager with a reputation of his own, a reputation that was perhaps not completely conducive to the club's style of play, and embrace that change which may well be the way forward. When they first set out on the post-Ferguson journey, continuation was the buzz word. 'Cut from the same cloth' was the headline used on United's official website to describe David Moyes's capability to continue the work done by Sir Alex Ferguson. There can be no question that the story of United's regeneration begins on 8 May 2013 — the day Ferguson announced his retirement from football.

The blood drained from my face

Shortly after 8am on Wednesday, 8 May 2013, following almost 48 hours of speculation, Manchester United announced that Sir Alex Ferguson would be retiring from his role as manager at the end of the season.

'The decision to retire is one that I have thought a great deal about and one that I have not taken lightly,' Ferguson said in an officially released statement. 'It is the right time. It was important to me to leave an organisation in the strongest possible shape and I believe I have done so. The quality of this league-winning squad, and the balance of ages within it, bodes well for continued success at the highest level, whilst the structure of the youth set-up will ensure that the long-term future of the club remains a bright one. Our training facilities are amongst the finest in global sport and our home Old Trafford is rightfully regarded as one of the leading venues in the world. Going forward, I am delighted to take on the roles of both director and ambassador for the club. With these activities, along with my many other interests, I am looking forward to the future. I must pay tribute to my family; their love and support has been essential. My wife Cathy has been the key figure throughout my career, providing a bedrock of both stability and encouragement. Words are not enough to express what this has meant to me. As for my players and staff, past and present, I would like to thank them all for a staggering level of professional conduct and dedication that has helped to deliver so many memorable triumphs. Without their contribution, the history of this great club would not be as rich. In my early years, the backing of the board, and Sir Bobby Charlton in particular, gave me the confidence and time to build a football club, rather than just a football team. Over the past decade, the Glazer family have provided me with the platform to manage Manchester United to the best of my ability and I have been extremely fortunate to have worked with a talented and trustworthy chief executive in David Gill. I am truly grateful to all of them. To the fans, thank you. The support you have provided over the years has been truly humbling. It has been an honour and an enormous privilege to have had the opportunity to lead your club and I have treasured my time as manager of Manchester United.'

Journalists were torn between writing plaudits and speculating as to who would be Ferguson's successor. Of the names suggested, Jose Mourinho and David Moyes quickly became the bookies' favourites from a list that included Pep Guardiola, Jurgen Klopp and Carlo Ancelotti. Most of the speculation as to who and why, and why not, turned out to be retrospective, as it quickly became apparent that it was Everton manager Moyes who would become 'The Chosen One'.

On 9 May, at 3.53pm, the club announced on their official website that the 'Manchester United Board unanimously approves the recommendation of Sir Alex Ferguson' in the appointment of David Moyes as the next manager. 'David Moyes will take over as the Manager of Manchester United from the 2013/14 season,' the club's statement to the Stock Exchange read. 'David, 50, has been the Everton manager since 2002, joining after a successful spell as manager of Preston North End.'

The statement included a number of endorsements from high-ranking officials at the club, beginning with the outgoing boss. 'When we discussed the candidates that we felt had the right attributes, we unanimously agreed on David Moyes,' Ferguson said. 'David is a man of great integrity with a strong work ethic. I've admired his work for a long time and approached him as far back as 1998 to discuss the position of assistant manager here. He was a young man then at the start of his career and has since gone on to do a magnificent job at Everton. There is no question he has all the qualities we expect of a manager at this club.'

Sir Bobby Charlton was quoted next. 'I have always said that we wanted the next manager to be a genuine Manchester United man,' he said. 'In David Moyes, we have someone who understands the things that make this such a special club. We have secured a man who is committed to the long term and will build teams for the future as well as now. Stability breeds success. David has tremendous strength of character and recognises the importance of bringing young players through and developing them alongside world-class talent. At United, I think David will be able to express himself. I'm delighted he has accepted and I'm looking forward to working with him.'

CEO Ed Woodward said, 'In David Moyes, we have secured the services of an outstanding manager who has all the skills to build on the phenomenal legacy in place today. I have no doubt that he will bring an energy and commitment to deliver winning football that is part of the fabric of this club. In this respect, he is cut from the same cloth as the Old Trafford greats who go before him. I have been very impressed by David's personal and managerial traits, which reflect the Manchester United values. I have no doubt that he will embrace, and soon become an integral part of, United's unique culture and heritage.'

Next, it was the turn of the Glazer family. 'I am very pleased David has agreed to lead Manchester United into the future,' said Joel Glazer. 'His hard-working style and steely determination are characteristics we value at the club. He has impressed as a coach for many years now and we strongly believe he will be able to take up from where Alex is leaving off by continuing this club's tradition of flair football played by exciting, world-class players.' Finally, Avram Glazer gave his opinion. 'The search for a new manager has been very short,' his statement read. 'Alex was very clear with his recommendation and we are delighted that David has agreed to accept the job. He comes to us with excellent credentials and a strong track record. I know he is keen to get started and Ed will be sitting down with him as soon as the season is over to discuss plans for the summer and beyond.'

All that was left was to hear from the man himself. Moyes's statement read, 'It's a great honour to be asked to be the next manager of Manchester United. I am delighted that Sir Alex saw fit to recommend me for the job. I have great respect for everything he has done and for the Football Club. I know how hard it will be to follow the best manager ever, but the opportunity to manage Manchester United isn't something that comes around very often and I'm really looking forward to taking up the post next season. I have had a terrific job at Everton, with a tremendous chairman and board of directors and a great set of players. Between now and the end of the season, I will do everything in my power to make sure we finish as high as possible in the table. Everton's fantastic fans have played a big part in making my years at Goodison so enjoyable and I thank them wholeheartedly for the support they have given me and the players. Everton will be close to me for the rest of my life.'

So far, so normal. With the benefit of nit-picking hindsight, one might look at the 'as high as possible' comment and think Moyes had made his first faux pas, but at the time nobody picked up on it. There were reservations, of course there were.

On 12 May, United defeated Swansea City 2-1 in Ferguson's final home game, fittingly enough, a victory delivered with a late goal. Afterwards, the club were awarded the Premier League trophy after a 13th successful league campaign under their retiring coach, and the man himself took centre stage to address the crowd. 'We've got a winner, that is really important for this club. To get a winner is the most important thing,' he said, before later telling the fans that 'their job now was to stand by the new manager.'

Moyes, of course, had never won a trophy in his career as a manager. The closest he'd come was in the 2009 FA Cup Final when his Everton team, who had defeated Ferguson's United side on penalties in the semi-final, came up short against Chelsea. Earlier in the year, Guardiola had announced that he would take over as Bayern Munich boss in the summer, following a short sabbatical after he had resigned as Barcelona manager. Some United supporters were unhappy, feeling that Ferguson and the also-outgoing chief executive David Gill might have been more proactive in sounding out the Spaniard. By far the most outstanding candidate, though, was Mourinho.

Having succeeded with Porto, Chelsea and Inter Milan (with European successes at the first and last of those clubs), Mourinho had spent three years at Real Madrid. In the 2011/12 season, Real enjoyed an incredible year, winning La Liga, scoring 121 goals and notching up 100 points in the process. The next season was not quite so outstanding; Mourinho described it as 'the worst of my career'. He had spent much of it battling with *Madridistas,* who did not agree with his treatment of goalkeeper Iker Casillas and his difficult relationship with defender Sergio Ramos. Mourinho also didn't cover himself with glory in an *El Clásico* where he poked Tito Vilanova in the eyes. It was obvious that his time in Spain was coming to an end, and 11 days after United's appointment of Moyes, it was announced that Mourinho was leaving Madrid by that old favourite 'mutual consent'. On the 3 June Mourinho was appointed by Chelsea for the second time.

Despite Moyes not officially starting in the role until early July, transfer speculation continued to rage, with most journalists suggesting similar names — Cesc Fabregas, Thiago and Mauroane Fellaini were all mentioned as potential midfielders, with Leighton Baines a possible addition at left-back. Tottenham Hotspur's Gareth Bale, who was destined to leave White Hart Lane, was the biggest name linked to United, if one is to accept and discount the yearly link of Cristiano Ronaldo. Meanwhile, the future of Wayne Rooney was the one pressing issue Moyes would have to deal with. Sir Alex had dropped a bombshell by revealing that Rooney had asked to leave the club — 'He came into my office the day after we won the League and asked away,' Ferguson said in his second autobiography, *My Autobiography.*

Ferguson's boast that he had left a squad in good shape was somewhat true, but it was a statement that came loaded with a million and one caveats. Moyes was, after all, inheriting the Premier League champions. Cynics had suggested that the most recent league successes in 2011 and 2013 owed more to the manager than the strength of the squad. There was undoubted quality within it, but it was clever management that optimised its capabilities. Here was a manager familiar with everything about his players. Most of them were young men he'd known for years — some, six or seven, others, ten or 11, or in the case of the likes of Ryan Giggs and Paul Scholes, over 20. He knew the condition of his veteran players, he knew the physical make-up of his squad, he knew the games they would be suitable for — in short, he knew everything you would expect a man who had been in charge for more than a quarter of a century to know.

When he was unveiled at a press conference at Manchester United's Carrington training ground on 5 July, David Moyes looked just as much the wide-eyed new boy as Sir Alex Ferguson had looked the relaxed and confident landlord of the joint in his pressers of recent years. The following is the transcript of Moyes's first press conference.

As you sit here as Manchester United manager, how proud do you feel?

'I am incredibly privileged to be given the opportunity to manage Manchester United and grateful to Sir Alex and the board for making it happen. It was a really strange situation for me. I had no idea whatsoever. I knew nothing until Sir Alex gave me a call and asked me to come to his house. I was expecting him to say "I'm going to take one of your players" or something along those lines. I went in and the first thing he said to me was "I'm retiring". I said when because he was never retiring, and he said next week. And his next words were "you're the next Manchester United manager". So I didn't get the chance to say yes or no. I was told that I was the next Manchester United manager and that was enough. As you can imagine, the blood drained from my face. I was really shocked. More shocked that Sir Alex had chosen to retire. But inside I was incredibly thrilled that I was going to be given the chance to manage Manchester United.'

Did you ever think that you had a chance at replacing Sir Alex as manager?

'For any football manager or coach who wants to manage, this is the place to be. I hoped when Sir Alex's days were up, I would be a consideration. I also think it's a plus for English coaches. You might have to work through the lower leagues, which I did at Preston, and if it goes well for you, you get an opportunity. From that point of view, people will think if I can do it, they can do it too.'

How daunting is it to take over from one of the most successful managers the world has seen?

'Whoever was going to take over this job knows what the manager did before. The manager before was incredible. His achievements, well there are no better. All I can do is what David Moyes has done before. I will definitely continue the traditions of Manchester United, but I have to put my own stamp on the club. I'm very fortunate I'm taking over the champions of England, so that gives me a great start, better than most would get. Sir Bobby Charlton came to see me and I was as thrilled about that as anything. He came in and saw me at the training centre and that was amazing for me.'

You have been given a long-term, six-year contract — how much confidence does that give you?

'I have found the people at the club fantastic. They want continuity and longevity — the Glazers and Ed Woodward see it as a long-term thing. I need to say a big thank you to Bill Kenwright and Everton. I'm sure he understands I had to make this move. The Glazers and Ed Woodward have been excellent. The players have too. You can imagine the size of the job. I need to say a big thank you to the former manager's old staff — Rene Meulensteen, Mike Phelan and Eric Steele, who have left the club. I asked Rene to stay but he felt it most fair that he moved on and let me stamp my own authority on the team.'

Can you replicate Sir Alex's success?

'Sir Alex will always be here — his stand and his statue are here — the supporters need to realise that it was Sir Alex Ferguson's time to go and someone needs to come in. To manage at this level for 25 years, I don't think another manager will ever do that at a club at this level.'

Have you managed to talk to Wayne Rooney about his future?

'I've had opportunities to speak with him, yes. It's interesting to think that Wayne is only 40 or 50 goals behind Sir Bobby Charlton and I think 40 behind Denis Law. I've had a chance to speak to Wayne. I'm sure it's a question on all of your lips, but the fact of the matter is Wayne is not for sale. He is a Manchester United player and will remain a Manchester United player. I've known Wayne since he was 16. I've had several meetings with Wayne. He's training brilliantly well. He's come back in good shape and I'm really looking forward to working with him. What we're looking to do is see how we can get Wayne Rooney scoring those goals, which will challenge the likes of Bobby Charlton and Denis Law's numbers. We are working and trying everything to get Wayne to the level where we think he should be. Not only that, this country will have a World Cup to play in next year, so for everybody's benefit, we are trying to get him back to the Wayne Rooney we all know.'

Has Rooney said that he wants to remain at the club?

'We have spoken several times. As far as I've seen it, whatever happened before is gone. We're working together now. I see a glint in his eye. He looks happy and he looks like he is going to knuckle down and get himself right.'

But has Rooney made it clear that he would like to stay at the club?

'I am looking forward to working with him and, as the club have reiterated, he won't be for sale.'

Sir Alex Ferguson said the player has asked to leave. Will the club have to go back on that?

'There was a private meeting between two people and I was not privy to that so whatever happened in that meeting was said. I don't know what those two gentlemen said. That conversation was private between them both. As far as I'm concerned, I'm really looking forward to having a go with Wayne.'

David, has Wayne Rooney categorically said that he wants to remain a Manchester United player?

'I can tell you categorically that Wayne Rooney is training fantastically well. That's all I can categorically tell you. I think if I was Wayne, I would look at the legends who have played at this club. You can see their pictures at the training ground — George Best, Bobby Charlton, Roy Keane, I could go on. And I thought to myself, Wayne is not too far away from that. It isn't too difficult to get the goals to reach the goalscoring record, and if he could do that he would be seen in the same light as those people. Wayne will not be sold by Manchester United.'

Are you intimidated by the presence of Sir Alex Ferguson watching on?

'I hope he is sitting in the directors' box because he has been so good. I have already called him two or three times for some advice. He's not there to pressure me. He said, "You were the name that I've told the board should be the next Manchester United manager." The big thing for me has been the players and they have responded well.'

Can you continue his success?

'I've come to a club where success is tattooed across its badge. This club is about winning trophies and I've come to continue that. It's something I'm looking forward to doing. It will not change me; I'm determined to try to get the first ones on the board this season.'

Are you inexperienced compared to other managers linked with the job like Pep Guardiola and Jose Mourinho?

'I'm inexperienced in a lot of things and there were some brilliant managers who could have quite easily taken this role, but the biggest confidence I got was that Sir Alex Ferguson said to me "you're the next Manchester United manager".'

Are you planning to strengthen the squad and, if so, where?

'They had a great season in the Premier League last year and it is something we will do everything we can to add to the squad. This club has done it, will always go after the best players and will always be interested in them and we will do everything we can to make sure we remain at the top.'

Have you identified particular players, Cristiano Ronaldo maybe?

'I would never speak about players at other football clubs because I think it's wrong and not my style. When people are in contract at other clubs I think it's wrong to talk about them. This club had a great season last year. I am taking over the champions and Manchester United are always interested in the best players available.'

Are you pleased to have Phil Neville and Ryan Giggs on your backroom staff?

'I wanted to make sure I had connections who know what the club is about. I spoke to Paul Scholes as well and he wanted to have some time off with his family. I spoke with Rene Meulensteen but he decided to go, so I thought the obvious person was Ryan and he's been great. I've only worked with him for two days but he's an incredible footballer and sometimes until you get really close you don't realise that. He's been on his Pro Licence course and taking steps forward, and with him and Phil Neville I wanted to make sure I had some young members behind me as well.'

What have been your first impressions of the squad?

'I've not got all of [the players] back yet as a lot of are coming back from different tournaments. But the biggest thing I've been really impressed with is their attitude and the way they have gone about their work. Total professionals.'

What are your thoughts about the start you face to the season?

'It's a tough start and I'm not convinced that's the way the balls have come out of the hat when that was being done. But you have to play everybody twice and I look back over the last five years and I've never seen Man Utd get a tougher start in any season.'

What style of play do you hope to implement?

'I hope we play the same way, with the same traditions and entertaining, exciting football. I've always said the biggest thing in football is to win, the job here is to win. I would always put winning at the top of the list. Sir Alex would as well. If you had a great entertaining team but didn't win the games, it doesn't quite get you anywhere. You have to get the balance right and hopefully I can.'

United had a great tradition of late goals under Fergie, the fans will expect that to continue. Can you do that?

'The players who can come on and win the games has been incredible and hopefully that won't change. Hopefully I will have that same magic touch Sir Alex used to have at times when he made remarkable decisions that got him results from nowhere at times. I hope I am able to do that.'

What did you immediately say to the players when you got them together?

'Not everybody's here and it wasn't as if I was able to go in there and say this is what we are doing. That will come in time. I had a word with the players the other day and said I was surprised that Sir Alex had chosen to retire. But I explained that when he had he had given me the opportunity to take the job and hope they respect that and we work together and try to be successful together.'

What advice have you had from Sir Alex?

'It was incredible when I met him. Within half an hour he was talking about the squad and the players and the staff and it was a period for me I couldn't believe it. At that time I was sworn to secrecy because Sir Alex wanted to keep his retirement private until the right moment. I only knew a couple of days before we played Liverpool when I got the call. He said a lot of things to me about the club and how great it was, the people who worked for it and felt I could take it on. He told me things that could be improved on as well so he was very honest.'

It must be strange — one minute you're targeting players for Everton — now bigger names for United?

'I've only been the manager since 1 July, but before that there was the month of June where I have had a chance to look at things, and yes it does change because it was a different window we would have been shopping in at Everton. That's why I said earlier, this club will always go for the best players, but it will always look to buy the best young players. And a big part of my job is to bring through the young players from the academy. I think we tried to do that as well as we possibly could at Everton, introduce young players to the team. And it is sort of in the DNA here, looking to bring through the young players.'

Who do you see as your biggest threat?

'I think there will be improvements from all of the clubs. I am really pleased to see Jose (Mourinho) back, he is someone who everyone will enjoy working in this country. He has been very successful and I think we will enjoy having Jose back in the Premier League again. I have come across Manuel Pellegrini a couple of times at Villarreal and Malaga, so it will be new to him as well. Probably for the first time there has been quite a big shake-up in the Premier League and because of that I think there are a lot of things unknown, how things will pan out. I don't think it's just at this club, I think there are a few other clubs where it is similar.'

What would be success for you in your first season in charge at Old Trafford?

'I actually think it is doing well in all the competitions, not just the Premier League. When you are at Manchester United, my thinking is that you have to go for everything, you attempt to win everything. Maybe you miss out sometimes, but you have to attempt to win all the trophies. I have done it everywhere else I've been, and I will certainly do it here because I have a bigger squad, quality players and a club with the tradition of being used to winning things.'

Will you look to get Paul Scholes involved at a later date?

'He has been fantastic, he wanted to give me so much help and direction on things. We spent over an hour on the phone, but he wants to give his family some time now after retirement. But there will be a place for him, we will look to bring him back in when he is ready.'

Could you have a new signing before United go on tour?

'I will try, but I couldn't turn round and say yes to that, but I will try if possible. The time is closing in a little bit just now. Always with a new manager, the players want to show they care. The players are working hard. To play for Manchester United, whether you are young or old, there is always a great pressure.'

Will transfers go down to the wire in this window?

'I think things might be done a little bit later this year, partly because there are quite a few new managers in so not everything will be done right away, but if you had the ideal position you would try to get the players in as soon as you could.'

Do you have an agreement with Everton and Bill Kenwright that you will not return to sign former players — Leighton Baines, for example?

'I don't think that is the case. Bill has been fantastic to me, they have got a great staff, a very good team and very good players. I've brought some of my staff with me as well, all I could ever say is thanks for what Everton did for me.'

Moyes was sitting alongside Nemanja Vidic, the club captain, who answered a couple of questions, and answered diplomatically. The new boss seemed quite insistent over his Rooney stance, but it seemed more in hope than expectation; his attempt at being convincing was never, well, convincing. As far as United supporters go, the majority just wanted that issue put to bed. There was talk of renewed interest from Manchester City and even a suggestion that Arsenal had made an inquiry, but the major link for Rooney was with Chelsea. On 15 July Chelsea made an offer for Rooney, believed to be around £20m, which was dismissed out of hand. When it was suggested that Blues playmaker Juan Mata and/or David Luiz may be part of the deal, Chelsea issued a statement. 'Chelsea Football Club can confirm that, yesterday, it made a written offer to Manchester United for the transfer of Wayne Rooney,' said a spokesman. 'Although the terms of that offer are confidential, for the avoidance of doubt and contrary to what is apparently being briefed to the press in Sydney, the proposed purchase does not include the transfer or loan of any players from Chelsea to Manchester United.'

By that point United had already kicked off their pre-season tour of Australasia; getting their preparation underway with the most underwhelming of starts, a 1-0 defeat to a Singha All Star

XI, marking the first time that a United team had been defeated by one of its sponsors. In fact, underwhelming was the perfect summary of the entire tour — the most memorable part of it being an announcement on 17 July that Ed Woodward had left the tour ahead of schedule to attend to, as described by the club on social media, 'urgent transfer business'. No explanation was ever forthcoming for what that business involved, but considering United did not make a signing in this transfer window for another month it seemed unlikely Woodward was jetting back to the north west of England to battle it out with Everton for the signing of Marouane Fellaini. If he had, perhaps United fans might have taken the Belgian's signing a little better; the pointless hesitation on this front meant that the club ended up paying far more than they might have earlier in the summer when Fellaini's release clause was considerably lower than the eventual fee. If only the United boss had some way of knowing the expiry date of said clause?

While it was much too early for genuine concern, eyebrows were raised at the club's persistence with offers for Barcelona's Cesc Fabregas. Fabregas had spent just two years back at Barcelona after seemingly spending twice as long pining for a move back there from Arsenal. The protracted nature of this potential deal meant United missed out on a £17m deal for Thiago, who did leave Barcelona, to join Bayern Munich. United were not presenting the impression of a club who knew how to do business and the new combination of Woodward and Moyes was not getting off to the best start in the eyes of fans, who were growing restless.

This was not helped by the fact that the channels of communication were seemingly more open than ever before; almost as soon as Ferguson retired, the club created an official Twitter account, and updates about the CEO's whereabouts presented the impression to supporters that activity was imminent. Instead, it all looked a little bit *Carry On*, particularly whilst the club were on their tour, with Moyes unable to provide any clarification on activity back in Manchester and thus presenting the impression of a person who did not have complete control and understanding of what was going on.

This period is looked back upon as almost humorous — in the way that if you don't laugh, you'll cry — but, the appointment of

Moyes aside (if we are to describe that as a mistake), the first public sign of United's slipping off the track was already evident. With the bids for Fabregas having been made public, the club were entering into unchartered territory — only once before had Sir Alex Ferguson openly coveted a player who had no intention of signing for United, and that was Alan Shearer. Then, though, United didn't quite have as much at stake. It was important for the club to make a statement in this immediate period of transition, whether that be bringing in a blockbuster name, or making a point of keeping the squad as it was. The tactic from the club was clearly to go with the former and so they had put themselves under pressure to deliver, armed with the reputation of the club and not the manager to attract players. If they had been more discreet, well, perhaps it would have been more forgivable. The damning thing was that Fabregas was obviously a 'gettable' player; United's pursuit of Gareth Bale later in the summer would end with the Welsh winger opting to sign for Real Madrid, which wasn't by itself a stick to beat Moyes and Woodward with, but on the back of the Fabregas and Fellaini sagas it was ammunition for more than just one or two to be worried.

Therein lay the first problem United faced — the club had moved with the times, it had even led and pioneered the evolution of the game, but in appointing someone who did not have a track record for success and did not even have a good track record for entertaining football, the club had only its, admittedly considerable, reputation to attract players.

Consider an alternate reality where Jose Mourinho had been sounded out for the job instead of David Moyes. With his future at Madrid more than uncertain, it would still have looked like a major coup on United's part — to hire the Real Madrid manager four years after they bought United's best player — and one suspects that Mourinho would have played every bit the showman.

In 2016 former Chelsea defender Marcel Desailly claimed Mourinho had long coveted the Old Trafford job. 'I was in Mexico with him at a FIFA conference,' Desailly told ESPN. 'Remember, when he left Inter Milan to go to Real Madrid [in 2010]? At the time, he said he would come back to England. But his plan was to go to Manchester United, not Chelsea. This was his main target. He respected the club. The worldwide exposure is through Manchester United.'

Had Mourinho left Madrid direct for Manchester instead of taking a detour to London, well, you can only imagine that it would have been the perfect case of promotion, and, with United being so keen on that aspect of the industry, it makes you wonder what on earth they were thinking when hiring Moyes, and that is said with absolutely no disrespect intended to the former Everton boss. Mourinho would have made it look like his decision, and in doing so he would have made Manchester United look like the desirable choice ahead of Real Madrid; this would have been a critical and pivotal moment in the club's history, as even if most in the media would have found those comments disingenuous they would have at least presented a far more convincing impression. And, as Mourinho showed when he eventually did end up at United, his transfer dealings are more direct. What do you have if you have a manager who left one of the biggest clubs in the world for another, a manager with a track record of winning things, who tells you he wants to play for his club, who had just won their domestic championship? You listen with a lot more attention than you do to a manager who hasn't won anything and doesn't seem that convinced that he actually wants you. Whatever the ifs and buts, United paid the price for the decisions made that summer for the following three years, and it was only when Mourinho arrived at Old Trafford and promptly convinced Zlatan Ibrahimovic and Paul Pogba to spend a year outside of the Champions League (with both players at ages where you would think they would flat refuse it) that the pulling power of the manager was truly recognised, and United had the same sort of allure as they had enjoyed under Sir Alex Ferguson. The lost opportunity to laud it over Madrid as the most desirable club in the world might not be something that the money-men at Old Trafford lose much sleep over, probably because it wasn't a thought that ever crossed their minds (although, *come on* — Mourinho would surely have made it look like a step up), but considering how close they were to a seamless transition in comparison to the shambles that summer became, the mind truly does boggle.

If the club did have a success that summer it was the retention of Wayne Rooney. The definition of success, however, must be explained in this instance. United rejected all further offers from Chelsea before the end of August, and so, true to his word, David Moyes did not sell

Wayne Rooney. This was a victory of conviction but not as emphatic as the manager would have liked; for, by now, there was not exactly the shock and upset about the possibility of a Rooney exit as there had been back in October 2010. Rooney didn't start in any of the last three games of the 2012/13 season and his place in the United first team had been under question since he was dropped for the second leg of the Champions League second-round tie with Real Madrid. There were in fact many supporters who believed Fergie had delivered a nice welcome present for the new manager — the opportunity to accept an offer for Rooney and start a new era. The forward's drop in form over the second half of that last season under Ferguson had been notable; in a game at Swansea three days before Christmas, Rooney put in arguably his most disappointing performance in a red shirt, and never picked up again for the rest of the campaign. However, with a frustrating transfer window drawing to a close, it is easy and understandable to see why David Moyes would have felt a move to Chelsea of all teams would have been perceived as a very poor move from United. They would have theoretically strengthened a rival, and United would look as if they were forced into selling. So Moyes stood firm; the following February, however, when Rooney was awarded a new five-and-a-half-year contract worth a reported £300,000 a week, eyes were watering throughout M16. By then, Moyes's reign was close to untenable anyway, and the deal was seen by most supporters as a financial nightmare for the club. Rooney's stock had fallen sharply to the point where the club would have been lucky to receive an offer of £15m for him — so in what scenario did it make sense to make a commitment to pay him that sum each year for the next six? The Rooney Conundrum was one that would dog the following management set-ups; by February, as stated, time was all but up for Moyes.

Rio and Chips

So, where did it all go wrong for David Moyes at Manchester United? To briefly return to the theme of understandable errors of judgement, it is worth mentioning the appointment of staff on his arrival. In the world of football management, coaches take their trusted staff with them into new jobs all the time. Yes, there is the cliché of 'jobs for the boys', but if a manager has been successful, then invariably they will stick to their trusted methods. David Moyes had done well enough at Everton so that his name was always in the frame for big jobs when they became available, and so, when it came to moving to Manchester United, who had been ruled by a single man for more than a quarter of a century, it is reasonable that Moyes would have wanted people around him who were familiar with him and therefore loyal to him rather than with and to Manchester United Football Club. He needed people he could trust and so those were the ones he employed.

Likewise, there was a perception from some that Ferguson ruled the roost to such an extent that some members of staff at United were undeserving of their role. Mike Phelan, the long-serving assistant, was let go following years of well-intentioned ribbing from supporters about wearing shorts and putting out the cones. Rene Meulensteen, upset at the Phelan decision, decided he too would leave. These were two crucial members of staff, but clearly two members Moyes felt were dispensable. It would be wrong to say these decisions immediately made a mockery of the 'cut from the same cloth' comments or that they created a contradiction of the idea of consistency, because change happens in football. Coaches get hired and fired. Ferguson had a number of different assistants over his tenure. Still, there's absolutely no point denying that with hindsight it was the wrong call and that the cracks which began to appear, appeared almost instantly.

Within a week, Moyes ruffled more feathers by banning chips from the club canteen. The issue infamously made its way into Rio Ferdinand's autobiography *#2Sides* in which the defender said, 'We loved our chips, but Moyes comes in and, after his first week, he says we can't have chips any more.'

Moyes later responded. 'Yes, I did ban chips,' he said in 2015. 'It was because a couple of players were overweight and I didn't think chips were good for their diet.'

Again, there was nothing theoretically incorrect with Moyes's decision, and it seems a petty thing to cause a disconnect, but what the example shows us is that the new manager had not taken the time to sit down and discuss changes with the senior players. Perhaps he didn't need to, what he said went, after all. But from this basic misunderstanding deeper problems formed. Moyes's 'my way or the highway' philosophy had a significant effect on Ferdinand in particular, so, when examining what went wrong, perhaps he is the best place to start.

Ahead of the tour of the Far East, Moyes admitted he would use the time to get to know the players. 'I don't know if it is useful to be away for three weeks but it is useful in terms of getting to know the players,' he said. 'They will get to know me and how I work, which is important. There are also two or three young players I might get a chance to look at. I am looking for Warren [Joyce] to give me direction on that and who should be pushed towards the first team. Maybe in some of the games I will have the opportunity to see them.'

One would presume that managers would get reports about their new squad, and in Steve Round, Moyes had an assistant who was supposedly ahead of the game when it came to tactical analysis. It would have taken the most casual of observations of United's team sheets from the previous campaign to notice something about the use of some of the senior players, most notably Rio Ferdinand, Ryan Giggs and Michael Carrick. The only time any of those players played consecutive games was when games were a week apart, and even then it wasn't all of the time. At only one point in the season did Ferdinand and Carrick respectively play consecutive games where the matches were closer than a week apart (that is to say, only once did either of them play a weekend and then a midweek game consecutively), and when they did, a long rest awaited them. Ferdinand and Carrick, when they did play, were exceptional in that last title-winning season. And, of course, when they did play, it tended to be together, and in the more important games.

There can be no doubt about it, Ferguson would have complained about the tough fixture schedule at the start of the season, and he would have felt it necessary to play Ferdinand and Carrick in consecutive games against Chelsea and Liverpool. One wonders if both players would have played in the opening league game against Swansea City, though. A draw at home to Chelsea and a limp away defeat to Liverpool were obviously upsetting, but Moyes was not about to be damned for his failure to win those games.

He responded by bringing in Fellaini from Everton, his sole signing of the summer window, and Fellaini went straight into the squad for the first game after the international break. How United might line up against Crystal Palace was an interesting one considering they had their first Champions League game in the midweek against Leverkusen and then an away game at Manchester City. When the team win, it would seem unfair to question the manager's selection. United did win 2-0, though the performance was not exactly inspired. Fabio started at right-back, after Phil Jones had played there since the start of the season. Not eyebrow raising on its own, but it was rather surprising to see Rafael missing out. The Brazilian seemed to have made the right-back position his own after being one of the best players the previous season, and now he couldn't get a game for love nor money. Ferdinand and Carrick were both made to play the full 90 minutes against Palace and again against Leverkusen in a game United won 4-2.

So far United had got away with it, but it was always likely that it would catch up with them, and so it proved to be on one of the most painful occasions possible, against Manchester City. The visitors looked leggy and tired against a vibrant City team that led 2-0 at half-time and scored two within five minutes of the restart. A late Wayne Rooney consolation could not paper over the cracks. United had been dreadful and the hiding had been coming.

Moyes's response for the next league game? Nemanja Vidic was rested and Patrice Evra was dropped from the team to play West Brom at home. Surrounding Ferdinand and Carrick were Phil Jones, Jonny Evans, Alex Buttner and Anderson. In those situations you hope the calming influences will win over but that was not the case; the veteran pair instead looked sluggish and out of place, slow to react to the erratic performance around them. Rather unfairly, their performances were singled out for criticism, and on the face of it it wasn't difficult to see why.

For Ferdinand, however, the repercussions were devastating. He had been the one constant in the club's worst start to a season since well before Ferguson's first title-winning campaign, and unfortunately, though the manager hadn't done him any favours, he was the figurehead and bore the brunt of the finger pointing. He's old. Slow. Past it. The solution was obvious, he must be dropped. The truth, of course, was that Ferdinand was still capable of brilliant defending. In this writer's opinion, Ferdinand is the finest centre-half to wear the Manchester United shirt, and in the opinion of many more, he walks into a 'best-ever United XI'. It is not an unreasonable argument to suggest he's the greatest English centre-half of all time. He didn't go from being a title-winning centre-half to a liability in just six months. Does Moyes avoid culpability here? Maybe, on account of not quite knowing the player as well as the previous manager did. But then again, that's simply *good management*.

Following the defeat to City, Moyes pulled in the squad to deconstruct the loss and run through why and how. His message was not clear to the players. 'You heard a lot of guys complaining: "I just don't know what he wants",' Ferdinand said. 'He had me doubting everything.' To further compound the defender's misery, following the West Brom defeat, Ferdinand was hauled in to watch another video. This time not of the game, but instead of Everton's Phil Jagielka. Moyes felt that Ferdinand — a six-time Premier League winner, a European Cup winner, with over 400 appearances for

United — could benefit from learning how to adapt his game to play like Moyes's former skipper at Goodison Park. It demonstrated a significant misunderstanding from Moyes about the defender he had at his disposal. Ferdinand may not have been as imperious as he was in 2008, but he had not reached Gary Neville's level of self-awareness where he himself knew the game was up.

The scenario had echoes of Dave Sexton pulling Gordon Hill into his office after training one morning and forcing him to watch tapes of the Hungarian wingers of the 50s — principally, their hard-working attitude. Sexton seemingly did not realise the value of Hill's natural game, even when the evidence of him being the team's top goalscorer from the wing made it easy to see. Hill, to give a modern example, had a goal record comparable with Cristiano Ronaldo, and didn't even take penalties. Instructing him to be defensive showed a basic misunderstanding of the manager, but, as always, the manager rules. Hill was sold and Mickey Thomas was brought in; the perfect summary of the difference between the Docherty side and the Sexton side. As George Santayana said, those who cannot remember the past are condemned to repeat it.

Instead of utilising him properly, Moyes — unwittingly — burned Ferdinand out, creating a significantly premature and sad conclusion to his Old Trafford career. The defender was brutally cut from United's starting XI, brought back for the occasional game before being recalled for a run in the late winter when confidence at the club was rock bottom. Moyes then told Ferdinand that he would not be playing in a Champions League game at Bayern Munich as the team trained in a public park in Germany — a moment the player described as one of the lowest of his career.

With his reputation damaged to the extent he knew the incoming manager would probably not renew his contract, Ferdinand signed a deal at Queens Park Rangers. It did nothing to restore any glory. On a tight pitch, in a team who were forced to defend for the entire game, Ferdinand was required to be more of a Vidic. He wasn't.

Ferdinand left with the blessing and good wishes of United fans, unlike Vidic, who left under a bit of a cloud when it was announced in early March that he had signed for Inter Milan. Vidic had become disillusioned with life under David Moyes, but the timing of the announcement, from the club captain of all people, coming at a stage when United were making a desperate last throw of the dice for Champions League qualification, was, for some, an unforgivable show of disloyalty. Time was almost up for Moyes, but the way Rio Ferdinand was handled was a case study for everything that went wrong for the Scot in those few months: the understandable misunderstanding, the questionable decision of resolution and the poor man-management that undermined all the work Sir Alex Ferguson had done. Twenty-seven years of work undone in roughly 27 weeks.

We will try and make it difficult for Newcastle

There was a palpable sense of the team having given up in consecutive 3-0 home defeats to Liverpool and Manchester City in March 2014 — losses which both flattered and humiliated United fans. By this point, the Manchester United team resembled anything but a team. It was 11 individuals who appeared to never have played together delivering a game plan that nobody seemed to understand.

'Moyes's innovations mostly led to negativity and confusion,' Rio Ferdinand said in his autobiography. 'The biggest confusion was over how he wanted us to move the ball forward. Some players felt they kicked the ball long more than at any time in their career. Sometimes our main tactic was the long, high, diagonal cross. It was embarrassing. In one home game against Fulham we had 81 crosses! I was thinking, why are we doing this? Andy Carroll doesn't play for us!

'The whole approach was alien. Other times Moyes wanted lots of passing. He'd say, "Today I want us to have 600 passes in the game. Last week it was only 400." Who cares? I'd rather score five goals from ten passes.'

Judging by how the team had lined up at the start of the season, one wonders if David Moyes had selected the 11 he *thought* had won the Premier League and that his minor tweaks would just make them better. And, when it became clear that this wasn't the case, the manager's unfamiliarity with his squad showed.

It wasn't just the players who had become bewildered by the statements made by the manager. United had two consecutive home games in December 2013, first against Moyes's former club Everton, and then against in-form Newcastle. Moyes's team had recovered from their shambolic start to go 12 games unbeaten, though, as well they might considering they had the benefit of a four-game run at home to build momentum. When qualification for the second round of the Champions League was assured thanks to a very impressive 5-0 win in Leverkusen, it seemed as if things were turning around. The jolt in confidence had been provided by a stunning double from Adnan Januzaj in a game against Sunderland; Januzaj was immediately thrust into the limelight of being a starter, and to be fair to the young Belgian he showed flashes of his potential.

With those three defeats in the first seven weeks of the season, United knew that they could not afford many more losses, but that's exactly what they got against Everton. Bryan Oviedo scored in the 86th minute of a game that United probably had the better of on the balance of it, but their inability to score meant that the Toffees registered their first win at Old Trafford since 1992. It was the second such record to fall, after West Brom's first win at the Theatre of Dreams since the late 70s. The loss put United 12 points behind league leaders Arsenal. Even accounting for the reliability of the Gunners' mid-season collapse, it still seemed an insurmountable gap, and for the first time since 1990 United supporters were approaching the turn of the year without their club being involved in a title race.

Objectives had been redefined. There were enough sensible heads to understand transition would be difficult, but Champions League would be the minimum expectation. With that, United supporters had essentially been willing to give David Moyes the chance to finish in fourth, which would have then been their lowest-ever Premier League position, and rebuild for the second year from there. There were still many who put the blame for the transfer mess-ups in the summer at Ed Woodward's door. The shambolic episode where lawyers claiming to represent United in the supposed pursuit of Ander Herrera attempted to negotiate a transfer with Athletic Bilbao summed up a difficult few months.

Newcastle's trip to Manchester came on the back of their own loss against Swansea City (which had ended their four-game winning run). Ahead of the game with the Magpies, Moyes faced the press, and gave a conference which left the United support open-mouthed in disbelief.

'They [Newcastle] also had a defeat against Swansea, but they have had four straight wins which is a great record to get. I know what it's like to try and win three or four games in a row, it's a hard thing to do in the Premier League, so congratulations to them. They come to Old Trafford and we're going to make it as hard and difficult for them as we possibly can,' Moyes said, before defending the performance against Everton. 'People who watched the game, they would have got lots of belief from it,' Moyes said. 'There were chances in the game we didn't take. It could quite easily have been very different. Unless you are someone who doesn't understand the game too much you would have seen that.'

The Newcastle game could barely have gone any worse. Yohan Cabaye scored for the visitors in the 61st minute. Robin van Persie pulled up with what appeared to be a groin injury, but when Moyes made changes — and he made all three within the space of eight minutes — the Dutch striker remained on the field. He was effectively a passenger, dropping back into midfield while Januzaj and Javier Hernandez played up front.

With Old Trafford used to late onslaughts, the Newcastle team would surely have braced itself for a surge in the last half an hour, but the truth was that it never materialised. United's response was abysmal as the game petered out in surely the most disappointing way one ever had at the famous ground in the Premier League to that point. Newcastle's win was their first at Old Trafford for 41 years — another wretched result.

After admitting his team could have done better, Moyes said that the plan was to bring Van Persie off. He told the BBC, 'I think if I'd have taken him off everybody would have said "what are you doing?!"

but in truth Robin had to come off after 70 minutes maximum. But we had to keep him on, we were chasing the game, we had to get a goal back.'

The bewildering statement was not bettered by his comments ahead of the last European game before the turn of the year. In his pre-match conference, the manager made comments immortalised in a tweet by the club's official account which still gets retweeted today — 'David Moyes says #mufc must improve in a number of areas, including passing, creating chances and defending.'

Moyes still played Van Persie in the next game, bringing him on in the effectively meaningless Champions League group game against Shakhtar Donetsk. The forward pulled his groin taking a corner and was subsequently out injured until late January.

At half-time in that game, Roy Keane, working as a pundit, said, 'They [United] don't look like a team, just a collection of individuals running around. You can defend players for making mistakes but you cannot defend players for not tackling and not getting close to people.'

Moyes suggested afterwards that he wasn't surprised with how poor United started. 'To be honest, it's been that way since I came here,' he said. 'We need to win matches and the players responded well to that encouragement. We passed the ball much better after we had given it away terribly in the first half, and that's not like us. I didn't think we were close enough to them early on when we gave them too many opportunities, and we were fortunate not to be a goal down. I think you want to try and win the group. It was a difficult group and a lot has been said, I was inexperienced in the Champions League … so to have my first experience, I am happy to top the group. We didn't play particularly well in the opening 30 minutes, we could have been fortunate still to be 0-0, but we missed a couple of chances just before half-time ourselves. We played much better in the second half.' Moyes was asked why his team had done so well in Europe and so badly in the League. 'If I had the answer I would have solved it by now and it would all be OK,' he said.

It was a disastrous few days for Moyes and United, and although he publicly insisted his objectives hadn't changed — 'We'll try to win the next match' — the mood around the club, and the support, certainly had. The most common complaint was that

Moyes's comments before the game were simply not befitting of the manager of Manchester United. Less than 12 months earlier, Newcastle's Boxing Day trip to Old Trafford had concluded with a last-gasp winner for the hosts, and the United manager dismissing his opponents as 'a wee club in the North East'.

Even if the fans were willing to cut the new man some slack and say that the previous manager had overachieved with the squad at his disposal, that was not exactly the same as accepting clear underachievement, and the public demeanour of the man leading the squad was not inspiring the fans with confidence. The Twitter account of the fanzine *Red Issue* reminded Moyes he was 'not at Preston any more'.

It had been a difficult few weeks for the United boss. Wilfried Zaha, the former Crystal Palace winger, had been Ferguson's last signing, and he arrived at Old Trafford in the summer of 2013. However, Zaha had endured a very tough start to life at United, too. He made his debut in the Community Shield win over Wigan Athletic, but it wasn't until the Newcastle game, where he came on as a sub, that he featured again. There was speculation that Zaha was being punished for an alleged relationship with Moyes's daughter, an allegation Zaha actually dismissed on his own Twitter account on the day before the Newcastle game, a statement which included the comment, 'I'll play when the manager thinks I'm ready.'

Rio Ferdinand had been interviewed by BT Sport that week and revealed that the squad were not kept in the loop when it came to selection. 'This manager's a bit different in that he doesn't name the team beforehand,' Ferdinand said. 'You don't really get to know the team. The old manager used to give you kind of a little bit of an idea if you'd be playing and stuff. When you know you're playing the intensity goes up a little bit more on match day and that's what you need to try and make sure you're doing, even if you don't know you'll be playing to try and get to that intensity you'd be at when you know you're playing. It's hard … it's hard to do that mentally because you spend a lot of nervous energy thinking, "Am I playing?" or "Am I not playing?" and you're just going round in circles in your head and turning into a madman.'

One might suggest that there was a benefit to that strategy; the squad players of before now had a genuine chance to stake a claim for their future. Admittedly, that was straw-clutching at its finest, with more than enough slack given to the new boss. Five months in, and he seemed no nearer to knowing who his starting 11 would be. Christmas, then, came at a good time. The fixtures coming thick and fast as they were, and the League Cup quarter-final on the 18th, meant that all of the squad knew that there would be changes to the team. It seemed to have a galvanising effect; the win in the Cup against Stoke served as a real shot in the arm with Sunderland the semi-final opponents, and when United turned around a two-goal deficit to win at Hull City on Boxing Day, there was renewed optimism based on the perception that United always finished the season stronger. The most fantastic thing to come out of this period was the form of Danny Welbeck, whose four goals in four games placed him in a prominent position to keep his place even when Robin van Persie returned. 2013 ended with Welbeck scoring the winner at Carrow Road; that 1-0 victory over Norwich was the sixth consecutive win on the bounce after the Newcastle defeat.

However, when that was followed up with three consecutive 2-1 defeats to kick off January — against Spurs at home in the league, against Swansea at home in the FA Cup third round, and at Sunderland in the first leg of the League Cup semi-final — the idea that David Moyes might not even see it through the first year of his six-year contract began to feel as if it could be a real possibility. By now, however, United's dilemma, even if they did sack Moyes, was who could they bring in? Jurgen Klopp had extended his contract at Dortmund and didn't seem likely to leave. With the season already feeling like a write-off, many in the United support suggested Ryan Giggs as a possible name to take over the reins until the end of the 2013/14 campaign. Others felt that six months was far too short a time to expect results from a manager who had taken over what was in effect a dynasty. He needed time.

In January the club seemed to reinforce that opinion, when the Glazer family allowed Moyes to spend almost £40m on breaking the club record to bring in Juan Mata from Chelsea. The signing came mere days after United's return game at Stamford Bridge where they surrendered rather meekly to a Samuel Eto'o hat-trick.

It also came two days after United had been eliminated from the League Cup in a farcical semi-final. They seemed set to go through on away goals after extra time at the end of an extremely arduous evening of football. However, in the 119th minute, former United right-back Phil Bardsley enjoyed what was one of the highlights of his career, making it 1-1 and seemingly sending Sunderland to Wembley. David de Gea, normally so excellent, made his one mistake of the season at the crucial moment. United somehow managed to find time to score a dramatic goal through Hernandez to set up penalty kicks. Thus followed one of the worst shoot-outs in the sport's history; Danny Welbeck, Phil Jones and Adnan Januzaj all missed their kicks, and, with one kick remaining each, Sunderland led 2-1. Adam Johnson stepped up and De Gea saved to give Rafael the chance to level it up and take it into sudden death. The Brazilian missed, and, barring the unlikely scenario of Champions League glory, United's awful January meant they were more than likely to end the season without a trophy.

Mata's arrival was seen as the boost which might see United make a late rally for the top four, but the truth was, after suffering seven league defeats already, it seemed a tough ask, even if the well-intentioned voices coming from the club maintained that they would keep going until it was mathematically impossible.

Mata made his debut against Cardiff City — United were disjointed and not convincing, but they grabbed a 2-0 win thanks to a goal from the returning Van Persie to move to two points behind Everton in sixth place. If Moyes thought his luck was turning, he was once again about to be cruelly mistaken; in the next league game, at Stoke City, neither of the centre-halves who started the game (Jones and Evans) made the second half. And by that point, Stoke had a 1-0 lead. Van Persie equalised in the 47th minute, but Charlie Adam got his second five minutes later to condemn the visitors to their eighth league defeat of the season — a third of their league games.

United set a new Premier League record in their next game, but once more it was a record of the unwanted kind. Fulham travelled to Old Trafford under the leadership of new manager Rene Meulensteen. The Cottagers were bottom and so a routine, morale-boosting win was expected. Just 19 minutes in, Steve Sidwell scored to give Fulham the lead, and the anxiety that had been tangible within Old Trafford in recent weeks was present once again. Moyes's team huffed and puffed and had 75 per cent of the possession but seemed to be doing nothing with it. The United boss threw everything at his opponents, making all three substitutes and pushing Rooney into midfield to make space for Hernandez up front. For all their territorial dominance, and despite the fact that United threw in a record 81 crosses, they were unable to find a way back into the game until Juan Mata's 78th-minute centre found Van Persie. Michael Carrick then put United in front in the 80th minute, but the last ten minutes felt strangely ominous; Darren Bent equalised in stoppage time and few were surprised. Afterwards, David Moyes was asked if it was a crushing blow: 'Yeah, it's been a bit like that so far,' he laughed with a brave face afterwards. 'Today was probably as bad as it gets, honestly.' Pressed on whether it was a confidence issue plaguing United, Moyes said, 'Well you've got to keep on trying to make it work and the players have done that today, they tried everything they could.'

Visiting manager Meulensteen twisted the knife into Moyes, claiming the game had been predictable: 'Their game plan was straightforward,' he said. 'They put crosses in from wide angles. We defended it well. If you are well organised, it can be easy to defend against. I do think that a few teams have come here with a different approach. Teams have come to Old Trafford and got something. Teams are thinking that there is a chink in United's armour. We set out as everyone can see, we made it very difficult for them. They have some problems of their own. They kept creating chances and crosses but we defended fantastically well. You think at the end all the hard work will slip away. But at the end, for Darren Bent to score that equaliser, it felt like a winner.'

Young Fulham defender Dan Burn, who made 22 clearances from those crosses, said it had been a comfortable evening: 'We knew that was going to happen and I was happy for them to play like that,' he said. 'I'm six foot seven so it helps when dealing with those sort of balls. Manchester United still have amazing players — on another day they could have scored more often but we defended really well.'

Burn then had an interview with Fulham's official website in which he insisted he didn't mean any disrespect to United, but still the comments didn't make any better reading. 'I didn't mean that quote to sound as disrespectful as it's been reported,' he said. 'There were a lot of crosses, statistically more than any game since stats started, so I just joked that I hadn't headed as many balls since the Conference.'

United did at least pick up two commendable results in London — a goalless draw at Arsenal and a 2-0 win at Palace — ahead of their trip to Olympiakos in the Champions League, but, as Moyes was learning, there was always a hiccup around the corner, and the Greek side secured a shock 2-0 win to increase the pressure on the United boss. 'I take responsibility for the result,' he said after the game. 'I'm just surprised that I didn't see that level of performance coming ... the players are hurting as well, they know how they performed.' Moyes talked up the idea of seeing another great night at Old Trafford and he was going to get that, but, frustratingly for him, a crushing blow was to befall his side beforehand.

United's plight had been exacerbated by two factors — the first, that Liverpool seemed to be on the cusp of recapturing some of their former glory. Inspired by Luis Suarez and a transitional Premier League, which Manchester City had inexplicably failed to dominate, Liverpool had slipped into the spot vacated by United. Worse still, it was plainly obvious that any hope of a result was in vain. United were not in the sort of form that was even capable of spluttering out a good performance — their wins had barely been convincing — and Liverpool took full advantage, pummelling the home side. Despite being by far the better team, they still needed the cushion of Mark Clattenburg's curious decision to award not one, not even two, but three penalties to Liverpool at Old Trafford (one wonders whether a referee would be brave enough to award three penalties against Liverpool at Anfield). Gerrard scored two and United supporters were saved the disgrace of having him score a hat-trick when he missed his third. Suarez did make it three shortly after and the 3-0 win flattered Moyes's team, who showed absolutely no fight.

Perhaps the most damning thing was the clearly evident way United were getting bossed from the first minute. Moyes did not make a change at half-time, and he did not even make a change after the second goal, incredibly waiting another half an hour to do so. When Vidic was sent off, Moyes hastily brought Rio Ferdinand on for Juan Mata, keen to avoid a scenario where blood-thirsty Liverpool might well have scored another two or three goals in the last few minutes, as Manchester City had done a couple of years back with that infamous 6-1 win. With defeat inevitable, Old Trafford was at its loudest so far this season, defiantly chanting, '20 times, 20 times, Man United' for the last 30 minutes of the game, pausing only to howl their derisive disbelief at the indecisive David Moyes, who stood on the touchline doing nothing. The loud support was more a case of the home fans reminding their hated rivals that even if they were to win the league, they'd still be one off the record.

'I thought there wasn't a great deal in it at half-time,' said Moyes, who may not have been watching the same game as everyone else. 'We had just started to play a bit better prior to the half-time whistle … the way the crowd reacted today, it was phenomenal support inside the ground here today, if they give us that level of support on Wednesday night we'll have a great chance of going through.' On United's faltering top-four chances? 'It looks as if we're a long way off it.'

United's supporters were in fine voice for the game against Olympiakos. Back in the starting line-up came Rio Ferdinand and Ryan Giggs, while Moyes's big gamble was to play Wayne Rooney, Danny Welbeck and Robin van Persie all together as he went for broke.

Prior to the first leg, United had met Olympiakos four times in their history, all four coming in the space of a year in October 2001 and October 2002; United did not concede a goal, and in their home games had won 3- and 4-0. To qualify, then, United needed only to reach par with one of their previous scores, but as we all know sport doesn't quite work like that and the pressure cooker that was Old Trafford threatened to boil over if the supporters didn't see their team get through to the next round. For a number of reasons, this game was one of the most compelling of the short Moyes era. When he needed a result, in came the players he had barely trusted to do a job, and the team resembled more of a Fergie line-up than most.

So how did it get to that point? Why did Moyes suddenly revert? Perhaps the former Everton boss had been influenced by the opinion of others when it came to assessing the quality of his new players. There was the often-suggested theory that Ferguson had overachieved, and if you wanted to find critical evaluation of United's players, you didn't have to venture too far. The majority of this squad had been together for five titles, and some maybe 'only' two, but to read the press in any of those campaigns would reveal opinion was split. Rafael would often be questioned due to his inconsistency and hot-headedness. Patrice Evra's susceptible games against Aaron Lennon had been blown out of all proportion so as to make the French left-back look overrated. You get the idea. And so you begin to understand why Moyes felt a blank slate in his first few months was the best way to go. He'd stick, essentially, with the team he felt had won the league, and make changes only when it became evident to him that they were necessary. He was too new in the job and too unfamiliar with the players at his disposal to understand and appreciate that the mistakes seemingly created by the individuals were made because of the shape and because of the selection.

By mid-March, even if he was outwardly projecting the idea that he could be the man to navigate positive change, internally he must have understood his own part in the malaise. Even accepting for some underperformance in transition, things should not have become anywhere near this bad. For supporters, it wasn't even the defeats — well, it wasn't *just* the defeats — it was the manner of them. The last 30 minutes against Newcastle had been the most limp United fans had seen their side as they accepted defeat, and the nature of the capitulation against Liverpool, whilst half-expected, was similarly alarming. Manchester United's reputation for not going down without a fight had seemingly vanished.

Where, then, did the remarkable turnaround come from against the Greek side? United scored twice in the first half before an early third in the second — all provided by Robin van Persie — which put them in the position they needed to be to qualify. The Dutchman was the figurehead of this turnaround but this was a pure victory for the likes of Ferdinand, Evra, and especially Giggs (in his first appearance for almost a month, and his first start for almost two), who was absolutely outstanding.

It is hard not to conclude that on the biggest stage of them all, with the world watching, United's proud players would not accept elimination at home against Olympiakos to be their final European game for the club. By now, it was obvious that Champions League qualification via the league was unlikely, so, with so many players in their mid-30s, and the club at this definite transitional moment, the idea that they would be around for Manchester United's next foray into the Champions League was unlikely. So, far from this being a display to vindicate any fantastic work on the training ground, or a victory to finally show that Moyes was steering his team in the right direction, it resembled something of a last hurrah from a team desperate to remind the world what they were capable of when playing to their own strengths. Of course, however, that didn't stop the manager believing this could be a turning point.

'I don't want to come out and say: "This is the moment",' he said after the game. 'But I hope it is. This is a work in progress and it will take time to get it as we really want it. It is a big job. I have got a lot of things I want to do, but the players gave the crowd something after we lost to Liverpool and we are delighted to see Manchester United in the last eight of the Champions League. There are stories of this player falling out, or that one falling out, but it is rubbish. People are looking for reasons why we are not doing well and it is only because we have not been playing well.'

Moyes had left Giggs out in favour of playing the inconsistent Januzaj, who had flattered to deceive since his autumn form, with his moments of promise presenting the genuinely bright times in these dark days. But after Giggs had rolled back the years, Moyes was full of praise, adding that it was in fact his instruction that he believed made a telling difference. 'Ryan's passing was fantastic,' said Moyes. 'His overall play was really good and he defies his age. He has not played much recently, but I felt, tactically, I needed him to play a certain role. He carried it out perfectly.'

Perhaps the words of Patrice Evra summed up how everything actually was at the club: 'Everyone thought we were out, but we showed Manchester United are still alive.'

The following weekend, a much-changed United side — with Michael Carrick in defence — won 2-0 at Upton Park. Wayne Rooney scored twice, one of them a stunning half-volley from the half-way line, suggesting that some of the old swagger was returning to the Champions.

Moyes's best days yet were followed by his darkest day yet, when United 'welcomed' Manchester City to Old Trafford. The majority of the 75,203 in attendance were probably not expecting a United win, but they were at least entitled to hope for something better than their game at City and recent game against Liverpool. Within

42 seconds City had taken the lead and were in complete control. It was no surprise when they extended their lead to 2- and then 3-0 in the second half. It could have been far worse, but the post-match analytics did nothing to make anything easy reading for Moyes. United were now guaranteed to finish with their lowest Premier League points total. With seven games left, they were 12 points off fourth position, and six points off fifth and even five points off sixth.

If United supporters thought at least it couldn't get any worse, then by the time they got home or read the morning newspapers they would have been absolutely stunned to have heard their manager's post-match comments. 'I think we've played a very good side and it's the sort of standard and level we need to try and aspire to get ourselves to at this moment in time,' David Moyes said. 'I think we need to play better. We're needing to come up a couple of levels at the moment and we're not quite there. We didn't start the game well, in the first 15 minutes they were very good and we've conceded a goal in 45 seconds so we've not given ourselves a fighting chance. I thought we grew into the first half and got better and until the second goal we had a chance, but on the night we didn't do well enough. I take responsibility for the team, I always will do. Everyone knows this is going to be a job which is going to take a little bit of time to get the way we would like it, but that is the job and I recognise that. I thought it would be a tough year for us, no doubt about that, but I hoped it would be much more competitive and closer to the top of the league than we are at the present time. We never started well. We never gave ourselves a great opportunity to get into the game. Manchester City started really fast, and conceding a goal after 30-40 seconds made it difficult. I just think we never came out of the blocks. You prepare the players, you warm them up, you do all the things to have them ready, but we just never started. It gave them a real big lift to get a goal so early on. We had to try to make sure we got through that 10 to 15-minute period when they were out of the blocks.

'After that, we weathered it and got ourselves back into the game and finished the half quite strong. The key to it was not to concede a second goal so we could always give ourselves a chance back in there, but I didn't think we started the second half well. We brought pressure on us by our play and in the end we conceded a corner just before that, and there was another one, and then that led to a goal. It was obviously poor marking and we should have done much better.'

Up until that point, Moyes's public statements had generally been met with some derision by United fans, who couldn't quite believe what their manager had said. The 'try to make it hard for Newcastle' was one thing, but suggesting United should aspire to be like Manchester City? (It seems like an opportune time to also note one of Moyes's post-match comments after the 4-1 defeat earlier in the season against City — 'It's going to get worse.')

Up until that point, supporters had been quite happy to allow Moyes to think the incredible support shown in the Champions League game and the game against Liverpool had been as much for him as it was for the team.

It should also be said that there were plenty of supporters who felt that March was too soon to condemn a new manager coming in, and so were hesitant to raise concern over the statements made to the press. Those wishing to defend him after the return game against City made a case for the point he had never actually said United aspired to be like City, and that those words had in fact been manipulated by the press. The fact of the matter was that Moyes had been around long enough to know just how the press interpreted statements, and anyway, in this instance, Manchester United supporters could hear the words for themselves and could draw their own conclusions. He must have known the way his words earlier in the campaign had been perceived by most, and, after the City game, a small section of the support chose to take matters into their own hands.

Before the next game against Aston Villa, it was revealed that some fans had paid for a plane to fly above Old Trafford with a banner declaring 'WRONG ONE — MOYES OUT' in seven-foot-high red letters. The wording was a play on the banner that had been present at Old Trafford earlier in the season. Fans' group Stretford End Flags had faced criticism of their own throughout the year following their decision to use donations to create a banner that had an image of Moyes alongside the words 'The Chosen One' and have it draped across the Stretford End. The organisation had faced fierce criticism and opposition from other supporters, who felt it was much too premature and had set United fans up to be a laughing stock, and, considering Moyes's failure, the banner had attracted a lot of attention.

'Hindsight is a wonderful thing,' Andrew Kilduff, spokesperson for Stretford End Flags, told the BBC. 'Do we regret making the banner? Absolutely not. David Moyes was chosen by the man who brought unprecedented success to Manchester United for 26 years. Maybe in hindsight we should have taken it down after that first home game against Chelsea, before such significance could be attached to it. But maybe, in hindsight, David Moyes would not have got rid of all the old coaches. Maybe, in hindsight, Sir Alex Ferguson would not have recommended him at all. We are going to do something but we will play it by ear a little bit. It is possible we could have a poll that will stay open for a week, which takes it past the Bayern Munich game, or maybe we will do it after the match has taken place. Whatever we do, we will make it clear that if the banner comes down, it will be seen as the fans turning against David Moyes. That is how it will be interpreted by the media and the fans have to understand that.'

Despite the annoyance over the banner, most supporters were against the idea of a plane protest. 'I can understand their feelings, but it is not the way I would do it,' Ian Stirling, the vice-chairman of the Manchester United Supporters' Trust, said. 'This is part of a bigger story about the appointment of David Moyes. The board laid down some criteria to Ferguson on choosing his successor and Moyes was one of the recommendations, but the owners should be taking responsibility for the appointment.'

To his credit, in his press conference ahead of the game, Moyes didn't shy away from the topic: 'I've heard of it, I've heard what was said about it,' he said. 'But it's a long journey here and this is only the start of the journey. People can do that, they're entitled to do that … everywhere I go I've got great support from Manchester United supporters. I was really fortunate to have been at a dinner last night for Darren Fletcher and the amount of Manchester United supporters who said "Come on, keep going," who understand exactly what the situation the club and team is in, they're really supportive. Every time I've gone to Old Trafford the crowd have been great. I'm seeing something different to what other people are saying. I understand results are what really matter.'

Despite the majority being against it, the spokesperson for the group paying £840 for the plane banner, Wes Jones, was insistent that it would go ahead. 'The rumblings of discontent have started in the stands,' said Jones. 'We wanted to show that support isn't as 100 per cent as Moyes would like to think.'

Ahead of the game, Moyes had a decent point to make. 'You just have to remain focussed on the game — and that's what we have done,' he told BT Sport. 'It is going to happen but I think, for the people who have spent money on the plane, it would have been better served by putting it into Darren Fletcher's colitis charity instead.'

Jones's feelings of what the terraces wanted him to do seemed to be horrendously misjudged, at least going by their vocal reaction at the start of the game. As the teams, and Moyes, came out, Old Trafford gave a rousing show of support, and the beleaguered manager waved a hand and gratefully applauded their backing. Even if it had become painfully obvious that David Moyes was not the man to bring success to the club and handle the post-Ferguson transition, most Manchester United supporters wanted to make it plainly clear for the world to see that they were disassociating themselves from the small-time attitude which was nothing but counter-productive.

Two minutes in to the game, the plane duly circled above the stadium, to audible boos and discontent. It was followed by the opportunist work of bookmakers who had sent another plane saying 'Fergie back in, 6-1'. United won the game 4-1 and the banner, instead, had the opposite effect of provoking the alternate reaction, thus giving Moyes the impression he had the backing of the majority of the support. 'I've found the support inside Old Trafford has been terrific and I think, if ever there was a show of support for their football club, it was today inside Old Trafford. It was terrific, it really was,' he said after the match. 'I've not found what people are saying or writing. I've actually found the majority of people are very supportive and understand the job we are doing. We know we have a big job and we are determined to put it right. You just have to remain focussed on the game — and that's what we have done.'

Of course, the reality of the situation was that most had lost their confidence in the boss (and even a comprehensive win over a dreadful Aston Villa team would not make a convincing case otherwise) but would still support their team.

Against Bayern Munich in the Champions League quarter-final, first leg, Moyes found himself again calling upon Ferdinand, Vidic and Giggs, who all played well enough from the start. Giggs was brought off at half-time after picking up a groin injury; one might suggest the scarcity he had been used in these top-level games meant he may well pick up a muscle injury. United drew 1-1, a credible result to take to Germany, but the performance was as comprehensively poor as it had been, and Moyes was perhaps spared a humiliation only due to the fact that Bayern paid a lot of respect to their opponents and didn't go for the kill. Still, the statistics made depressing reading. United recorded just 26 per cent possession — the lowest for a home team in the competition that season; and, really, in any season in any situation, for Manchester United, that is a shockingly low figure.

A 4-0 win against Newcastle United gave the impression that Moyes's team were heading into the return game in good form and, incredibly, there was a 60-second spell where United dared to dream in the Allianz Arena. Patrice Evra, one of those who had endured spells on the sideline, scored with a stunning long-range drive just after half-time to give United the advantage in the tie. The goal, however, was like prodding a nest of angry wasps — 20 minutes later, it was 3-1 to Bayern, and United were reeling. Their 35 per cent possession stat was a marginal improvement but the shot statistics — 25 to the hosts, six to the visitors — tells everything about the gulf in class between two sides who were heading in very different directions.

Moyes insisted that allowing Mario Mandzukic to equalise less than a minute after going in front was the turning point: 'It's the sort of thing you learn as a schoolboy — once you score a goal, make sure you don't concede,' he said. 'You get into position and do your job. We had concentrated so fabulously well throughout the game, for us just to give it up on that moment was really disappointing.'

That seven-point gap between United and Arsenal hadn't closed, and with five games remaining for Moyes's team it was looking like an insurmountable task. Certainly, the manager was being realistic: 'We've not got Champions League football but I believe it's not far away and hopefully it's only one year,' he added. 'We've got to rebuild and our focus now is getting a team together to get back in this competition because it's a really good competition and we've really enjoyed it.' He insisted that the summer transfer plans would not be affected. 'Any players we've quietly discussed it with are more than happy to join Manchester United,' he said. 'The club have never had any problems. We're looking to spend the right money on players who are available and it's not anything to do with the Champions League.'

There could have been no way of Moyes knowing how close he was to the axe swinging. As Manchester United prepared to visit Goodison Park, they were boosted by Everton's defeat at home to Crystal Palace. Surely, if Palace won there United could too?

It was fitting that this should be the final game of Moyes's reign. Few games demonstrated the apparent lack of understanding of the squad as much as that match did. In defence, Chris Smalling, Jonny Evans, Phil Jones and Alexander Buttner lined up, a complete change from most people's first choice defence from less than a year before. Maybe only Michael Carrick, David de Gea and Wayne Rooney could be said to have been first-team starters under the last manager, and the latter was on his way out. To make matters much worse, Everton had progressed under Moyes's successor Roberto Martinez. They looked more vibrant than they had in recent years, and with a victory would pretty much guarantee that they would finish above United. By half-time it was a case of the same old story — United were two goals down and looked absolutely toothless. Supporters didn't expect a comeback, and it never threatened to materialise. When the final whistle blew, the 2-0 scoreline was kind to the visitors. For the first time in history, both Everton and Liverpool had beaten United home and away, and to compound matters they'd done so without conceding a single goal, or ever looking like they would. The United team was anything but a team; they looked like a bunch of strangers, strangers to supporters who had seen these players do much better in recent years, and strangers to each other. There was no attacking verve, no self-confidence, no fight for the shirt, and, most damning of all, even the bare minimum that was expected from Moyes — that he would at least have United playing aggressive football, in the way his Everton teams had — was painfully notable by its absence. It was now mathematically certain that Manchester United could not qualify for the Champions League.

'We controlled big majorities of the game, but we didn't have the cutting edge and were vulnerable to the counter-attack,' Moyes said.

'More importantly than that, we gave away two dreadful goals today and if you do that against any team you'll lose ... I thought we were the better team, we came in 2-0 down at half-time and I thought we were the better team, we got done with two counter-attacks and that's part of football.' With Champions League qualification dreams over for certain, Moyes was asked if he had already begun the rebuilding plans. 'Yeah I've said for a while, we're underway with what we're doing and we'll try and make sure we get the right things in place for the start of next season and get ourselves a better chance of competing nearer the top end of the league,' he said. Finally, asked if the remaining four games of the season were important, Moyes said, 'If you play for Manchester United every game is important.'

Ironic, then, that he should finally say something that resembled a statement you'd expect a Manchester United manager to make after so long. There were still the odd voices shouting support but tellingly these opinions centred more around the general knee-jerk reactions of modern football and how it was a ridiculous thing to sack a manager at a big club particularly after less than a year. And particularly at Manchester United.

Speaking in his role as a pundit for Sky Sports, former United defender Gary Neville voiced his opposition to increasing speculation that Moyes's job might be on the line after the meek surrender at Everton: 'I've been associated with the club for 30 years and that's what I've always believed,' he said. 'From Dave Sexton to Ron Atkinson — people will say those are different times — and Sir Alex Ferguson himself got time in his early years when it was difficult for him. I genuinely believe that when you give a man a six-year contract that he deserves an opportunity and the time. The reason we are sat [in the Sky studios] is because we look at football management and think of it as being a world of madness, an absolute world of madness where the average manager gets sacked every 12 months. I've always felt that Manchester United should be different and hold itself up as a club that basically stands against what is happening in the game. We used to laugh at Italy 20 years ago and say it was ridiculous what's happening there, but now we have almost become accustomed to it. I think fans are well within their rights, but I don't like it when professional people — people inside the game — come out with statements that suggest a manager should be sacked. It's not something you'll ever hear from me because it's a difficult job, something that I've never done. Sunday was a really poor performance, make no mistake about that. The idea that they had possession is a waste of time; I called it meaningless during the match and I don't change my stance on that. That's not Manchester United. Manchester United have cutting edge, brutality in attacks and they go and win games. They go and destroy teams with that level of possession. The idea that you just keep the ball and faff around in the middle of the pitch looking pretty is a waste of time to me. We had a go at Arsenal a couple of weeks ago when they went to Goodison Park and did some similar things, exactly the same as what I saw on Sunday. Not good enough. There's no doubt that this transition from the end of Sir Alex Ferguson has been tough, make no mistake about it. For ten years everyone at the club feared what would happen when Sir Alex Ferguson left and when David Gill left. If you think about it this year, David Gill was probably needed by David Moyes and Ed Woodward probably needed Sir Alex Ferguson to bed in. They have both had to get used to their new jobs together and it's proven to be tough for them both. I would personally always think that managers should be given time over a couple of years to bed their own team in.'

The problem was, even with the best will in the world, David Moyes hadn't just underachieved at United, he'd failed spectacularly to reach even the minimum of expectations. Even accounting for squad regeneration, even accounting for some overachievement under the last manager, and even accounting for the unpredictability of transition, Moyes had inherited a title-winning squad, and, more than that, a team who hadn't finished outside of the top two for years. Maybe some supporters were spoiled, maybe some might have expected a title push. Most accepted that maybe a year out of the title picture would be necessary, but results and performances had been abysmal, so abysmal in fact that it was probably unfair to compare Moyes's tenure to that of Sexton or Atkinson. If the situation at the club resembled anything familiar to its history then it was in the latter days of the reigns of both of those mentioned bosses, when things had spiralled out of control and simply seemed to be issues beyond repair under the current management. Worse still, at least under Sexton and Atkinson, the malaise had been caused over a significant period of time and the reasons were understandable. United's decline under Moyes had been so sharp and so significant that it was difficult to argue anything other than the manager was the main cause. In Atkinson's case, even if he did lose the support of some senior players, at least that took five years to happen — with Moyes, many senior players had become disillusioned within the space of five months. Some may say that even that length of time is a generous assessment.

Sure, it would be nice to be virtuous and say Manchester United were not like Manchester City or Chelsea, and would not just sack their manager after a year of underachievement, but there are two points to that — how bad would it have had to become, and how true is it anyway? Neville's Italy reference is interesting, as you would have to think he was responding to former Chelsea manager Gianluca Vialli's February comment — 'David Moyes, in Italy, would have been sacked three times by now.' Maybe three times is a push, but one can see the argument. Some big clubs would have axed their manager after the Newcastle game in December; with five league defeats before Christmas, and a title race over for the defending Champions, perhaps the manager's position could be seen to be untenable. Then the run of three defeats at the start of the year, which included two Cup eliminations, when it seemed clear to all that United's issues were perhaps more pronounced now *because* of the person they had chosen to become the new boss. Maybe the 2-0 defeat to Olympiakos would have been the third.

In any event, there was, unfortunately, absolutely no sign of progress for anyone who was going to defend Moyes. Every area of the club had stagnated or regressed. The league position. The cup exits. The performance of the team. The performance of individuals. The long-term status of those individuals. The potential of the club to attract players to improve the situation under the current management. How bad would it need to be for Neville to accept that the time was right?

And, after all, which principles of the club were being upheld? Sir Matt Busby and Sir Alex Ferguson had, as their noble titles suggested, earned the right to decide when to call it a day.

When it was clear the step up from reserve-team manager to first-team coach was too much for Wilf McGuinness, he was sacked (or demoted, depending on how generous you are). He had 18 months as manager, in much more patient times. Frank O'Farrell lasted the same amount of time, roughly. 'It wasn't so much I got the sack but the way they behaved as people,' O'Farrell said in his autobiography. 'I can never forgive them for that — they were nasty beggars.' In 2008 O'Farrell also criticised Matt Busby's interference: 'He was always about somewhere where the players could find him ... after one game he told me I should have dropped Bobby Charlton,' he said.

On the morning Ron Atkinson was sacked he arrived for training and was told he had to report to Martin Edwards's office. Atkinson remembered joking to assistant Mick Brown that he wouldn't ask for a raise after the team's recent form but was stunned to hear he'd been sacked. And, of course, there was the to-ing and fro-ing over Tommy Docherty's affair in 1977. After being told by Martin Edwards it was a personal thing and wouldn't affect his position at the club, Docherty was called to a meeting where he was asked to resign after breaking the moral code of the club. The 'Doc' refused to resign, and so Louis Edwards told him he would have to sack him. When it was revealed some years later that Atkinson had an extra-marital affair whilst manager of United, you can perhaps appreciate Docherty's bitterness which remains.

Certainly, if there was a moral code, it was ever-shifting and inconsistent with itself. Only in the case of Sir Alex could it be referenced that the club really did stick by a man in tough times, and by that point Ferguson had enough of a winning track record elsewhere, and had worked so tirelessly at rebuilding the infrastructure at the club, that to have sacked him mid-season in 1990 wouldn't really have been fair.

Ferguson later insisted he did not interfere with the day-to-day management of David Moyes; in the 2014 updated version of his autobiography, Ferguson also tried to refute the suggestion that Moyes had been hired solely on his recommendation. He additionally said that he had not been part of the decision to sack David Moyes but did at least reveal the decision appeared to have been taken regardless of what happened against Everton. The relevant extract from Ferguson's book reads, 'On the Monday, I was flying back to Manchester and sitting next to me was a lad with a newspaper with a headline that ran: "David Moyes to be sacked". At the same time, David Moyes texted me. I wasn't sure what to say to him because I was unsure what was happening at that exact moment. Ed Woodward had recently spoken to the directors to update us on the club's thinking and gather everyone's views individually, before he went on to manage the process with the Glazers. I spoke to Ed when I got back to Manchester and established that a final decision had been made. I knew that Ed wanted to tell David Moyes in person the following day and that we had come to the end of David's time at Old Trafford.'

At 8.30am on Tuesday, 22 April 2014, Manchester United released an official statement. It said, 'Manchester United has announced that David Moyes has left the club. The club would like to place on record its thanks for the hard work, honesty and integrity he brought to the role.'

The rumours initially broke some 18 hours earlier, as fanzine *Red Issue* ran a poll on their website which revealed only 6 per cent wanted the manager to stay on past the summer; Moyes had reportedly been talking to officials from Southampton to try and finalise an agreement on the transfer of left-back Luke Shaw, whilst tentative talks over a club-record £40m move for Bayern Munich midfielder Toni Kroos were apparently underway. He was reportedly incensed when he heard the rumours breaking as he left work that day. Perhaps Moyes was justifiably annoyed at the apparent lack of communication, or, perhaps, he was just hearing what he wanted to, and not hearing what he didn't want to.

A case in point was the revelation that Danny Welbeck had told some members of the press that he was 'considering his future' at United. Earlier in the season Moyes told journalists that he had talked to Welbeck about his attitude: 'I've got to say we had a word with him about a month ago and we said that he needs to be the last off the training field,' he said in December. 'Wayne's out there practising his finishing each day, whether it's taking free kicks, shooting from tight angles or bending them in, whatever it may be Wayne's practising.'

Welbeck, however, objected, saying, 'I have been doing that ever since I have been at United. I have been injured this season so maybe the manager has not seen me on the training pitch as much.' The news that he was considering leaving was a huge blow for Moyes, and not necessarily because Welbeck was such an indispensable member of the team. The Longsight-born forward was hugely popular but still had plenty of divided opinion regarding his potential as opposed to his ability but the idea that United's own stock had fallen so badly that Welbeck would be the one to call time on his career at the club, and not the manager, was such a terrible indication of the state the club was in. The story had been leaked on the morning United went to Everton; it is unthinkable to consider such a thing happening under Sir Alex's stewardship.

Less than two hours after the club announced Moyes's sacking — or, departure — they also released a statement announcing his immediate successor. It read, 'Following the departure of David Moyes as manager, Manchester United has announced that Ryan Giggs, the club's most decorated player, will assume responsibility for the first team until a permanent appointment can be made. The club will make no further comment on this process until it is concluded.'

The following day, David Moyes released his own statement through the League Managers Association. 'To have been appointed as manager of Manchester United, one of the biggest football clubs in the world, was and remains something of which I will always be incredibly proud,' he said. 'Taking charge after such a long period of continuous stability and success at the club was inevitably going to be a significant challenge, but it was one which I relished and never had a second thought about taking on. The scale of the manager's job at United is immense, but I have never stepped away from hard work and the same applies to my coaching staff. I thank them for their dedication and loyalty throughout the last season. We were fully focussed and committed to the process of the fundamental rebuilding that is required for the senior squad. This had to be achieved whilst delivering positive results in the Barclays Premier League and the Champions League. However, during this period of transition, performances and results have not been what Manchester United and its fans are used to or expect, and I both understand and share their frustration. In my short time at the club I have learnt what special places Old Trafford and Carrington are. I would like to thank the United staff for making me feel so welcome and part of the United family from my first day. And of course thank you to those fans who have supported me throughout the season. I wish you and the club all the best for the future. I have always believed that a manager never stops learning during his career and I know I will take invaluable experience from my time as United's manager. I remain proud to have led the team to the quarter-finals of this year's Champions League and I remain grateful to Sir Alex Ferguson for believing in my ability and giving me the chance to manage Manchester United.'

Richard Bevan, the LMA Chief Executive who had been called to Old Trafford on the morning of Moyes's sacking to help negotiate the terms of the settlement, also made a comment. 'Throughout his time at United, David, as he always does, has conducted himself with integrity and professionalism, values that he believes in and that have been strongly associated with the club and its rich tradition,' Bevan said. 'It is therefore sad to see the end of David's tenure at United being handled in an unprofessional manner.'

Certainly, it did feel as though the club could have handled things in a much more dignified manner. The world knew, as Moyes went into work on Tuesday, that he would be told he would be unemployed, and that much should at least have been communicated to him personally before it was leaked to the media.

Was there a scenario where David Moyes could have succeeded at the club? Let us give him the benefit of the doubt and say Luke Shaw and Ander Herrera, who had been close to signing in 2013, would have been two of the signings who came in anyway. In the interest of fairness, it has to be said that those two players, as of 2017, have been popular with fans. Herrera in particular really seems to have taken to the club. It would be a stretch to suggest he would have been able to convince Kroos to go to Old Trafford ahead of Real Madrid. Instead, you would have to think that the exodus of senior players — Ferdinand, Vidic, Evra and Giggs — would tell its own story, and cause some players to think twice. Of course, you would always be able to attract players to United by the name alone, not to mention the money, but at this late stage, you would also presume that the board had been working alongside Moyes on the list of names and had not been convinced by the overall quality or realistic aim of the list.

No projection of the future was rosy enough to paper over the cracks of the damage already caused, and, most crucially of all, the new manager was deemed to be responsible for causing that damage.

Without any shadow of a doubt, the manager succeeding Sir Alex would have had the futures of the senior players as one of the most pressing pieces of business to resolve. United have had that issue before, when Tommy Docherty took over and had to deal with the likes of Best, Law and Charlton. If you want a contemporary example then look no further than Chelsea, who, for a long period of time, allegedly had John Terry ruling the roost in the dressing room at the price of the careers of some of the managers who followed Jose Mourinho after his first stint in charge at Stamford Bridge. There was no suggestion that there were such power struggles at Old Trafford, but, then again, it could be said that Moyes never had the dressing room to lose it. Things had become so bad that those senior players no longer wanted to be around the club anyway. This was a problem Moyes inherited, but one also made worse for the incoming manager, whoever it may be. Nemanja Vidic was definitely off while the future of Ferdinand, Evra and Giggs remained in the balance. It was an awful lot of experience to delete from the squad in one fell swoop, particularly when you would need to find a replacement for it from elsewhere.

The signings of Marouane Fellaini and Juan Mata did not appear to have been well thought out or strategised. Fellaini played alongside Carrick in midfield and the two appeared to be incredibly incompatible; their lack of pace and movement was an irritating problem for United supporters. Maybe they were the kind of midfield who might be able to control the pace of a game if United were leading, the only problem being that Moyes's team rarely imposed themselves on a game of any importance where that midfield could prove to be a winning solution. Juan Mata, a brilliant schemer, was brought in with no real idea in place. Wayne Rooney and Robin van Persie would be the first-choice front two so there was no place for Mata in his preferred number-ten role. This meant he played on the right. United's midfield against Liverpool was Mata, Carrick, Fellaini and Januzaj. After picking up an injury following that hat-trick game against Olympiakos, Van Persie didn't play again for Moyes, temporarily solving the Mata problem, but leaving it behind for the new manager. Shinji Kagawa, a gifted playmaker capable of excelling in that number-ten role, hadn't been given enough of a chance in that role to shine. And that, ultimately, was the major issue for the next boss — not enough players with credible winning experience to depend upon, and too many players who were filed in the 'Might be good if …' category. The squad was now essentially composed mostly of players of that latter quality, and those who had demonstrated enough promise to suggest they would break out of it and establish themselves as proper first-choice players had found themselves hampered by the new manager (Rafael and Welbeck, for example). This was an incredibly serious problem for a new manager as a clutch of these players, in the absence of those established winners, would be automatically depended upon to form the backbone of Manchester United's first team in the short term.

Ryan Giggs — Football Manager

The decision to give Ryan Giggs the job as interim boss for the last four games was met with universal approval. At this point it should be said that Giggs was the number-one choice for many in the United support. Pep Guardiola was also pointed to, but the history of Giggs as someone who understood what it meant and what it took to be a winner at Manchester United gave him a theoretical edge. The Welsh legend clearly wanted the job.

Perhaps, in hindsight, putting him in charge in late December 2013 might have been the best solution. He would have had a transfer window to bring in a player or two and by the end of the campaign there would at least be the opportunity for him to have the team playing in the way he wanted them to. Four games wasn't going to be enough time for him to really do that.

On the morning of 25 April, Giggs faced the press as United boss for the first time and made sure his first port of call was to pay some credit to his predecessor. 'I'd like to thank David for giving me my first chance in coaching,' he said. 'It was something I'll always remember when he rang me in the summer and asked me to come on board. Obviously I was still playing but he's given me my first opportunity of a coaching role. Secondly, to say how proud I am to be managing Manchester United for the remaining games. It's a club I've been associated with for 25 years and it's a proud moment for me and one I will enjoy. I've enjoyed the week and I'm proud more than anything. It's probably the proudest moment of my career and one I'm going to enjoy for the remaining two and a half weeks of the season and bring back some smiles onto the faces of the fans.'

Giggs was asked what his first business had been and he joked, 'I've just given myself a five-year contract! While I can! I haven't done much this week but am still involved as a player as well. I've trained okay this week and looked sharp, to be fair! No, everyone has looked sharp, 20-odd players are in with a chance.' The left-winger confirmed he had made a phone call to Paul Scholes to ask him to come and help out with coaching, and he'd also asked Nicky Butt to work more closely with the first team rather than the reserves, but insisted his mind was only on the last few games of the season when asked if he wanted the job permanently. 'I'm just concentrating on a short time, the four games remaining, that's the main focus on Saturday and Norwich as it's going to be a tough game with them fighting for their lives,' he insisted. 'After that, I've not really thought about it.'

With United's general performance levels being so poor, and even their victorious games not really resembling the classic style which the club was associated with, it was suggested to Giggs, as someone who liked to play with flair, that he would be the man to bring some swagger back to the team. 'I'll tell the players just to try to enjoy yourself, express yourself,' he said. 'I don't know if I'd be saying that as manager last week because the performance wasn't great, but I've come into the job and my immediate aim is to win on Saturday, and I felt just the way to do that is to make training as enjoyable as I can so they can go out and play and they have done that. It's going to be my philosophy, obviously the Manchester United philosophy as I've been here for all my career. I want players to play with passion, speed, tempo and be brave with imagination, all the things that are expected of a Manchester United player. To work hard but, most of all, enjoy it. As a player, I know if I'm enjoying the game I can express myself a lot more and that's what I'll be doing with the team tomorrow. It's been a frustrating season for everyone. We win together and lose together, and in these remaining four games I want to bring the positivity back. Three home games at Old Trafford, where the home form hasn't been great, and I want to see goals, tackles, players taking players on and getting the crowd up. I want the passion that should come with being a Manchester United player ... we have the players to do it, we have players in that dressing room who are winners, used to winning and have a winning mentality. They will show it on Saturday. I trust the players, I know what they are capable of and I want them to go out and show it against Norwich.'

Giggs revealed he'd already spoken to Sir Alex Ferguson to get advice. 'He has given me advice and told me he is always at the end of the phone,' Giggs said. 'He was the first person I picked up the phone to. Why wouldn't I? It's good to know I can turn to the manager if I ever need him. He's been everything you can be as a manager — a young manager, an experienced manager, a successful manager.' The new man admitted it'd been a busy few days, but he'd had a little help from his friends. 'It's been chaotic,' he admitted. 'You get pulled from pillar to post. I sit in the office to write notes because I'm trying not to forget anything. It's a pretty lonely place at times, but I keep saying I'm enjoying it. They [Phil Neville, Paul Scholes and Nicky Butt] are Manchester United fans and have played for the club for the majority of their careers. Myself and Scholesy have been at just the one club. I've had great help from them. It's a tough job and you need as much help as you can get. Phil has been brilliant. He's organised everything and taken the weight off my shoulders.'

Positive words which were well received by fans, but already other names were being touted as candidates to take the job in the summer. Antonio Conte was one name mentioned, Carlo Ancelotti another, while Louis van Gaal, the Holland coach, was the early favourite. Dutch newspaper *De Telegraaf* reported that a deal had already been agreed for Van Gaal to take over after that summer's World Cup in Brazil, but United issued a statement: 'There is nothing to report. We have not signed a new manager. When we have something to report, we will announce it.'

Giggs gave an exclusive interview to MUTV where much of the same information was discussed as with the general assembled press, but he did say a few extra things such as sharing his expectation that

Old Trafford would be 'rocking' against Norwich. 'I have got to say it is the proudest moment of my life,' he told the club's official channel. 'I have supported Manchester United all my life, I have been a part of the club since I was 13. I am proud, I am happy, a little nervous and, just like playing, can't wait for the game on Saturday.'

All eyes were on what Giggs would be wearing; when he emerged for the pre-match interviews wearing a suit, it was clear he hadn't selected himself to play. Giggs made six changes from the team who were defeated by Everton, and within the first few minutes it appeared clear that the United players were freed and liberated, playing with some of that old style and movement the fans had been used to seeing. Four minutes before the break, the recalled Danny Welbeck was felled in the box and Wayne Rooney scored the penalty. Rooney scored early in the second half and some gloss was added to the scoreline with a Juan Mata double to make it 4-0. During the game, another plane flew over the stadium, arranged by a small group of Maltese supporters, with the sarcastic message 'Thank U Moyes' on a banner.

Afterwards, Giggs described it as the best feeling of his time at United. 'All the years I walked out at Old Trafford, I've never felt like that,' he said. 'I felt ten feet tall. I enjoyed it and 4-0 is a dream day for us so I'm really pleased. Obviously I was happy we were 1-0 up at half-time but not particularly with the performance. I said to the players they had trained hard, maybe too hard, and it's been an emotional week. I reminded them we play with speed and tempo and when we do, not many can live with us. They reacted well to that. All of us have let ourselves down this year, we haven't played to the quality we are capable of but we did that this afternoon. The standards they set here, they need to keep for Sunderland. I think every player has a point to prove. Only David de Gea has performed to his ability this season. The rest have fallen below those standards. It's not about playing one good game. Every time you put a United top on you have to keep to those standards.'

The following week, Giggs made another five changes, but United lost against a Sunderland team enjoying a mini-revival in their annual relegation fight. Sebastian Larsson's 30th minute goal gave the visitors the lead and, with a cause to fight for greater than United's, their concentration and commitment levels were higher.

United had more chances but not the better ones, the flat afternoon the product of the reality of the preceding nine months rather than the temporary boost of the last nine days. 'Yeah, I feel flat, the players are a bit flat, why I don't know,' Giggs admitted. 'But credit to Sunderland, they're in good form and they probably created the best chances even though we had the majority of the ball. We lacked that bit of quality in the final third.' The interim boss repeated that he wasn't aware of any developments in the search for a permanent manager, but did say that he would give himself a fitness test before deciding whether or not he would play in the next game, the final home game of the season against Hull City.

By the time he did come on as a substitute, United were winning. Giggs had given young players Tom Lawrence (who he replaced) and James Wilson (who scored twice) their senior debuts in a little bit of a nod to the club's tradition for bringing through youngsters, but the biggest cheer of the night was reserved for the man whose brief cameo made him the second player-manager in the club's history after Clarence Hilditch. Every Ryan Giggs touch was greeted with a loud cheer as if it was a testimonial. With five minutes to go, Robin van Persie scored to make it 3-1 and add a bit of gloss to the result. Giggs came close to scoring with a long range free kick — after the game, he was asked if he had been playing with the thought this might be the last time he pulled on a United shirt. 'Not really, I think my concentration's not changed, I'll do my job on and off the pitch as best I can,' he said. 'We'll see what happens after Sunday.'

It became apparent that ahead of the season's closer at Southampton, Giggs had been informed that a new man would be given the job, and in his last pre-match press conference he said he was giving some thought as to whether or not he would continue to play on. 'With all the things going on, whether to carry on playing or not, there are a lot of things to consider,' said Giggs. 'This experience has definitely helped me, I have loved it, but there is no major disappointment. It [playing on] will depend on if the new manager wants me. Do I want to put my body through another year of eating the right things, the discipline, another pre-season? Do I want to go out still enjoying it and not go on a year too long. These are all the things I have to consider. I loved coming on the other night. I still enjoy training, even though I have not done much of it over the last couple of weeks.'

Giggs didn't play as United finished their campaign with a 1-1 draw; technically, the result meant the club would not play in Europe for the first time in 25 years, though he could hardly be blamed for that as the damage had been done well before he took the reins on a short-term basis.

Before the dust had even settled on the 2013/14 season, the BBC reported that Louis van Gaal had told them he would 'love' the United job. 'It's a fantastic challenge and I hope that I shall be the one,' the Dutchman told their news channel. On 19 May 2014, the appointment was confirmed, and Ryan Giggs was named as his assistant.

* * *

To conclude this chapter, it's worth just jumping a little ahead of time to evaluate Giggs's prospects of managing the club on a long-term basis. It was alleged by some that Giggs coveted the job even after Van Gaal took over, and there were still many who would have been happy if that was the case. The period Giggs had in charge most certainly whetted his appetite but was simply not enough to draw a conclusion either way.

The Welshman admitted after the game with Southampton in May 2014 that, with his future uncertain, he was overcome by emotion. 'I was saying goodbye to the players, thanking them,' he said. 'Potentially saying goodbye to a lot of the players for the last time, a bit of the staff and I'm not emotional, at least I didn't think I was. My car was parked right outside and I thought I need to get in my car here. I could feel myself getting emotional. So I get in my car and I just went, started crying, getting really emotional. It was a mixture of saying goodbye to people for maybe the last time and the pressure that I put myself under. Sounds stupid now. I come out of the airport and at the lights Nicky Butt pulls up next to me and I'm thinking fucking hell, I can't let Butty know I've just been crying … it's been a difficult year playing-wise … if I'd retired last year I'd have gone out on a high, you know, it was the 20th title and everything would have been rosy, but life isn't like that. I think Manchester United symbolises, for me, the bedrock of my life. It's been there since I was 13. I learnt so much, you know, winning, never giving up.'

As Giggs discussed the future plans with Louis van Gaal, he was informed that the new manager would like to keep him on as assistant. Giggs accepted and announced his retirement from playing. 'Today is a fantastic day for Manchester United,' he said in a statement on the club's official website. 'Louis van Gaal is a great appointment and let me begin by telling you how delighted I am to be working with someone of his calibre. His credentials are second to none and I'm positive the club will thrive under his leadership over the coming years. I would also like to take this opportunity to announce my retirement from professional football and embark upon a new and exciting chapter in my life, as assistant manager of Manchester United. I am immensely proud, honoured and fortunate to have represented the biggest club in the world 963 times and Wales 64 times. My dream was always to play for Manchester United, and although it saddens me to know I won't be pulling on a United jersey again as a player, I have been lucky enough to have fulfilled that dream playing with some of the best players in the world, working under an incredible manager in Sir Alex Ferguson, and, most of all, playing for the greatest fans in world football. I have always felt and appreciated your support. I want to also give a huge thanks to the backroom staff and support teams we have and have had at Manchester United over the years. I would not have achieved the success I have without your continuing dedication and commitment to creating the best environment to enable the players to thrive. I would not have won 34 trophies in my career without you. I would also like to say a special thanks to my friends and family for all your love and support. For me, today is a new chapter filled with many emotions — immense pride, sadness, but, most of all, excitement towards the future. United fans I hope will share and echo my belief that the club, the management and owners, are doing everything they can to return this great club to where it belongs, and I hope to be there every step of the way. To the greatest fans in world football, thank you, I have loved every minute of playing for you and representing the biggest and best club in the world. See you next season. Ryan.'

Considering the rigidity of Van Gaal's approach, which is about to be evaluated in full, it seems unfair to suggest Giggs had any hand in the frustrating brand of football United would play over the following couple of years. One might use that to question Giggs's own influence and contribution, but the fact of the matter is that Van Gaal's reputation for having everything at the club his way was well documented. Even after two years as assistant, we are no closer to knowing just how well equipped the club's most decorated player is to be its manager.

The romantic in any United fan sees Giggs one day returning to the club as manager and winning league titles and European cups, but shortly after Jose Mourinho took charge in 2016 a 29-year association with Ryan Giggs and Manchester United came to an end.

'After 29 seasons at Manchester United as a player and assistant manager, I know winning is in the DNA of this club — giving youth a chance, and playing attacking and exciting football,' Giggs said in a statement as he left the club. 'It's healthy to have high expectations, it's right to expect to win. Manchester United expects, deserves, nothing less. This is why it is a huge decision for me to step away from the club that has been my life since the age of 14. It has not been a decision that I have made lightly. I'll take away so many special memories as well as a lifetime of experiences that will, I hope, serve me well in the future. However, the time feels right and, although I have no immediate plans to step into management, it is where I want to be. I've been extremely fortunate in having two great managerial mentors — first in Sir Alex, who I've spent the majority of my life working with and learning from and who I believe will remain as football's greatest-ever manager, and, in more recent times, Louis van Gaal, whose CV speaks for itself. The knowledge I have gleaned from them has been invaluable. I want to reiterate my thanks to the backroom staff and support teams at Manchester United I've worked with over the years. The results on the pitch are a reflection of the hard work off it. I would not have achieved the success I have without the dedication, sacrifice and commitment of these people in creating the best environment for the team to succeed. I want to congratulate José Mourinho on his appointment as manager of the world's biggest club. There are only a handful of proven winners at the very highest level and José is unquestionably one of them. I know the fans will welcome him. My final thank you is to the fans. I cannot begin to tell you how much I will miss walking out at Old Trafford in front of you. It's extremely difficult to say goodbye after 29 years. I have loved every minute both as a player and assistant manager. The support you have always shown me has been phenomenal — thank you. It's time for a new chapter and a new challenge. I'm excited about the future — I've had the best apprenticeship into management anyone could ever ask for.'

In January 2018, Giggs was hired as the Welsh national team manager, succeeding the hugely successful Chris Coleman.

The future is Orange

The announcement of Louis van Gaal's arrival at Manchester United did not come without many caveats. In March of 2013, Manchester City chief executive Ferran Soriano lifted the lid on what Van Gaal was like to work with at Barcelona. 'If you treat people badly they remember. One day you make an error and they will kill you. I've seen this in many clubs,' Soriano said. 'Louis van Gaal has been a very good coach in many clubs but his style is very difficult. The same thing happened to him in Barcelona as in Bayern Munich. He is very tough, people don't like him but he wins. And one day you won't win — and when you don't win everybody that is angry with you will come back and try to kill you. In the movies this works but in real life it doesn't.'

Van Gaal had been sacked from his job at Barcelona and also from his job at Bayern Munich in April 2011. Bayern president Uli Hoeness said that the decision was one that had been a long time coming. 'Football should be enjoyable, but there has been nothing enjoyable about football at FC Bayern for a while now,' he said. 'And to say that he had the players behind him was a myth.'

Still, the reputation of the man chosen to be David Moyes's permanent successor at Manchester United was hardly unknown in the world of football. On 19 May, after a temporary delay as Van Gaal was working with his Holland team as part of their World Cup preparation, the appointment was made official. The club's official statement read, 'Louis van Gaal will take over as manager of Manchester United from the 2014/15 season. He has signed a three-year contract. Louis, 62, has managed at the top level of European football for over 20 years and in that time has won domestic titles and domestic cups in three countries, as well as the UEFA Champions League, the UEFA Cup, an Intercontinental Cup, two UEFA Super Cups and domestic Super Cups in Holland and Germany. He will take up his post after the FIFA World Cup, where he will manage the Dutch national team.'

Ed Woodward said, 'In Louis van Gaal, we have secured the services of one of the outstanding managers in the game today. He has achieved many things in his career to date and Old Trafford provides him with a fitting stage on which to write new chapters in the Manchester United story. Everyone is very excited about this new phase in the club's history. His track record of success in winning leagues and cups across Europe throughout his career makes him the perfect choice for us. People know him as a larger-than-life character, but I have also been extremely impressed by his intelligence, thoughtful approach to the role and his diligence. I'm looking forward to working with him. I'm delighted that Louis has chosen Ryan as his assistant. Ryan's association with the club spans over two decades and his knowledge and stature will be of great use to Louis. In addition, this is a fantastic opportunity for Ryan to learn his trade alongside a world-class manager whose attacking instincts and belief in youth are tailor-made for Manchester United.'

The Glazer family also made statements. 'I am delighted that Louis will be our next manager,' said Joel Glazer. 'He has an outstanding pedigree as a coach, both as a man who motivates his teams to win trophies and as someone who believes in giving young players a chance to prove their worth. I am sure he will make a big impression on the club, the players and the fans.' Avram Glazer said, 'Louis joins us at an exciting time and has already communicated some great ideas for how the club can move forward. The board is right behind him in his plans and everyone here is already looking forward to the start of next season.'

The club's official website also carried a short statement from the new manager: 'It was always a wish for me to work in the Premier League,' Van Gaal was quoted as saying. 'To work as a manager for Manchester United, the biggest club in the world, makes me very proud. I have managed in games at Old Trafford before and know what an incredible arena Old Trafford is and how passionate and knowledgeable the fans are. This club has big ambitions; I too have big ambitions. Together I'm sure we will make history.'

Before he officially took charge in mid-July, there was plenty of activity. The work already done on the deals for Luke Shaw and Ander Herrera was given the thumbs up, but Van Gaal immediately ruled out the idea of signing Toni Kroos. Just as important as any transfer activity, however, was how the new manager would get Manchester United playing, and whether or not the ideas of the Dutch coach would be compatible with the way supporters at Old Trafford were used to watching their football. It's fair to say the appointment was greeted mostly with positivity and high expectancy. Van Gaal, after all, was credited with at least some work in the foundation of the modern successes of Bayern Munich and Barcelona. Those two clubs had not only enjoyed glory days and acclamations of being the best side in Europe, but they had done so with a certain reinvention of their own identity. For Manchester United supporters, they could get on board with the idea of a new style of football, so long as it was entertaining and attacking. Bayern and Barcelona were impressive models to acknowledge, though how much of that was down to the new manager at United was up for debate; so, inevitably, eyes were keenly trained on the World Cup to see just how well his underdog Holland team might fare.

When Holland took on Spain in their first group game out in Brazil, they were cheered on by most Manchester United supporters; after an even first half, which finished 1-1, United fans were given cause for extreme optimism by a stunning second-half display which saw the Netherlands hit four more goals without reply. Their 3-5-2 system looked fluid and devastating on the counter-attack.

Holland won their other group games and in their second-round game against Mexico displayed a little of the Manchester United spirit, coming back from a goal down to equalise in the 88th minute from one-time rumoured target Wesley Sneijder and then winning the game in injury time. It was, however, the quarter-final against Costa Rica that attracted most attention aside from the Spain game; after a goalless game looked set to go to penalties, Van Gaal took off goalkeeper Jasper Cillessen in injury time after extra time and replaced him with Tim Krul. Krul was not a better goalkeeper than Cillessen but it was clear the idea was to project the impression that he was a better penalty stopper, so as to get under the skin of their opponents. Holland won on penalties, and Van Gaal was heralded a genius by his waiting fans back in Manchester. The Dutch went out in the next round against Argentina after another goalless draw (perhaps it was these points that should have been more picked up on by United fans) and another penalty shoot-out which this time didn't go their way.

Eight days after the World Cup exit, Louis van Gaal was unveiled to the press back in the UK. 'First of all, I want to thank Sir Bobby Charlton because it's a great honour to come into this stadium and be guided by Sir Bobby Charlton,' he told journalists. 'My first steps ... okay, my first ones were with Bayern and Barcelona [as a visiting coach], but as a coach of United these were my first steps and I was very proud to do that with Sir Bobby Charlton. I have the age to have seen him playing so I know what he means for Manchester United and English football. It was a great honour to do that with him.'

Van Gaal was asked what he hoped to achieve at United and his response was almost instantly more impressive in its authority than what Moyes had said when he first faced the press. 'I will do my utmost best,' he said. 'That's what I can give. I cannot give predictions because you never know. It's the biggest club in the world. Within two days, I know already how important Manchester United is but also how important the sponsors are. I have to work, I have to prepare a team, I have to adapt to this big club. It shall not be easy but I will do my utmost best and, when you see my career, you can see what I have won. That's all I can say. The future shall show if I can do that again. It's the biggest club because of how well it's known around the world. In sport, you are never the biggest club because every season you have to be prove [*sic*]. Last year, you were seventh so then you are not the biggest club. But it's well known all over the world. When I was in China or Brazil, people are talking about United when I was the coach of the Dutch team. That's the difference. There's a lot of expectation but it's also a great challenge because of that. Therefore, I have chosen this club. I worked for Barcelona — in my opinion, number one in Spain. I've coached Ajax — number one in the Netherlands, and I've coached Bayern Munich — number one in Germany. Now I'm in Manchester United — number one in England. I hope I fulfil the expectation but it shall be difficult.'

The expectation was that the new United boss would be given over £100m to spend on new signings but he insisted he would first look at his squad. 'My method is always the same,' he said. 'I want to look at the players now, the players present. Of course I know how the players play. But I don't know the players under my training or coaching. In the first three or four weeks, I want to see what they can do. Then maybe I will buy other players. The players we have bought now — Shaw and Herrera — they were already on the list. I gave my approval because I like them. First I want to see the players performing under my philosophy. The owners and the CEO have a lot of confidence in me. They have come to me and I explained my philosophy and they were excited. Because of that I'm here. We have to wait and see if I can fulfil this expectation of those people and the supporters. The fans are very important, I know that. You cannot predict. In the world of football you cannot predict.'

Van Gaal's most famous success had come with Ajax when a team comprised predominantly of young players developed by the club won the European Cup, and, with youth being so important to his new club, he was asked if he had been given any direction as far as that was concerned. 'The owners and the CEO, Ed Woodward, have asked me to give advice but the main project is the first team,' the new boss said. 'That's more of a short-term thing than the youth — that's a long-term project. The first year or two years we have to separate them. Now, I need all my knowledge to transfer my philosophy into this selection. You have to give me time to do that. Not only you, but also the CEO and the owners. Nicky Butt is already assisting us, Paul Scholes we shall find a role for him and also for Phil Neville, I believe. That's what we want. But it has to also be possible and we have to look at that. We have to adapt to the qualities of these people. It's not an easy job. We have to speak personally with them — that's why we have to wait and see ... you have to know that I'm not always convinced of the experience of players. I've said a lot of times, a boy like Clarence Seedorf was 16 years old … I gave him his debut for Ajax at that time. At 16 he was sometimes more experienced than a player who was 30. It depends on the personality. You named Rooney. For example, Michael Carrick has been injured the day before and that's a blow for me because he's experienced. It's very important we have experienced players, but not only in age and football experience but experience as a human being. My philosophy isn't only the football player but in total. Then there are not so many experienced players.'

Asked how he would describe his strong personality, Van Gaal said, 'I'm democratic, empathetic to human beings. Of course I have a strong personality, but the other characteristics are more important. That's the key of my personality … the media wants to show that part of the personality [that he was autocratic]. But that part of the personality is small. But when you repeat that everybody thinks like that. I'm always the same person. When I was 39, when I began at Ajax — I played professional football until I was 37 and an assistant — the personality hasn't really changed. It's the same. But autocratic and strong personality is not the same thing and a lot of people think it's the same. I have a strong philosophy. Every year I've trained, it confirms this philosophy. Sir Alex also had a strong philosophy and it was always affirming that because he won a lot of titles. I hope I can do that.' Van Gaal confirmed he had already spoken to his former opponent. 'Sir Alex called me to congratulate me and we have spoken about getting a coffee or to eat with each other. We were always invited to UEFA forums and we would always have a glass of wine. We know each other very well. I shall drink coffee and wine with him — maybe the best wine I can imagine.'

After a year of underwhelming performances, Van Gaal was tasked with bringing success back to United — so, what would success represent for the manager? 'I don't know,' he confessed. 'First, what I've already said, I have to see how the players perform my philosophy and how quick they can pick up this philosophy. Then I can answer. Now, I haven't worked with most of them so we have to wait and see. It's very important there's a click between players and the manager. For me, the challenge is always to come first. Not fourth. But when you have to analyse after one season, it's dependent on the click between the players and the manager. I have never worked in the Premier League so it's a big challenge I wanted to take. I have worked in Spain and Germany and in my time at Barcelona I think at that time the Spanish league was the best league. And in my time in Germany we were the best league. And maybe, when I work here the Premier League is the best league! It's difficult to describe. I've only been here two days. I've met a lot of people and when you see those kind of people who love the club, you see it's a big family and they expect a lot from me. They are very excited to meet me. Can I fulfil that expectation? I think I can do it. But because of the greatness of this club it's also much more difficult than in another club. Also, this club is also guided in the commercial way and we have to fulfil that also. And that's not always possible to fulfil both commercial and football. That's my big challenge after two days. Maybe it will be changing after the US tour, but I don't think so!'

If there was one thing to take from the conference it was Van Gaal's self-confidence; there was no wide-eyed disbelief at the size of the task he'd taken on, no admittance that he had felt nervous when approached about the job, and no flinching when it came to stating the ambition for the future, because the demands and expectations of the club were the same as his own and he had the track record to back it up.

Perhaps that self-belief was assisted by the fact his name had been mentioned in the media as a strong candidate to replace Ferguson after the then-United boss announced his intention to retire the first time in 2001. Van Gaal was one of a number of names alongside the likes of Martin O'Neill, Ottmar Hitzfeld and Sven-Göran Eriksson tipped to replace Ferguson. In 2013 Eriksson claimed he had signed a contract to succeed Ferguson back then and had been willing to break an agreement with the FA to manage England. In 2017 Martin Edwards revealed in his own autobiography that the first choice had actually been Arsene Wenger, and that he and then-chief executive Peter Kenyon had even been invited to Wenger's house in London to discuss the possibility before the Frenchman's loyalty to Arsenal executive David Dein won out. Van Gaal was the bookies' favourite — betting firm Blue Square suspended betting at one point in January 2002, as the Dutchman's contract with the national team was due to expire at the end of that month, and some media sources had put two and two together and suggested that he may be unveiled as the incoming boss as early as February. 'I knew I was first on the list last year,' Van Gaal had told reporters. 'I don't have any contact with them now because I am coach of the national team but I can imagine that a club like Manchester United are still interested in Louis van Gaal.'

Of the names still around, Wenger of course was still managing Arsenal, but Van Gaal was the only other to remain at the top level. In the interim, he returned to coach at Barcelona, signing a three-year contract in the summer of 2002. His previous spell at the Nou Camp had ended acrimoniously when he told Spanish journalists, 'Friends of the press, I am leaving, congratulations!' During the 1999/2000 season, Van Gaal had famously rowed with star player Rivaldo, and upon his return, despite the Brazilian having a year left on his contract, he was released on a free transfer. 'Rivaldo was only interested in making more money and playing less,' the manager said. 'He was chosen as the best player in 1999, but he has not handled himself well since then and has not behaved like a footballer should. He had illusions about Barca and was requesting to take holidays when important Champions League games were approaching. He then hides back home in Brazil. He plays for Brazil like we needed him to at Barcelona, and he has proved this in the World Cup finals, showing he reserved himself for Japan.'

Rivaldo retorted, saying, 'I don't like Van Gaal, and I am sure he doesn't like me either.'

On 28 January 2003, just five months after his return, and with Barcelona just three points above the relegation zone, Van Gaal left by mutual consent. His next managerial role was far more successful, taking AZ Alkmaar to only the second league title in their history in 2009. At the start of that season, Van Gaal had actually said he would leave the club, but the players had convinced him to stay and he in turn said he would give them a chance to prove themselves. Their Eredivisie success came off the back of a club-record run of 28 games unbeaten.

From there, Bayern Munich had been sufficiently impressed to hire Van Gaal but suffered a difficult start. The new manager had made a number of changes, bringing the likes of Thomas Muller into the team and moving Bastian Schweinsteiger from the right wing into central midfield, and the early results were less than convincing. Sports Director Christian Nerlinger heaped pressure on the boss when he said, 'We need short-term success, which means we need immediate results.'

Van Gaal's response? He said he was a process trainer, and everybody knew that. 'We're just starting, we're not ready yet,' Van Gaal said, adding that he felt his new team were doing well mostly but not in 'Phase Four', which was effectively being proficient enough in the style to create that final pass to create a goalscoring opportunity. At the end of the season, Bayern won the Bundesliga and DFB-Pokal Cup double. They also got to the Champions League Final, where they were defeated by Jose Mourinho's Inter Milan. Van Gaal was named Manager of the Year in Germany and there was some discussion that his contract would be extended; less than 12 months later, he was sacked, with Bayern trailing third-placed Hannover by a point and thus being in severe danger of missing out on Champions League qualification. Bayern did qualify but did not win the League again until 2013 — since then, as of 2019, they have won it every single season, and they also won the 2013 Champions League, defeating Barcelona by an aggregate score of 7-0 in a staggering display of football. Despite a very fractured and difficult relationship, Van Gaal — perhaps generously — was credited with having created the framework for the modern success of the German giants. Their brand of football, at least in 2013, was seen as a style which could better that of Barcelona's. It had all the same elements and principles in terms of keeping possession but seemed more powerful and physical. How much of that was down to Van Gaal?

When David Moyes took over the year before, the best-case scenario was that he would manage the transition smoothly; the necessary evolution of the squad so that the experienced players were gradually phased out and replaced with new stars, staying true to that 'cut from the same cloth' idea. In the summer of 2014, with Manchester United's present identity resembling little more than a hollow shell and the perception of what it should be, most supporters were on board with the idea of change. Perhaps change would not only be good, but it could be necessary. It was clear that some of the senior players did not take to Moyes but when those players had diminishing contributions on a short-term scale, if at all, to the incoming boss, then perhaps it was for the better that there was a clean slate.

Manchester United's tradition may have been a counter-attacking 4-4-2 with wingers, but, just as Sir Matt Busby had to move with the times in the 1950s and 1960s when teams became more focussed on defensive strategies and started playing with the conventional four-man defences as they are found today, perhaps it was time to shake that up. So long as United played attacking and entertaining football, and did so with as many young, home-grown players as it was possible to balance in a team that was successful, then how much did it *really* matter what shape the team played? Van Gaal had played a 3-5-2 with Holland, and the highlight of that formation had come when a long ball from left wing-back (and rumoured United target) Daley Blind was met with a superb diving header by Robin van Persie.

Moyes's United had played 4-4-2 for the most part, with some brief flirtations with 4-3-3, but the Scot's ideas could never be mistaken for being radical in the same way that Van Gaal's ideas might. Whether you were for or against Van Gaal's methods, it's almost beyond reasonable argument that a shake-up had become necessary. United had become pedestrian and predictable (that these same accusations would still be levelled at the team some years later is a whole different ball game, as we'll come on to later), so much so in fact that their approach now appeared archaic. Antonio Valencia was perhaps the only component in United's front six who resembled something close to what he might in an Old Trafford team near its reputable best; an out and out right-winger who was direct and fast. Notable by their definite absence were the box-to-box midfielders; in their place, there weren't even like for like complementary players, a tackler and a schemer, for example. Instead there was Michael Carrick, the potentially beautiful passer who would generally be a capable defensive screen but rarely likely to punish the opposition in the last 40 to 45 yards. Alongside him had been Marouane Fellaini, whose hard-man description alongside the likes of Roy Keane was only justifiable in the Vinnie Jones-esque context that his physicality was a nuisance for opponents. In a deep midfield role, Fellaini's limitations on the ball (and, truth be told, as a natural tackler) often left him open for criticism as the mistakes he would tend to make with clumsy tackles or misplaced passes would, that far back, be costly. New boy Ander Herrera and long-term servant Darren Fletcher had the tools between them to at least come close to resembling a combative midfield in the way United fans were used to seeing, but that depended a) on whether Herrera could hit the ground running, b) whether the two would even have the chance to strike up a partnership due to Fletcher's ongoing illness issues which restricted his availability, and consequently c) whether the qualities of each respective individual would complement Carrick and/or Fellaini considering that either might *have* to play.

With Ryan Giggs retired, United had the option of Nani, Adnan Januzaj and Ashley Young on the left. Surprisingly, Nani, as frustrating and inconsistent as he was, was still arguably the best choice to play that role. Januzaj was more inconsistent and less effective on his good days; Young had periods of great form but his tendency to cut inside was sometimes to his downfall. Up front, the oft-injured Rooney and Van Persie lacked the mobility of previous great partnerships and, after a difficult year, Danny Welbeck and Javier Hernandez no longer appeared to be the fantastic second-choice options they once were. All four forwards were different, and so the manager, whoever he may be, could be content with the diversity, if not the outstanding quality. Juan Mata was the extra ingredient in this mix; could he play off the right, or would there be a role for him in the number-ten role? Just six months into his career at United it seemed as if David Moyes had landed his successor with a £40m headache. Indeed, in the summer of 2014, Jose Mourinho was being lauded for acquiring such a large amount of money for a player essentially surplus to requirements at Stamford Bridge. The biggest issue for United was the lack of speed, penetration and consistent quality in the final third; Valencia had two but not the third of those attributes, though it has to be said that the natural wingers were rare in the game. Generally, the better ones had been converted into strikers or deep-lying forwards, Cristiano Ronaldo and Lionel Messi the most prominent examples, whilst Gareth Bale had also made that transition too. Maybe it was true; maybe instead of sticking round pegs in square holes, Manchester United needed to demonstrate fluidity in order to evolve to catch up with the modern game.

Louis van Gaal also inherited further problems, though. In Chris Smalling, Jonny Evans and Phil Jones, he had three players all tipped to succeed Ferdinand and Vidic one day. One day was now here and none of the three had yet provided a compelling case for their selection as the senior one of the trio, and, further to that, there was no obvious pair from that selection.

In United's first pre-season game, against Los Angeles Galaxy, all three played together as Van Gaal played a 3-5-2, with Valencia and Luke Shaw as wing-backs. Fletcher and Herrera played in midfield, with Mata slightly more advanced, and Rooney and Welbeck played as the strike pair up front. United won 7-0 and looked lively; perhaps they had been cajoled into performing by an angry team talk in training the day before, where Van Gaal had dressed down his new players for an apparent lack of intensity in their play. Before that training session, he had been asked by reporters about potential signings.

'At this moment, I cannot say anything about the squad and additions,' he said. 'I want to learn about my players and get to know them. When I am the coach and when I give the orders to my players to play a certain way, I want to see how they perform. That is why I cannot answer this question just now. I want to give all players the chance to show themselves under my guidance.'

With speculation raging, as always, about who United might sign, some of their current squad players were looking forward to a new start. Shinji Kagawa said he couldn't wait to get started back at Old Trafford after a very disappointing World Cup with Japan. 'I feel incredibly excited,' the former Dortmund forward said. 'It's a new start and I feel re-energised. It's up to the players to get the results we need. I have a strong desire to do well. I'll look more closely at my game and accept the challenge filled with passion. It [the World Cup] was the most disappointing experience of my life. How I can use that as a plus will depend on how hard I work.' Kagawa, however, was the final player to leave Old Trafford that summer, returning to Dortmund for an undisclosed fee. The Japanese international was a high-profile casualty of the humiliating 4-0 League Cup defeat at Milton Keynes Dons; Anderson and Welbeck two others, while Jonny Evans's reputation at United never recovered.

There was a mass exodus of players. Ferdinand and Vidic were gone, Giggs had retired, Patrice Evra joined Juventus for £1.2m,

Alex Buttner was sold, surprisingly at a profit, to Dynamo Moscow, while Bebe also finally left to join Benfica, and Federico Macheda, for whom great things had once been expected, was allowed to join Cardiff City on a free transfer. Danny Welbeck was allowed to join Arsenal for £16m. Youngster Tom Lawrence joined Leicester City, while Nani, Wilfried Zaha, Javier Hernandez, Michael Keane, Tom Cleverley and the highly rated striker Angelo Henriquez were all allowed to leave on long-term loans, to Sporting, Crystal Palace, Real Madrid, Burnley, Aston Villa and Dinamo Zagreb respectively. From those outgoings at least 11 could be said to be serious members of the first-team squad, and with Darren Fletcher and Anderson leaving in the winter window, that made 13 senior players all out.

An overhaul of the squad was necessary, with many fans feeling there was too much dead wood at the club, although the big broom sweeping through Carrington did seem as if it had pushed out plenty of vital experience too. Still, by the time the start of the Premier League season kicked off, there was a real sense of optimism despite the lack of new signings. United's pre-season tour of North America had been a resounding success. Back-to-back 3-1 wins over Real Madrid and Liverpool were achieved by a United team playing outstanding football.

Against Madrid, young Tyler Blackett had impressed as a substitute, as did Jesse Lingard, while Ashley Young's adaptable performance at left wing-back clearly gave the new manager plenty of food for thought. The shape was kept for the win over the Scousers in Miami, with the only disappointing note being an early injury picked up by Valencia on his birthday. It would keep the player out of the start of the season.

With the start looming, United announced that Wayne Rooney had been named the new club captain. 'For me it's always very important the choice of captain,' Van Gaal told manutd.com. 'Wayne has shown a great attitude towards everything he does. I have been very impressed by his professionalism and his attitude to training and to my philosophy. He is a great inspiration to the younger members of the team and I believe he will put his heart and soul into his captaincy role. Darren Fletcher will become the vice-captain. Darren is a natural leader and will captain the team when Wayne isn't playing. Darren is a very experienced player and a very popular member of the dressing room, I know he will work well alongside Wayne.'

Rooney, who a year ago was close to leaving the club, now had the security of a long-term contract and the honour of leading the team into its new era. 'It is a huge honour for me — and for my family — to be named captain of this great club,' Rooney said. 'It is a role I will perform with great pride. Team spirit has always been very high in our dressing room and I am very grateful to the manager for the faith he has shown in me. I look forward to leading the team out on Saturday at our first match of the new season.'

United kicked off their season against Swansea City at Old Trafford and went with the 3-5-2 which had served them so well in pre-season. Van Gaal was good to his word and gave the players who had impressed the chance to earn their place, resulting in a very unfamiliar team. David de Gea, the subject of speculation linking him to Real Madrid, was in goal, while Chris Smalling, Phil Jones and Tyler Blackett were the defence. Deprived of Valencia and Shaw, Van Gaal deployed Young and Lingard as wing-backs. Herrera and Fletcher started in midfield, with Mata behind Rooney and Hernandez. When Lingard was forced to come off with injury in the 24th minute, he was replaced by Januzaj who was forced to play in that unfamiliar left-sided role.

Up until that point, United's confident and assured pre-season form looked to have completely abandoned them. Ki then scored a shock goal for the visitors in the 28th minute and the host's response was agitated at best. The issues caused by the 3-5-2 due to the limitations of the players within it seemed immediately obvious. Van Gaal's ideas of possession and ball circulation depended hugely on the confident footballing ability of all of the players, but without an assured defence to build on an entire game plan can be undermined. It seemed evident that the instruction for the players was to move the ball on with the second touch, and third at a push, and this was clearly something which Smalling, Jones and Blackett were uncomfortable with. It led to unnecessarily hesitant passes which too often were well telegraphed by a Swansea side fully deserving of their half-time lead.

Despite having stuck to that 3-5-2 system all through pre-season, Van Gaal immediately switched to a 4-4-1-1 in the second half, bringing off Hernandez for Nani and playing Young and Blackett as full-backs. Eight minutes after half-time, United's pressure earned them a corner; Mata's kick was flicked on by Jones and met by a cute overhead kick by Rooney at the far post. Three minutes later, Rooney's long-range free kick smacked the outside of the post; the new captain clearly revelling in his role as the leader of his team. With 18 minutes to go, Gylfi Sigurdsson scored a goal against the run of play; this time, United were unable to muster an adequate response, and succumbed to a disappointing defeat in Van Gaal's first game in charge.

Following the game, Van Gaal had a sit-down chat with Gary Neville for *The Telegraph*. 'My teams shall improve through the season,' Van Gaal told him. 'That is not a question. They shall improve.' Neville asked the manager if he thought the players were finding the transition to Van Gaal's tried and tested ideals of football difficult. 'As coaches we have to give a lot of information,' the boss said. 'Too much, I think. Compare it to when you go to an airport for the first time. If I go to Manchester, what terminal, where is my flight, where do I have to park? How long is the queue at the desk? You know that. You know the place. All that information, you have to tell me. I go away and know one or two things. It's the same with the players. I have to drive on the other side. Now I have to watch the road. That's the process my players are in and it's not so easy. Sometimes I speak with them interactively because you want to know what the players are thinking. I ask questions and then they speak. Not only me but also Ryan and Albert Stuivenberg and Frans Hoek. Ryan gives the analysis of the opponent, for example, Albert will do the evaluations and I do the tactics before the game. I'm always present and I always interrupt my assistants.' The manager insisted that his approach would never change. 'Only the contents of my philosophy,' he said. 'I evaluate the game with all the players. I always did that. I also picked up the midfielders and defenders for extra sessions [after losing against Swansea]. But it is only the contents of my philosophy. So, where [Juan] Mata has to play, or where the defenders have to play, and communicate, and cover the space. That's the only way to improve. It [the success] always depends on the level of the players. I'm not a magician. It depends on the personality. At the end of the three years we shall have that kind of player. And I shall select them through. I say that to the players. I have said from the beginning — I have not shouted — "We shall be the champion." I have said we need time. We need time to build up a new team, and that cannot be in one day. It's a process, and the process is starting now. All my teams in the beginning were not good. They have to switch from instinctive to thinking brain. It's very difficult. I train in another way to the former coaches, and that's difficult. [I play 3-5-2] because it's more easy to defend. You have to defend the space and the player who is coming into it. When you play like that it's always less than 15 metres [between the three centre-backs], and then it's more easy to defend when you communicate well. And there are always wide players. And they are always free when they move well, in the right tactical way at the right tactical time. When I play with three strikers, they are also wide. When you play with full-backs, they are also wide, but they cannot always go. When you play with three defenders, they [the wing-backs] can always go. Both at the same time. That is a risk, but I am a risky coach. Then you have to switch the play. And you know that all the wide players are free. Now, we have to look more for the free player. I could also play 4-4-2, which I played at Bayern Munich in the beginning. They wanted me to play 4-4-2, but then I played in a window [diamond] because I liked that more, between the lines, because I had Gómez, I had Klose, I had Olic. Gómez was £35m — at that time a lot of money. After two months I changed it in spite of the £35m, and played 4-3-3. I bought Robben for that reason, because he could play that way. You can communicate it in the first meeting you have. And I have said everything about how I am … they have hired me for my philosophy. They have said that. I think I shall be supported.'

The loss prompted some difficult decisions and revealed a harsher truth; fair as the new manager had been to his new squad, many of them just weren't ready for the test of representing United at this stage a) in their career and b) in the redevelopment of the club. It was harsh, for example, on Tyler Blackett and Jesse Lingard to make their debuts in such circumstances. It was harsh to expect Chris Smalling and Phil Jones to automatically become Ferdinand and Vidic just because the established pair had now gone.

The next game — a draw at a very average Sunderland — exposed further issues in United's approach. Defensively uncertain, unimposing in midfield and pedestrian and predictable up front, it seemed as if the previous 12 months had sucked all of the confidence out of the talented players still at the club. There was hope, rather than expectation, that Van Gaal's Dutch connection with Van Persie would revitalise the former Arsenal forward to show the kind of form he had in his first season rather than his second. There was expectation rather than hope that Wayne Rooney's decline may ultimately prove to be a major point of contention as far as the manager was concerned. Whilst not exactly *persona non grata* at Old Trafford, and whilst his appointment as captain was the sensible one in so much as he was the most senior player apart from Darren Fletcher still at the club, Rooney's days as a fan favourite were long gone. To many, those days were as far as four years before, and to most of the rest it felt like another of Moyes's wrong calls to have kept him on. As this book suggests, it was an understandable decision taken at a time when United were under significant pressure to make a transfer statement; less understandable was the decision to anchor the club with a five-year contract given to a player who would be over 30 for the majority of it. This is not a slight at Rooney; regardless of the player, it seemed remarkably bad business and had backed the club into a corner as his annual wages already dwarfed any prospective transfer fee. United were stuck and had to make the most of Rooney; furthermore, due to the weekly pay-packet the new captain was pocketing, there was some pressure to play him. And to be fair to Rooney, for the first part of the Moyes era he had shown surprisingly good form; there were goals and there was also a little bit of the all-action player who seemed long gone.

When United lost at MK Dons it made two things very clear — for one reason or another, the squad inherited by Van Gaal was not good enough, nor did it have potential to really improve to the standard required to return the success in the way supporters had become accustomed to. Of those who played in that game, only David de Gea could claim to have escaped with his reputation relatively unscathed.

It was a dark day in the recent history of the club; the tumultuous nature of events at Old Trafford was summarised by the news coming in just before kick-off that United had broken their transfer record to sign Angel Di Maria. Di Maria had been named the man-of-the-match in the Champions League Final earlier that summer after his pivotal role in Real Madrid's victory, but he had become disillusioned at playing second fiddle to the likes of Bale and Ronaldo; this was not a player Madrid wanted to lose, and, despite strong interest from Paris Saint Germain, the winger moved to United for a fee of £59.7m.

'I am absolutely delighted to be joining Manchester United,' Di Maria insisted, though it had been suggested that only concerns about breaking Financial Fair Play rules had deterred the French club from making a serious offer. 'I have thoroughly enjoyed my time in Spain and there were a lot of clubs interested in me, but United is the only club that I would have left Real Madrid for. Louis van Gaal is a fantastic coach with a proven track record of success, and I am impressed by the vision and determination everyone has to get this club back to the top — where it belongs. I now just cannot wait to get started.' Six days before that, Marcos Rojo, the Sporting defender, had signed for the surprisingly high sum of £16m.

Di Maria made his debut on 30 August against Burnley in a goalless draw. The Argentinian looked positive and lively, creating his team's best openings; it was easy to come away with the impression that United had secured themselves a massive upgrade in terms of creativity, whilst maintaining the concern that the team didn't have the firepower to benefit from their new playmaker's ability.

That worry was seemingly eased on a remarkable transfer deadline day; early that morning, news broke that United were interested in Radamel Falcao, the superstar Monaco striker who had missed the second half of the previous season after suffering an ACL injury. He had returned ahead of schedule and demonstrated his ability by scoring twice in three games — but United's interest had previously been completely unreported, due to the fact nobody expected the Colombian to leave the French club. The deal was officially confirmed by United in the early hours of 2 December, a loan transfer with the option to buy for £43.5m. 'I am delighted to be joining Manchester United on loan this season,' Falcao said in an official statement. 'Manchester United is the biggest club in the world and is clearly determined to get back to the top. I am looking forward to working with Louis van Gaal and contributing to the team's success at this very exciting period in the club's history.'

And United fans were excited. Their glum start to the season suddenly had an injection of Latin flair and, there's no doubt about it, their transfer activity had stunned the football world. Di Maria and Falcao were two of the most highly rated players on the planet and to convince them to come to Old Trafford was a major statement from Van Gaal, at a time the club desperately needed it.

Frustratingly, United fans would have to wait a couple of weeks to see these new players in action — when they next took to the field, against Queens Park Rangers on 14 September, they were given a treat. Van Gaal went with a 4-1-2-1-2 system, with Daley Blind operating as a holding midfielder, and Herrera, Mata and Di Maria playing further forward with Rooney and Van Persie up front. Di Maria was the star of the show, opening the scoring with a free kick in the 24th minute, before playing a part in two more of the goals as United helped themselves to four on the day. It was an impressive showing, the only disappointing mark being the inability of Falcao to get on the scoresheet following his cameo as a substitute.

Seven days later and Manchester United raced into a 2-0 lead against Leicester City at the King Power Stadium after just 16 minutes. In the 13th minute, Falcao, making his first start, spun past former Red Ritchie De Laet with extravagant style. His cross to the far post was met by the head of Robin van Persie; the former Arsenal man had just missed a great opportunity after a fantastic through ball from Di Maria, but made no mistake this time around to put United into the lead via a deflection.

Three minutes later, Di Maria picked up the ball in his own half. He went past two players and then played the ball to Rooney; United's number ten waited until the number seven had advanced far enough to play him the return pass. Di Maria moved into the penalty area and from 16 yards — an area he had absolutely no right to do so — he lofted the ball above Kasper Schmeichel and under the crossbar. Only the identity of the player and the events of the future have diminished the memory of this goal, but recalling it as it was thought of at the time, and how really it ought to be thought of, this was one of the most exquisite goals in Premier League, and even Manchester United, history. At the time it seemed as if it would be much more — if it is hyperbole and overreaction with hindsight, then at least at the time it seemed as if Old Trafford was set for a glorious new era of attacking football.

Out with the old

There are individual moments in football matches which supporters argue the toss over, particularly if those moments served as the defining separator or the pivotal moment. That's football, and the sport is all the richer for the conversation inspired by these episodes. You know how they go — if only the referee hadn't given that decision against my team, if only the opponent had not cheated, if only our own player had performed to either the higher standard he's been capable of previously, or, if only they'd played to the potential we have collectively deemed appropriate to project upon him. If for this, but for that.

In the 57th minute of United's trip to Leicester on 21 September 2014, Ander Herrera scored to put Louis van Gaal's team 3-1 up. It would be premature to say United's supporters were lumping their mortgages on a title win, but it would be a fair assessment that there was at least some expectancy that the soulless days of the winter and spring of that year were long gone. It would also be a fair assessment to suggest the following 30-odd minutes of football demonstrated to United's new manager why he would be unable to trust his team to play such an open style.

Just after the hour mark, Rafael and Jamie Vardy contested for the ball; Vardy clearly barged Rafael over, and the Brazilian full-back did admirably well to recover lost ground after referee Mark Clattenburg bizarrely allowed play to continue. The decision was made all the more infuriating as the tussle continued into the box and Rafael then brought Vardy down; Clattenburg remembered where his whistle was and blew for a penalty. One-time England striker David Nugent scored the penalty; United's defending from that point was shambolic, with Chris Smalling, Tyler Blackett and Marcos Rojo an erratic trio who did not cope with Leicester's energetic trio. Blackett was sent off in the 83rd minute when his foul gave away another penalty; when Leonardo Ulloa scored it, it was Leicester's fifth goal of the afternoon, finalising a miserable capitulation for the visitors.

In the immediate aftermath of the game United fans were determined to give their team the benefit of the doubt, blaming Clattenburg and the first penalty decision. Perhaps they had a point, but it was easy to see that with the defence in its current shape, a free-flowing Manchester United team was not sustainable without consequence. At Old Trafford it may work but on away grounds it appeared to be a gamble almost always with severe repercussions, and Van Gaal's post-match comments gave an indication into his long-term view: 'We started the last match against QPR very good with a new team, new players and then we played very well here, but we gave the game away,' he said. 'Leicester had five shots on goal, and that was it. These five goals were existing because we made errors in ball possession. We created a lot of chances and made superb goals but you have to do that over 90 minutes, not 60 minutes. It was not enough.'

Despite his reaction, it was injuries and not form which necessitated some defensive changes for the next game against West Ham. Jonny Evans and Chris Smalling were injured after playing at Leicester, as was Phil Jones, and so promising centre-half Tom Thorpe was called into the squad. He was, however, only brought in to the game as an injury-time substitute; Patrick McNair, a fellow youngster, and a midfielder in his usual deployment at lower levels, was surprisingly given the nod alongside Marcos Rojo in central defence.

After a quarter of the game, it seemed as if United fans would be settling for fine home performances and inconsistent away displays;

Wayne Rooney and Robin van Persie scored to suggest there may be a repeat of the four goals which were scored against QPR. But with eight minutes to go in the first half, Diafra Sakho scored, and a quarter of an hour after the break, Rooney was sent off, leading to a very nervous remaining half an hour.

It was a mixed afternoon for Rooney, who was under pressure to score goals. On that front he had finally delivered but he now faced a three-match ban where Radamel Falcao could be expected to cement his place as first-choice striker alongside Van Persie. Theoretically, then, it meant there should be a fight for a place for Rooney — not so. Before the Leicester game Van Gaal had essentially guaranteed the number ten a place in the team, much to the dismay of United fans. 'Only the captain has more privileges,' he said. 'No other player has privileges. There are always players we put in the line-up in a team — my captain shall always play. I don't think that Falcao interfered with Van Persie or Van Persie interfered with Falcao. I think Falcao is a very good striker. I also said when he was coming in his first press conference that I like Van Persie also. Then we have Rooney and Januzaj and we have [James] Wilson. We have five players for the two striker positions and I have to choose.' The former Holland manager said that Rooney's apparent versatility was an advantage. 'We have played well but can improve and I was not so satisfied with Rooney as a striker and Mata as midfielder and that's why I'm changing,' he said. 'Rooney can play in more positions, he's a multifunctional player and I have tried him in a striker's position. He's played well but not spectacular and Falcao is a striker and I think he can do it better.'

After the West Ham game, Van Gaal praised his team for their efforts in getting the win — Kevin Nolan had seen a late goal disallowed, controversially, but United's makeshift defence more or less held out otherwise. 'The win is very important, you can imagine that,' the United boss said. 'We played a very good first half with attractive football. We conceded again a goal from a set play. But OK, I am very happy that we held the result until the end because it is very difficult to play against a team who not only have one more player but who also play a lot of high balls. I am very pleased with the attitude of my players.'

However disjointed, there were signs of progress. And, in the grand scheme of things, considering how disastrous the past year had been, United fans were willing to be patient. It is worth noting that there was still a section of the support — and there probably still is — who believed Moyes was a fall guy. He was a convenient scapegoat. Nobody could possibly have succeeded in those circumstances. You wouldn't blame Moyes if he felt like that; he may have felt anxious when he was told he was going to be the next United manager, but over time, before he started work, there must have been moments where he was feeling like he had experienced every Christmas in his life rolled up into one. David Moyes may well have been the *Chosen One*, but he must have felt as if he was given a poisoned chalice at some point. As already explained, just as many, if not more, of the things that went wrong could be put down to poor management as they could be attributed to understandable misjudgements (hiring his own staff, for example), but when you're in the eye of the storm and everyone is blaming you for everything, well, you wouldn't blame Moyes for feeling he had not quite been dealt the hand he thought he had when he took the job. The longer the 2013/14 season wore on, and the more the issues worsened, even the buffer of familiar faces on the staff wouldn't have been enough to stop Moyes feeling like the loneliest man in the world. In some respects, then, plenty had sympathy for him. It was always likely that the manager who followed Ferguson would not be able to replicate the success — who could? But there was a school of thought that factored in the idea that Ferguson's management skills had seen him overachieve, and suggested whoever followed him would have his work cut out.

By then the squad was in need of such severe regeneration, not necessarily in the way that it was devoid of talent, but the age of the invaluably experienced legendary figures and the flattering to deceive quality of the squad players meant a huge turnaround over a relatively short space of time was probably necessary. The suggestion that Ferguson had identified this and got out while the going was good is surely absolutely without foundation; it was one of Ferguson's classic qualities to oversee such transitions, and one got the feeling it was one of his most enjoyed aspects of the job. Vocalising that idea was a man once identified by the former United boss to be a major part of a transition: Mark Bosnich, the former goalkeeper whose controversial career included two newsworthy stints at Old Trafford.

'For me, it was quite telling that the guy he chose … when there were rumours going around and mounting pressure, he stayed completely quiet,' Bosnich told Fox Sports in the immediate wake of Moyes's sacking. 'It's a great, abject lesson for all sporting clubs around the world not to let your ex-manager choose the one who is coming in. I think Sir Alex Ferguson chose David Moyes because he knew that David Moyes would've taken a lot of time to get up to speed to what Sir Alex did and he knew during that time people would still be thinking of him. He knew that if he chose a manager like a Jose Mourinho or a Carlo Ancelotti that they would have made sure his memory would have eroded much quicker than a David Moyes would have in terms of the success they would have had. He's got a lot to answer for.'

Did Bosnich have a point? Had Ferguson developed a protection complex about his legacy? Even if one can understand the logic behind the theory it just seems ultimately implausible. Yes, there is the idea suggested earlier in this book that hiring Jose Mourinho would have possibly, if not probably, had a short-term galvanising effect on the club to sustain its lure and possibly even improve its cosmopolitan attraction considering the club he would have been coming from, and there is certainly a sensible and logical argument to suggest Mourinho would have handled the transition better than Moyes. Still, it seems unlikely that such a cynical route would have been taken when the decision was of such magnitude; it was not as if David Moyes was managing a Sunday League team before arriving at United, and it wasn't as if Moyes wasn't linked with every top job in the country, even if it was as an outsider. It was an appointment that made sense to many at the time, even if it was, with the benefit of hindsight, the wrong appointment.

Overseeing change is just one element of football management and so it stands to reason that David Moyes could have taken over in any summer and there would have been a similar scenario. Ferguson had boasted that he had left a squad in rude health and there is nothing to suggest that he was being disingenuous; for that critical area of central defence, even with Ferdinand and Vidic reaching the end, there had been Smalling, Jones and Evans, all of whom Fergie had rated highly. Indeed, Phil Jones had performed well in a man-marking role in holding midfield against Real Madrid in the final

Champions League tie under Ferguson, showing a) that the manager trusted and depended on him, and b) that the player could in fact be trusted to excel. The transition to phase Ferdinand and Vidic out was handled terribly and none of the other centre-halves were quite ready to make the step up. Perhaps they might never have been, regardless of who the manager to replace Ferguson was, but, then again, that's the point — whoever came in the door after him had to be skilled in the art of redeveloping an experienced squad of winners, and Moyes had no experience on that front. As soon as he alienated the senior players it was difficult to get them back, and with most of them gone in September 2014 Louis van Gaal had a blend of a few of his own players, that main core of squad players who were not quite at the level to take the mantle of the likes of Ferdinand and Giggs as leaders, and young players who had the heart but not necessarily the talent. On those three points — Van Gaal was certainly trusted to bring in his own players, and at that point, there was genuine belief that his signings were a significant step up in quality. As for the squad, well, the manager had already offloaded a sizeable number to cut numbers down, and even if some disagreed with the identity of those — for example, there was genuine sadness when Welbeck was allowed to go, and some frustration that Rooney was retained and even elevated in terms of importance — the new manager had to have some backing from day one, with the long-term future of the club more important than short-term loyalty to players. It was good to have a manager who was ruthless. On the final point — even if the likes of Blackett and McNair were not obvious names from the reserves who stood out, it was promising that the manager was giving them a chance, and so long as they performed, then they deserved their place in the side. Blackett's league form had been sketchy but he had impressed in United's fantastic pre-season form, and, crucially, he seemed to fulfil the expectations of the manager, and it was quickly becoming apparent that it was working to instruction that impressed the boss. It was at least some indication of consistency in a club that sorely needed it.

Next up was Everton; the team who had defeated United twice without conceding a goal in the previous campaign, including that win which rammed the final nail into David Moyes's managerial coffin at Old Trafford. Moyes might have been the happiest man watching the game, as United continued to illustrate their problems ran deeper and Everton's second season form under Roberto Martinez looked far less impressive than their first. The Toffees had won just one of their opening six league games and United played without a conventional midfield again, with Blind at the anchor point of a diamond and Mata at the spearhead of it with Valencia and Di Maria the wide options. The more cynical might have said United had played without a central midfield for the past year anyway so what was the point in putting any players there; it was not exactly the most physical combination Van Gaal could have fielded, as he continued to familiarise himself with his options. Again, though, the supporters remained optimistic, and patient; as part of this transitional process, and the genuine lack of an established first-choice 11, experimentation was to be expected.

Against Everton it paid off, but only barely. Angel Di Maria continued to dazzle as United's best player and scored the opening goal. As half-time approached, Luke Shaw clumsily tackled Tony Hibbert in the box and referee Kevin Friend awarded a penalty. Leighton Baines had a fine track record from the spot, but missed for the first time here, or, to put it more accurately, his effort was saved by David de Gea. Everton were beginning to impose themselves on the game and got the goal their efforts deserved when Naismith headed in a Baines free kick in the 55th minute. Seven minutes later, though, and United were back in front; Di Maria, the home side's main outlet, was always likely to be the person who forced the breakthrough again and he did when shaping up to hit a long-range effort to test Tim Howard. The shot was poor, but worked out to be a brilliant pass into the path of Falcao, who diverted the ball into the net to open his account for the club. If the nature of the goal was fortuitous then so was the win itself; De Gea was forced into action in injury time, making two outstanding saves to preserve the three points. The manager was full of praise for the goalkeeper, calling him 'fantastic', and said the game had been similar to the win over West Ham. 'It's the same as last week, first half very good, we had a lot of chances, more than against West Ham, they get a penalty, their only chance, and the second half is very different,' Van Gaal said. 'We were not any more in our organisation and so I made changes to improve it, but even after the changes we weren't [organised], so it was again waiting for the signal of the referee to finish the game. It was a good victory. Of course [there were nerves], always.'

United's back-to-back wins had pushed them into the top four for the first time since David Moyes's second league game in charge, a time of the season when it should be deemed wrong to publish league tables as if they stand for anything. It was a suggestion of things coming together after a mixed start under Van Gaal, best summarised by the staggering statistic made true when James Wilson came on as a late substitute for Falcao. Wilson became the 30th different player to be used in the league for United after just seven games. To put this into historical context, only twice before in full seasons had United used more players — 31 in 2011/12, and 33 in 2008/09.

In his book *Leading*, Ferguson had rightly boasted about how it was effectively his title-winning team in 2012/13 that began the following season. The point he was making was about continuity; we all know how it unfolded under Moyes, and opinions of the quality of that squad differ, but the fact remains that the former Everton boss did inherit a title-winning team which more or less selected itself for bigger games and had a core of senior players who understood that they would be rested for at least a quarter of the campaign. There were no such luxuries for Louis van Gaal; David de Gea essentially picked himself but after that the genuine experience was not really on offer for the new manager. Michael Carrick had been absent since suffering an ankle injury in pre-season, and Wayne Rooney and Robin van Persie had spent a significant enough portion of the previous year out with injuries and underperforming compared to their previous levels. The new signings were still bedding in and, on the right-hand side, Rafael was still trying to recover from a very difficult year under Moyes, with the Leicester game having done him no favours at all. There was no obvious first-team selection and from the side who played against Everton, six of the first team — Shaw, Blind, Rojo, Falcao, Mata and Di Maria — were new to the club that calendar year, another starter, McNair, was new to the senior set-up, whilst none of the substitutes who played (Blackett, Fellaini and Wilson) had featured for the first team before the 2013/14 season.

It was an absolutely staggering turnaround of players before even beginning to consider the loss of experience of Ryan Giggs (963 appearances), Rio Ferdinand (455), Patrice Evra (379) and Nemanja

Vidic (300) over the summer and Paul Scholes (718) the summer before. Collectively that was 2,815 appearances, 2,815 times playing for United, almost all of them spent challenging for honours. Even if you exclude Community Shields (the trophy but not the appearance record), Giggs's trophy record stood at one won for every 38 games. For Vidic it was one every 30 games. When you consider that United's most successful seasons were generally 60 games long, then you have some kind of perspective of just how prolific a group of winners had been lost by the club.

United and Van Gaal (and Moyes before him) had spent approximately £213.2m since Sir Alex had retired and so, to some, it was justifiable to expect that the club would be able to challenge for honours. That kind of expectancy also existed amongst supporters, but it was slowly becoming evident that the scale of the transition and the necessity for change was far greater. So while United fans expected to challenge for trophies because that was what the tradition of the club dictated they should do, by and large there was an appreciation for what was lost and just how profound the scale of the transition was.

The sum of £213m reads like an awfully large amount of money and there is no escaping from the fact that it is. The truth is, though — and you can blame inflation if you like — that even that large amount of money was not enough to even begin to replace what Manchester United had lost. Knowing what we know now, and how badly it turned out, the idea of Angel Di Maria being a Ryan Giggs replacement is laughable, but the idea behind the transfer was sound. At the age of 26, it would have been reasonable to suggest Di Maria could provide maybe six years of service playing at the top level, and at a cost of almost £60m, only then does the concept of the cost of replacements start to make sense. Over time it would become clear that Ferdinand and Vidic would need replacing because their successors were not at the club. Eric Bailly seemed a snip at £30m and there are hopes for Victor Lindelof to solidify that defensive partnership at £5m more. Patrice Evra cost United £5.5m in 2005; his replacement cost almost six times that amount in 2014. When Paul Pogba returned to the club in 2016, he cost them £89m, and a year later United bought Nemanja Matic for £40m to finally have a midfield where all of the parts could (theoretically, at least) function cohesively for the first time in almost eight years. Time would tell if that collection of players would turn out to be adequate replacements for just those experienced players listed above — if they did, collectively it would have come at a cost of £284m. If not, the cost would continue to rise.

Then, of course, there is the matter of the squad regeneration, where the majority of that money went. United needed a midfielder and Moyes felt Fellaini was the answer. When they needed creativity he chose Mata. It is a popular modern trend to reel off the numbers of squad costs without taking into effect the variables. '*The most expensive squad ever assembled!*' some would complain. Maybe so, but was it Louis van Gaal's choice to spend around £70m on the above pair? Did he wait until Fellaini's contract clause expired to then spend almost £5m more on getting him? And just because he *cost* £28m, did that make him worth that amount of money? Was it worth breaking the club's transfer record for a player Chelsea were clearly happy to allow to leave? Are Manchester United the only club spending money, however absurd the fees are deemed to be? These partially explained, selectively handpicked statistics, which help benefit the agenda someone is trying to push on any particular day, does little to explain the full truth. In these line-ups, Wayne Rooney would also be included, and the inference of the point that if United failed to get a positive result was absolutely clear — the club had wasted their money. But Wayne Rooney cost £30m in 2004 and had won numerous trophies on the way to a record-breaking career for club and country. Had he not been well and truly worth it? And just because he was a £30m player in 2004, was it worth labelling him as a £30m player in 2014? Sergio Aguero cost Manchester City £38m in 2011 — money well spent, without question. He would keep out any other forward City bought because he was better than them. Likewise Yaya Toure in their midfield. The cost of other midfielders and forwards City spent on potential alternatives ran into the hundreds of millions, but, of course, when Toure and Aguero took to the field, only their cost was factored into the figure for the line-up on that day.

To categorise United's recent — and many would say well overdue — overspending as gross underachievement is almost wilfully playing ignorant to the circumstances in which it occurred and demonstrates an acute lack of knowledge about the sport.

Then there are those squad players. Putting aside United's tendency to have to pay over the odds, thanks in no small part to the not-so-private boasts about the club's status, and putting aside the fact that different managers have different ideas and so Louis van Gaal's perception of what he wanted from his squad composition was likely to differ from David Moyes, whose own ideas would have differed from Ferguson's, and *even* putting aside the probability that there were still plenty of squad players surplus to requirements (as would become apparent from Van Gaal's next summer transfer window) who were having to be fielded as first-teamers, then it should also be considered that inflation in football was scaling new heights.

Manchester City had won the title in 2014; this had been the lesser of two evils for United fans considering that Liverpool had been the other contenders. It was less than a vintage year, but considering City had spent £154m strengthening their previous title-winning squad with none of the regeneration issues similar to United (of course, every team has regeneration by virtue of time, but City's heavy spending was a consistent thing and not forced by a mass exodus of experienced players), their title win wasn't a surprise. As annoying as it was, and certainly more annoying than Chelsea's triumphs, there was a similar air about their successes; they are somewhat easier to stomach, considering the manufactured way the clubs have been artificially propelled, than a Liverpool success would have been, as is obvious by the lack of intensity often seen in those big games featuring those clubs. United and Chelsea games, over time, became a barometer for the standard bearers of the top team in the country between 2006 and 2013, but there was a certain sterility in the fixtures that was tangible and undeniable. The counter-effect of their respective takeovers was the long-term rise in the cost of players who would not be expected to be named as 'premium' stars.

The likes of Samir Nasri at £22m and Javi Garcia at £16m saw the prices creep up slowly; then it became £20.6m for Alvaro Negredo and £26m for Stevan Jovetic. In the summer of 2014 City spent £28m on Wilfried Bony of Swansea City and an eye-watering £40m on Eliaquim Mangala. In their defence, Mangala *was* at least expected to be a first-team player from the off, and it was only his poor form which eventually cost him his place, but the standard was set. As United had seen with their purchases of Rojo and Blind,

the negotiations for buying any player were now likely to start at
£10m. Regeneration was already proving to be a costly exercise and
United were entering into a crucial period of their history at the worst
possible time in terms of value.

One of the most prominent criticisms of United was that for a
club who apparently based their ethics and identity on developing
their own players, they were now betraying that with their high-
profile signings, breaking the club transfer record as they had twice in
2014. More than that, it seemed as if the football world was waiting
with bated breath for United to spend heavily as they had been
predicted to do because this would apparently serve as undermining
some perceived moral high ground, particularly amongst supporters.
These arguments are an exercise in futility for most; on the one hand,
many United fans have spent years criticising the owners for taking
money out of the club and away from football, and, when the owners
finally *did* acknowledge the need for a substantial investment, those
same fans were faced with criticism from supporters of other clubs
who seemed to only notice when Manchester United spent money.
Their own money, let it be added. Football is unique in that it is
littered with hypocritical fans who have a flexible and ever-changing
set of moral values depending on the opponent of any given week and
their own plight. Nobody batted an eyelid when City spent £40m
on Mangala, but as soon as United paid £59.7m for Di Maria they
were ruining football.

It should be noted at this point that of course it would be all well
and good to suggest that United's regeneration had historically at
least partly come from within. There is another tremendously unfair
stick to bash United with and that is the fact that since 1992 another
group of similarly talented players hasn't broken through. This of
course is neglecting the fact that they haven't elsewhere, either. For
Arsene Wenger's much-lauded work producing young players, only
Ashley Cole and Jack Wilshere could be said to be genuine stars, and
that is being kind to Wilshere in the respect that it is recognising
the potential he had and not the player he became. West Ham came
as close as anyone when they brought through Joe Cole, Michael
Carrick and Rio Ferdinand. The fact of the matter is that United's
development line has still been better in terms of prolific generation
and quality of players than any other club in the country. Wes Brown,

John O'Shea and Darren Fletcher might not have been as illustrious as Giggs, Neville and Scholes, but between them they still clocked up more than 1,000 appearances for United. That's before numbering the players who went on to have hugely successful league careers elsewhere, such as John Curtis, Danny Higginbotham and David Healy, who became Northern Ireland's record goalscorer.

In 2014 Manchester United's youth resources were not quite as strong as they had been in the past. The club had had to contend with the nouveau riche Chelsea and Manchester City at junior level as well as senior level. United won the FA Youth Cup for a record tenth time in 2011 and so it could be reasonable to expect that a number of the players from that squad would be around the first team. And, to be fair, many had chances to be. Sam Johnstone, the goalkeeper, was often the reserve or third goalkeeper with the senior squad, which was historically as close as anyone has come (Gary Walsh and Kevin Pilkington made a number of appearances, as did record-breaker David Gaskell much earlier, but reserve/third goalkeeper was probably their squad status at the club). High hopes were still held for Tom Thorpe and he had recently made his debut — it would have been irresponsible to thrust a 20-year-old into such a crucial position at such a tumultuous time, no matter how highly regarded he was. Besides, David Moyes had at least five senior players to choose from before taking a needless risk with Thorpe, and Moyes was not a manager known for his risks. Michael Keane's rise to prominence due to his form with Burnley, which earned him a big move to Everton (and a rumoured return to Old Trafford, at one prolonged point), has identified him as a 'Gerard Pique' in that he was one who got away, and maybe that's fair. However, with hindsight, Keane did not cover himself in glory in the MK Dons game, however unfair it is to only have one match to view a player. Paul Pogba, Ravel Morrison and Ryan Tunnicliffe were the three prominent names from that team, with Will Keane the master goalscorer. Historically, it was always difficult for strikers to break through, but high hopes were held for the midfield trio to be the heartbeat of United in the future. By 2014 none were at the club. Pogba's exit had been acrimonious and as controversial as his initial arrival at United, and the French midfielder was now showing off his skill at Juventus. Tunnicliffe's progress had stalled and with United's need for new blood in midfield reaching desperate levels,

Moyes instead sent him on another loan, to Ipswich Town. In January 2014 Rene Meulensteen made Tunnicliffe one of his first signings at Fulham, showing how highly regarded he was. Indeed, Tunnicliffe played in every game he was eligible for until Meulensteen was sacked in mid-February and was deemed surplus to requirements by incoming boss Felix Magath. From there his career has stagnated with various loan moves, a shame for a midfielder who promised more.

However, if that is a case of lost potential then it is nothing compared to Ravel Morrison, whose talent was still so clear that he was given a chance at Lazio in 2015. Morrison joined West Ham in January 2012, with Sir Alex Ferguson hopeful that his long-term friend Sam Allardyce would prove a suitable mentor. There were flashes of brilliance — Morrison scored a stunning solo goal at White Hart Lane in a 3-0 win for the Hammers — but for the forward it was never a case of his talent being in question. Personal issues, and suggestions of a lack of discipline, led to him being sent on loan to QPR and Cardiff City. Shortly after moving to Lazio, the player was criticised by club officials for his inability to speak Italian. In 2017 he signed for Mexican side Atlas on loan. In 2019, after a short spell at Swedish side Östersund, he was released. At the age of 26, you hope that the best is yet to come, although it does appear as if Morrison's will be another lost star lamented.

Compare that, then, to Jesse Lingard; the sole remaining member of the 2011 winners still at the club at the time of writing. Accusations of inconsistency and, according to some, simply a lack of ability to play at the level required for United, have dogged Lingard; perhaps writing this in 2019, referring to 2014, is using the benefit of hindsight, but the winger has valuable traits which must have been endearing to his new boss back then. His perseverance and dedication serve as honourable traits and desirable qualities and his inclusion in the squad is a good example of how other players should apply themselves. Still, the prevailing point is that, from the 2011 winners, there were not the number of graduates one would hope in the United squad, and that is a salient point. Then again, Chelsea have won five of the following six tournaments, and how many of their first-team players are from any of those sides? The 2015, 2016 and 2017 finals have all been contested between Chelsea and Manchester City. City, too, have such a dreadful record of promoting youth players that there has not been a single notable academy graduate in their squad.

Chelsea won the 2018 FA Youth Cup to tie United's 1950s record of five consecutive triumphs, a shining example of why artificially creating these records is not comparable on any scale whatsoever to the achievement of Jimmy Murphy and Bert Whalley back in the 50s. Even Chelsea's own Youth Cup winners of 1960 and 1961 are more renowned for their achievements. This is not to make the point about how football was back in the day; it's more a point to say how much more valuable the achievement is when it is earned through toil and hard work rather than simply throwing money at it. The proof of this is not in my writing the words on these pages, the proof can be found in how those successes filtered up to higher levels. In the 1950s, as it did in 1992, the nucleus of home-grown players graduating to the first team had a significant benefit. Firstly, with the majority being local, there was a greater inclination for supporters to become endeared to them. This translated into more vociferous support and a collective sense of identity, and the value of this surely speaks for itself. Secondly, with a number of players all schooled on the same way of playing with the same sort of standards, their move into a first team based on those same principles was a smoother transition than it might be for a young player being moved from, say, a 4-4-2 or a 4-3-3 into a 3-5-2, where the requirements and responsibilities of almost every single player in the team are different. The knock-on point from this is that if a number of players break through at the same time, then there is the benefit of familiarity, and an instant awareness of the movement of those players. Sir Alex Ferguson developed that idea further still when he hired the optometrist Gail Stephenson to improve the peripheral vision of players, but there is still an unquantifiable benefit that comes from naturally knowing the movement of your team-mates as learned through the two or three years' experience before the move to first-team level.

Beyond the thrill of individual flair, which results in a trick, the beating of an opponent or a long-range goal, there is nothing quite so exciting as a team that plays with such cohesion and fluidity. One would presume that creating a team which possessed such qualities would be the Holy Grail for any coach. Certainly, if one was to list

Louis van Gaal's own achievements, the Ajax European Cup win sits at the top for those very reasons listed above.

Conversely, and somewhat straying away from the point for a moment, perhaps there exists an insight into the value of the so-called lesser lights, such as Lingard, for example. Let us rewind to 1992 and use the example of the Neville brothers, and, to a lesser extent, though arguably a better illustration of the point, Nicky Butt. Those three players were deemed to be the lesser talented of the group that broke through. In the case of the brothers this was largely a projected perception of the media — you simply can't sustain careers at that level without having talent, and one would have hoped that perspective would have been realigned in their retirement so as to pay due credit to their actual ability, but you still get the impression that isn't the case. The point is, even if it was true that they weren't quite as gifted as Beckham and Giggs, their role in the United first team was generally just as valuable due to the partnerships established thanks to their familiarity. Beckham needed Neville working alongside him to help create the space for him to cross. Giggs needed to be able to depend on a defender behind him, and more often than not it was Denis Irwin, probably the most dependable player in the club's history, and certainly at that point, but many a time Giggs played in front of Phil Neville. Nicky Butt is the name most often left out of that all-conquering midfield of Beckham, Keane, Scholes and Giggs, but the truth is that, particularly in big games away from home, Butt would be called upon to play instead of Scholes. The Gorton lad was as worthy of mention as any other and was finally given credit for his contribution when he was roundly deemed to be England's best player in the 2002 World Cup. A Nicky Butt at his peak would easily walk into any modern United midfield and improve it. What Butt brought — and, when he was called upon in an emergency midfield role in the winter of 2002, Phil Neville, too — was an appreciation and understanding of the work of his team-mates, and so the players automatically played well.

United legend Gordon Hill has worked for years developing young players in the United States and one of his most favoured phrases is that you can't put a player into a microwave and expect them to gain, say, five years of experience in five weeks. The same principle occurs when considering the benefit of playing a group of players together for a long period of time. Of course some players are more gifted than others, but does that make those so-called lesser talented players less crucial to the system? They arguably become just *as* important due to their presence, being one of the reasons their team-mates are able to display their full range of talents. If one needs a contemporary example then look no further than a point we will return to later — the acquisition of Nemanja Matic and the instant liberation that afforded Paul Pogba. It is not quite the same, as those players did not have a long history of working alongside each other (and, of course, it wouldn't be a combination that was effective for a long period of time), but the principle of components of a team working to make a whole unit remains almost the same. It is entirely possible, in theory, that in resisting pushing a huge influx of these players into their senior squads, both Manchester City and Chelsea are missing out on a significant long-term benefit.

In 2014 Lingard may not have had the connections and relationships with the players in the same way as those who came through the system together, but he embodied all the traits which had been passed down through the club. In the short term, picking young players by virtue of what he had seen was all Louis van Gaal could reasonably be expected to do. Individually, they did not have the cohesion that previous groups had, but, then again, such cohesion is notable by its rarity, and expecting United to constantly have on tap a quality it has only been able to call upon in two periods in its entire history is both unfair and unreasonable.

No other English club has enjoyed a period like that even once, so to suddenly accuse a brand-new manager of abandoning an unreasonable and impractical level of seamless youth development is playing ignorant to the problems which were already clearly prohibitive to that development prior to his arrival. Simply put, Manchester United had been forced to spend big and spend quickly or risk falling further behind, and the short-term responsibility of the manager was not to appease accusations of betraying the club's heritage, nor was it fair whatsoever to suggest that was what he was doing.

It is often said that teams are shaped in the identity of their manager, an idea which brings to mind the comments at the very start of this book about the individual qualities each manager brings to his work in conjunction with the historical values of the club he is working at. It is also an unavoidable truth that in order to survive, much less thrive, you have to adapt to your surroundings and your circumstances.

Van Gaal's summer spend of £145.5m (net, approx £100m) was ostensibly competitive with United's rivals (Man City £87.5m, Arsenal £95.6m, Liverpool £117m, Chelsea £118.3m) but that, as has exhaustively now been explained, is to consider all clubs on an equal footing and does not factor in the requirement for regeneration at Old Trafford. Unwittingly, the same issues for Van Gaal would consequently be presented for the following manager, but that time was some way off.

The rebuilding work at Manchester United had only just begun, but awaiting the new-look team shortly after the October international break (following a 2-2 draw at West Bromwich Albion where a late point was rescued after a poor performance) was a strong looking Chelsea team — the first test against a genuine title contender, for Van Gaal to assess the quality of his side, and for United fans to see just how close or how far away they were. As is always the case when the suggestion is made that definitive answers are forthcoming, none arrived.

After having the lion's share of the chances, United succumbed to a goal in the 53rd minute from Didier Drogba; the striker was somehow left unmarked at a corner and thundered in a trademark header. A point was rescued when Van Persie lashed in the rebound of a saved Fellaini header in injury time. Statistically, it looked okay for United; they had more than double the amount of shots on goal than Chelsea did and even edged possession. Yet there was an undeniable and distinct difference between the two sides; Chelsea, in their second year under the new Mourinho era, were in a smooth groove and played with the assured style that was giving them a solid lead in the league. In some ways it bore some resemblance to the 2005/06 game between these clubs, decided by a Darren Fletcher looping header. Then, as now, United were some way away from matching the fluidity of their opponents, but they at least showed promise that it wasn't a million miles away. United were playing in fits and starts and their achievement of a point from this game was gained from endeavour more than it was from quality. Even if the media and some pundits believed United should be showing more quality, well, profit from endeavour was at least a step forward from the sorry capitulations to the likes of Newcastle and Everton on this ground less than a year before. A late goal at Old Trafford was reassuringly familiar.

Still, the league table revealed its own story after nine games. Chelsea had 23 points and United had 13. Van Gaal took his team to Manchester City hoping that the two consecutive draws were just hiccups. He was boosted by the return of Wayne Rooney after his suspension but was left cursing ill-discipline from another of his players at the Etihad. It was a bad tempered first half; City's title defence had got off to an inauspicious start with two defeats already, and they were coming into this game on the back of a 2-1 loss at West Ham and a League Cup home defeat to Newcastle. Additionally, although it would ultimately improve, their Champions League group stages had started very poorly, and the pressure was already mounting on Manuel Pellegrini. With both sides below par and both desperate to get a big victory, the mood was fractured and the opening 45 minutes were difficult for referee Michael Oliver to manage. Daley Blind kicked the ball away and was fortunate enough to not have his petulance punished in the most severe way considering he had already been booked; Oliver's attempts to keep a lid on proceedings meant he did not show a second yellow, and this decision did not go down well with the City goalkeeper, who not only confronted the referee but went head-to-head with him. It was not quite the headbutt some would make it out to be, but it was certainly aggressive enough to warrant a red card. Hart was let off without even being cautioned, but it was apparent that the referee would not need an excuse to pull out his card for any further misdemeanours. It didn't take long. Chris Smalling was booked for charging down Joe Hart's clearance — slightly harsh, but given the climate, a decision the referee was always going to take. If that was a reckless decision, what followed bordered on completely irresponsible. With James Milner going nowhere on the left, Smalling launched into an over-the-top challenge which was inevitably going to see Oliver reaching for the red. He did. As Smalling left the field, the United coaches didn't even look at him, so incensed were they by his attitude. Michael Carrick was hastily brought on to fill at centre-half and Adnan Januzaj was taken off.

In the 56th minute, United's issues were compounded when Marcos Rojo was stretchered off. It meant Van Gaal was forced to bring on Paddy McNair, who was presumably deemed too green to have come on immediately after Smalling's indiscretion. This new central-defence partnership of Carrick and McNair, more suited to midfield, was hardly likely to hold out against a City side growing in their own momentum, and when Aguero scored just seven minutes after Rojo's exit, the hosts had a secure lead that was never really threatened, despite a tangibly anxious five minutes of stoppage time.

'In a derby you have to be careful — the second yellow card is a stupid yellow card,' Van Gaal told BBC Sport after the game. 'The sending-off is not *"one of those things"*. As a player you have to control your aggression. I didn't see the first yellow but with the second, you know you already have a yellow, so have to handle it differently. I said that to the players. The red card had an influence on the game but, despite being ten men against 11, we played better in the second half than the first because of the willpower of this team. They fight until the last moment. We are very close, but it's not enough, and it's not good.'

Van Gaal was not holding back in his blast for Smalling. 'It's a disaster, and we will have to play another week with a [new] defence, so the automatism is not growing,' he complained. 'But in spite of the result we are very close. You saw it against Chelsea and now against Manchester City. They are the two best clubs in this league and the difference is zero I think. It is a little bit of luck. When you see what we did with ten men you can be proud as a coach then, but, we have nothing.'

The United boss might well have been pleased with his team's response, but one former player felt that questions should already be asked of the Dutchman following the defeat. 'Manchester United are level on points with West Brom,' Robbie Savage told the BBC. 'Don't get me wrong, I think Alan Irvine is doing a great job there, but United have spent £150m on new players and that is unacceptable. When are we going to start asking serious questions of Louis van Gaal in press conferences because I haven't heard it yet.' Those questions were not far off, and in Savage's position as a pundit, he was arguably the first to raise them. The real question, though, was surely, 'Isn't it tremendously irresponsible and short-sighted to question the capability of a manager three months into his new job on the back of one defeat?'

Following the City defeat, the United support was most certainly disenchanted with Smalling rather than the manager. The news that Rojo had a dislocated shoulder was even more problematic. With their early exit from the League Cup and their complete absence of any European competition, United were playing once a week. The benefit of the rest was contradicted by the fact Van Gaal was unable to field a consistent 11, and injuries had already made that difficult before you factored in suspensions.

United's response to the City setback was better than anyone could have expected and made a mockery of Savage's knee-jerk response. They recorded six wins on the bounce, including a victory at Arsenal and a 3-0 win at home against Liverpool; both of those results were big boosts. First of all, was the win at Arsenal, which was Van Gaal's first away victory at the club at the seventh attempt. Chris Smalling was back in the defence — a case of needs must, and you would have thought in normal circumstances he would have been dropped for a prolonged period if United were not in urgent requirement of senior defenders. He was leading a three-man defence which contained McNair and Blackett; Fellaini and Michael Carrick anchored midfield behind Angel Di Maria. It was a bold move for Van Gaal to go 3-5-2 again. Not only had their experience with it in the league been unconvincing, it seemed as if the club were just historically doomed whenever they chose to use that shape. Even Sir Alex Ferguson had, on the very rare occasion, decided to go with a three-man defence before quickly realising it wasn't going to work. Van Gaal's selection, though, was not one he would have wanted to make, and when Luke Shaw was injured in the 16th minute Ashley Young was brought on to play left wing-back and give an even more unfamiliar look to the defensive unit.

Despite all of this, the game followed a familiar pattern. Arsenal dominated the ball without penetrating, and on a counter-attack early in the second half, Valencia's hammered cross was diverted into his own net by the hapless Kieran Gibbs. Angel Di Maria turned provider for Wayne Rooney in the 85th minute. The goal was reminiscent of the counter-attack goals scored by Ronaldo and Rooney at the same stadium in 2009 and 2010 respectively. Arsenal

scored in injury time but it should have been 3-0 before that —
Di Maria contriving to miss when in a similar position to Rooney
earlier. The 2-1 win was more than fans expected going into the
game, considering the line-up. David de Gea was the man of the
match, with several crucial saves, and he was arguably the best player
again despite a comprehensive looking 3-0 win over Liverpool in
December. This win went some way to cleansing the memory of
that miserable reverse by the same scoreline back in March. Wayne
Rooney, Juan Mata and Robin van Persie got the goals. United had
again played an unfamiliar system, with Carrick almost playing
as a sweeper alongside Phil Jones and Jonny Evans, both of whom
had recovered from their own injury problems. De Gea's form had
been fine, but it was Michael Carrick's return to the side which
had coincided with United's upturn in fortunes. That was almost a
curse as much as a blessing. At the age of 33, Carrick could not be
depended upon to be the mobile player who got around the pitch,
and, at the same time, his confidence in possession was crucial to
Van Gaal's game plan being successful.

That win over Liverpool pushed United into third position, eight
points behind Chelsea, but nonetheless a position most fans would
not have been too dissatisfied with considering everything. One thing
they would have been dissatisfied with was Falcao's underwhelming
contribution since arriving in that blaze of deadline-day glory. He
scored United's goal in a 1-1 draw with Aston Villa before Christmas,
and again in the same scoreline at Stoke City on New Year's Day,
before a goal in the 3-1 win over Leicester City on the last day of
January. This may paint the picture of a player entering a richer
vein of form, but the reality was different. He lacked a shadow of
the devastating forward he had been at Monaco, an understandable
consequence of the injury he had suffered. United's gamble had
been effectively risk-free, aside from the striker's wage packet, and
it became evident that they were not going to pay a fee in excess of
£40m to keep him at Old Trafford.

There were disjointed performances. The 1-0 defeat at home to
Southampton on 11 January was as poor as anything witnessed under
David Moyes. Just one of those days? United bounced back to be
unbeaten for their next four games, but then lost at Swansea before
an embarrassing exit in the FA Cup a couple of weeks later at home to

Arsenal, courtesy of a goal from returning forward Danny Welbeck. Following that game, Van Gaal selected Falcao to play in a reserve game against Tottenham, prompting former Liverpool midfielder Dietmar Hamann to go public with his criticism of the United boss: 'The best players have got huge belief in their own ability and they have got a certain standing and you can't treat a Falcao like you treat a Chris Smalling or Jonny Evans,' Hamann said. 'He may have lost the player now and I will be very surprised if he plays a role between now and the end of the season.'

United were going to finish trophy-less for the second season in a row, and with ten games remaining and Tottenham, Manchester City and Arsenal still to come to Old Trafford, as well as visits to Liverpool, Chelsea and Everton, their two-point buffer in fourth place did not suggest the club had a secure enough hold on their Champions League spot — the minimum requirement — to endure a run of bad form. United's injury list included Luke Shaw and Robin van Persie, while Angel Di Maria was forced to sit out the game against Tottenham due to picking up a red card against Arsenal. Like Falcao, Di Maria's own winter form had been disappointing, although the player hadn't been helped by the manager's inability to pick a consistent line-up. The nadir up until that point had been an isolated performance as striker in that awful Southampton game.

After an ineffectual performance by the winger at Sunderland, which saw him substitute his star man, Van Gaal admitted that the bright start had been followed by a difficult acclimatisation period. 'When a player is not in a match, I have to do that [bring him off],' he said. 'I'm the manager and I cannot deny what I see. We have to give Angel a little bit more time to adapt to the Premier League, the high English rhythm. It is not so easy.' There was that, and also another important factor to consider — Di Maria had gone from being the underrated star of a Real Madrid team boasting star names in confident and all-conquering mode to the figurehead of a new period in the history of Manchester United, a club in crisis in a country where he did not speak the language. Di Maria's season had been pretty good regardless — he was the second-highest 'assister' behind Cesc Fabregas of Chelsea, and that was impressive considering he didn't have a striker in the same vein of form as Diego Costa had been playing in front of him. The issue was that on his off days, Di Maria was less ineffectual, more anonymous. And for the money he had cost and for everything he represented, there was no hiding place from that.

The player's family had also become unsettled in the Manchester area. In late January an attempted burglary at his mansion set off the alarms and Di Maria and his family were immediately moved by the club into a hotel, where they were also given around-the-clock security protection.

When it came to game day against Tottenham, only Daley Blind from the manager's signings (if we don't count Ander Herrera) made it into the starting line-up. Blind lined up at left-back and his defensive colleagues were a new assembly again. Rafael's run in the side post-Leicester had ended after the Chelsea home game. From then on, Antonio Valencia had more or less nailed down that spot after being selected to play there against Crystal Palace in November. Valencia's sporadic appearances at right-back in the past had showed he was capable, but performing there well on a consistent basis was still a surprise. Not as surprising, however, as Chris Smalling's rapid ascent to good form. After the Manchester City debacle, as soon as he was able, Van Gaal dropped the defender — but was forced to call him back into the side against Sunderland on 28 February. Smalling had performed very well in that game and then in the following game at Newcastle, with United keeping consecutive clean sheets for the first time since those early season games against Burnley and Queens Park Rangers. Partnering him was Phil Jones and in front of them was another new set-up — a three-man midfield of Carrick, Herrera and Fellaini, and a three-man attack of Mata and Young either side of Rooney, with the idea being that Fellaini would serve as a focal point for long balls. That, however, was doing the Belgian a disservice going by his early contribution to this game; before it was ten minutes old, he latched onto a brilliant through ball from Carrick and finished incisively with his left foot in the style of Van Persie. In the 19th minute, Carrick turned goalscorer, heading in cleverly to make it two. When Wayne Rooney scored a third in the 34th minute — a fine solo goal followed by a 'knock out' celebration in reference to a video that had been shared online which saw him being knocked out by a punch from former United player Phil Bardsley

— it completed the finest half of football United had put on show arguably since the Ferguson era. It also gave United a buffer to take it easy in the second half and Van Gaal that rarest of luxuries — the ability to name an unchanged side against Liverpool the next week, the first time he'd been able to do that. The comprehensive nature of the win and the style of the performance against Spurs meant that Angel Di Maria had to make do with a place on the bench at Anfield. These back-to-back games were even more crucial considering the presence of Spurs and Liverpool as contenders for the Champions League positions. So the 2-1 win which followed at United's most bitter rivals was crucial on result alone, before even considering the style in which it was accomplished.

Juan Mata had survived the transition from being the record signing that the buying manager wasn't quite sure how to use, to being an expensive squad player who didn't seem to have a purpose under the new boss. The injuries to some players and inconsistency of others meant Mata had to be patient, but his performance against Spurs meant he had earned his place against Liverpool. His first goal, in front of the Kop, was a clever right-footed effort, but it was his second that is permanently embedded in the minds of all United fans; an exquisite acrobatic volley which turned out to be the winner. By that point, the game was already well on the way to becoming a fondly remembered one for the visiting fans considering Steven Gerrard's cameo — he came on as a half-time substitute and was sent off within a minute. Having already announced that he would be leaving Liverpool at the end of the season, the dismissal marked his last involvement in this fixture, and it was a welcome memory for United fans who waved him off safe in the knowledge that it was another Liverpool icon who would go without winning a league winner's medal. Crucially for the current season, the win put a five-point gap between the clubs in fourth and fifth with eight games remaining. Had the result gone the other way, Liverpool would have been on 57 points and United on 56. It really was a huge result, and perhaps more positive than anything was the style the team played with and the comfort they seemed to have playing the system. In both of these wins, they had deployed a game plan to pressure their opponents high up the pitch and it was paying dividends in its watchability and results. Two weeks later, United comfortably saw off Aston Villa, though they were forced to play Rojo in place of the injured Smalling. The England defender was back in the line-up for the game on 12 April against Manchester City, with Van Gaal going with the same side that did so well against Spurs and Liverpool. It meant a place on the bench once again for Di Maria and Falcao. To return to that earlier point about Blind being the only Van Gaal recruit in the side, what we had learned from this was that the group of players, even without the vastly experienced stars that David Moyes had at his disposal, were not only more than capable of good performances, they were capable of good performances in big games, and even more than that, they were capable of good performances in big games in systems that had been unfamiliar to them beforehand. If anyone wanted vindication of whether or not the club had got the right man in to succeed Moyes, well, they seemed to have it, and when United secured a stunning win over City, that vindication was stronger still.

City took the lead at Old Trafford after eight minutes. In all honesty, their start to the game was blistering in its speed and quality, and their goal, through Sergio Aguero, was richly deserved. You wouldn't have blamed any home fan in the stadium for abandoning all memories of their recent good form and instead bracing themselves for a defeat which may fall anywhere in between the 3-0 defeat of the previous year or even the infamous 6-1 loss of 2011. That would have been doing a disservice to the new-found resilience of this team, who were cajoled into life by the concession of the goal; six minutes later, Ashley Young levelled the scores, and in the 27th minute, Young's cross was headed in at the back post by Marouane Fellaini. United got the goals their dominance deserved in a crazy six-minute spell in the second half — Juan Mata beat the offside trap (or, should that be, the assistant didn't put his flag up despite the Spaniard being marginally off) and then beat Joe Hart before Chris Smalling headed in another Young cross. Aguero's late consolation goal did nothing to take the gloss off the win as United moved four points clear of their cross-city rivals and, most importantly of all, nine points clear of Southampton in fifth place. With six matches remaining, the primary objective of returning to the Champions League was more or less secured and had been delivered with a stunning run of form which gave supporters renewed optimism for the future. The win also meant that the club had already achieved more points than they had in the previous campaign with six more games to spare.

This was, to repeat, a testament to good management. No United fan thought that the idea of Fellaini, Rooney and Young in tandem was a long-term solution, but its short-term benefits in these games had demonstrated that the manager was capable of finding solutions to help them challenge. If he could get these players working well in the big games, what might he achieve with bigger and better players that the club might be able to attract with their return to the Champions League? Young was a particular example. A player who might well have found himself discarded was in fact fairly valuable to the post-Ferguson squads because he was one of the best crossers in a group of players who were not exactly blessed in that area. Those crosses had certainly made their mark against Manchester City, and Young was one of the players as far back as October 2014, just as the club were starting their good run after an early wobble, who came out offering complete vocal support for the new regime. 'I just want to play the best I can,' Young told the *Manchester Evening News*. 'The manager has shown faith in me and I want to go out there and play well. The new manager has his methods and philosophy and everyone has bought into it. We've shown we can go into games and play different formations. It isn't any different for me. It was new things in the role I was playing, but, like I said, the manager changed the system and we're capable of changing the system against different teams.'

Van Gaal appeared to be happily preparing for the next season as the club announced their pre-season tour plans of the United States. He revealed that the likes of Nani and Javier Hernandez had continued to be watched by United's scouts in case their form warranted a recall rather than a sale. 'Already in January [we began thinking about the following season] because we have to prepare our pre-season and Manchester United will go to America,' the boss said. 'The aim is of course that we have to train and not only play matches. Already for three or four months we are talking about our pre-season. We also think about the scouting of players, the scouting of our own players because we have a lot on loan and then we have to analyse their performances, so it's a lot of work. It's not only the present season but also what we have to decide for players next season.'

There would be no such reprieve for the clutch of players offloaded in the January transfer window; Michael Keane and Wilfried Zaha left, bringing in £9m between them, while Darren Fletcher and Anderson both departed on free transfers.

Van Gaal did not have the luxury of an unchanged side again — Carrick, Blind and Jones were all missing from the game against Chelsea at Stamford Bridge, with Rojo and Van Persie still sidelined as well. Despite that, there was still no recall for Di Maria, with Mata and Young continuing in the wide roles and Fellaini retained in the 'number-ten' position. Herrera was given an unfamiliar job as holding midfielder. It may have been asking too much on the balance of probabilities for United to earn a seventh successive win at Chelsea of all places, but on the balance of play they certainly deserved more than the 1-0 defeat they ended up with. Eden Hazard scored a first-half goal, but United had enjoyed most of the ball; overall, they had 70 per cent possession and had twice as many efforts on goal, but this was a Chelsea side schooled in the traditional Mourinho method of late-season lockdowns, and their defensive organisation was simply too strong for the visitors.

Asked if he felt unlucky not to win, Van Gaal bluntly told the post-match interviewer, 'It doesn't matter how I feel, I think ... I don't have to say it, in football it's only counting the goals, they scored one goal from one shot. I'm not frustrated, I'm very proud of my team, we played our best performance of the season today ... we are in a process but you have seen my team is always growing, improving every week. It is amazing how we have played here. It is unbelievable that the result is 1-0 but that's football. Our fans are disappointed we lost and I am disappointed we lost. That is a pity, especially after we played so well. I have very disappointed players. And I'm very disappointed. But I see that we are improving every week. When you can play at Chelsea, like this — as the dominant team — then I'm very happy with that. But I'm also very disappointed. And that's the ambivalence in my feelings.'

The reporter asked if that was genuinely how highly he rated the performance. 'Yeah,' Van Gaal replied. 'You don't? Okay. That's good, that you're interested.' The Dutchman seemed particularly annoyed about a foul on Falcao in the build-up to the goal, especially considering his team were denied a late penalty.

His anger was redirected to his own players after they followed up that loss with another two defeats, sparking genuine concern about a late season collapse. First of all they went down 3-0 at Everton, and Van Gaal told Sky Sports that he had a bad feeling about the game as soon as he saw his own players in the warm-up. 'You shall always be compared with your opponent in aggression and motivation, and Everton really wanted to win this game, and I don't think we equalled it,' he said. 'The fighting spirit of Everton was higher, and when they scored the first goal it became difficult for us. I already had the feeling and my colleagues Ryan Giggs and Albert Stuivenberg had the feeling because the warm-up was not as good as usual. In the last minutes before the game you hope you can recover and stimulate your players, but then it is too late. You have to prepare the match already two or three days before and Everton have done that and they have won because of that. In phases we played well, and created chances, but I did not see the belief that I have seen when we were behind in matches. We need that aggression and a little bit of luck. It is of concern that we have not scored for two games in a row. We lost three duels in a row, and that was the first goal. You cannot start a game like that. When you are 1-0 ahead, you can defend how Everton and Chelsea did. You play compact and have a lot of players behind the ball. In the second half, we didn't create as many chances. It is very important that you score a goal and get belief from that. I am manager of Man United and the players shall use my words and think and communicate with each other, and I hope it shall not happen again, but as a coach I know it shall happen again. But we are human beings so it can happen once but when I see my season until now I am very satisfied.'

The manager apparently singled out Valencia and Blind in training at Carrington for what *The Express* described as 'particularly harsh criticism' about their performances. Their next defeat — a 1-0 home loss to West Brom — appeared to be the consequence of a loss of confidence in front of goal. United had an incredible 80 per cent possession rate, and 26 shots on goal (one of which was a penalty) and still couldn't find a way to get a single goal. Van Persie's spot kick was saved, missing a chance to level up a game which United were already trailing. 'We knew in advance that they'd park the bus, we have to deal with that,' said the United manager. 'In the second half we had enough chances — you have to finish. It's now the third match we have lost in a row. We have to take care of that. It's very difficult. You have to also give credit to the goalkeeper, but it was our biggest chance as it was without a lot of bodies in front of you. It's also a concern now because it's not a coincidence and, in spite of the way we have played against Chelsea, Everton and now against West Bromwich Albion, we have created a lot of chances and still we don't score. So you can say, as manager, we were not unlucky in every match. It's also that you have to finish these chances. We have lost three times in a row so it's also in the hands of my players. It [Champions League qualification] is less secure.'

Those three losses meant United were now just four points in front of Liverpool with three games to spare. They had been fortunate in the respect that Liverpool's own form was patchy enough to render United's a mere hiccup; Van Gaal's men won at Crystal Palace thanks to goals from Fellaini and Mata (some irony in the Moyes signings being the players who scored the goals to put the club back into the top competition) meaning their remaining games against Arsenal at home and Hull City away would mean little.

The club certainly seemed confident enough ahead of the Palace game, as they announced that PSV winger Memphis Depay would be joining for the 2015/16 season. Depay was clearly a Van Gaal buy due to the relationship between player and coach, and perhaps the promise of security for the following campaign helped relax United's players to get the necessary result at Selhurst Park. 'He [Depay] is a goalscoring winger and there aren't so many of them in the world,' van Gaal told MUTV. 'I was forced to handle [the situation] as a manager because, otherwise, he was going to PSG, that's why I had to sign him and we've done it within one day.' The manager was asked if this was an indication of his transfer activity — that it might all be done early. 'I want to do this [make signings] early but it's not always possible,' he added. 'When there's a chance, you have to handle that and manage it directly and that was the case. I want to purchase players after our season and not during the season because it disturbs our concentration for the match.'

Transfer talk was not limited to incomings. David de Gea came off in the game against Arsenal and gave the supporters a pointed applause amid speculation he was going to be the subject of a transfer bid from Real Madrid. Victor Valdes, who had signed on a free transfer in the January transfer window, came on and played from the start in the last game against Hull. United fans were preparing for life without their number-one goalkeeper, who had been the club's best performer over these two difficult seasons.

Another player rumoured to be close to the exit was Angel Di Maria. The poor form, the changed position of the player and the changed shape of the team, the red card against Arsenal as well as the burglary, had all contributed to make the winger's year in Manchester a miserable one, despite the promising start. After ten minutes of the game against Hull, Di Maria sat on the turf and signalled to the bench that he had to come off. *The Telegraph* did a study and between 5 July 2014 and the same date the following year, the player had missed 75 days through injury. Considering new boy Depay mainly attacked from the left, it seemed as if Di Maria's days may be up, although there was still the hope among some United fans that they would see better days from their record signing.

In many ways it mirrored the situation of Juan Sebastian Veron; the primary point being that there could be no doubting the star quality of the player. Di Maria was unquestionably the best player at the club in terms of pure talent. However, the manager's most effective selection when keeping the overall qualities of his squad in mind did not seem to have a place to accommodate the player. In the case of Veron that was understandable, to an extent. It was a winning strategy and Veron's arrival upset the balance. Ultimately, on that occasion, balance won out, even if in the years that immediately followed Veron's departure United were ironically crying out for that kind of midfielder. The unexpected upturn in form towards the end of the 2014/15 season, considering the identity of the players, meant that the effective system in place had no place for Di Maria. Could he have played the Mata role? Maybe, and maybe he could have done it better. Mata's consistency and reliability, however, placed him in favour with the boss. In this case the long-term prospects of the club might have been better served building around Di Maria considering that United were hardly likely to threaten for a league title relying on the combination of Young, Fellaini and Rooney for a full season, but what this had provided the boss with was a stunningly effective Plan B to fall back on with proof that it already worked in the big games.

Following the last home game of the season the club held its internal awards night; an apparently slightly worse-for-wear Louis van Gaal took to the stage to give a seven-minute speech where he insisted his team were very close and 'could have been champions'. It was rousing and drew a great response from those in attendance, and many more on social media. United's little wobble meant that they would still face the prospect of pre-group qualifiers for the Champions League, but it was a steady enough progress for all to believe the club were ready to challenge for the top honours again.

Cracks

On 15 July 2015 Louis van Gaal announced that he would be happy to allow one of his Spanish goalkeepers to leave — Victor Valdes. Valdes had apparently refused to play for the reserves and Van Gaal blasted the ex-Barca stopper, saying, 'He doesn't follow my philosophy. There is no place for someone like that. Last year he refused to play in the second team and there are other aspects you need as a keeper at United. When you are not willing to follow those principles, there is only one way and that is out. It is a big disappointment. It is a pity because we have given him the opportunity to rehabilitate, gave him a contract and then he is fit to play. I played him at Hull because I wanted to help. I am always a very social human being.'

The Manchester United manager was speaking in Seattle after the club had announced three signings which had happened in rapid fashion. Matteo Darmian, an Italian full-back, was brought in, as well as Morgan Schneiderlin, the Southampton midfielder who had played so well at Old Trafford in January, but the biggest shock was Bastian Schweinsteiger, Bayern Munich and Germany legend, who had been convinced to move to Manchester for what seemed to be a bargain fee of £6m. Despite these new arrivals, Van Gaal was mostly fielding questions about players who were rumoured to be leaving or had already left, such as Robin van Persie, who, the boss revealed, had learned he would be sold before the summer. 'He knew already what was coming from the day we played golf,' Van Gaal said. 'After we played golf, we talked about the perspective for him at Manchester United. I think he made a very good choice [to join Fenerbahce].' The boss was also questioned on Di Maria's future and was non-committal. 'No idea,' he said. 'We shall see. Now, he is still a member of Manchester United.'

The second phase of the club's transition under their Dutch 'trainer coach' was well underway. Despite the suggestion he would be recalled, Nani was also sold to Fenerbahce for a little over £4m. Tom Cleverley was permitted to sign for Everton on a free transfer and Tom Thorpe was surprisingly released.

Much more transfer activity was to follow, and it seemed as if the major business was destined to include David de Gea. Importantly, United didn't seem to be prohibiting the move, but the valuation they had of their player seemed to fluctuate wildly from Real Madrid's. In a summer where Raheem Sterling had joined Manchester City for £50m, and Kevin De Bruyne went there for £55m, United's insistence that Madrid break the world-record transfer fee for a goalkeeper (which was still Gianluigi Buffon's £32.6m move to Juventus in 2001) did not seem unreasonable in the least. However, the Spanish club were sure they could force United to sell for much less and started offering derisory sums of less than £20m.

Complicating matters further was Sergio Ramos; the Real Madrid defender was apparently disillusioned with life at the club and wanted to move. 'With everything that has happened it will be very difficult for Sergio Ramos to stay at Madrid,' the player's agent Pedro Riesco told journalists. 'Sergio is a symbol of this club. He has nothing to prove. But so many things are being said about him. There is so much manipulation to discredit his name via spokesmen who behave like puppets saying he is not respecting the club and that he is just a money-grabber.'

United responded to the comments by submitting a formal £35m bid, which was stressed to be unconnected to Madrid's interest in De Gea.

Their tour of North America was largely successful, with wins over Club America and San Jose Earthquakes followed by two games against European sides — a 3-1 win over Barcelona was then followed by a 2-0 defeat to Paris. In between the last two games, United announced the signing of Sergio Romero, the goalkeeper for the Argentina national team, who was available on a free transfer after leaving Sampdoria. 'I am absolutely delighted to join Manchester United,' he said. 'To play for the biggest club in the world is a dream come true for me. Louis van Gaal is a fantastic manager and I cannot wait to get started on this new and exciting challenge in my career.'

Romero was going to go straight into the team for the season's opener against Tottenham Hotspur on 8 August. Before that first league game, there was enough time in the month to offload two players, both to France, both to mixed reactions. Rafael was sold to Lyon, a true fan favourite whose place in the side had been lost to Valencia. Some supporters were upset as Valencia didn't appear to be a long-term solution for that role, but the idea was that the former Torino defender Matteo Darmian would be the first choice there and the manager had at least earned the right to make such tough calls. Perhaps he earned kudos with the sale of Angel Di Maria; the rumoured fee of £44m meant United took a £15m hit on the player after just a year, but it was a show of character from the boss to admit it wasn't working. That does not mean it couldn't have worked, but it was at least an indication of how the team might shape up going forward.

Against Tottenham, United appeared to play a 4-2-3-1. Romero was in goal, with Darmian and Shaw at full-back and Smalling and Blind in defence. Carrick and Schneiderlin partnered in midfield behind Juan Mata, with Young and Depay flanking Rooney. Their performance was not convincing, but they won 1-0 thanks to an own goal from Kyle Walker. It was the same story the following week against Aston Villa, with Adnan Januzaj (given the nod in the place of Young) scoring the only goal of the game.

These were baby steps and so issues about the fluidity in United's attacking play were not so problematic, even if they did cause some concern. Of course, the jury was still out on Januzaj, but particularly with Nani, Di Maria and Van Persie all having left, and Falcao returning to Monaco (and then joining Chelsea on a similar loan deal) supporters were convinced that some movement in the remaining weeks of the transfer window would be inevitable. It did seem a little worrying that the manager had clearly identified the centre of defence as an area that needed strengthening and no name had come in, particularly when it was announced that Sergio Ramos had signed a new deal to stay at Real Madrid, painting a picture that United had been foolish to become drawn into a political affair between the player and his club which was always destined to end one way. Still, if there was one thing the manager had done which could not be questioned, it was the organisation he had instilled upon his defenders. United's defensive record hadn't been *awful* under Moyes — their 43 conceded in 2013/14 was the same as the previous year's tally — but it was more the nature of the defending and how, when a goal was conceded, the team tended to capitulate. Under Van Gaal the tally improved to 37, which was even more impressive when you consider the Leicester capitulation is included. Without that freak game, United were as solid as they had been in defence since Ferdinand and Vidic were at their peak, and that was some achievement when considering the collection of defenders Van Gaal had been left with.

United secured qualification to the Champions League group stages with wins in both legs over Club Brugge, which were just about as routine as the club had managed anything in its post-Fergie slump. First of all, Memphis Depay scored two in the home leg, and then Wayne Rooney scored a hat-trick in the away game to help the club register a 7-1 aggregate win.

Goals were much harder to come by on the domestic front. A frustrating 0-0 draw against Newcastle could have been put down to just one of those days if it was a result in isolation. United had more than two thirds of the ball and had 20 efforts on goal — they started well enough, putting their visitors under pressure and even scoring a goal which was ruled out for offside in the fourth minute. In the first quarter of this game, United had registered more shots on target than they had in the entire opening two games. The closest Van Gaal's team came to scoring was a late header from Smalling, which hit the post, but their play was not cohesive. Schneiderlin and Schweinsteiger controlled the game in the middle of the park and United comfortably set a new record of three consecutive clean sheets at the start of the season — a record, consequently, for new goalkeeper Sergio Romero, who had yet to really be tested — but this was at the cost of the attacking fluidity which United seemed capable of just a year ago. Pragmatism had won out.

The more concerning thing for United was the likelihood that they couldn't now play expansive football even if they wanted to. Without Di Maria's penetration bridging the gap between midfield and attack, the team were overly reliant on the creativity of Juan Mata, who was an admittedly brilliant footballer, yet less effective against teams who made it a point not to afford any space.

Van Gaal's comments after the match suggested he felt it had been just one of those days. 'We can be satisfied with the performance but not with the result — we were unlucky,' he said. 'We did not make the right choices in the final third but we played fantastic as a team. I like these kind of games when we work like this, but not this result. The performance was one of the best in my period, but we don't reward ourselves and there was only one club that wanted to win and that was us.'

Perhaps the manager was vindicated by the four-goal win over Brugge which followed, but when attentions were redirected back to the Premier League and Swansea City, United's domestic start suddenly went from 'Okay' to 'Indifferent'. The Swans registered a third consecutive 2-1 win over Van Gaal's side. Bafetimbi Gomis's effort to win the game was a tame shot which Romero arguably should have done better with. His fine start to the season had suddenly been undermined by a costly error, provoking a sharpening of the lens. The business of being a goalkeeper, or defender for that matter, can be cruel, as the perception of competence is more harshly defined. It was one error in his first six games, but because it was not one you would expect David de Gea to make, naturally, the manager's decision to omit the want-away Spaniard from his starting line-up was called into question. Also notable by his absence against Swansea, particularly given United's need for a late goal, was Javier Hernandez. The Mexican had missed a penalty against Brugge, and, despite it not coming at any cost to the result, Van Gaal had clearly seen enough to know there would be no place in his squad for the striker who had done so well earlier in his Old Trafford career.

Van Gaal was again insistent that his team deserved more from the game. 'We dominated for 85 minutes and you have to have a result that is better than this, because we lost it in five minutes and that cannot happen in my eyes,' he said. 'They changed the shape and because we didn't know that we should have become compact it was more difficult to beat us. We were very dominant, but we didn't create enough chances. To score goals you also need a little bit of luck and we don't have that at the moment. The most important thing also is to react when an opponent changes their shape and we didn't react quickly enough.' When asked if that was a fault of the manager or the players, the manager seemed to suggest his players were not proactive enough. 'I can only change, and when I make the changes, within five minutes we were dominating the game again. The players have to read the game for themselves and I said this in the dressing room. We need players to keep the team together. It is difficult to say I am happy with how we are playing because today I enjoyed watching the way we played football, but we lost again, and again against the same opponent.'

Former Premier League striker Jason Roberts offered his opinion on United's goalscoring issues. 'There is absolutely no doubt in my mind that Manchester United need to buy a new striker before the transfer window shuts on Tuesday,' Roberts told BBC's *Match of the Day 2*. 'From watching United in their 2-1 defeat by Swansea, and what I had seen of them beforehand this season, they desperately need someone dynamic to lead their line. To have a chance of finishing in the top four, and qualifying for the Champions League, they need a top-class striker who can run — someone fast and mobile enough to stretch opposition defences. Wayne Rooney is still a wonderful forward player, but he is not that man. In an ideal world for Rooney and United, when the Premier League restarts after the international break, he will still be an integral part of their attack — but as a number ten, with a new number nine playing in front of him.'

It was now ten league games without a goal for Rooney and the common consensus from supporters was that, rather than get a player to partner him, they needed someone to replace him. There would have been a definite split of opinion if you asked fans if they would rather he or Hernandez was sold; with the deadline looming large, it was 'Chicharito' who was one of three squad players sold on. He left for Leverkusen, while Jonny Evans and Anders Lindegaard both joined West Bromwich Albion. Adnan Januzaj was also surprisingly allowed to join Borussia Dortmund on loan.

The major story of deadline day threatened to be that of David de Gea. With news leaking out of Old Trafford that United had reluctantly decided to sell the goalkeeper to Real Madrid, supporters were waiting to hear details of that agreement when they were caught cold by the announcement that Anthony Martial, the Monaco forward, was heading to Manchester. Martial had scored 12 times for his club the previous season and, while there was no doubting his potential, many eyebrows were raised at the size of the fee. An initial £36m was paid for the player who only cost Monaco £3.5m in 2013, with the potential for the fee to rise to almost £60m after add-ons. 'Is he worth that amount of money? If you ask the people back in France, they will say no he's not,' journalist Philippe Auclair said. 'This amount of money leaves people speechless in France.' The deal was announced later that day.

'I am so excited to be joining Manchester United,' said Martial in a statement released by the club. 'I have always wanted to play in the Premier League, and to join the biggest club in the world is what every young footballer dreams of. I am looking forward to meeting my new team-mates and working with Louis van Gaal, who has achieved so much in his career.'

After wrapping up that signing, United then entertained conversations with Real Madrid. Madrid's offer was reported to be a '£29.3m player-plus-cash' deal which included their goalkeeper Keylor Navas; according to *The Guardian*, the offer valued De Gea at just £22m. Regardless, United felt they had to conclude the deal rather than risk losing the best goalkeeper in the world for nothing. The twist in the tale came when Real officials claimed they had received the fax from United with all the required documents too late. United's response was that all of their paperwork was time-stamped and filed through FIFA's official systems. Madrid appealed to La Liga but their pleas were rejected. The blame game was played through the media over the coming days, with various 'sources' on either side suggesting the other was at fault, but even if there was an element of truth to be found in the theory that United had been mischievously dragging their heels with registering the paperwork, then the finger ultimately should have been pointed at Madrid for firstly offering sums which were completely unreasonable and secondly for not seriously engaging United's earlier attempts at negotiating (they had responded to the first offer by tentatively suggesting Gareth Bale be included, and then again during the Sergio Ramos farce).

United were clearly weaker after the summer considering the number of squad players who had left and the number of forwards who hadn't been replaced, but it was seen as something of a power move to have retained De Gea and then brought in Martial. It almost gave the impression of a successful transfer window and this feeling was strengthened by the news that De Gea had signed a new contract. Presumably offended by the fact he had quite openly invited the move and Madrid had not quite valued him as highly as United clearly did (and maybe even motivated by the fact that in his prior refusal to sign a new contract, he was still earning considerably lower than he might expect to), he agreed terms on a new four-year contract with a new expiry of 2019. 'I am delighted to be starting this new chapter in my United career,' De Gea said. 'I have always enjoyed playing with these great players in front of our fantastic fans. Manchester United is a special club and Old Trafford is an ideal place for me to continue to develop my career. I'm looking forward to putting a difficult summer behind me and concentrating on working hard to improve and help my team-mates to be successful.'

All of which sounds very positive, and just the kind of news United fans needed going into their game against Liverpool as the first match after the international break. Less welcome was a report in the press on 10 September, the day before the new contract announcement; it was rumoured that there had been a bust-up in training in August where senior members of the squad had confronted the manager about the methods he was using. A 'source' told the *Daily Mail* that the players 'felt like robots'. 'Nobody is allowed to take a chance,' the unnamed person said. 'They feel like they are wearing straitjackets. Everything is in zones. It's a case of "you can only go this far". The feeling is that they are being turned into robots.'

At a dinner that evening for executive season-ticket holders, Van Gaal told fans that he felt the fee the club had paid for Martial was 'ridiculous' and an indication of 'the crazy world we are in'. This was not a slight at the player but rather an exaggeration of market prices Van Gaal had experienced at United, where the club were quoted, in his words, '£10m more' for players than other clubs. He said that he felt 'everything must go for us' for United to win the league and admitted he would be satisfied with a top-three finish, and also suggested that Martial was in fact not his choice at all. He said, 'I have not bought Martial for me, I have bought him for the next manager of Manchester United.' He then nodded to Ryan Giggs who was sitting alongside him and said, 'I feel I am introducing the next manager of Manchester United.'

It was not the long-term ambitions, but the rumours of the fall-out, which were the most prominent questions from journalists' mouths in the pre-match conference before the Liverpool game. Further details had been leaked — it had reportedly been Michael Carrick and Wayne Rooney who had approached the manager after the Tottenham game to air their frustration about supposed restrictions on attacking play, but the boss was putting a positive spin on it when forced to talk about it. 'I think I have a superb relationship with my players,' the 64-year-old insisted. 'Maybe you have to consider how many players are coming to the manager to say something. In my career as a manager, I didn't have so many come to say something about the atmosphere in the dressing room or the way we train, or something like that. But it is very positive that they are coming to you and that they trust you. I have read things that we haven't talked about. It is the same story as last year, but the consequence of the philosophy is that we have to release players. The whole dressing room has been changed. Can you imagine when your friend must leave? What are your feelings then? Rooney and Carrick came to me and said the dressing room is flat — they told me to help me. I communicate not only with my captains, they try to warn me. I then go to my dressing room and discuss with my players and we discussed a lot of aspects — but not what some have written. The fans are shouting every week "Louis van Gaal's army, Louis van Gaal's army". They are very satisfied and the players are satisfied. Some players are coming to me to apologise about what has been said in the papers. I can say only that I have a very good relationship with my players, but it is logical now that only nine are left from the initial group. The others I have bought will not say I am a lousy manager!'

Van Gaal also took the extraordinary step of publicly elevating Rooney. 'Wayne Rooney is the best captain [I have coached],' he added. 'That is something I mean because Danny Blind was always my best captain and when I say Wayne Rooney is my best captain,

I say something about Danny Blind and he shall read that and be disappointed.'

Speaking about the meeting in March 2017, Michael Carrick told ESPN, 'We just spoke to him as the senior players, to have a conversation to say that everyone wanted to be better. We weren't having a great time in terms of results and it happens to a lot of teams, but you just have to do something about it. It was a fair conversation, nobody went in there fighting or anything, and it wasn't really a big deal. It probably sounded like a big deal, but it happens all the time at clubs all over the country. Sometimes a manager will pull you aside in training or in his office, but it just so happened that me and Wayne went to chat to him. It got built up to quite a big thing, but that's just the way it is.'

The truth, as it often does, surely falls somewhere in the middle. Meetings like that may well occur on a regular basis but there had to be something different about this one. If they happened all the time, why was this the only one to make the news? Furthermore, this was done on behalf of the players, not the manager, so why did it come out a few weeks after the meeting apparently took place? And why *was* it newsworthy? The answer is surely because the outcome of the meeting had not been to the satisfaction of the party who felt they were aggrieved; in this instance, the players. The fire-fighting exercise from the manager was fairly refreshing in its honesty but left everyone feeling that the coach was perhaps more respectful of his players than they were of him. Stories of similar incidents at Chelsea down the years — with players obviously familiar to Carrick and Rooney from international duty — usually led to widespread talk about dressing room revolts and player power down at Stamford Bridge becoming stronger than the word of the manager. Whenever those stories emanated, they ultimately ended with the manager losing his job.

It prompted an interesting political question for supporters: did they agree with the players? Had they been brave enough to articulate something which needed to be said? You could probably argue fairly on both sides of the coin when discussing Van Gaal's pragmatism and whether or not it was necessary or over-cautious. There was certainly something not clicking about United's attacking style, but then again, even if Carrick and Rooney had a point, were they two players who supporters would want to win a long-term power struggle considering their own futures were hardly likely to be integral to the next generation of success at the club? At the very least, it suggested a resistance to the changes Van Gaal was trying to make, and if there was such resistance, then surely that in itself was conducive to ineffective performances? In any ordinary circumstances this would have been a fairly logical chain of events: team underperforms, manager is under pressure, and then manager is sacked. It was not quite fair to attribute all of United's issues to the manager. As he rightly pointed out, he had overseen a huge turnover of players — a necessary turnover, too. How many tears would have been shed if Rooney and Carrick had been part of that turnover? There is hardly any doubt that, of the two, Carrick's influence on the performance of the team was more pronounced, and, indeed, his return to the team the previous season had helped instil a calm air. And yet it was clear to everyone that, if only because of Old Father Time, United would need to find another way to reinvent their midfield without Carrick. With Schneiderlin and Schweinsteiger, and Herrera, United had the personnel to control games from the middle of the park and were doing a fairly good job in that regard. Schweinsteiger was not a long-term solution himself, but he was an indication that United would be a little more aggressive in their play in that area. The remaining issue was moving the ball quickly enough to the forwards and in that sense there had to be some responsibility on the shoulders of the forwards. There was certainly criticism of the mobility of United's forward play even with Van Persie, Hernandez and Falcao to call upon, and the idea of over-reliance on Rooney was not a prospect supporters were overwhelmingly positive about.

Rooney and Carrick *had* been a part of the glory days at the club. They'd also been a part of its decline and hadn't exactly demonstrated the sort of form that, say, De Gea had, to suggest that they were immune to criticism. On the other hand, if something needed to be said, you could not have picked two more suitable figures to step forward and speak up. Perhaps the issue is whether or not it needed to be said, or whether, at that point, it was an unnecessary issue raised at an unnecessary time.

A game against Liverpool is not the best occasion to observe whether the criticism was fair; the unique atmosphere of this fixture, could, however, help to provide a shot in the arm when it was definitely needed. And to be fair, United were well on their way to achieving that boost with a 2-1 lead in the game before the late introduction of Anthony Martial, which stole all the headlines. Martial's embarrassment of Martin Skrtel made him an instant hero at Old Trafford, and the 3-1 win was good enough to take United back into second place, behind a City team who had won all of their opening five games.

The way Martial had exploded onto the scene gave supporters the belief that the Frenchman possessed all of the dynamism the team had been lacking in forward positions. It also provided the manager ammunition to suggest maybe he did know what he was doing. You didn't have to look too far to see signs of progress. Van Gaal, like Moyes, brought in his own coaches, and there could be no denying that De Gea's general level of performances were better than they had ever been. If you were being cute you might say the player was always destined to reach that level and it was little to do with goalkeeping coach Frans Hoek. You might also suggest that the management had had as much of an impact on stunting Luke Shaw's career as it had on its apparent progression at the start of the 2015/16 season, though to the credit of the manager he had declared that the forthcoming season would 'be the season of Luke Shaw'. It was clear to all that the left-back had all the talent and potential to be a long-term successor to Patrice Evra, but fitness issues meant he had only made 20 appearances overall in his first year at the club. His start to his second year had been far more convincing, and then disaster struck as United kicked off their Champions League campaign at PSV Eindhoven. Just 15 minutes had been played when Hector Moreno scythed down Shaw; the full-back was on one of the marauding forward runs which were becoming his trademark, and he was hauled down on the edge of the box. It was clear from the reaction of the players that this was a serious injury and play was stopped for ten minutes while Shaw was stretchered off. Shockingly, Moreno was allowed to remain on the pitch, and PSV literally added insult to injury when the Mexican scored the equaliser after Depay had opened the scoring. A second-half goal from Narsingh won the game for the hosts, and United's performance had been understandably subdued, though they still might have felt unlucky both to have been defeated and in the nature of it, thanks to the goalscorer.

'It is awful. It was a very bad tackle. He had the oxygen mask on and was crying in the dressing room,' said a furious Louis van Gaal after the match. 'A boy who came to Manchester United at 18 years old, it was very difficult, and the next season he plays fantastic and then that happens like this. When I say it is a red card and penalty, you will say I am a bad loser. Every word I say is taken in the wrong way. It was in the 18-yard box and it was a very bad tackle with two legs. I'm not a doctor so I cannot say, but when you have a double fracture it is four to six months. But you can never say that in advance. He won't play in the group stage, I don't think. I hope he will play again this season.'

It was a bitter blow for United, Shaw and the manager, who was always keen to play a side whose abilities complemented each other. Balance was a key factor in the Louis van Gaal philosophy, as illustrated by his consistent selection of a right-footed and left-footed centre-back pairing. That defensive unit so far had been Smalling and Blind and this had been another positive element of Van Gaal's management. Blind was a versatile player, capable of playing in holding midfield — as he had through most of his first season at the club — left-back or centre-half. There were reservations about his ability to do that on a long-term basis, but concerns over his pace were counter-balanced by his quality on the ball. Blind was the best passer of the ball in United's defence and so it was a boost to have someone comfortable at bringing the ball out. Smalling, alongside him, had enjoyed an upturn in form and also fortune considering how close to the brink he must have been after the red card against Manchester City the previous season. In fact, Smalling's form was universally applauded, with the common consensus being that he was now fulfilling the potential many thought he was capable of. Some of this credit was given to the manager, but few were considering the underlying reasons for this sudden improvement. Van Gaal's teams generally lined up with two holding midfielders, particularly after the Leicester 5-3 game where he realised that something would have to give. This offered a level of protection, helping the defence more than it did the attack. And, even then, the defence was relatively porous; there was a reason that David de Gea's form was noticed.

Underworked goalkeepers rarely tend to get the same amount of praise, much less get voted Player of the Year. Smalling's form — and Blind's, beside him — was praised for much the same reasons as United's attacking form was criticised. The club simply did not appear to possess a squad of players with the skillset of playing confident attacking football whilst maintaining an organised defence.

The primary reasons for this were the wholesale loss of experience and the present lack of leaders in the dressing room. Bastian Schweinsteiger's arrival was presumably to address some of that; the idea of Sergio Ramos as another was a sound one. In Rooney and Carrick, United had players who had the experience but even though Rooney had long been touted as a captain for club and country, now that he actually was, he was not exactly the leader in the form many anticipated he would have been. There was none of the Keane or Robson approach of leading by example by performance; maybe some of the old fire had been rekindled under David Moyes, but to most Rooney was now no longer a player going through a bad period of form, he was a player in decline, however understandable it was and whatever the reasons for it were. The Old Trafford, Cliff and Carrington changing rooms had contained some remarkably large characters over the years; never, certainly in the Fergie era, did it come to light that players were confronting the manager over style of play or training methods. There were stories of bust-ups between players which were later revealed, but not reported at the time. The closest anyone had come to criticising the players was Roy Keane — he was club captain and even he wasn't safe from getting axed. Tellingly, the only other notable time that anyone had publicly questioned the club's direction was Wayne Rooney in October 2010. It didn't appear as if United had the sort of on-field leadership they required and without that it was crucial that they played to the instruction of the manager, whether he was right or wrong.

If there was one place they could boast some form of authority it was in midfield, with Carrick's pedigree, Schweinsteiger's mere presence and Schneiderlin's potential to emulate either of them. This provided a buffer to protect a defence which was desperately lacking in leaders.

The composition of the squad *was* at least now something the manager could be taken to task for. Three transfer windows and the freedom to oversee and instigate so much change was enough time for United to be assuming the sort of identity you would think the manager wanted, even accounting for the odd disaster like the injury to Shaw. To be generous, Van Gaal's record in the transfer market was a mixed bag and at best seemed to be at odds with the meticulous planning the Dutchman seemed to be famed for.

The indecision over the future of De Gea was primarily down to Real Madrid, but even if he was to go then you get the impression that under Sir Alex, for example, the deal would have happened early in the summer and the club would have got on with it. There was a lack of conviction on both sides, which ultimately reflected poorly on each party. It didn't appear to be a strategic move, and the fact that so many different types of player had been identified as potential swaps for United's goalkeeper was testament to the erratic nature of their planning. Bale, Ramos and Navas were all suggested by Van Gaal as possible exchanges, and in the end, not only did none of those players come in, but nobody of equivalent stature arrived in their place, as you would expect that they might if United were needing that quality. It left the manager open to a fair accusation that the signings of Di Maria and Falcao had not been well thought out, either. Coming as they did so late in the window, it seems a reasonable enough conclusion to arrive at that these players were not top of the manager's wish list. Falcao, as already explained, was a gamble more or less worth taking, while signing the man of the match from that year's Champions League Final was hardly a 'poor' move. But there was nothing to suggest that either player were primary targets and the relative ease with which the moves were conducted at least suggested they could have been done much earlier.

Van Gaal's other transfer activity seemed to generally centre around players he was familiar with. Schweinsteiger and Valdes were players he had worked with before at club level, while Daley Blind and Memphis Depay were players he knew from his time coaching the national side. Alongside Ramos, the biggest transfer rumour of the summer had involved a mooted £100m move for Thomas Muller, another Van Gaal protégé. Was this an indication of a manager not entirely sure of his long-term strategy at the club? Perhaps it was an indication of another structural problem he had inherited. Things had become almost autonomous under the Ferguson reign and scouting was included with that. Over time, the reputation of the club under the manager spoke for itself, and it was a reputation rich enough to rely upon, especially when attracting young players. In recent years the club's infrastructure hadn't changed even with the new money coming into the game, and inevitably some talent had been lost elsewhere.

In fairness to Van Gaal, he was clear in his very first press conference that he had been told not to have too many short-term concerns with the youth system at the club. And criticism of the success of his transfers was only truly justified with hindsight; strong arguments for why each of them were necessary and promising at the time were not any less valid just because they didn't work out. The club needed a boost to its profile without Champions League football, so being able to attract two of the best players in the world at their respective peaks was a statement to that effect. When experience was needed in the middle of the park, Bastian Schweinsteiger was almost over-qualified. If there was a genuine concern to be levied then it would be that the club hadn't got enough bodies in. David Moyes had infamously been dubbed as 'dithering' at Everton and the club's procrastinating in his summer, which potentially cost them Thiago, Fabregas and Herrera, did nothing to alter that opinion. The failure to land Sergio Ramos was perhaps not something the club could be criticised too heavily for, except to say that perhaps they could have realised they were a pawn in a political game much earlier. With the need for defensive reinforcement having been made so public then (especially when considering Mats Hummels had also been a reported target before he moved from Dortmund to Bayern), the decision to not test the waters for Ramos's Real team-mate Raphael Varane or Athletic Bilbao's Aymeric Laporte seemed to be an opportunity missed. It makes for interesting conversation, but one thing that can be taken from the period was that there was no clear strategy with regards to recruitment.

The strategy which was clear — *the philosophy* — was beginning to divide supporters' opinions with regards to its effectiveness. United bounced back from the PSV setback with four consecutive wins — scoring three goals in three consecutive games, and then defeating Wolfsburg 2-1 thanks to a goal from recent hero Chris Smalling.

Before that game, they had eased to a 3-0 victory over Sunderland and went top of the table. City's perfect start had been dented by a defeat at home to West Ham and then a 4-1 surrender to Tottenham. Here was another thread influencing United's own chances of success — the fortunes of others. City boss Manuel Pellegrini was almost always suffering speculation over his future and his team always seemed to play as 11 expensively assembled individuals. This is what they were, of course, and by and large that method had been somewhat successful for City, but the clear lustful longing for Pep Guardiola was to the perennial undermining of any attempt Pellegrini could have on making his own statement. He was perceived by the footballing community as little more than a caretaker of that role and that was now coming at a clear cost to the form of the first team.

Liverpool's own poor start to the season (they had lost 3-0 at home to West Ham before the defeat at Old Trafford) had put Brendan Rodgers on the brink of the sack following their spectacular fall from grace after selling Luis Suarez. In early October Rodgers would be dismissed and so the Anfield side's search for a renaissance would begin again. If their start to the 2015/16 season was poor then there is barely a superlative extreme enough to describe Chelsea's early campaign form. *Dreadful* might suit; they had lost three out of their first seven league games. When they were defeated 3-1 at home to Southampton on the evening before United travelled to Arsenal, the severity of this indifferent form at Stamford Bridge under Mourinho was clear enough to illustrate to everyone that there were huge problems at the champions. Naturally this meant there was intense speculation over Mourinho's future, and after the defeat against the Saints the Chelsea boss faced the television cameras for a staggering seven minutes when he explained how his team had 'mentally and psychologically collapsed', but said he would not 'run away from his responsibility' and also that 'this is a crucial moment in the history of this club. If they sack me, they sack the best manager this club has had. And the message they send is that bad results [mean] the manager is guilty. But everyone needs to take responsibility — me, the players, everyone.' Chelsea's 'collapse' would continue and by mid-December Mourinho would be sacked. Tottenham's relatively poor start to the season — that opening day at Old Trafford was followed by three draws — had picked up but, the huge win over City aside, no one had them down as potential champions yet.

It meant a huge opportunity was opening up for someone to take advantage; the aligning of so many big clubs in transition at the same time was so rare. And so Arsenal versus Manchester United was propelled into the position of being bigger than it had been for a while. Van Gaal's team included Smalling and Blind at centre-half, Ashley Young at left-back and Michael Carrick and Bastian Schweinsteiger in the middle. Before a quarter of this game had been played, United were three goals down, with Arsenal fans baying for revenge for the 8-2 loss of 2011. The full-time statistics, which showed Van Gaal's side to have had 62 per cent possession and as many shots on target as their opponents, only go to prove the ease with which Arsenal were able to protect their lead. Half-time substitutes Valencia and Fellaini were unable to have a positive effect but did at least help prevent the defeat becoming even more emphatic. 'It was a very bad start, without aggression and the will to win. That is the first time I have seen that from my team. I did not expect that,' Van Gaal said afterwards. 'We have won our last four matches — I gave the players a day off because they were tired. On Saturday the training was normal, I was very amazed to see that. When you give a team like Arsenal so much space to play football, then you know that you shall lose. But all teams will have a dip.'

United's tactical issues in this game were exposed too easily. Their midfield was too slow and Arsenal took advantage of the fact that the left side of their opponent's defence featured players more suited to playing further up the pitch. It was by no means a false result, but it was the sort of result you can expect when coming up against a top-six team in the Premier League if your line-up is not mindful of the opposition's strengths. A harsh lesson learned for Van Gaal — for once, he made a tactical misjudgement. The size of the defeat predictably cajoled Arsenal sympathisers into full voice, who — as they tended to do with any early-season victories against big opponents — were quick to assume this was an indication of Wenger's team coming good rather than a blip of their opponents. The first goal came about as a result of poor organisation on the left side of the defence. The second goal was a result of pressure on Smalling, forcing the defender into a hasty punt which went straight to an Arsenal shirt; from the resulting counter, Smalling and Blind were caught completely out of position. The defending could have been better for the third, too — it was an opening period which substantiated some of the hype around Alexis Sanchez and Mesut Ozil, players understandably deemed as the stars of this Arsenal side. Great players they certainly were, although the fact that they were surplus to requirements at Barcelona and Real Madrid respectively perhaps gave a truer reflection of why Arsenal would persist at the level of pretenders rather than genuine contenders. In the aftermath of this result in October 2015, it wasn't only those with an Arsenal persuasion who could make a case for their 12-year wait for a league title possibly ending. Their settlement under Wenger in this tumultuous, unpredictable season could easily have served to be their ace card. It wasn't, of course. Arsenal were stuck in their own perpetual cycle of underachievement.

United's own underachievement on the day was not fatal to their title hopes. They dropped to third but were only two points from the top place. The mistakes at the Emirates were emphasised further by the corrections for United's next game, at Goodison Park. In came Phil Jones into defence and Marcos Rojo came in at left-back. Schneiderlin and Herrera were brought in to offer bite in midfield. The result? Both of the recalled midfielders scored in an impressive 3-0 win. Gary Neville took the time in his punditry role to both praise the response and criticise the Arsenal game: 'Against Arsenal, for some reason, and I don't know why, it was like, has Schweinsteiger gone rogue?' said Neville on Sky Sports. 'But the more you watch the clips back, you think it must have been a tactic. In this game they got concerned about Cazorla. And Cazorla, he had him on a lead. It was like a man with a ball saying to a dog "come to get it off me, come to get it off me", and as soon as he gets near him, he throws it off to Mertesacker. The contrast on Saturday was absolutely dramatic. It was a case of Manchester United being patient, compact. It was a completely different thing to that Arsenal game. I'm sure Van Gaal, when he thinks about the Arsenal game, will think, "if we'd done this, would it have been different?" even though Arsenal played brilliantly well. It culminated in United dominating the game. It was typical of how an away team would create a perfect away performance. Against Arsenal it was a complete blip, in terms of the tactics.'

That Everton game was the first result of an 11-match unbeaten run, which sounds much less impressive when revealing that seven of those games were draws, and even worse when revealing that five of those draws were goalless. Van Gaal's assertion that his team hadn't played to win at Arsenal was followed by murmurs that, in fact, they weren't playing to win for him. It had been a statistical anomaly that Memphis Depay's goal had been the only one scored by a United player in front of the 'K' stand at Old Trafford (Kyle Walker's being an own goal) that season, but the trend seemed to evolve into a problem and then it became something of a disease. The psychological impact of that seemed to have a definite effect on the players, who were not giving convincing performances, and consequently results suffered. A scoreless 120 minutes against lower-league Middlesbrough in the League Cup was followed by a penalty shoot-out defeat; in late November, another goalless game against PSV Eindhoven in the Champions League put their place in the competition in a precarious position. It meant they needed to win against Wolfsburg in Germany or match PSV's result to avoid the ignominy of Europa League football after the turn of the year. Before that final group game, United faced West Ham at home, and drew 0-0. The hosts had 63 per cent of the ball and 21 efforts on goal, but, most revealingly of all, only managed to get one effort on target. 'The most important thing is you dominate, create and you finish,' Van Gaal said after the game. 'Football is scoring goals. The first two basic aspects of football we have done. When you don't finish from a metre in front of an empty goal you can say nothing any more. You have to finish and that's the only problem we have. We played very well especially in the second half — but you have to finish. The goals are coming. That is my strong belief.'

Dark December

Louis van Gaal was right. Goals were coming. Not exactly, however, in the order he would have liked. December 2015 will go down as a very dark period in the history of Manchester United Football Club, not only for the results but for the sour taste of the events. Poor runs of form in football — most sport for that matter — can generally be explained and you don't usually have to be an expert to work out why. Perhaps there has been a tactical shift which is unfamiliar to the players; perhaps there appears to be no direction. The latter point seems to be a criticism levelled at David Moyes when attempting to acknowledge how unfamiliar his Old Trafford team was from a traditional Manchester United side, despite having all of the same players.

Other factors come into play. Injuries that prevent a manager picking his strongest 11 had certainly appeared to restrict Louis van Gaal's chances of success in his first year in charge. External factors, such as the then-ongoing legal battle at Chelsea with former physiotherapist Eva Carneiro, can cast a dark cloud over the entire club and have an impact on morale. Whether or not the Carneiro episode, ugly as it was, was enough of a reason to justify such a pronounced underachievement from title-winning players, that by

Christmas some were wondering if they might become the first Premier League champions to be relegated. That alone can surely not be a good enough reason, but there can almost be no denying that there exists, to some extent, a political battle at most sporting clubs which can manifest itself in the team's performances. Mourinho's impending, inevitable sacking from Chelsea had implications at Old Trafford.

The early season reports of player unrest at United had surfaced in the first international break. Their form after the second international break seemed to take a drastic downturn and it was almost unexplainable. Defensively, their recovery after the 3-0 defeat at the Emirates had been as resolute as one might expect from a Louis van Gaal team. The 12-game unbeaten run that followed included eight clean sheets. Clearly, then, it was the attack that was an issue. Earlier in the season, there had been no suggestion that scoring goals would prove to be such a difficult task. In the eight games played between 12 September and 17 October, United scored at least three goals on five occasions. It was hardly likely that there had been a change in Van Gaal's methods; firstly, he was too long in the tooth and his training techniques had such emphasis on rhythm. Perhaps injuries had played a part.

Against West Ham, Rooney had missed out, and problems in defence meant that, in addition to Shaw, the manager had Valencia, Jones and Rojo unavailable. To the team's credit, there had been no notable loss of form defensively; maybe the constant changes did, however, provoke a conservative approach from the forward players in order to provide further protection, but the statistics from the games generally showed the same pattern — United with most of the ball and most of the chances and yet a staggeringly low number of goals to show for it. Perhaps the options should be considered: Martial had started life at the club well but appeared to be absorbing most of the responsibility as the attacking outlet. Depay had obvious talent but his level of inconsistency would make Nani blush. Jesse Lingard was getting chances and his locality bought him praise and patience from home supporters even though there was an existing concern that he might lack the ability to be a top-level player for the club. It meant for a difficult introduction to genuine first-team rotation for Lingard, who had earned his chance but was probably expected to deliver more than he normally would have. It was unreasonable to expect Juan Mata to have developed an extra couple of yards of pace and the other forward option was Rooney, who had scored just two league goals so far.

If the quality of players at his disposal was the reason why United looked so poor in attack, then it was probably a fair time to say the manager must take some responsibility. Three transfer windows in (including two summers; and even if one gives the caveat of the first one being shortened due to the World Cup, the second one did not have such a headache) was a long enough time for the squad to resemble something like the one the manager wanted, even accounting for the turnover of players. Still, that didn't explain how the same group of players could go from having a fairly handsome goal return to looking like strangers.

And so we return to the early season 'revolt', if it was strong enough to be called that. These leaks to the press did not end there. First of all, let us deal with the small matter of United's embarrassing Champions League exit. They took an early lead through Martial and, despite falling behind, equalised through an own goal in the 82nd minute to put qualification in their own hands again. Two minutes later, Naldo scored his second, and Wolfsburg held on to win. Earlier, Van Gaal's substitutions had confused everyone when he brought on Nick Powell to try and help United get back into the game. Powell had not played a game for the club since the MK Dons humiliation and his last appearance prior to that had been in December 2012. His introduction — for Mata, of all people — was perceived as one of the most bizarre changes in modern United history.

United had been knocked out of the Champions League and into the Europa League and there was no shortage of ex-players lining up to take a pop. Paul Scholes, who had been infamously renowned for his lack of public presence in previous years, had said in October that he would 'not have enjoyed' playing for Van Gaal. 'There's a lack of creativity and risk,' Scholes said after the League Cup game against Middlesbrough. 'It's a team now you wouldn't want to play against because they're tightly organised. But it seems he [Van Gaal] doesn't want players to beat men and it's probably not a team I'd have enjoyed playing in.' Scholes defended Rooney's poor form at the time.

He said, 'The hardest thing to coach is scoring goals and creativity. I was at the derby on Sunday [a 0-0 draw with City] and Rooney's movement was brilliant, but when he's playing in that team there's no one prepared to pass to him. I think after 20 minutes you'd be tearing your hair out. I played with some brilliant centre-forwards and I don't think they could play in this team — the likes of Ruud van Nistelrooy, Andy Cole, Dwight Yorke, Teddy Sheringham.'

Scholes was just as scathing in his role as a television pundit after the Wolfsburg game. 'They spend £250m and can't qualify from a shocking group,' he said. 'It is more of a disaster when you are surprised. It was a shocking group. Will Wolfsburg and PSV get to the last eight? They will get knocked out in the next round.'

Rio Ferdinand concurred. 'It's embarrassing,' the recently retired defender said. 'I was in a squad that went into the Europa League and it's an embarrassment. You don't want to come out of your house, you don't want to walk around Manchester. People look at you and think "you're not good enough", questioning you as an individual and as part of a team that didn't get through the group stages that you should have. If you strip it back, this squad needs a hard look. There is no pace or power. People are looking around at each other rather than saying, "I will drag you through."'

Michael Owen, working with the pair for BT Sport, went as far as listing the players who he felt would still get a game for United. 'Rafael, Nemanja Vidic, Jonny Evans, Patrice Evra, Nani, Shinji Kagawa, Robin van Persie, Javier Hernandez, Adnan Januzaj and Danny Welbeck would all get in to that side,' he said.

In his post-match conference, the United boss was questioned about the club's direction under his stewardship, and whether or not they had progressed at all. 'When you see the facts, we got further in the Capital One Cup, we qualified for the group stage, we have played all of these matches and we are still in a very good position in the League, so the facts are saying we are better than last year,' he said, defiantly. 'That's my answer, I can only give facts, I am also disappointed we are out of the Champions League of course.'

The identity of Van Gaal's critics gave some cause to ponder about the harmony at the club. Scholes's close relationship with assistant manager Ryan Giggs provoked some suggestions that perhaps the pressure on the current boss wouldn't be the worst thing in the world as far as Giggs's managerial ambitions were concerned. The lineage had already been publicly established; Van Gaal himself had even declared Giggs as his successor. Furthermore, there were some journalists whose reports seemed to carry weight because of the nature of their connections with the 'Class of 92' and some players still at the club. It's jumping ahead of time, but a report in *The Independent* from February 2016 revealed that 'the often critical opinions of former United midfielder Paul Scholes, who has described Van Gaal's football as "boring" and "lacking creativity and risk", are shared by influential voices in the dressing room who crave a return to the free-flowing and free-thinking football of the Sir Alex Ferguson era.' The report continued: 'The emphasis on possession and the manager's instruction not to shoot first time have led to players becoming hyper-conscious of the consequences, with some fearful of being singled out for censure during the evaluation sessions, which are overseen by video performance analyst Max Reckers. There is also concern within the squad that United's opponents have now become so familiar with the tactics employed by Van Gaal that they are able to predict where the ball will be played and therefore to nullify any attacking threat posed by United.'

Comments similar to this were already widespread in December, and whilst there was no denying that United had not been enjoyable to watch so far that season, it seemed unnecessarily harsh and quick to blame the manager. The club's form had deteriorated so quickly that it almost seemed illogical to put it down to the manager and his philosophy.

Defeat at Wolfsburg was followed by an abject surrender at Bournemouth, though the extenuating circumstances surely absolved the manager of the same sort of blame he'd assumed for the European defeat. Lining up with a defence that included Varela, McNair and league debutant Cameron Borthwick-Jackson, with Daley Blind the most senior of the back-line, was never likely to end well and it didn't. United lost 2-1 and it explains much about the state of the league that season when acknowledging that victory would still have put them level on points at the top of the table.

Much less forgivable than the loss at Bournemouth was the following result against Norwich City, which served as a memorable low moment.

Thankfully — or, it *should* have been thankfully — Van Gaal's side resembled something close to normal. Ashley Young was a makeshift right-back alongside Smalling, Jones and Blind, while Carrick and Fellaini played as holding midfielders. In Rooney, Depay and Martial, there should have been enough mobility and menace for United to overcome a team who had lost six and won just one of its previous 11 games. Certainly in the apparently improved Smalling and Jones, United had a defensive unit that ought not to be troubled. However, prior to the game, Cameron Jerome must have been given acknowledgement for some hitherto unrecognised supreme act of bravery considering he was given the Freedom of Old Trafford. It seemed the only justification for what was about to transpire. Jerome was a decent striker who had burst on to the scene with Cardiff City, but in subsequent spells at Birmingham and Stoke he had only once scored more than ten goals in the league. At Norwich, he'd been revitalised, scoring 18 league goals in their 2014/15 promotion campaign, but his return to the Premier League was looking par for the course. He had scored just two league goals so far. After latching on to a through ball, Jerome was followed by Smalling, who had no urgency in his pursuit, even when Young missed his tackle. The forward continued unchallenged and finished past De Gea. Early in the second half Jerome found Alex Tettey. United's closing was again lethargic and effectively non-existent. Tettey was allowed plenty of time from the edge of the box to pick his spot past the goalkeeper.

The pair of goals rank up there with the most astonishingly poor goals ever conceded by a Manchester United team, particularly at home; even if there was some vindication in the criticism of their attacking fluidity over their pragmatic manager, there was absolutely no explanation for the betrayal of the basic principles of defending as witnessed here. Martial scored but United never even threatened to get a result from this game and the team were booed off the pitch after a performance which was even more disappointing than the late-Moyes losses against Liverpool and Manchester City. Then, at least, credit could be given to ruthless opponents. Here, there was no such excuse, though it was obvious now that the rot had set in.

Chelsea's defeat at Leicester the previous week had been the end of Mourinho's second reign at Stamford Bridge. United's run of form meant the speculation was natural and perhaps not quite what had been anticipated at Old Trafford from the players. The seeds of discontent which had been sown in those early weeks were done when there were few available successors to Van Gaal. The natural replacement, then, stood to be Giggs, and one would presume that the appointment would have been a popular one. If the cynical observer might suggest that such a scenario had been engineered, then, if that theory had any truth, it was instantly looking as if it would backfire, as Mourinho would emerge as the prominent name linked to Van Gaal's job.

At the very least, Giggs's voice had been notable by its absence during the poor run of form. If he was a popular choice as manager with the players then they weren't alone; fans were keen for him to be given the reins, with many already having seen enough of Van Gaal's football. However, in the same way as Mike Phelan was roundly pilloried, and the involvement of Steve Round had been questioned, it was also notable that Giggs had largely escaped any criticism or had his reputation damaged by association. One might have cause to think that as assistant manager perhaps it was part of his responsibility to spot and nip any underlying issues in the bud, issues such as senior players raising their concerns about training — particularly if they were so familiar; particularly before any talk of disharmony reached the newspapers. Likewise, there was more than enough time for concerns about the style of football to be communicated and discussed. It was peculiar that those hopeful that Giggs would be named as the new manager if Van Gaal was sacked were so ready and willing to simply ignore the fact that he had been part of the coaching set-up under the Dutchman for 18 months. Against Norwich, Giggs marched to the touchline to remonstrate with the players; compared to the stationary Van Gaal, who had been criticised for his studious note-taking approach, it appeared that the Welshman was more passionate and more affected by the team's display.

Giggs was not responsible for the underperformance of the players any more than Van Gaal was; and by the same token, Van Gaal, who had deserved so much praise for restoring a sense of discipline and organisation to the defence, could not be faulted for their sudden dip in form. Were Jones and Smalling good defenders playing poorly, or average defenders playing above themselves? The answer to that question now appeared to be that they were potentially good defenders with the right coaching but simply, going on the evidence of the preceding weeks, not good enough to play for Manchester United. And, if it *was* coming to the crunch, and the players were unhappy with the manager, then the underperformance of some other players (the decline of Carrick and Rooney, for example) surely propelled those men in line for the exit before the manager. Of course, football doesn't work like that, and the manager is always the one who pays the price, but ask a Manchester United fan if they had any faith in that squad of players to achieve the glory expected of the club under a different manager and the answer would likely have been no. Coming short of being the best is no disgrace. Never before had the supporters been subjected to witnessing a performance as dismal as the Norwich game.

What was abundantly clear was this: there was little chance of Manchester United being successful under Louis van Gaal. The statement is almost undeniably true, whoever or whatever was to blame. And, knowing that in football, it is managers and not dressing rooms which are forced to change, even those who supported Van Gaal and could still see the positive things he had done had now accepted that change was necessary. With Mourinho available, the idea that he might be hired as United manager before they played against Chelsea at the end of the month was even suggested.

After seeing his team lose against Norwich, Van Gaal conceded he was concerned that he might be sacked. 'Yes of course I am worried about that because I know that belief in a manager is very important,' he said. 'That's the football world. I know that, my board knows that, my players know that. I don't think a change of management shall bring direct success — but that is what I believe. Maybe that is not so interesting. I am always evaluating myself because I think that is an aspect of the philosophy I have. But the philosophy is also making an evolution — I am not the same coach I was 25 years ago. So, you are always evaluating and of course that philosophy is very important for me. Because of that I am — or maybe I have to say now, was — a very successful manager.' When asked about the performance, he admitted he wasn't happy: 'The main thing is that you have to be professional and do the things that you have to do and work very hard to come out of this bad period. It was not good enough. You have to win against Norwich. We know that. Now we prepare for the Stoke game with professionalism and spirit, that is the only message I can give.'

Van Gaal's position appeared to be untenable. Yet, two days before Christmas, he faced the media at Carrington, clearly preparing to face Stoke City and armed with confidence.

'Has anybody in this room not a feeling to apologise to me? Nobody has that feeling?' he asked the gathered journalists, one of whom had asked him on his thoughts about Arsene Wenger's comment earlier in the day that the speculation had been disrespectful. 'That's what I am wondering. I think I was already sacked, I have read. Or have been sacked. My colleague [Jose Mourinho] was here already. What do you think happens with my wife or with my kids? Or with my grandchildren? Or with the fans of Manchester United? Or my friends? What do you think? They have called me, a lot of times, and also Arsene Wenger is saying something about that. Do you think that I want to talk with the media now? I am here only because of the Premier League rule. I have to talk with you. But I can only see when I say something, you use my words in your context. I want to say only, I have tried to lift the confidence of my players, I have done everything this week, I hold meetings, evaluation meetings with the players and members of staff. I held a Christmas lunch, I held a speech and I feel the warmth and the support of everybody in Carrington. But I didn't feel that in the media. Of course I can imagine that you can write about that subject. We are not in a good position, but four weeks ago we were in first in the Premier League and in about four weeks we can again be in that position.'

He was told that speculation was inevitable at a big club if results didn't go the right way. 'No, no,' he interrupted. 'I don't think you can do that. You have to stick by the facts, and when I get calls from Ed Woodward, Sir Alex Ferguson and David Gill, because you are creating something that is not good, what is not the facts, and now I have to answer questions. I don't think I want to do it. I only say now I am focussed on Stoke City, I wish you a Merry Christmas and maybe a Happy New Year when I see you. Enjoy the wine and the mince pies. Goodbye.'

United were poor against Stoke and lost 2-0, and still Van Gaal's position remained unchanged. He took charge of the goalless draw against Chelsea and at the turn of the year was still in charge to oversee the club's win over Swansea City. It seemed unlikely that a change would be imminent, even though supporters had spent the Christmas period expecting an announcement to that effect at any time. Against Sheffield United in the FA Cup third round, United's performance was again abject. Memphis Depay, who had taken the only shot on target so far in the game, was felled in the box in injury time. Wayne Rooney's penalty kick decided the tie but it did not protect United from Paul Scholes twisting the knife in again. 'The players looked bored themselves,' Scholes told BT Sport. 'There's no spirit, there's nobody having a go at each other, there's no smiling, there's no entertainment. I think even Van Gaal on the bench looks bored, but he'll come out and say he's happy. It wasn't a great performance, will he be happy with it? I think he probably will be. I think that's the way he likes to play football. We haven't seen anything different now for the last six months, that's the way this team plays football and he'll be happy with the 1-0 win. We don't see anything else, and he constantly comes out and says he's happy with his team, he's happy with the way they've played. But they didn't create a chance, had to win a game against a League One side with a penalty in the 94th minute. In my eyes it's not good enough. As players sometimes you have to lift the crowd, whether it's a tackle, whether it's a shot on goal. You need to make something happen as a footballer at this club. To just go through the motions like they did, people need digging out sometimes, it just seems to be accepted. I'd be depressed [after playing like that]. It would take me two or three days to get over that performance. You've just seen 90 minutes of boring, defensive … I've tried to defend this team now for the last two or three weeks; it's getting more and more difficult to do it because every time you come to Old Trafford this is what you see — negative football. I see square pegs in round holes with players in the team. There's so many question marks over the team. The only thing I can say is I'm glad I don't have to go to Sheffield a week on Tuesday.'

Asked if he felt the way forward was a change in manager, Scholes surprisingly said no. 'It's time for a change in style of football, pass the ball to Wayne Rooney,' he said. 'I think he had 34 touches today in the whole game. This is Wayne Rooney, get the ball to your best players. I'd never call for a manager to be sacked. He's got some really good players there. His style of football is not suited to Manchester United's football, but he's going to argue that they've got through, they are fifth in the Premier League and only nine points off the top. And he has got a case for that, but I think fans would rather see a bit more excitement rather than be in those positions.'

Rooney's form had come from nowhere; he scored twice at Newcastle in a 3-3 draw and then scored a late goal (United's only effort on target) at Liverpool to earn his team a 1-0 win. With 22 games played, United were in fifth, and seven points off the leading pair Arsenal and Leicester. The winless December had seen United throw away 13 winnable points, points which would have given them a healthy lead. Nonetheless, Van Gaal's comments after the win at Anfield suggested he was optimistic about where the turnaround in form may lead. 'We know Wayne Rooney has played for Everton and now plays for United so he wants to score against Liverpool, it means a lot for him,' he said. 'We have made a good start in 2016, to beat Liverpool for the second time in a row is marvellous, it gives a big boost to the players and the fans so I hope it shall continue with winning. That is why we are here, to win our games and at the end of the season to be in the first three positions of the league.'

The fans, however, were booing after the following 90 minutes of football; a second consecutive 1-0 home defeat to Southampton after the previous year's loss to the Saints. If possible, this performance was even poorer, and for the second week in a row United managed only one shot on target. It was also the 11th home game in a row when United had failed to score a goal in the first half, though, increasingly of late, the second halves hadn't been much better. 'They are right to boo. I cannot deny that, I saw the match,' said Van Gaal. 'For better or for worse we have to stick together. We are working very hard, but we have had a lot of injuries. That you cannot change.'

Despite the injuries, Van Gaal decided not to make a signing in the January transfer window. For a squad with Valencia, Darmian, Jones, Rojo, Shaw, Depay and Schweinsteiger all out, it meant having to again call upon Varela and Borthwick-Jackson to play at full-back in the FA Cup fourth-round game at Derby County. Wayne Rooney scored his 243rd goal for the club, continuing his recent run of form and suggesting that it wasn't an unrealistic target for him to break the club's goalscoring record of 249, set by Sir Bobby Charlton, in the coming weeks and months. 'It was obviously a better performance than last week's game,' Rooney said afterwards. 'But the manager gave us a lot of freedom to go and play, and you can see the difference in the team. You can see we were enjoying it, scoring some good goals, and thoroughly deserved to win, so hopefully we can put in another performance like this on Tuesday and take this into the game against Stoke.' Rooney was asked if the manager deserved criticism for the perceived negative style of football: 'It's unfair to say it's the manager — we're on the pitch,' he said. 'The players have to take a lot of responsibility for performances and results. We have to stand up and take criticism when it's there. We want to win, of course we always want to win, and we're trying. Even when you're giving 100 per cent, it doesn't always come off, and thankfully against Derby it has.'

United were in fine form against Stoke City in their next game at home, turning up early for once and playing some great football. The highlight was a swift move which led to Martial's brilliant finish from 15 yards to put United 2-0 up after Jesse Lingard's earlier goal. Lingard had scored a header from a fantastic cross by Cameron Borthwick-Jackson; having started the season behind Shaw, Blind, Rojo, Darmian and Young in the pecking order in that position, Borthwick-Jackson had actually emerged as a surprising talent, with his crossing ability as good as any senior player had shown that season. Rooney scored in the 53rd minute to round off a convincing 3-0 win. 'I think we have played in the first half attacking-wise very good,' Van Gaal said. 'In the second half we were more controlling and we didn't give any chances away against a team like Stoke. That is remarkable because they always make it difficult.'

His post-match comments were markedly different to his mood ahead of United's next game, away at Chelsea. Despite the relative upturn in form — and the team were almost unrecognisable from the one that had capitulated to Norwich four weeks prior — the United boss appeared to still be sensitive and defensive. 'You want to repeat every time the same question in every press conference?' Van Gaal said to *The Guardian*'s Jamie Jackson about Wayne Rooney's comments about the improved form against Derby coming following the team apparently having been given more freedom. 'I'm not agreeing with that remark of Wayne Rooney because it's only because they have more confidence. Especially Rooney because he has scored seven goals in a row, then he can say he is playing with more freedom, because he has more confidence, but you want to write tomorrow in your paper that it is because he got another training session in another style, or Louis van Gaal gives more freedom, no, it is still the same, we train still the same, the same way, it is not because of the change of attitude of Mr Louis van Gaal or another way of training, no, I am sorry to say that. We are working very hard and very professional in the philosophy of Louis van Gaal.' When asked if Juan Mata's form in the number-ten role was the reason for the upturn in form, Van Gaal again stood firm: 'No, because I have played Mata in the same role. Maybe you remember that? I have not changed him, he has changed himself, because at that time he was not good enough. That is the reason. When he is playing like he plays now he plays at number ten.'

The manager was quite right to be annoyed. With it now becoming increasingly obvious that the board would back the manager until either the end of the season, or at least until it was mathematically impossible to qualify for the Champions League again, it was now time to identify a reason for that December collapse. Against Chelsea, United should have won — Jesse Lingard scored a fine goal, before the hosts grabbed an injury-time equaliser to get a draw they scarcely deserved. The performance was not quite vintage United, but it was difficult to comprehend how this could be the same side of six and seven weeks before. As Van Gaal had said quite firmly, his approach hadn't changed.

Were the players simply in 'a bad moment'? Had they been caught out by an opponent on the top of their game? It was such a difficult thing to argue, because the issue argued by the majority of the United fans during the past two and a half years was the trend of visitors to Old Trafford not really having to be brilliant to achieve a result. Those home defeats to West Brom and Newcastle under Moyes were infuriating to supporters, not because of the result but the manner of it. The teams hadn't had to be at their best. They may have prepared for an onslaught in the last ten minutes but it never came.

Even if every single criticism otherwise was justified, nobody could have contested that Van Gaal had at least instilled a defensive discipline into a team who had looked chaotic early on in his reign.

Prior to Wolfsburg, the club had kept 14 clean sheets in 24 games. Against Liverpool, Stoke and Chelsea, that defensive organisation seemed to be present once again. This positive run of results (with the caveat that the dreadful Southampton game was amongst them) suggested that perhaps the manager wasn't completely wrong with his methods. If the Norwich game was a blip, albeit a significantly damaging one-game blip from which some players' reputations are still struggling to recover at the time of writing, then it was still a blip that was all on the players and not the manager. It was not a performance which highlighted everything wrong with the Van Gaal reign; rather, it was a performance which went against everything he had taught.

United's brief recovery had been played out against a backdrop of never-ending speculation about Mourinho taking over at Old Trafford, and that speculation probably came to a head in mid-February. United lost their two games after Chelsea, first of all going down 2-1 in an inept display against a poor Sunderland team, and then losing by the same scoreline against Danish minnows FC Midtjylland in the first leg of their round of 32 Europa League tie. Van Gaal could have complained about a worsening injury crisis at the club — he did say he had 13 players injured, and after being forced to select Donald Love and Paddy McNair in defence, David de Gea then picked up an injury in the warm-up — but mitigating circumstances were now being perceived as excuses. A bad result against Shrewsbury Town in the FA Cup may prove to be the end for the United manager, with the *Daily Star* reporting an exclusive the day before the game that claimed 'even the club's staff have lost faith in the manager'.

Van Gaal insisted that the club could still compete on three fronts even though their post-December league form now saw them in fifth place in the league, six points behind City in that last Champions League spot and a huge 12 points behind unlikely leaders Leicester City. In many ways, the identity of the league leaders was the most damning indictment of all for United's stars. Okay, so this was not the best Manchester United team ever, but it was also far from a good Premier League. Champions Chelsea were in 12th position. Arsenal, those consistent underachievers, were occupying third place. What had happened to this same group of players who were so full of

Sir Alex Ferguson thanks the travelling United fans in his last game at West Bromwich Albion.

Sir Alex Ferguson prepares for his last game as a manager.

David Moyes is all smiles on his first day as Manchester United manager.

'Wrong One – Moyes Out' – A controversial banner flies above Old Trafford.

All over – Moyes is helpless to prevent Bayern Munich eliminating his team from European football.

Ryan Giggs, football manager. Giggs sees his United team win 4-0 against Norwich.

Changing of the Guard — Van Gaal poses with his record signing Angel Di Maria after a blockbuster spending spree.

Louis van Gaal amuses United supporters with a theatrical tumble on the touchline during a game against Arsenal.

Louis van Gaal poses with Marcus Rashford and match-winner Jesse Lingard after the 2016 FA Cup Final.

Louis van Gaal shows signs of the strain getting to him at White Hart Lane.

The smiling executioner – Ed Woodward happily greets Louis van Gaal, while the media is already speculating that the legendary Dutch coach has been sacked.

Uneasy bedfellows — Mourinho and Woodward's relationship would dominate talk from 2016–2018.

The first of many? Jose Mourinho celebrates with the League Cup.

Completed it mate — Manchester United celebrate their Europa League success in 2017, a victory which meant they had won every major trophy available to them in football.

No place like home — Mourinho is involved in an altercation with staff at Stamford Bridge as speculation about his future at United rumbles on.

End of days — Jose Mourinho and Paul Pogba share a bench in December 2018.

The smiling one – Ole Gunnar Solskjaer cannot hide his delight as he returns to take charge of the club he represented with distinction.

Glory days — Ole Gunnar Solskjaer celebrates with Marcus Rashford after a famous night in Paris.

confidence that they defeated Spurs, Liverpool and City in the same run of games, playing attacking football and turning their fortunes around? Most of those players were still at the club and, as stressed to the point of risking overstating it, the manager's demands had not changed. It was a fair observation to suggest that if Sir Alex Ferguson had been in charge, even with this squad, the Premier League would have already been talking to the trophy engravers about perhaps getting an early discount.

It was becoming clear to all that a change in management was needed and, again, not necessarily completely *because* of the manager. When a team loses faith it is difficult to recover, though there was a section of the support who felt that if the manager was to be kept on for the summer, as unlikely as it seemed, it would be an opportunity for him to be ruthless and cut out those players who did not enjoy playing for him. The unlikelihood of a turnaround in such a short space of time led to fingers being pointed at the board, with the question essentially being 'how long' could this be allowed to go on? Had the change been made at Christmas, Mourinho might have been able to motivate this clearly capable group of players into a title challenge. Now, in mid-February, it was going to be three years without a title and there was also danger of a third year without a trophy.

The defeat in Denmark meant that Van Gaal had no option but to admit in his pre-match press conference that the mood in the camp was low before that crunch FA Cup game. 'When you see the last two games it's maybe like that but maybe we have to make them fear again, because we lost the first match in the Premier League also, Swansea City when I came,' the coach said. 'But then still we had a very good home record last season and we can do that again, it's a question of winning matches in a row. You cannot continue with losing games and the question is how we lift ourselves because Shrewsbury Town will fight for the second balls and play direct and that kind of thing. You have to cope with that but you have to keep the ball better and not give unnecessary losses away. I think the first goal [against Midtjylland] was an unnecessary loss and the second goal we could have won that duel much more easily but that was the substitute who came in [and scored the winner].' Would United's recent woes mean Shrewsbury might fancy their chances? 'Maybe. I hope so. Because then it is a benefit for us,' Van Gaal said. 'It's not a question of being the favourite for the Cup. It's a question that you have to see every match as a match that you have to win. So OK we have lost 2-1 but we can overcome [it], and also Monday we have to win. And when we win we are in the next round and we are becoming capable of winning the FA Cup. When you see Chelsea against Paris Saint-Germain it is 2-1 but still Chelsea has a chance to overcome so that's football.'

The pressure was at its peak. Harry Redknapp had a column in *The Telegraph* and even the experienced coach broke rank from the manager's union and admitted he couldn't believe what was going on at United. 'The word in football is that Jose Mourinho and Manchester United is already a done deal, so it is a question of how much longer Louis van Gaal can survive as manager,' he wrote. 'Mourinho is expected to go in at the end of the season and faces a huge rebuilding job to turn United into a force again because these last few years have been desperate … I fully expect United to beat Shrewsbury and Midtjylland to avert the crisis for a few more days, but what does it prove? Van Gaal's time is coming to an end regardless of what the next two results against minnows are.'

Rio Ferdinand tweeted on 20 February, two days before the game, 'Given LVG loads of time … the team have gone backwards since his arrival. The style of football has no resemblance [*sic*] to @ manutd at all.'

United's game with Shrewsbury was as straightforward as one would expect, despite the injuries. Chris Smalling, Juan Mata and Jesse Lingard scored the goals to achieve a 3-0 win in a team that included Varela and Borthwick-Jackson from the start and Joe Riley, Andreas Pereira and Will Keane from the bench. Keane pulled up with a groin injury five minutes after coming on and United had to finish with ten men. Following the final whistle, Van Gaal took time to sign autographs for the travelling fans. One shouted, 'All the best for the rest of the season!' to which the manager responded, 'We need it, otherwise I shall be sacked.' Speaking to the media, Van Gaal was pleased with the response. He said, 'I think the performance was very good. I said that already at half-time to my players. They were very committed, they performed our game plan very well and the consequences were we were ahead 2-0 at half-time — a lucky goal from Smalling I think but a very good free kick from Mata … Everybody shall say it is easy against Shrewsbury Town and Manchester United has to win but we have seen very difficult results in the FA Cup, not always the top team is winning, so I think we have done it fantastically. I have congratulated my players, I was very pleased but now we have to beat Midtjylland because it's also possible to beat them. But it is not easy because Midtjylland are very well organised, we have seen that in the away game. But still everything is possible, we're still in three competitions, so we have to fight for a lot of chances I think.'

A temporary reprieve then, although the axe was still swinging as United prepared to overcome their European embarrassment. Romero would again have to play in goal, while Borthwick-Jackson's injury against Shrewsbury meant a first start for Joe Riley. Michael Carrick would have to move into defence, but at least Van Gaal was able to keep Jesse Lingard in the side after the winger overcame a knock. Having named his team, Van Gaal was given yet another warm-up blow when Anthony Martial picked up a knock and had to be withdrawn from the team. With no Wayne Rooney, no James Wilson and no Will Keane, it meant a debut would be given to untried Marcus Rashford as the centre-forward. This was truly a case of needs must, and Rashford was only this high in the pecking order because Ashley Fletcher, another rookie forward, but slightly ahead of Rashford in his development, was on loan at Barnsley.

A versatile player, 18-year-old Rashford had not exactly been knocking down the door to the first team. His sole goal for the reserves had come as a substitute in a 6-1 win over Leicester City early in the season and he had not made an impact in his handful of appearances since. That goal and appearance came as a result of a reward for some fine early academy team form — he scored eight goals in September, including three in the UEFA Youth League, but since then he had only registered on the scoresheet three times. The third of those was in the penultimate academy league game against Manchester City and, with resources thin on the ground, Rashford was pulled from the last game against West Brom to keep him around the first team in case he was needed. He had been suddenly thrust into a position of responsibility; a player who had not been renowned for his clinical ability was now required to be just that.

The team sheet against the Danish side read: Romero, Varela, Carrick, Blind, Riley, Herrera, Schneiderlin, Lingard, Mata, Depay, Rashford. It was not a line-up that would have inspired many with confidence, but perhaps it was the best Van Gaal could have hoped for. Of that team, only Michael Carrick and Juan Mata could be said to have been established players prior to Van Gaal's appointment. Romero, Blind, Schneiderlin, Depay and technically Herrera were all Van Gaal buys. Varela, Riley, Lingard and now Rashford were youngsters who were keen and grateful to have been given the opportunity. If most of the senior players were not convinced of the manager, well, he had a collective in front of him who should have had good cause to play up. As we know, that was eventually the case, but it did take United some time to get going. They went a goal down in the 27th minute, equalised through an own goal in the 32nd, and then when Juan Mata had a penalty saved towards the end of the first half it felt as if it might be one of those nights.

Just after the hour mark, Old Trafford was sparked into life — amidst cries of 'shoot', United's midfielders looked for an opportunity to create an opening on the edge of the area. The ball was swung into the box by Varela and Mata pulled it back, right into the path of Rashford, whose instinctive finish was perfect. Twelve minutes later, Varela's cross needed no middle man — his hooked left-footed ball went over the head of everyone and landed perfectly for Rashford to finish first time again at the back post. United were now ahead in the tie and had the momentum. With three minutes left, they were awarded a second penalty, and this time Herrera stepped up and smashed it in. There was still time for a fifth, scored in style by the impressive Memphis Depay. Depay may well have been the man of the match, but the headlines belonged to just one person.

'I wasn't worried about him. I'm always confident for that,' Van Gaal insisted about Rashford afterwards. 'He was the best option.'

Old Trafford had bounced in the second half and that was perhaps thanks in no small part not only to Rashford, but Riley, Lingard, Pereira, and 17-year-old Regan Poole, all of whom were players developed at the club. Perhaps Van Gaal had been left with little choice, but nobody could accuse him of being neglectful of fielding young players wherever he had been, and so he obviously understood the intangible benefits of including them in the team rather than, for example, rushing Marcos Rojo back from injury. Consequently, even if the philosophies were one and the same, Van Gaal had stayed true to the identity of the club and had reaped the short-term reward. Simon Stone of BBC Sport suggested that these values of the Dutchman may well be valuable: 'If there is a reason why Van Gaal has lasted through such a traumatic campaign, and now seems likely to reach the season's end, this could well be it,' said Stone. 'And before Mourinho comes in, it needs to be carefully considered what could be being thrown away.'

Rojo was fit enough to take up a place at left-back in the next game against Arsenal, but with Varela and Carrick continuing to play in defence and Rashford, Depay and Lingard up front, United fans were bracing themselves for a difficult afternoon against a visiting team who would have fancied their chances. More than just the pride of victory, which is a little added bonus in this fixture, Arsenal knew that victory would take them to within two points of Leicester at the top and would have felt their chances of three points had never been greater since their last win in the league at Old Trafford almost ten years prior. Rojo's selection was complemented by David de Gea's own return to the side, but this did little to instil much confidence, especially considering the lack of senior options on the bench. Adnan Januzaj, whose loan at Dortmund had been a disaster all around, had returned to United and he was subsequently injured. He was fit enough to be named among the substitutes and, alongside Paddy McNair, represented the most senior option. Riley and Pereira had seen some first-team action but James Weir and Timothy Fosu-Mensah had only played in different roles for the reserve side. Fosu-Mensah had joined the club in September 2014 and was very highly rated — some wondered why he hadn't yet had an opportunity with so many defensive injuries.

Arsenal's bench, by contrast, was full of international players. Early on, Arsenal sought to expose the right side of United's defence and the hosts had De Gea to thank for a great save to deny Monreal. This makeshift United team were sporadically thrust into life by the galvanising encouragement of the crowd, who were getting behind the younger players in particular. A roar went up as Varela charged forward but his cross was met by a defensive foot; the clearance, however, was poor, and it dropped straight to Rashford, whose sense of timing was proving to be impeccable. He finished with some aplomb into the top corner.

United's youngsters seemed to gain confidence and Varela, Lingard and Mata were involved in a fine one-touch passing move on the right-hand side, which Arsenal found difficult to cope with. Varela hit it back to Lingard, who waited and then clipped a left-foot cross in. Rashford was there to divert the ball in from around eight yards with his head. Danny Welbeck scored, just as he did in the FA Cup game the previous year, but United's two-goal lead was re-established when Rashford showed fine intelligence in his build-up play to hold on to the ball and lay it into the path of Herrera, whose deflected effort flew past Cech. Mesut Ozil scored four minutes later, with United struggling to adapt defensively after Fosu-Mensah came on for Rojo, but as the game wore on, Old Trafford was in full voice. Fosu-Mensah was showing plenty of promise with his confidence on the ball, and when Van Gaal started remonstrating with Wirral official Mike Dean on the touchline, the manager threw himself to the ground in emulation of what he perceived to be a dive from an Arsenal player, and the United supporters went crazy in support of their boss. There was a loud ovation for the players at full time. Starting the week on the brink, somehow Louis van Gaal was now basking in a positive glow.

It wasn't quite enough for all to suddenly forget the tumultuous events of the past few months, but there was a general level of acceptance that the manager would remain in charge until the end of the season at least.

Spring

Manchester United faced Liverpool in European competition for the first time ever. In 2007 and 2008 the clubs both qualified for the semi-finals of the Champions League against other teams, and this was as close as they'd come to meeting before the 2016 Europa League quarter-final drew them against each other. Liverpool's 2-0 win at Anfield meant that the second leg would be an uphill struggle if the visitors scored just once — and when Coutinho equalised Martial's 32nd-minute penalty just before half-time, United couldn't get going in the second half.

Some joy was restored three days later when Marcus Rashford was back on the scoresheet for the first time since his exploits against Arsenal, this time in an even bigger game, at Manchester City. The goal earned United a 1-0 win, but hopes of a renewed late push for the fourth spot in the league were given a severe blow when Louis van Gaal's team went down 3-0 at Spurs. Their performance was more or less reflected with Timothy Fosu-Mensah; the young Dutch player had coped so admirably with the step up to first-team football that he was as deserving of his place in the team as Rashford, and he was playing well at White Hart Lane before being substituted in the 68th minute with the score goalless. Within eight minutes, it was

3-0 to Spurs — hardly the sort of preparation United needed before travelling to Upton Park for the FA Cup quarter-final replay.

That Spurs game was not without its controversy. Rashford was substituted at half-time for Ashley Young (more on that later); Young, a winger by trade who had started to make a name for himself in either full-back role, came on in the central striker position despite Anthony Martial being on the pitch. *The Telegraph* listed this as the fifth in a series of 'baffling tactical decisions' by Van Gaal at United, a list which included the ill-planned high-pressing game at the Emirates, the substitution of Mata for Powell in Wolfsburg, and the deployment of Jesse Lingard and Wayne Rooney as right-back and left-winger respectively against Southampton.

West Ham were enjoying their last season at their famous ground and this game would be their last Cup tie there; likewise, their last home league game would also be against Manchester United. It seemed as if the fates would conspire to give a romantic end to the Hammers' stay there before moving to the Olympic Stadium. Van Gaal, however, was the party pooper — the rest for Fosu-Mensah seemed wise considering how colossal the defender was. Nine minutes into the second half, Rashford scored a stunning solo goal, and then Fellaini made it two in the 67th. West Ham rallied, pulling a goal back and then forcing De Gea into a magnificent double save towards the end.

Rashford was at it again three days later, scoring the only goal in United's win over Villa. The hosts played their second consecutive game at Old Trafford four days after that, easing to a 2-0 win over Crystal Palace, which put them one point behind fourth-placed Arsenal, though having played a game more.

There was a definite sense of the 1990 FA Cup run attached to the competition in 2016, with the extended stay of execution it had seemingly given the manager, even if this story clearly was going to have a different ending. Here was a team that was, in general, appearing to underperform, a team who had suffered through a bunch of injuries and had enjoyed some fantastic away days in the run. The atmosphere for the games at both Derby and West Ham were two of the best of the campaign so far and the idea of taking on Everton at Wembley with a couple of rookies playing so well almost cultivated the idea that United were underdogs, even if that wasn't strictly true. On the big occasion both Fosu-Mensah and Rashford had subdued days, but it was the former whose performance was more note worthy. United were in the lead, thanks to a first-half goal from Fellaini, when Ross Barkley went on a charge forward. Fosu-Mensah slid in on the midfielder and his tackle looked good — the defender clearly got the ball first, but his trailing leg wrapped around Barkley's to effectively make it a scissors challenge, and the referee deemed that it was a foul. Romelu Lukaku's kick, however, was brilliantly saved by De Gea. Almost immediately, Fosu-Mensah was hauled off and found himself harshly out of favour. The Toffees were motivated by their miss and came at United, finally getting their reward in the 75th minute when Chris Smalling put the ball into his own net. In injury time, Anthony Martial showed composure that defied United's jittery end to the game by playing a smart one-two with Herrera and then finishing past the Everton goalkeeper to send United into the final.

There, they would face Crystal Palace, in another nod to the 1990 FA Cup Final run; though this time the idea that winning the trophy would serve as a saving grace for the manager was fanciful at best. Since December, when it had become fairly apparent that United would struggle to win a league title under their manager, the relationship between the manager and the club had begun to disintegrate. Like a friendship that turns sour, with every fault of the other becoming blown up out of all proportion, the supporters had become disillusioned with the style of football and the buck stopped at the coach. According to *The Independent*, Van Gaal was apparently approached by United players after the 2-1 defeat to Norwich, insisting that they wanted him to continue. But by the time the team lost to Southampton a month later, the manager even seemed to agree with the supporters, who booed the team off the pitch. 'I am very disappointed that I cannot reach the expectations of the fans,' he admitted. 'They have — or they had — great expectations of me and I cannot fulfil them. I am very frustrated because of that. I agree with the fans booing so it doesn't have any impact. I have also a knowledge of football, of entertaining football, and you have to play football to entertain the fans. I don't think we have entertained the fans against Southampton, so they can be very angry, but when we won [against Liverpool] they were not so angry any more. But now we have lost in the last minute.'

These were the remarks of a man who clearly felt as if the club might bow to the external pressure, the remarks of a man who had been in that position before. If they sounded flat and defeatist it is at least important to differentiate them from the style of comments made by David Moyes, who had been castigated for the way he spoke to the media. Moyes's comments generally came before games or, in the case of the home defeat to Manchester City, courted blasphemy by suggesting United should aim to be like their neighbours. Whilst no more inspiring, Van Gaal's comments were impassioned reactive statements and the outspoken nature of his personality had, up until January 2016, been an attribute which endeared him to United's supporters. In fairness, too, there were moments of genuine hilarity which came after January. There was the February slapstick routine against Arsenal and then, when United drew 1-1 with Leicester in the first game after the semi-final, Van Gaal made many more laugh with his assessment of a foul on Marouane Fellaini where the tall Belgian had felt his hair pulled. Fellaini had reacted by swinging an elbow and, although the incident was missed by the referee, it meant he was likely to suffer a three-match ban after an FA review. Van Gaal was in defence of his player. 'Every human being who is grabbed by the hair, only with sex masochism, then it is allowed but not in other situations. They did it. They did it several times I think,' said the United boss. 'Huth was the guy who grabbed the hair of Fellaini. I think the reaction of Fellaini is like a human being.'

United supporters were less amused by Van Gaal's comments the following night, at the club's in-house Player of the Year award ceremony. The draw with Leicester would ordinarily be viewed as a bad result, not only in respect of the opposition but also because it was another blow in the race for that last Champions League spot. It was compounded by the fact that Leicester were about to be crowned champions of the Premier League, a sure sign that no so-called big club had benefitted from the transition of others. Aside from the occasional show of dissatisfaction from supporters, their response had been more apathetic than vitriolic, but the response to Van Gaal's comments at the dinner was certainly rooted more in the latter camp. 'We have to meet the expectations of the biggest club in the world,' said Van Gaal. 'Expectations are too high. We are in a period of transition. It is not so easy. When the media is writing for six months I am sacked already. I can cope with that. It is not new for me. For my players, it is not so easy. They are reading every day. What do you think about my authority? What do you think about the way they want to follow my advice, when their coach is showed like a nobody because I cannot do anything? But I am not like that. I am very arrogant. I am one of the best managers of the world.'

On one hand you can sympathise with Van Gaal and it is easy to see where he was coming from. Perhaps the speculation had been unsettling on the squad, and, certainly, the manager was not the cause of that. Nor was he responsible for the sheer scale of the transition, although it was his remit to oversee that period. It could also be said that the nature of the defeats in December, with performances that abandoned even the rigid defensive principles that Van Gaal's United team had been renowned for, were not a product of poor management. However, sympathy can only stretch so far, and if the blame rests on the shoulders of underperforming players, then the finger keeps moving and ultimately lands at the manager, who is responsible for the composition of the squad and the team. In fairness to him, again, it was clear from the pursuit of Mats Hummels and Sergio Ramos that the vulnerability of the team at centre-half was a huge issue at the club and one he was aware of; so, those two players didn't arrive, but they were far from the only two players capable of making a significant improvement to United's defence.

There was a blunt point which overrides each and every argument underneath it. At the end of the first year, Van Gaal had managed to get Manchester United back into the Champions League. Even if we disregard the notion that Leicester City as champions was a source of embarrassment for United's own season, then, still, it was surely not unreasonable to have expected improvement. The manager should have had a strong enough familiarity with his squad to have known what it needed in order to make the move forward, and, while there was a genuine buzz for the club's first FA Cup Final since 2007, the likelihood of missing out on a Champions League place was a clear sign that the team had regressed from that promising first year. Whether or not that was enough to justify sacking a manager, well, the club had already made clear the consequences of failing to qualify for Europe's premier competition. Even *if* it was unrealistic to have expected United to have challenged for the league — and everything about the quality of the league suggested otherwise — then simply expecting more was surely, well, to be expected. That was one thing, but to actually publicly criticise supporters for expecting more was a crossing of the line that they would not take kindly to.

Later in the week, Paul Scholes was back in the media, expressing his dissatisfaction over the manager's comments. 'It makes you wonder if he realises the size of club he is at,' rapped Scholes. 'Finishing fourth or fifth in the Premier League and winning the FA Cup is probably not good enough for Manchester United. All right, I think the fans will accept it this year, but if he is here next year I think standards have to be raised and he has to realise he is at a club who needs to win.'

In keeping with the theme of that year's league, Manchester City had contrived to throw the race for that final Champions League spot back into the mixing pot. They lost 4-2 at Southampton and then could only muster a 2-2 draw at home to Arsenal, meaning that it was back in United's hands. If they won their final two games, at West Ham and at home to Bournemouth, they would get that fourth place. Their preparation for that game at Upton Park was disrupted as kick-off was put back an hour following an attack by Hammers fans on the United team coach.

The game went ahead, and, roared on by a rowdy support, West Ham took an early lead. When Michael Carrick came on at half-time, United had a greater assured quality about their play, and scored twice through Anthony Martial to turn the game on its head. That second goal, in the 72nd minute, appeared as if it might prove to be the crucial goal in United's season. Eight minutes later, though, West Ham had performed a turnaround of their own and were leading 3-2. This time United's response was not quite so impressive. The final match statistics show that the visitors scored with their only efforts on target and even then only managed one more shot at goal; they could have no complaints about the defeat. 'It is very disappointing because we were ahead and changed the match,' Van Gaal said, refusing to blame the coach attack for distracting his players. 'They were two very good goals and then we give it away because of the set plays. We knew that in advance, we have to organise it, but we don't have the centimetres that West Ham did.'

The BBC reporter then asked the United boss if the club 'needed to look at' when they were scheduled to arrive at the stadiums, following the late kick-off here and their recent late arrival at White Hart Lane. 'I think you are now a little bit exaggerating,' he said. 'When you see the circumstances you see it is not normal, and you think it is normal, otherwise you would not put this question, I am very disappointed now that you put a question like that. We were a hundred yards behind the West Ham bus. I am very disappointed that you ask.' Asked, finally, if there was anything he would improve, Van Gaal admitted, 'As a manager you are never satisfied, but if you are winning 2-1 after 70 minutes, you have to make the pitch bigger and play the ball better.'

Trailing Manchester City by two points now, United were hoping Swansea would get a result on the final day. They did that, but could only get a draw from City, and the superior goal difference of 30 as opposed to United's 12 meant that any win over Bournemouth, unless it tore up the record books, would be inconsequential. For the second time in five years, United would suffer the consequences of not being as prolific as their newly rich neighbours. As it transpired, there were more pre-match disturbances, as the Bournemouth game was postponed due to a suspect package in Old Trafford. It turned out to be much fuss over nothing and the game was rescheduled for the Tuesday evening — United won 3-1. Their top-four hopes had been effectively denied by poor defending in one game and poor finishing over a few. If this writer's assessment of Van Gaal's work in improving United's defence is glowing then it does at least come with the caveat of a) as mentioned, failing to bring in a leader and b) playing Rojo in the centre of defence as not exactly being the wisest option. Rojo and Smalling (who scored an own goal against Bournemouth) were both prone to rash decisions at the best of times and neither stood out as a leader. Having those and Phil Jones as United's selection of senior centre-halves could only reasonably hold out for so long before proving costly. The manager could well have done all within his power to improve that organisation, but the games where the organisation had been notably absent — Norwich, Stoke, Tottenham and West Ham — had cost the club a place in the Champions League despite all the other problems that were present at the club. If the harsh truth is that you can only improve players so much before they plateau, then the difference between qualifying and not qualifying for the Champions League was represented in the ability of United's squad.

'I want to thank you for the unconditional support of you,' Louis van Gaal told the United fans, who stayed behind after the Bournemouth win to see the players' lap of honour and hear the manager's address. 'Whenever we have played, however the things have gone on the field, you never let us down. Thank you for that and we want to bring the FA Cup home. You deserve it. Thank you.' The Dutchman's words about support came against an ironic backdrop of boos from home fans.

Speaking to the media after the game, he addressed that reaction and whether or not he expected it. 'Of course, because as I have said the expectation is very high, especially the fans,' he said. 'They are expecting a lot but I think these expectations are much too high. We are a team in transition and this I said when I started here in Manchester United. Maybe I have to bring over the message much clearer than I have done. More or less [not scoring enough goals] is the issue, but I think the issue is the amount of injuries in the months of November and December. It was particularly in two positions — the two full-back positions. That was very tough at that time. I have also said in the season that we need creative, fast attackers. I said that, so we have to take care of that. But nevertheless, when everybody was fit we were first in the league and these are the facts.'

On the morning of the game, Jose Mourinho had again been linked to the job, with the narrative now becoming that Van Gaal was indeed entering the 1990 Ferguson territory of needing a victory in the number-one domestic cup competition to save his job. Lose it, and he would definitely be sacked. Even winning was not a guarantee that he would be at Old Trafford for the 2016/17 season.

For this most crucial game of his reign, Van Gaal selected Wayne Rooney and Michael Carrick in midfield, with Marouane Fellaini playing off Marcus Rashford up front. Their central area was hardly energetic or inspiring, with the emphasis instead being placed on experience. A disappointing first half was followed by a more authoritative second; United hit the woodwork twice through Fellaini and Martial but when Jason Puncheon scored a fine angled half-volley with 12 minutes left it was beginning to feel as if Van

Gaal's reign would end with the underwhelming feeling that had seemed to dog most of this second half of his second season. Such pessimism lasted less than five minutes; if Wayne Rooney's time as captain of the club offered nothing more inspiring, then his contribution to the equaliser still shouldn't be understated. His cross-field run with the ball was dogged and persistent in the style of old, coated with the relentless perseverance which had famously been his trademark. His cross was met by Fellaini's chest, and before the midfielder could react, the ball had fallen kindly to Juan Mata, who thrashed the ball in via a deflection. Having dragged themselves back into the game, victory was again thrown into risk when Chris Smalling was caught out by Yannick Bolasie near the half-way line. Despite the size of the pitch, Smalling had a rush of blood and hauled down Bolasie; having been booked in the first half, it was inevitable he would be sent off. Perhaps Smalling, more than any other player, personified the Van Gaal era — having seemingly been the biggest beneficiary of the teachings, his stock was now similarly low to the time when he was dismissed at Manchester City the previous season. Palace looked to make their numbers count and had an early chance in the second period of extra time, before United counter-attacked. Valencia's cross hit a Palace defender but the loose ball bounced into the path of Jesse Lingard. Lingard had been inconsistent in these positions throughout the season but his finish here was impeccable, driven like an arrow with ferocious speed into the top corner before any Palace defender or the goalkeeper could react. Ironically, it was the first time since that 1990 win that a Manchester United youth product had scored the winning goal in a cup final.

'It is fantastic to win this title for the club, for the fans, and also for me because I now have won the cup in four countries, and not many managers have done that,' Van Gaal said on the pitch after the game. 'We had ten players, and we have played Tuesday evening also, but we have deserved it I think.'

Afterwards, the manager gave a short press conference to journalists. Almost as soon as the final whistle went, there was widespread speculation through the press that Jose Mourinho would be announced as the new Manchester United manager in the coming days. The whispers had already made their way to Van Gaal as he sat at the table with the FA Cup. 'I show you the cup and I don't discuss it [the speculation] with my friends of the media who have sacked me for six months,' he said. 'I can be happy because I have won something. I gambled with youngsters this season. I thought we needed the spirit of the youngsters. I believe in refreshment of my squad but it depends on what players we purchase, you cannot stay with the same squad. Last summer I wanted fast wingers and we didn't do that. You are thinking everything is possible at Manchester United but it's not. We have a bigger chance than others because we are a rich club. I don't want to talk about leaving the club. I said when I started as manager that we are in a process of transition. I have already said this a lot of times and I am repeating myself. I have to refresh my squad and I have done that in spite of many injuries this season and I have lifted the cup and that's a title. Which manager could do what I have done? It was three years ago United had the title and I'm very proud that I'm the first manager after the period of Sir Alex Ferguson [to win a cup]. I have made a picture with him and that's history. Thank you for the congratulations.'

If there was criticism about how David Moyes was sacked then that was almost classy compared to the regretful manner of Louis van Gaal's departure. First of all it ought to be stressed for the avoidance of doubt that absolutely no blame could be attached to the club for the timing of the leaks coming as they did. It did appear to be an engineered announcement to make Mourinho's arrival appear to be more newsworthy than United actually winning the FA Cup, but, engineered or not, it did have the effect of undermining a fine and proud achievement after a difficult time. Even that positive shining light of playing so many young players had been manipulated into being something the manager was forced into doing.

The widespread reports from all sections of the media appeared to be confirmed as reporters flocked around Van Gaal the following morning as the Dutch coach left the team hotel. 'It's over,' he told one reporter for Sky Sports.

As the football world waited for confirmation of the managerial change, many were already analysing where everything had gone wrong. Daniel Taylor of *The Guardian* wrote about how journalists had been so stunned when they had heard Van Gaal say in an early press conference that he did not want players to be intuitive, they had to go back and check the tapes to make sure he did actually say that. 'Other sources have revealed how players became so frustrated with Van Gaal's instructions they took matters into their own hands and told him they wanted to play their own way,' wrote Taylor. 'In one case, that player is said to have improved markedly as a result. It has also become apparent that a lot of players wanted Ryan Giggs to take over on the basis that he has a better understanding of the club than Mourinho, as well as being less likely to fall out with everyone a couple of years down the line, and it will be intriguing to see whether the Welshman remains at Old Trafford or decides to break free now he has been overlooked for the role that Ferguson, among others, wanted him to inherit. Giggs's own thoughts about Van Gaal's managerial style are understood to fall roughly in line with those of Neville and Scholes, his close friends, and the last couple of years have been exceedingly awkward for him as assistant manager, brought up on the old United principles but having to adhere to a different way of thinking and not wanting to rock the boat. It partly explained why Giggs stopped doing interviews if it meant discussing the team and why his body language often looked so stifled on the bench. Every Thursday, United had an 11-versus-11 practice match and it was Giggs's role to set up one side in the formation of the team they were about to face and talk about set pieces. Beyond that, however, he did not have a significant say in tactics and was unable to convince Van Gaal to switch to a more entertaining style of football.'

Sunday passed without any formal announcement, and when most of Monday went by, most were wondering what the hold up was. This time there was to be no unexpected stay of execution, no next game for Van Gaal to put things right. At 8.30pm the club made the official announcement that Louis van Gaal had 'left' the club. 'I would like to thank Louis and his staff for their excellent work in the past two years, culminating in winning a record-equalling 12th FA Cup for the club (and securing him a title in four different countries),' Ed Woodward said in a statement released by the club's official website. 'He has behaved with great professionalism and dignity throughout his time here. He leaves us with a legacy of having given several young players the confidence to show their ability on the highest stage. Everyone at the club wishes him all the best in the future.'

One would imagine that Van Gaal was feeling less diplomatic than his own statement seemed to suggest. 'It has been an honour to manage such a magnificent club as Manchester United FC, and in doing so, I have fulfilled a long-held ambition,' he said. 'I am immensely proud to have helped United win the FA Cup for the 12th time in the club's history. I have been privileged during my management career to have won 20 trophies but winning the FA Cup, which is steeped in so much history, will always be one of the most special achievements of my career. I am very disappointed to be unable to complete our intended three-year plan. I believe that the foundations are firmly in place to enable the club to move forward and achieve even greater success. I hope that winning the FA Cup will give the club a platform to build upon next season to restore the success that this passionate set of fans desire. Having managed in Holland, Spain and Germany, I had always hoped for the opportunity to manage in English football and be part of English culture. Both of these experiences have lived up to expectations and been fantastic.

'I thank my players and wish them well for next season. It has been a pleasure to work with them and it has been particularly rewarding to see so many young players take their chance to break into the first team and excel. I look forward to watching the continued development of these young players next season. Thank you to the owners and board of Manchester United for giving me the opportunity to manage this great club. I would also like to express my gratitude to the amazing United supporters. They are truly the best fans in the world. I am indebted to my support and coaching staff, who have given me their all during their time at the club. I am deeply grateful to each and every member of the club's staff — the sports science team, the medical team, the kit and laundry department, club administration, the press office, the manager's team, the academy team, ground staff and the catering team, both at Old Trafford and the Aon Training Complex, all of whom have given me their unwavering support in my time at United. Never in my 25 years as a manager have I been so well supported in my role. Finally, my special thanks go to Sir Alex Ferguson and Sir Bobby Charlton for always making me and my family feel so welcome throughout my time as Manchester United manager.'

* * *

Perhaps Daniel Taylor was right. Certainly, no supporter has fond recollections of the style of football played in the two years under Louis van Gaal. The style which promised so much in that first pre-season never really materialised in competitive football. The most exciting moments of that first year were firstly provided by Angel Di Maria before the manager deemed an attacking style of football was not sustainable in the long term. It appeared that there was not the technical ability within the squad to replicate the teachings of Rinus Michels, as interpreted by Louis van Gaal. The most effective run of form came in the early spring when Young and Fellaini were the star performers, which gives some indication as to how far United had come. When star names were allowed to depart in the summer of 2015, supporters hoped for stability and consistency. It seemed as if that might prevail in those early weeks of the 2015/16 season but very quickly internal conflicts became prominent and manifested themselves in the disastrous form of the winter.

If the identity of the complainants early in the 2015/16 season — Carrick and Rooney — revealed the frustration of creative players who were instructed not to play on instinct then the otherwise well-known aspects of the philosophy explained the rigidity elsewhere. Whereas the last training session before games under Sir Alex Ferguson had been a bit of a relaxing run-through when the players were encouraged to express themselves, under Moyes, those occasions became last-minute opportunities to run through rehearsed drills. This became less fun for United's stars and also had the counter-effect on their self-confidence. Ferguson's methods were not quite as cavalier as Tommy Docherty and Tommy Cavanagh's routine of screwing up the team sheet of the opposition to emphasise the idea that the identity of the opponent did not matter at Old Trafford, but it was close enough in that it had its roots in the players believing in themselves. That was nullified with Moyes's good-intentioned preparation but even that was a world away from Van Gaal's pre-match drills where defenders were instructed to stand in certain positions in proximity to each other. This was not an unfamiliar trait in Dutch football coaching, though Van Gaal went further still. He had such a strong belief in the parallels and crossovers between hockey (owing much to the fact that the Dutch men's and women's national sides were so successful) and soccer that he hired two former professional hockey players, Hans Jorritsma and Max Reckers, to help at the World Cup in 2014. Reckers joined up with Van Gaal at United.

Marc Lammers, former coach of the Dutch women's hockey team, suggested that 'total football' had evolved from hockey. 'Hockey in Holland at that time was all about speed, creativity and individual skills,' Lammers told the *Wall Street Journal* in 2014. 'They interchanged positions constantly. Dutch hockey has brought a lot of innovation and football has learned from it ... Van Gaal is someone who is always looking to get a two per cent improvement in his team. So of course he wants to know why Holland is always winning the Women's Hockey World Cup and the men are always in the top three [in the world rankings]. He is always watching other sports and looking at their processes.'

The ironic thing of course is that some players benefitted from this extra discipline, though it seemed any benefit was under threat of evaporating, and it was almost for the good of what was left from Van Gaal's positive work that he should leave before it was completely gone. It was telling that the most electric moments of those last few months of Van Gaal's reign came from the young players, most notably Marcus Rashford; the manager had said after the stunning first few games that he was allowing the forward to play without instruction.

However, by the Spurs game, that too had changed. At half-time at White Hart Lane, Van Gaal was so unimpressed by Rashford's performance that he gave him a vicious dressing down in front of his team-mates and brought him off for Ashley Young. Rashford's subdued performance might have had something to do with the fact that he was playing against the league's most miserly defence as a solo striker, but this was no excuse for the manager; many senior players were allegedly very upset by the way the boss tore into the youngster.

When Rashford scored that stunning goal against West Ham in the cup, the manager felt as if it was partly the product of the player taking on board his advice. 'It was a great goal,' Van Gaal said. 'I was behind it on the bench and saw the gap in the corner and shouted "shoot", but to do it is much more difficult. A great goal and the dribble, also. He has that quality and he can score a lot of goals. He has no nerves, he's very focussed on his work. I admire [that] when you are so young and with so much attention now. He's scoring important goals. He can cope with that attention and focus on the next match. When he has criticism, he can cope with it. He can say, "Yes manager, you are right, I have to do that." It is fantastic. There are not a lot of players who can see their self-image in a match. He is very focussed on his work and I admire that when you are so young.'

Perhaps the above story makes one less sympathetic to Van Gaal's comments of September 2017, as he spoke in detail for the first time about how disappointed he was with the manner his exit was handled. 'United put my head in a noose and I was publicly placed on the gallows,' he told *The Mirror*. 'The pressure was enormous with my head in the noose and they went right behind my back. I think it was all orchestrated like a film and it was done very much behind my back right from January. My wife, Truus, told me that the attitude of the board had changed. Women have this intuition. They smell it. I denied it, even to my wife, because between me as a manager and the chief executive Ed Woodward, everything was running as normal. Suddenly former players started to yap in the media that we were playing boring football and Mourinho's sacking made it very attractive for everyone to keep bashing me. I do understand that choice of United to get Mourinho. I never wanted more than two years anyway. Man United wanted three years. Suddenly, Mourinho was out after one-and-a-half years of my contract and I knew United wanted him one day. They told me only after it was leaked out and it was the biggest disappointment of my life. United did not discuss this with me. If they had come to me with the Mourinho plan then I could have said "okay, let's give it everything for the last six months, complete commitment to each other and the team and then Jose Mourinho can take over." They could have saved the last year of my salary by doing that, but after what happened I made them pay every penny.'

However obvious it had become that Van Gaal's position had become untenable and however much he had been culpable for the seemingly irretrievable situation at the club (which seems like a remarkable statement considering the FA Cup win), it bears repeating that the mess he inherited meant that Manchester United was not an ideal job for any manager. These days taking a big job is almost easy by comparison because the previous managers would generally not have had anywhere near the longevity and success that Ferguson had; David Moyes had attempted to make changes but had only served to alienate most of the senior players, leaving a club without many of its major stars and most of its core identity by the time Van Gaal took over. To the credit of the board, he was given enough time to implement his philosophy, and, who knows, with a different group of players, at a different time, perhaps he could have had a more successful time. In the world of football it is much easier to dispense with the manager — whether they have five years or one year remaining on their salary — than it is to dispense with the playing squad, and so when Jose Mourinho was available, United finally did what many thought they ought to have done three years prior, and hired the Portuguese manager to hopefully bring the glory days back.

Summer

Manchester United revealed the worst-kept secret in football at 9.30am on Friday, 27 May 2016, when they released a statement announcing the appointment of Jose Mourinho as their new manager on a three-year contract with an option for a fourth.

'José is quite simply the best manager in the game today,' said Ed Woodward in a statement. 'He has won trophies and inspired players in countries across Europe and, of course, he knows the Premier League very well, having won three titles here. I'd like to take this opportunity to welcome him to Manchester United. His track record of success is ideal to take the club forward.'

Mourinho's own statement, released by the club, was as saccharinous as such comments tend to be. 'To become Manchester United manager is a special honour in the game,' he told ManUtd. com. 'It is a club known and admired throughout the world. There is a mystique and a romance about it which no other club can match. I have always felt an affinity with Old Trafford; it has hosted some important memories for me in my career and I have always enjoyed a rapport with the United fans. I'm looking forward to being their manager and enjoying their magnificent support in the coming years.'

Having analysed the condition of the squad Louis van Gaal inherited, how about the one he left behind? He deserves some credit for helping the development of David de Gea, who had been named the club's Player of the Year again, even if the truth was, had all gone to plan, the goalkeeper would have already been playing for Real Madrid. Nonetheless, it was what it was, and Mourinho was inheriting the best goalkeeper in the world approaching the peak of his career. Other than that, it would probably be a fair judgement to say that United's squad basically comprised mainly of players who, if all were on form and fit, could challenge for the League title, but would be some way away from a Champions League-winning team. Antonio Valencia, Luke Shaw, Ander Herrera, Juan Mata, and Anthony Martial would not have looked out of place in a team competing for honours while Marcus Rashford was emerging as a star. In Wayne Rooney, Michael Carrick and Ashley Young, United had three long-serving players with bags of experience, and in Bastian Schweinsteiger, another player with tremendous pedigree, even if he had a very questionable injury record which had not improved at United (he made just 13 league starts). In Morgan Schneiderlin there was a midfielder with the potential to succeed Carrick in the holding role. The jury was out on Phil Jones, Chris Smalling, Marcos Rojo, Memphis Depay, Jesse Lingard, Adnan Januzaj, Daley Blind, Marouane Fellaini and Matteo Darmian in terms of their capability to hold down a starting role in a Manchester United team that had ambitions of the highest honours. Alongside Rashford, Tim Fosu-Mensah, Cameron Borthwick-Jackson and Axel Tuanzebe were three highly rated prospects for whom high hopes were held, though the long-term prospects for Guillermo Varela, Paddy McNair, James Wilson and Tyler Blackett didn't seem brilliant.

It looked like a squad that was in the midst of a transition because that's exactly what it was, but without the lure of the Champions League, one wondered how much Jose Mourinho would be able to use the name of Manchester United (and an open chequebook) to attract the names required to add a little stardust to a club in desperate need of its reputation as an attractive outlet being given a public polish.

Of course, such an approach wasn't without its potential pitfalls. Even before Mourinho's appointment was made official, there was plenty of speculation about who would become his first signing. The most prominent name was Zlatan Ibrahimovic, the legendary Swedish striker who was set to leave Paris Saint-Germain after his contract had expired. His record of 50 goals in 51 games in the 2015/16 season was exceptional but the standard of the French league and the player's age — 34 — stood out as red flags. Additionally, the track record of United buying established world-class stars and expecting them to make a lasting impact was not exactly brilliant. However, the link was so strong that there seemed to be no smoke without fire. Ibrahimovic may have passed his peak but the status of his potential acquisition — a player who could have had his pick of Premier League clubs, except for Manchester City, due to the manager and the player's past disagreements — was at least a step in the right direction for a club without Champions League football for the forthcoming season.

The jury would remain out until later in the summer when the allure of club or manager couldn't be questioned. In fairness, if that was just about the only part of Mourinho coming to United that wasn't really in doubt, it was still questioned. After all, the end of his second spell at Chelsea had ended so acrimoniously that Mourinho's stock had fallen. He was damaged goods. He was even presented as yesterday's man in a league with the bright new things, Jurgen Klopp and Pep Guardiola. In December 2015, shortly after Mourinho was sacked, Chelsea fans booed Cesc Fabregas and Diego Costa, and one supporter was pictured with a banner declaring the pair and Hazard as 'the 3 rats'. In January 2016 a Chelsea steward was sacked after being captured on video calling Fabregas a snake. The implication was that those players in particular had disappointed from their high standards the previous season, with the suggestion being that they were not keen to perform for their manager. After the year he'd had, some observers wondered if the top players in the world would want to play for a manager who had a knack of making himself the main event.

One more obvious point which had been made for many years about Mourinho, and a reservation held by many, was the style of football the manager would supposedly bring with him. By reputation, it was unapologetically defensive. His first Chelsea team broke records for clean sheets and fewest goals conceded. He had famously coached Inter Milan at the Nou Camp in one of the most stubborn defensive displays in modern memory. His achievements with Porto were more fondly remembered because of the size of the club rather than the style of the victory. Regardless of how much many wanted it to happen in 2013, including, probably, the man himself, perhaps the best time for him to have taken over at Old Trafford was in the summer of 2016. Or worst, depending on which way you looked at it. Louis van Gaal had been sacked as much for the style of play as he had for United's underachievement; that much was made clear by the merciless way he'd been disposed of hours after the club had celebrated winning the FA Cup.

Theoretically that meant Jose Mourinho would immediately be under scrutiny because, not only was there an expectation to win, there was an expectation to win well. The first thing to do when considering this is to evaluate the truth of the reputation. It serves no purpose to be so sycophantic that we pretend those past instances of defensive teams and performances did not occur; it is also going close to rewriting history to wax lyrical about the offensive qualities of those teams. The hallmark of Chelsea's 2005 title-winning side was the rapid wing play of Arjen Robben and Damien Duff, while their 2006 side had a Didier Drogba fully in tune with English football. In that second season they handed out some comprehensive beatings, winning 2-0 at Tottenham and Arsenal and 4-1 at Anfield. Their 2015 title was achieved by playing some storming football in the first half of the campaign and then tightening the noose (five 1-0 victories were recorded from 11 February to the end of the season, as opposed to none before it). Chelsea could be brilliant under Mourinho; more than often, it was enough to simply be better than their opponent.

If there was one job Mourinho had where all of those expectations were blown away, then it was his time managing Real Madrid. It all ended rather spectacularly — more on that in a second — but the peak undoubtedly came in 2012, when Madrid had a fair claim on being the best side in the world. They not only won La Liga against a Barcelona team at its peak, they did it breaking all manner of offensive records. Their 121 league goals was an incredible return, with a staggering 174 registered over every competition. They lost just two league games — the second of which was a 3-1 home reverse to Barcelona in the December (a defeat they exacted revenge on with a 2-1 win at the Nou Camp in April) — and scored four or more goals in 18 of their games.

A year later and everything appeared to have gone sour; Real were eliminated from the Champions League at the semi-final stage again and were on course to finish second in La Liga. If that continental underachievement wasn't enough for a club who were traditionally ruthless with managers who didn't win the big one in Europe, then the politics had made Mourinho's potential at the Bernabeu almost untenable. Whether it was poking then-Barca coach Tito Vilanova in the eye, or continued arguments with journalists and repeated suggestions to the press about supposed favourable treatment from UEFA to Barcelona, or alienating club legends Iker Casillas and Sergio Ramos, Mourinho had not been shy during this spell in Spain and towards the end was openly courting a return to England, saying, 'I want to be where the people love me to be.'

While the majority of the weight favoured the argument about Mourinho's pragmatic style, there was at least enough evidence to suggest Manchester United would not be without their entertaining football. And with that, we are provided with a pertinent reminder to revisit that topic again — in the summer of 2016, what *was* the Manchester United way? What were the standards Mourinho must meet, where Louis van Gaal failed?

Many referenced those late season wins by Chelsea in 2015, where they closed out their title success with clinical ease. Was this not a hallmark of United under Sir Alex Ferguson in more fruitful times? Were those games not a benchmark of brilliance which United hoped to once again achieve? The 2-0 processions with pedestrian second halves? Surely, at the very least, the landscape of modern football dictated that the identity of Manchester United had to evolve too. The idea of wingers has already been discussed, though it's worth returning to the point to say they were just as rare, if not even more so, in 2016 than they were in 2014. Most wingers had been trained into central players, with the more successful ones providing penetration that was devastating. The idea of an old fashioned quick player who liked to run down the touchline and whip the ball in now applied more to full-backs; the lower quality in dribbling ability and crossing ability was the compromise for greater defensive assets.

United's crossing ability in recent years had not been the greatest. The nadir was Phil Jones taking corners in January 2015. Ashley Young was not exactly the most consistent, but was generally the most consistent at United, though selection of the former England international in the team at all was generally a sign that it wasn't the strongest side available to the manager. Cameron Borthwick-Jackson, a left-back, had showed great promise in this area, but again was considered more of a back-up player, or one for the future. The prevailing point here was that the days of Beckham and Giggs (though the latter received his own fair share of critics for his delivery) swinging in balls from the right and left were gone. In the 1980s, Gordon Strachan and Jesper Olsen frustrated as many as they entertained with their over-deliberation. In the 1970s, Steve Coppell and Gordon Hill were fondly revered for their consistency of performance. The 1968 European Cup Final is remembered most of all for Bobby Charlton's header and George Best's rounding of the goalkeeper, but the most illuminating feature of the game was John Aston racing up and down the left wing in a man-of-the-match appearance. Aston, it should be noted, was arguably only playing due to Denis Law being injured.

The overriding point is that although using wingers was a definite feature of United's play, and a hallmark when available, formations and team shapes had evolved so much that it wasn't not playing a conventional 4-4-2 that eventually did for Van Gaal. Indeed, Van Gaal had publicly explained he wanted wingers at United, and had just not been able to get the right players in. Would they have thrived in his system if he had? Maybe, but it's an 'if' which will never get an answer. And, returning to the point, it was the philosophy and not the shape of the side which supporters opposed. If one wanted to get to the real nitty and gritty about what Manchester United supporters expected from their team, there were some basic elements. Their team should play attacking football. This was a basic philosophy put in place by Sir Matt Busby who insisted that the Manchester working public should be entertained on a Saturday. Where the influence of Jimmy Murphy came in was the attitude; no ball, or cause, was lost, an attitude which resulted in a relentlessly dominant team in the mid-50s and an attitude which almost took on an ethereal quality after the Munich Air Disaster in February 1958. Yes, the training routines were simple and based on repetition, but they were successful. After 1958, the players representing Manchester United were also playing for something greater than themselves; it was that never-give-in attitude which manifested itself in the greatest night in the club's history.

The abandonment of an attacking attitude in favour of a patient build-up had probably been given more patience than most would have thought from 2014 to 2016, but it was clear that it was an alien strategy simply incompatible with Old Trafford. If that was just about tolerated, then the meek surrenders under David Moyes which then began to seep back in under Van Gaal were the unforgivable straws which would break the camel's back.

It would not be entirely fair to say that by the summer of 2016, Manchester United supporters were prioritising success over style by welcoming Jose Mourinho, but it does nonetheless ring true that having sat through three years of football that Alan Partridge might describe as 'moribund', those fans would rather be having that discussion with trophies in the bank rather than not. That is not to say that there weren't hopes of Mourinho putting together a side who did play good football, and if he managed to replicate something resembling his last Chelsea side — potentially brilliant, but always professional — then it was a fair trade-off if it brought success with it.

Another reservation over the new manager was his tendency to take trouble with him. Those aforementioned spats at Real Madrid, and the rapid disintegration of relations at Chelsea, did not exactly bode well considering that he was heading into a dressing room with strong and vocal personalities. Another year on and the senior players Michael Carrick and Wayne Rooney were another year older; and another manager coming in, it did now seem that if there *was* a lack of harmony in the Old Trafford dressing room, this time the players wouldn't survive it. Still, the concern remained that Mourinho was an unpredictable enough character that he might be the cause of disharmony. The most-uttered theory was that Mourinho was probably the right man to bring ultimate success back to United (if ultimate means a league title) but that it would probably all end spectacularly within three to four years. By that time, even if Mourinho was on his way, if all went to plan before that he would have overseen a transition where the club was fully in tune with modern football's cycles. A new generation of players with a winning attitude, and not necessarily held back by a certain way of thinking, all prepared for the short-term cycles of playing under a few managers as opposed to just one or two. There was a crucial element missed out in the general observation of most of this — considering that there had been revolts in the last couple of years, it wasn't as if Mourinho would be upsetting a perfectly balanced squad. Perhaps it needed someone with his personality and reputation to sort out something which was threatening to spiral out of control.

So it's fair to say that many of the reservations about Jose Mourinho were based on somewhat archaic and incomplete perceptions of United's own current standing; that of a romanticised history, both recent and long-term, of the club and that of a manager whose apparently incompatible qualities were being overblown. Were Manchester United problem-free? Were Manchester United not a side who had a history of good defences? Didn't they set records in the 2008/09 season? And was it not true to say that the majority of United's post-Ferguson issues stemmed from the fact they lost Ferdinand, Vidic and Evra in one fell swoop? Van Gaal had done a fair job at fixing that area of the squad (more than any other, at least) but it seemed clear that the defence Mourinho inherited came with about half a dozen caveats. Potentially they were very good, if they were all in form, if they could all stay fit, if the right combination could be settled upon and if none of the centre-halves had rushes of blood to the head. Chris Smalling's FA Cup Final red card suggested that it was still a work in progress, but a Van Gaal signing, Marcos Rojo, seemed even more unpredictable due to his aggressive manner of defending. It brought him many fans but was very much 'defending on the edge'.

Amidst all of these reservations, perhaps the most valid one was the idea of young players getting opportunities. United's run of games featuring a youth product in their team famously stretched back as far as the end of the Second World War and it wasn't just a gimmick. As far as Van Gaal was concerned, he had enough miles in the bank that nobody could accuse him of being fortunate with the form of Marcus Rashford. There was some suggestion that the selection of the young forward was one he had no choice but to make, and, even if that was true, at least his track record clearly showed a faith in young players.

Perhaps what did save Van Gaal for a few months was the fielding of players like Rashford and Fosu-Mensah. It helped turn a volatile atmosphere at Old Trafford mostly in favour of the team, and the frustrations which threatened to boil over never really did as the fans passionately got behind the young players.

Mourinho would later claim that he had a very long list of young players he had brought through, and, while you couldn't say he was being disingenuous, a look at the Real Madrid team and most recent Chelsea team in particular provided more than enough reason for concern. Okay, so Real Madrid had the reputation of signing big-name players for most positions, but Chelsea had that FA Youth Cup record, and their recent reputation had been repeatedly mocked due to the vast number of young players farmed out on loan with no clear path to the first team. This was not necessarily a Mourinho issue because he wasn't at Stamford Bridge when that particular trend started, but one would assume that the number of FA Youth Cup-winning teams might at least have provided one or two players for the first team by now. The relatively short shelf life of a Chelsea manager might make blooding those kids a risk not worth taking, but the reasons were not convincing ones to placate concerned United fans.

Marcus Rashford had enjoyed a decent summer with England at Euro 2016 — in so much that he was one of the few players to emerge with any credit — so surely he wouldn't be thrown to the side by Mourinho, but the speculation about Ibrahimovic coming in gave many cause for concern. United didn't boast a wealth of attacking riches but both Rashford and Anthony Martial had provided the spark of enjoyment and entertainment that the club otherwise missed in a miserable campaign in terms of attacking football. With the world waiting to see how Mourinho would handle Wayne Rooney's status at the club, it stood to reason that one or both of the young forwards would have their progression stunted. Clinically speaking, United needed a proven goalscorer, so it was time for them to make a step up.

If Rashford's emergence had just about protected his position as a member in the first-team squad, there were no such guarantees for the likes of Fosu-Mensah, the Dutch utility player who had been so brilliant since coming in. Would he too become collateral damage? And, even if it meant the worst for Fosu-Mensah and Rashford, was this simply the compromise worth making to bring in Jose Mourinho?

Even with all these points of contention, many more were to reveal themselves as the new boss settled into life at Old Trafford. The club announced that Jose Mourinho would face the media for the first time on 4 July; before that, on the 2nd, it was revealed that Ryan Giggs would leave his position as assistant manager and in doing so end an almost 30-year association with the club. Regardless of your opinion on the politics of Van Gaal's second season, you couldn't help but feel Giggs had been misled. Clearly, the intention had been to eventually name him as Van Gaal's successor; the Dutch coach had said so himself. When it became clear that United's board members were instead attracted to the idea of Jose Mourinho, you wouldn't blame Giggs for being disillusioned, and certainly — going by his official statement upon departing (mentioned earlier in this book) — the Welsh legend was keen to try his hand at being the gaffer someplace.

It was a busy week for United. Giggs's departure was the biggest news, but it was rivalled by the announcement that Zlatan Ibrahimovic had signed a one-year deal at United following weeks of speculation. 'I am absolutely delighted to be joining Manchester United and am looking forward to playing in the Premier League,' Zlatan said. 'It goes without saying that I cannot wait to work with Jose Mourinho once again. He is a fantastic manager and I am ready for this new and exciting challenge. I have thoroughly enjoyed my career so far and have some great memories. I am now ready to create more special memories in England.'

Zlatan's arrival followed that of Eric Bailly, the Villarreal defender, who arrived for a fee of around £30m. His combative and proactive defending approach seemed to suggest he could be the aggressive leader United had been crying out for in their back-line. On the morning of Monday, 4 July 2016, there was no doubting who was the main event: Jose Mourinho took his first press conference at Carrington.

'You've been the special one, the happy one, what does Manchester make you?' asked James Cooper of Sky Sports.

'I don't know, really,' Jose said. 'The other two times, I was arriving at the country, this is a different one. I was sacked by Chelsea and then I stayed in the same country, the same competition with the same faces in front of me basically, so it is nothing new for me really, it is just to arrive into a club which is difficult to describe, to find the right words to describe this club. I don't like the denomination many times people use like "dream job", it is not a dream job, it is reality, I am Man United manager but the reality is I think it is a job everyone wants and not many have a chance to have and I have it and I know obviously the responsibility, the expectation. At the same time I know the legacy, I know what is behind me, the history of this club, I know what the fans expect from me and I think this challenge doesn't make me nervous because my history in the last ten years or more was always to live with big clubs' expectations and I think it comes in the right moment of my career, I feel very prepared. Very stable and with a great motivation. I am where I want to be in this club, in this country, in the Premier League and in the domestic cups, I feel a bit frustrated I am not playing Champions League. I don't hide that I chase Sir Alex's record in the Champions League for matches as a manager, I am around 130 matches. Hopefully it is only one season I am not there. When I say we, obviously the club is more important than myself, Man United is a Champions League club and we have to make sure July 2017 this club is where it has to be in the Champions League.'

'The reality is Man United have finished seventh, fourth and fifth ... is the realistic aim to compete or win these trophies?' Simon Stone of the BBC asked.

'Depends on the way you want to face it,' Jose said. 'I was never very good playing with the words or hiding behind words and hiding behind philosophies. In fact, I never tried to be good at that. I was always much more aggressive in my approach with the risks that can bring, and it would be easy and even honest and pragmatic to focus on the last three years, on the fact that we don't qualify for Champions League and so on and so on, and be quite pragmatic to say: let's work and try and be back to the Champions League, try and be back to the top four, try and be back to the Europa League. I prefer to be more aggressive and say we want to win and I can anticipate any one of you will come later with a question about style of play and a question about what is before, and I can imagine one of these questions is around the corner, and I can anticipate by saying you can win a short competition, a couple of matches without playing well, but you cannot win competitions without playing well. What is playing well? It is scoring more goals than the opponent, conceding less, making your fans proud because you give absolutely everything and you win. We want everything at the same time. It is an aggressive approach by myself. I want *everything*. I want to win matches, I want to play well, I want to play young players, I want to score goals. I want the fans to be behind us because in the last ten minutes we are chasing a result or defending a result. Of course we are not going to get everything but we want to.'

Martin Samuel of the *Daily Mail* asked Jose if he had a point to prove after what had happened at Chelsea. 'You know, there are some managers that the last time they won a title was ten years ago,' Mourinho responded with a not-so-subtle dig at Arsene Wenger. 'Some of them the last time they won a title was never. The last time I won a title was one year ago, not ten years ago or 15 years ago, so if I have a lot to prove, imagine the others. But the reality is that was never important for me. I play against myself. That is my feeling many times. I feel I have to prove not to the others but to myself. I would never be able to work without success. That is my nature and I have to always find the reasons why I have always many questions towards myself and the people working with me. That is my nature. That's why I could approach this job in a defensive point of view by saying the last three years the best we did was fourth. I can't go. It is my nature. I work in some big clubs before. Obviously Manchester United, by the social point of view, is a completely different dimension but the reality is that when people have year after year a certain kind of menu, the menu has to change for better or worse. Manchester United, for many years success was just routine and in this moment the last three years are three years to forget. I want the players to forget. I don't want the players to start the season thinking we have to do better and finish fourth. To finish fourth is not the aim. This is what I do with myself. I am 53, I am not 63 or 73. Maybe you are tired of myself because I started so early at the highest level. I am a young manager. If I don't go for big challenges I am in trouble. The reality I was in trouble for the last five months.'

Ian Irving from Premier League Productions observed that the manager had already made signings and asked how many more might be expected. 'I don't know,' the new manager admitted, before slipping up about the imminent arrival of Borussia Dortmund playmaker Henrikh Mkhitaryan. 'I think the third player is official or not yet? So the third player will be official, when? Soon. I can try to make you understand the profile. We made a nucleus of four priorities, four positions to give a certain balance to the squad, to give a certain push in terms of quality and the qualities I need and want. Especially the ones with more vision. I am more a manager that likes specialists and not so much the multifunctional players because I am very clear in my approach. Multifunctional players are like one or two, when you are in trouble during the season you always need someone who can fill but basically I want specialists. We decided four targets. From these four, we have three and until we don't have the fourth, we are still working hard; myself, the structure, Mr Woodward, the owners, we are working hard on that. When we have the fourth, I breathe and then the market will be open. We are not going to get the fourth on 31 of August, we will get the fourth before then. There is something for me which is very important, that the players I keep are all happy. Imagine first match I don't select somebody, he gets disappointed, he has the chance to go to another club. If he leaves, somebody else has to come in. There is a fundamental market and there is a supplementary market. We are doing well. We are getting the players we want and now we have the third and hopefully we will have the fourth.'

Neil Custis of *The Sun* asked Mourinho about Pep Guardiola, who had taken over as Manchester City manager, and how excited he was about taking him on again. 'I think Leicester's legacy was not just the happiness around the country,' Mourinho said. 'The legacy was we are in a competition where 20 teams are fighting for the title. That is their legacy. Next season if you have another team who win the first five matches, it doesn't matter who they are, you will consider them candidates. It is over the time you say they will collapse in December. Leicester killed the collapse word. To speak about one manager, one club, one enemy, I hate the word in football and life, I don't think it is right. It is one thing to be in a two-horse race like I was in Spain, or in Italy it was three teams fighting for the title, then that kind of approach makes sense. In the Premier League it doesn't make sense at all. If you focus on one opponent, the others will be laughing, they'll be so happy with that, so I am not going to be part of it. I am Manchester United manager, with all the respect to all the other clubs in the country, especially one that was my house for seven years, and I share so many special moments with their fans, I have to say that I am the manager of the biggest club in the UK so I don't have to be looking at the others so much. I am going to focus on our job and our club. Thanks to what Leicester did. One of their legacies is to change forever the competition.'

Dom McGuinness of talkSPORT asked about Ryan Giggs leaving the club and then spoke about Mourinho's reputation for not playing young players. 'I have no time to answer it. To answer it would take ten minutes. I knew that was coming,' Jose said, pulling out a sheet of paper from his pocket. 'You know how many young players I promote to the first team from academies? 49? Do you want to know who they are? If any of you is interested I can give you that [the sheet of paper]. I promote 49 players from the academies from the clubs and with two factors, sometimes you promote players because you don't have another choice because you have so many injuries. That is one factor and the second factor is when you are not playing for big targets, it is easier to bring them up outside the pressure of the big moments. My record of injuries is very very low. Even in many years from the Champions League studies about every team, my teams were many times the teams with less injuries. I never promote players because of a need, I did it because of conviction and decision. The second factor is that last year was the only season of my career when I was not fighting for the title, in every other season, I was winning or finishing second or third once, so it was never a situation of stability and no pressure to promote players. I did 49. Some of them, we are speaking about big names, they are today Champions League winners, they are in the Euros, playing for national teams and 49 is a lot. So one lie repeated many times sometimes it looks true but it will never be true. 49. Many times, many of you, with intention or without intention … If you want the names, I'll give you the names. About Ryan, let me finish with it. I want to make it clear, I never run away from my responsibility. The reality is it is not my responsibility that Ryan is not in the club. The job Ryan wanted is the job the club decided to give me. It is not my fault. Ryan wanted to be Manchester United manager and the club, the owners, Mr Woodward decided to give the job to me. From this moment, Ryan wants to be a manager. Like in 2000, I decide I want to be a manager. For many of us, we start as assistant coaches and, for many of us, arrives the moment where we make a decision. So when you are speaking about did I offer him a job. He could be what he wanted in the club. The club wanted to give him any important job in the club. He made a decision, where you have to be brave. It happened with myself in Barcelona in 2000, I had a contract for another two years to be assistant. It was not easy to go to another fight. For Ryan it is not just the step from assistant to manager, it is the step to leave his house of 29 years. He was brave, he is honest, so good luck so if one day he wants to come back while I am here, I will always say yes and if one day the club offers him the chance to be manager, I think it will be something natural and the consequence of his success in his career.'

Paul Hirst from *The Times* asked if Mourinho had sought advice from Sir Alex Ferguson. 'Yes — bring the umbrella!' Jose laughed. 'Yesterday I couldn't believe it was raining in the training ground. It was great advice. The second advice was to bring my typical bottle of wine. Now we are going to have many occasions to be together. At the moment Sir Alex is on a bit of a holiday at the Euros so I cannot see him this week but when his holidays are finished we will have lots of time to meet. He will always be welcome to the training ground obviously and we will have a lot of time to share our personal stuff. His opinion is important to me, the same way so many legends love this club and they are in the pundits industry and every opinion will be important to me. I will try and learn from them.'

The last question put to the new manager was the Rooney one; Mark Ogden of *The Independent* referred to the earlier comment about specialists and asked if Rooney would be a striker or a midfielder. The response? 'I think in football there are many jobs. There are many jobs on the field. The one that is more difficult to find is the guy who has put the ball in the net. The players change during the years, their qualities, their characteristics. It is normal a player at this age change a bit but there is something that will never change which is the natural appetite to put the ball in the net. Maybe he is not a striker, not a number nine any more, but for me he will never be a number six, never somebody playing 50 metres from the goal. You can tell me his pass is amazing but my pass is also amazing without pressure. To be there and put the ball in the net is the most difficult thing. For me he will be a nine, a ten, a nine and a half but never a six, not even an eight.'

The last answer was perhaps the most telling remark of the entire conference. To the United supporters watching and listening, it was the clearest indication yet that time was ticking on Wayne Rooney's omnipresence in the first team. If Jose Mourinho was going to line up like he normally did, and there was nothing to suggest he wouldn't be, his team would be a 4-2-3-1 or a 4-3-3. Traditionally, most notably at Chelsea, Mourinho had a strong spine. In his first spell it was Cech, Terry, Makelele, Lampard and Drogba. In his second spell it was Courtois, Terry (or Cahill), Matic, Fabregas and Diego Costa. At Old Trafford, the new boss already had David de Gea and Michael Carrick but the identity of the incoming players and the roles they played said much. The fourth player was clearly a strong and combative midfielder (though many thought Schneiderlin fit that role perfectly), so, if Mkhitaryan was to play the number-ten role, or wide right, it meant five players for two positions — Rooney, Mata, Lingard, Rashford and Martial. The strength in the competition for places in that area of the pitch meant there was no room for underperformance. There were no special privileges remaining; if Rooney wished to keep his place in the first team, it meant a recovery of his best form, and so, with that in mind, it was the best possible situation for fans who just wanted to see a team picked on merit and not reputation.

Considering his existing familiarity with the English game, and considering the possibility that he had been identified for the job as early as January 2016 (a theory backed up by the rumour that Mourinho had sent a multipage dossier on how he would improve United to Ed Woodward), Mourinho likely had a fair idea of the quality of the United squad and the capabilities and areas which needed improvement. While the hiring of Louis van Gaal had very much appeared to be a case of getting the best man available, Mourinho was simply the best man for the job, available or not. It was a considered decision which appeared to be thought out and rational. Still, there is observing from the touchline as an opposing manager, and there is observing from the stands in the stadium as a spectator, or on the television, but it would be quite a different thing for Mourinho to work closely with his new squad for the first time. He would have unquestionably preferred a much more settled pre-season than he got; United's tour of China was supposed to take in games against Dortmund and Manchester City, and the game against the Germans ended in a 4-1 defeat while the City game was cancelled due to terrible weather.

Back in Europe, United's preparations would conclude with a game against Turkish side Galatasaray in Swedish town Gothenburg and a testimonial for Wayne Rooney against Everton, four days before United were due to face Leicester City in the Community Shield. If describing the pre-season as inadequate is a little harsh then saying it wasn't ideal certainly isn't.

That preparation was played out against a backdrop of the biggest transfer saga of the summer. It had become apparent that Paul Pogba was Mourinho's first choice as the creative and combative midfielder, but the prospect of the French star returning to Old Trafford seemed remote. For a while, it appeared as if Real Madrid's overtures would win out; Zinedine Zidane, the Real manager, openly coveted his compatriot and in late July confirmed that the club were in negotiations with Juventus. 'In this moment we are still working, and I cannot say anything more,' Zidane told the press. 'Until 31 August anything can happen, but today he is not a Real Madrid player and I cannot talk about what will happen. I always say how things are, but now is not the time to talk about this. A lot of clubs are interested in Pogba. Real Madrid always want the best players. But we owe Juventus respect, and I can't say anything more out of respect.'

With Real Madrid as European Champions, it very much appeared as if United would be as embarrassed as they were the previous year when they went after Sergio Ramos. Everything seemed set for Pogba to follow in Zidane's footsteps and it was generally accepted that United should pursue a more realistic target. Perhaps Wesley Sneijder, who had worked with Mourinho before, might finally make his move to Old Trafford after years of speculation, or Kevin Strootman, the Roma midfielder who had suffered multiple injury problems since being linked with a move to United ever since the early days of Louis van Gaal's reign.

United persisted with the Pogba deal and in late July widespread reports suggested their official opening offer would be around £87m. Their willingness to break the world transfer record was a game-changer in the negotiations as Madrid were not willing, or able, to match such a fee. Their 2014 signing of James Rodriguez for £67m had been their only signing over £30m since Gareth Bale's world-record transfer move and their transfer activity in the summer of 2016 saw them actually make £6m more than they spent. The low-ball offers for David de Gea appeared to have been made because they couldn't afford to go higher. For years Real Madrid had rode roughshod over the Premier League, using their apparently limitless spending power and illustrious lure to snare the world's top stars. Their purchases of the likes of Kaka, Ronaldo, Benzema, Kroos, Modric and Bale made them very much the modern day Galacticos. Their status was enough to seemingly convince De Gea to yearn for a move, if not enough for him to completely ruin his status at Old Trafford by requesting the transfer.

Keeping De Gea was one thing and attributable to a comedy of errors more than the player's desire to stay at United, but convincing him to sign a new deal was another, as Real officials privately hoped that the Spaniard would run his contract down and sign for them for nothing. It meant returning to try and sign him in 2016 would be prohibitive; another player of the year campaign at United had elevated the goalkeeper's status to being widely acknowledged as one of the best two, if not the outright best, in the world. This meant United would not budge on their expectation of a world transfer record for a goalkeeper and it appeared that Madrid did not have the money and were not willing to part with one of the players they had who would match that valuation in exchange. It appeared that Juventus, too, were not keen on any player that Madrid were willing to offload to them in order to bring the price for Pogba down.

However, convincing Paul Pogba to move from a team widely considered as one of the best in Europe, to return to a club who weren't even in the Champions League instead of joining the winners of that elite competition, was something that seemed beyond all realistic ambition. Quite beyond anything else, beyond the 'untouchable' number of players — Ronaldo, Bale, Messi and Neymar — Pogba was the most highly rated 'next big thing' who would command a huge transfer fee and break into the world's elite. It had almost been taken for granted by the footballing community at large that he was destined to end up at Real Madrid.

This was arguably when Mourinho's political masterpiece really revealed itself. As reports emerged that Pogba had always been the manager's primary target, the stakes were raised — surely United wouldn't put themselves at the risk of such huge embarrassment, weeks into the new manager's reign? The key figure in this transfer saga was revealed to be not Mourinho, or Zidane, or even Paul Pogba himself, but Pogba's agent, Mino Raiola.

Raiola was one of the most heavily photographed figures of the summer, his movements followed by the football media, and he had already been in lengthy negotiations with Mourinho and Ed Woodward throughout the year. Raiola, of course, was the agent of Zlatan Ibrahimovic and Henrikh Mkhitaryan, both of whom were settling into life at Old Trafford. You couldn't help but get the impression that the success of the earlier conversations had helped to sweeten the potential path for Pogba's return to Manchester. It was all wonderfully convenient for United and Mourinho, as well as Raiola — you would get the impression that this would have been an opportunity seen as missed by Manchester City, though one the circumstances of their new management simply prohibited them from seizing. City, with Guardiola's non-existent relationship with Ibrahimovic (the Swede called Pep a 'spineless coward' who spoke 'advanced bullshit'), were not in the race to sign the legendary striker after his contract expired at Paris. They did, however, want to sign Paul Pogba, and, alongside Paris, were one of the few clubs with the kind of disposable income to put towards a deal that would attract Juventus.

United's move for Ibrahimovic was a marriage of convenience for a whole raft of reasons. It was a move which suited both parties. There is no use pretending that the striker was in demand by every club in Europe but his status was such that even if, for example, Real Madrid had made a move to sign him, one would imagine that the player would not have moved back to Spain a) because of Ronaldo's status as the star man and b) because he wouldn't have been guaranteed regular football, never mind a starting place. Barcelona were out of the running for similar reasons and so the major destinations appeared to be MLS, probably with Los Angeles, or China, with all their new money. He could happily go into retirement in either place and say he had 'conquered' each country he'd played in. However, once Manchester United expressed an interest — how better to stroke his ego than to move to England to play for the most famous club and complete a set? United needed a talisman and on a free transfer, even with the 'big name' failure reputation of recent past, Zlatan was worth the gamble, especially as a short-term signing. Mourinho's ambitions were apparently longer term. Having made Zlatan and his agent two very happy men, Raiola was happier still when Jose identified another of his clients as the number ten he wanted. Mkhitaryan's transfer was completed with little difficulty and, despite the concerns about Shinji Kagawa's identical path and underwhelming time in Manchester, the Armenian's reputation in Germany was solid enough for United fans not to necessarily expect a repeat.

The furore caused by Ibrahimovic's transfer in particular revealed an avenue of marketability which would have not gone unnoticed by Raiola. Having been so heavily involved with United over the summer, and with United so publicly courting Pogba, the agent would not wish to sabotage this new relationship by instead welcoming any interest from Manchester City, and when the prospect of a world-record transfer fee was raised, again, it began to feel like a transfer that would suit all parties. Remarkably, it seemed as if the move may actually happen, and as United prepared to kick off their season against Leicester at Wembley, all the talk was about players in the Mino Raiola camp.

Call The Doc

A couple of themes of this book have been the habit of repeating the past and the idea of Manchester United requiring major surgery. Before assessing Jose Mourinho's attempt on the latter, perhaps we should take one final walk down memory lane to more historical times.

To some with enough life experience to know first hand, the 2013 selection between David Moyes and Jose Mourinho was like choosing between Dave Sexton and Tommy Docherty in terms of personality. If we are indulging in comparisons, perhaps it is far more pertinent to actually compare Moyes to Frank O'Farrell, and Louis van Gaal to Dave Sexton. Like Moyes, O'Farrell was the man who took on the job of Manchester United manager the first time it was offered 'out of house' following Wilf McGuinness's reign and Matt Busby's short return.

O'Farrell's recollections of his time at United generally paint the picture of a man who felt he had inherited a club in a bit of a mess, and the chapter in his autobiography which describes how he was sacked is titled 'A Nice Day for an Execution'. In it, O'Farrell described how Matt Busby sat across from him and avoided eye contact (as per the quote mentioned earlier in this book). Perhaps he had a point about the way United handled the sacking, and the story told by Tommy Docherty about being offered the job after the team had lost 5-0 at Crystal Palace in December 1972, while O'Farrell was still manager, certainly corroborates the theory that it could have been handled much better.

O'Farrell had come from Leicester City and had no experience of handling footballing superstars like Denis Law, George Best and Bobby Charlton. He was supposed to deal with the outward transition of Law and Charlton while also keeping George Best under wraps and was unsuccessful with all three. Even with these players in the side, Manchester United as a glamorous footballing entity were almost unrecognisable from the team which had won the European Cup four and a half years earlier. They were not only poor to watch (that Palace game was the tenth time in 26 games that season when United had failed to score), they were prone to suffering heavy and embarrassing defeats. A 4-1 home defeat to Tottenham and a 3-0 capitulation at Maine Road had preceded that Selhurst Park humiliation in recent weeks.

Maybe making comparisons such as this can be a relatively lazy way to point out issues because there are likely to be a multitude of goings-on which are relevant and specific to those personalities, those players, that manager, that era of football; then again, there are repeated scenarios which happen time and time again. It is a truism that most football managers are hired because the previous manager underachieved, and in that case a manager will inherit a mixture of personalities and most of them will feel as if they have something to prove. It is the manager's responsibility to identify which players will be good enough for him moving forward, which players won't be, and who he will have to bring in.

Twice in Manchester United's history the opposite has happened; a manager has retired after overseeing a generation of success, and not only that, but a generation clearly defined by the methods he put in place. In 2011 O'Farrell predicted that the Manchester United left by Sir Alex Ferguson would be in much better health than the one he inherited from Busby. 'He will leave the club in better shape than Sir Matt did,' said O'Farrell. 'He won't let it be fragmented like it was then. He is already bringing in younger players to replace the ones that are there. He is constantly doing that. Whoever takes over won't have the pressure of chasing around, trying to find replacements quickly. They will take over an established team — one that is competing in Europe and challenging for titles. They will have time to settle into the job.'

On his disappointment with Busby, O'Farrell continued: 'I was more disappointed in him than anything else. He wasn't true to his word. He handpicked me. He outlined what needed to be done, which is why I had a five-year contract. I couldn't do it in just 18 months. He was around the place and all the players had grown up with him. He was a father figure to them. The alarm bells started ringing when he questioned my decisions. After we lost a home game against Tottenham he started finding fault with Martin Buchan. He also said that he wouldn't have dropped Bobby Charlton. If he wouldn't have dropped Charlton, why didn't he stick in the job himself? That to me was interfering and that made the job untenable. He wouldn't accept culpability for what he'd let happen at the club. Wilf McGuinness had been sacked before me. We paid the penalty for not being able to produce success straightaway. He admitted he'd let things go, so he should have realised we needed time to do it. There were no youngsters coming through — only Sammy McIlroy — that must have been down to Sir Matt.'

Certainly as far as David Moyes was concerned, there was no reason to fault Ferguson for alleged interference, as he kept out of all matters. As has already been discussed, some suggested he had retired at the right time for himself, but really, what *was* the right time? Suggesting it in such a way presents the theory that Ferguson knew a dip was coming — but that has to be nonsense. This was a manager who had overseen transition so many times he could have done it in his sleep. Whenever a new manager takes over at a football club, there will inevitably be some regeneration, and wouldn't it have been far worse if Ferguson had gone out and bought some more senior players and *then* retired? Moyes had an open chequebook, and perhaps if there is a criticism that deserves to be placed elsewhere, maybe the board incorrectly presumed that the incoming manager would just continue with the minor changes that Ferguson had become famed for, concentrating on one area of the team for regeneration as and when it was required rather than making wholesale changes. The make-up of the first choice XI he left behind represented exactly that. There was De Gea (bought, and made his debut in 2011), Rafael (2008), Ferdinand (2002), Vidic (2006), Evra (2006), Valencia (2009), Carrick (2006), Scholes (1994), Giggs (1991), Rooney (2004) and Van Persie (2013). Clearly 2006 had been the major year for that side seeing reinvestment but even those players had been at the club for seven years. There is a lot of truth, or at least there are many similarities, nonetheless, about the Manchester United team David Moyes inherited in comparison to the one O'Farrell inherited, especially when it comes to squad composition. However, it must be said that the side O'Farrell coached was already well on the way to its decline, while Moyes was, no matter which way you dress it up, taking on a title-winning team.

When Tommy Docherty did take the job, it took him a considerable amount of time to turn things around, a period of time which included relegation to the Second Division in 1974. Docherty expected to be sacked and instead, when he and Busby next met following the demotion, the 'Doc' was presented with a case of champagne and told to get on with the rebuilding of the team.

Comparisons between Docherty and Mourinho are natural because both are immensely quotable characters, as well as outspoken. Another thing that can certainly be said to be true is that wherever they were the manager, they were clearly the figurehead of the club, and even after a tumultuous beginning, it was clear that Docherty ruled the roost at Old Trafford, and, importantly, that he was allowed to. This writer has had the pleasure of working closely with Docherty (and in the interest of full disclosure, the books we worked on stand as records to support the opinion that the manager did an excellent job when it came to shaping a side which later successful United sides closely resembled) and, amusingly, he shoots down any talk about he and Mourinho being similar characters.

Soon after Mourinho was confirmed in the job, the *Manchester Evening News* talked to Docherty about the appointment: 'Mourinho now has the biggest club job in football and with that comes responsibilities,' said the man who won the FA Cup in 1977. 'You can't be having petty squabbles, poking opposition coaches in the eye and keep picking fights with referees and the FA. Every United manager handles themselves differently. Dave Sexton was very quiet and Sir Alex Ferguson was an authoritative figure who took control.

But I'd be surprised if Sir Bobby wasn't a bit worried by Mourinho's appointment. His comments a few years ago suggest that. They would have asked him to use his head and think of his actions. His track record as a manager is great but off the pitch it certainly isn't and he must improve his image. You can't get away with such things at Manchester United. United have looked stale in the last few years and have needed a change. The playing style under Van Gaal was drab at best. Some players must go and they need to play with more pace.'

While the similarities certainly exist between the two controversial characters, one can certainly see why Docherty rejects it. And with that in mind it's worth pointing out that there are big differences. Mourinho's reputation as a manager was to plan every detail and concentrate on game management. Docherty, whilst not quite so flippant as many would make out, encouraged more freedom and creativity, placing the trust in his team to express themselves. As far as Mourinho was concerned, it initially appeared that his front players would have permission to roam and seek opportunities and openings in a manner which suggested that they were not bound by any tactical instruction (though, of course, there were always occasions where this might not be the case), but as far as his defence and midfield were concerned, his preparation was meticulous. Docherty's side, certainly from 1974 until the end of his reign, were regarded as spectacular and cavalier, and, although Mourinho's work deserves numerous accolades, rarely have those two superlatives been associated with the Portuguese manager.

Having said that, prior to his own arrival at Old Trafford, even if he *did* favour attacking football, then Docherty's own reputation was again not too far away from Mourinho's. At Chelsea, he was known as a master motivator, shifting out a significant number of older players and putting together a young nucleus who believed in their coach and his instruction. In 1965 Docherty unintentionally destroyed his own team's title chances by putting principle and discipline first, when he sent home eight senior players for breaking a curfew before a crucial game at Burnley. He resigned from his position at Stamford Bridge, where the team left behind was picked up by Dave Sexton and won the FA Cup and European Cup Winners' Cup. It wasn't in spells at Rotherham, QPR, Aston Villa and Porto where Docherty carved out his reputation for attacking football, either, nor was it prevalent in United's relegation year where it is widely accepted that it was the lack of goals scored — at one point, in January of 1974, goalkeeper Alex Stepney was joint-top scorer with two goals (both of them penalties) — which did for their chances of survival.

Docherty's reputation for that free-flowing football was more or less developed at Old Trafford; not that there is anything wrong with that, for it was a tremendous side, but it's a point worth making when considering Mourinho's reputation and the idea that he would not play attacking or entertaining football at Old Trafford. The pair are similar and different in many ways and the strongest reason for the comparison is because of their strong, and outspoken, personalities. Of course, one could say the same about Louis van Gaal, and that episode tells us that simply having the cojones to walk into Old Trafford and assert authority is no guarantee that everything will go swimmingly.

So why the comparison to Dave Sexton when, in terms of personality, he and Van Gaal were almost chalk and cheese? How are they possibly alike? Well, first and foremost, let us consider their reputations prior to getting the United job. There is no questioning the work done by Louis van Gaal at Ajax, but the suggestion that he was the mastermind ultimately responsible for everything good Barcelona and Bayern Munich have done in the years after his management is almost insulting the work he *did* do and deserves credit for. He clearly had a nous for developing young players and for seeing things within them that perhaps they didn't even know they had — the repositioning of Bastian Schweinsteiger at Bayern, for one — but it would be completely disingenuous to say that the 'tiki-taka' style of Barcelona was the product, long term or otherwise, of Van Gaal's methods, even if his teachings about positional discipline do deserve credit. He arrived at Old Trafford with the reputation suggesting that he would rip up everything we thought we knew and create a new blueprint and modern identity for the club, which Ryan Giggs would be able to take over, and achieve similar success to Van Gaal's previous clubs. Perhaps Sexton too was the beneficiary of generous praise considering the circumstances of his own success.

Having inherited a clearly talented side from Docherty at Chelsea, Sexton's reputation as a manager increased considerably following the success at Stamford Bridge. However, late into his reign, public fallouts with some players and a drop in the team's form led to Sexton's dismissal in 1974. A few weeks later Sexton was appointed manager of QPR, where his reputation would be restored and sufficiently improved to the extent that he would be hired as Docherty's successor for a second time, this time at Old Trafford, in 1977. However, once again, Sexton had essentially won a lottery ticket when he took over at Loftus Road; previous manager Gordon Jago had assembled a fantastic team and only quit following repeated fallings out with the Rangers chairman Jim Gregory. Under Sexton, the team made up mainly of Jago's men went within a point of winning the First Division in 1976. If this is doing Sexton a disservice then it should be pointed out that his ability as a coach had never been questioned and so, in complete fairness, he did deserve some significant credit for his own contributions.

It could not be ignored, nonetheless, that he did take over two clubs where everything seemed to be in place for success to be achieved, and so when it duly came (*success* being achievements which were relative to the size of the respective clubs) it is only fair to ask the question: was the potential of the squad that good anyway, or was it the coaching which had the telling effect? Certainly in the mid to late 70s, the general consensus was that Sexton had improved what he had taken over and so when he was given the United job a couple of months after the club had won the FA Cup, the expectation was that he would deliver what Bill Shankly had been afraid of — a Manchester United team who would end his Liverpool team's period of dominance. Sexton couldn't make it three times lucky as his influence on the team's chemistry came at a detriment to their performance. He sold Brian Greenhoff and Gordon Hill — two players who essentially summed up, between them, Docherty's United team — Greenhoff the ball-playing defender who had been converted from a midfielder, and Hill that rarest of winger who was a triple threat, a great goalscorer, a scorer of great goals and a consistent supply line. Both players were attack-minded and neither of them could get along with Sexton's conservative approach.

Of course, even if these comparisons and analogies make any sense, there is one significant and key difference. Chronologically, if O'Farrell = Moyes, Docherty = Mourinho, and Sexton = Van

Gaal, then, in the modern era, Van Gaal was inheriting Moyes's 'O'Farrell's' United rather than Mourinho's 'Docherty' team.

It meant Van Gaal was not taking over a team who were successful, rather one that was in some strange transitional phase. Maybe, had Van Gaal taken charge in 2013, United's senior players might have been more receptive to his methods given his track record. Then again, considering how Rooney and Carrick spoke out, maybe not. It is an inconsequential point, really, and one can reason that Van Gaal was never considered in 2013 because the club wanted to appoint a younger man with years ahead of him.

What happened between then and 2014 that the owners felt experience was necessary? Maybe the need for authority was evident; maybe it was clear to them, as it was to most, that it needed a stronger character to take on the transition, and, let's be frank, characters barely come any stronger than Van Gaal. The players' reluctance to adhere to his methods, which almost threatened to become a revolt, meant that when push came to shove, it was going to be the coach nearing the end of his career who would be leaving the club. One could argue with some confidence that in so many respects, the board would not have viewed Van Gaal's tenure as much of a disappointing one as the directors would have viewed Sexton's when deciding to dismiss him in 1981.

In 1980 the club finished second, two points behind Liverpool. One might argue that a United side with Hill and Brian Greenhoff would have been enough to have bridged the difference. Either way, the general consensus was that the 1977 FA Cup win was the start of something (the average age of that side was the same as United's 1996 team) rather than, as it came to be, the end. In 1981 the club could not shy away from acknowledging that a change was necessary and that Sexton's reign had been one where potential had not been realised. In 2016, when Van Gaal was dismissed, even though the style of football had become deeply unpopular, it may not be too far a stretch to suggest that the owners would have felt it was still the right choice and still the necessary appointment. The team that started the FA Cup Final contained just four players who could say they were starters in the team which had won the League title just three years before — De Gea, Valencia, Carrick and Rooney, and Valencia had moved position in the team in that time.

Sacking Van Gaal after victory was ruthless and went against the grain for many, but perhaps it was simply a case of history repeating itself, going back to Dave Sexton winning his last seven matches in charge. This was simply as good as it was going to get, and in order for Manchester United to move on to the next level, the directors needed to be ruthless and get in the best man for the job.

In 2016 that man was Jose Mourinho. If these things are cyclical and history is doomed to repeat itself, then whether it was following the Docherty pattern, or Mourinho's own, at least two things were true — an eventful time was to follow, as well as a successful one.

A New Era

Most of the morning headlines on the day of the Community Shield were about Paul Pogba's seemingly imminent return to Old Trafford, but that afternoon transfer speculation took a back seat as another of Mino Raiola's men, Zlatan Ibrahimovic, took centre stage and gave a solidly emphatic response to those who wondered if he was past it, or whether he could thrive in the physical English game. His record against English clubs in European competition was not great, but against Leicester City he scored a late winner with a great header, which also suggested he had the endurance to last full games even though he was rapidly approaching his 35th birthday.

Jesse Lingard had scored a fine first half solo goal before Jamie Vardy equalised early in the second. United's first official line-up under Jose Mourinho was an interesting one. Eric Bailly lined up alongside Daley Blind in defence, with Marcos Rojo on the bench and Chris Smalling out with that suspension from the FA Cup Final. Michael Carrick and Marouane Fellaini were the midfield two, behind Lingard, Wayne Rooney and Anthony Martial, who provided support for Ibrahimovic up front. It suggested that Rooney would at least start the season as first choice, which had been more or less what Mourinho had said earlier in the week when he said Rooney was 'the club captain, the players' captain and my captain'. Lingard's selection was perhaps a surprise, but then again, considering he'd scored the winning goal in the Cup Final, nobody deserved their place in the Community Shield more. Juan Mata's selection as a substitute appeared to confirm the widely held theory that the Spaniard — having already been sold by Mourinho once, at Chelsea *to* United — was likely to be the highest profile casualty of the new shake up. And when Mata was brought off in injury time (having only come on in the 63rd minute) the substitution was portrayed as all the evidence most needed that he would definitely be shipped out by Mourinho again.

The 2-1 win was a positive way to begin the new era, but the manager wasn't getting carried away with the performance. 'A good first half in my opinion, in the second half they showed they started [their preparation] before us, we showed we need more time, and we had a bad pre-season,' Mourinho said. 'We desperately need the next week to bring our conditions up, because in the second half we suffered a little bit with the intensity of the game. We recovered the intensity when we made the substitutions. Defensively we were very good, so I'm happy, but I know we have work to do.' Asked on the Mata substitution, Mourinho said the schemer had played well, but stressed the precariousness of the lead meant he could not take off Fellaini or Ibrahimovic due to their height, with the boss expecting Leicester would come at them from set pieces. 'I knew the end of the game would be a nightmare, and it was a nightmare, so I'm happy I made that decision, Juan understands and I'm very happy with his performance,' he said. Mourinho attempted to remain coy on the Pogba speculation but was pressed by the BBC reporter who told him the club had announced that the player was undergoing a medical. 'If it is announced and he is with us next week, perfect,' the manager said.

At 12.25am on Tuesday, 9 August, Mino Raiola posted 'THE MAN IS UNITED' on his Twitter account. At 12.35am, with most of their home-based supporters fast asleep, Manchester United announced that Paul Pogba had completed his £89m move back to the club, breaking the world transfer record by £4m. It was the first time since the year 2000 that a club other than Real Madrid had broken the world record (that year, they paid £37m for Luis Figo, shortly after Hernan Crespo had moved to Lazio for £35.5m).

United released an official statement on their website, with comments from both player and manager, announcing that Pogba had re-signed on a five-year contract. The news was accompanied by promotional videos from United's kit manufacturers Adidas, featuring grime and hip-hop artist Stormzy.

'I am delighted to rejoin United,' Pogba said. 'It has always been a club with a special place in my heart and I am really looking forward to working with Jose Mourinho. I have thoroughly enjoyed my time at Juventus and have some fantastic memories of a great club with players that I count as friends. But I feel the time is right to go back to Old Trafford. I always enjoyed playing in front of the fans and can't wait to make my contribution to the team. This is the right club for me to achieve everything I hope to in the game.' His return to United's first team would have to wait, however, as the FA announced he would be suspended for the season's opener against Bournemouth due to having accumulated two yellow cards in the 2015/16 Coppa Italia with Juventus.

Despite those pre-season weeks not going according to plan, at least Mourinho now had all of his planned targets at the club and Manchester United had four significant improvements in their squad from the previous year, four players who were likely to go straight into the first team. Only Victor Valdes and Nick Powell of the senior squad had been allowed to leave, while young striker Ashley Fletcher had also departed. The manager's transfer activity meant an increased level of competition for first-team spots and a gentle easing out for some players. For example, with Eric Bailly coming in as first choice, it meant the place alongside him would be hotly contested. Daley Blind had taken that spot in the Community Shield but Jones, Smalling and Rojo were waiting in the wings. It was a smart move by the manager because it stood to reason that with the prospect of it being a 'survival of the fittest' scenario, performance levels would improve, as would concentration levels, at least theoretically. All of those players had the potential to come in and be an effective partner for Bailly and the gauntlet had been thrown down to them to earn a permanent place.

Pogba's arrival would do the same thing for the midfield. For years United supporters had bemoaned the lack of investment in that area and now there was Pogba, Herrera, Carrick, Schneiderlin, Schweinsteiger and Fellaini as senior figures contesting for three or maybe even just two positions. Likewise, Ibrahimovic's instant status as the senior striker meant an interesting selection poser in the forward positions, and, as described earlier, presented a situation where Wayne Rooney's critics would finally get their wish or they would have to eat their words. This was no guarantee that the squad players would definitely raise their game, but it was the first time since Sir Alex retired that there was a definite benchmark for quality and a pretty much settled system the manager would use. There was a level and a profile to aspire to and Mourinho had quickly managed to make that an internal issue rather than referring to a hated opponent as David Moyes did or dismissing them as unrealistic expectations as Van Gaal did. The new man had instead used United's profile to attract Ibrahimovic and, whether or not money played a part in convincing Pogba to sign, the status of the two players — unquestionably the highest profile transfers of the summer — had consequently restored and reset the level of what it meant to be a Manchester United player and what was expected. Complemented by the fact that Mourinho's style and system had been successful everywhere he'd been, and the fact it was so clear what that system was, there was a sense of routine which the players could familiarise themselves with instead of the unpredictability of the previous two managers.

Whether or not even the new star players would perform to the standards expected of them, and whether or not Mourinho's system could be successful at Manchester United, were two topics the jury was out on, but for the first time in a while there seemed to be a sense of stability and structure at Old Trafford rather than consistent insecurity.

Einsteins

The way Manchester United's latest new era started gave many the ammunition to suggest that any concerns about the manager's reputation conflicting with the supposed historical values of the club were unfounded. In August 2016 United got off to the perfect start. Their first two games were won with ease, 3-1 at Bournemouth and 2-0 against Southampton. Zlatan Ibrahimovic followed up his debut goal at Wembley with a long-range strike against the Cherries and both goals against the Saints.

One of the goals in the latter game was a penalty — notable because with Wayne Rooney on the pitch, and Zlatan already having scored, Rooney took a back seat to allow the Swede to assume spot-kick duties. Rooney had scored against Bournemouth himself and provided the cross for the opener against Southampton. So far, at least, if Rooney's was the position most at risk, then his form was justifying his selection. Paul Pogba made his second United debut against Southampton and, despite ring-rust, showed some exceptional touches to demonstrate his progress in the intervening years since he had played on the Old Trafford pitch. Ibrahimovic's form had quietened doubts of his own acclimatisation to the British game and it meant Mourinho had his own justification for not yet giving Marcus Rashford a taste of action in the league. The left-side spot had been given to Anthony Martial, and United supporters could hardly complain about that. Harsh as it may have been on Rashford, and as easy as it was for the remaining critics of Mourinho to use the forward's absence as justification for their own concerns about the lack of game time being given to those kids who had done so well at the back end of the previous season, the team's form was more than enough to back up any selection grumbles.

When Rashford *was* called upon, as a substitute at Hull City in a game where the opponents unapologetically sought a draw on their own pitch, he scored a late winner to give the manager a headache; though, of course, the kind of headache every manager would prefer to have. Likewise, another player who seemed crucial to the win was new signing Henrikh Mkhitaryan, who so far had had to settle for cameo appearances from the bench. It may have taken the full 90 minutes to break down Hull, but the movement of Mkhitaryan and Rashford was instantly too much for the tired home defenders to cope with and it should be said that United were far more adventurous than they had been under Louis van Gaal.

That was thanks in no small part to the settled nature of the side. De Gea in goal was as reliable as ever and in front of him he had enjoyed the rare luxury of a settled first-choice defence. Valencia and Shaw were looking good at full-back and the first partner for Eric Bailly was Daley Blind. They seemed to be a good fit — Blind the calming influence who could read the game, and Bailly the aggressive enforcer who would go in to tackles and was proving to be pretty good on the ball himself. Indeed, it was Bailly who was really impressing in the early weeks, with many fans going as far as to say that the Ivorian was the most impressive and most necessary signing made by Jose — praise indeed considering the stature of the other players.

The Hull win was followed by an international break, a punctuation in momentum which would have been unwanted ahead of the game that came straight after it — Manchester City at Old Trafford, and a first head-to-head clash with City boss Pep Guardiola in England. Guardiola had spent £168m (with £37m of that amount committed to the January 2017 signing of Brazilian player Gabriel Jesus) with the most noteworthy additions being the £48m defender

John Stones and goalkeeper Claudio Bravo. Bravo's arrival was protracted and so, when City started the season with Willy Caballero instead of regular number one Joe Hart, the writing was on the wall for the England goalkeeper. Bravo would become first choice in front of Hart and Hart was forced to join Italian side Torino on loan; Bravo, known to Guardiola since their days together at Barcelona, was far from a fantastic goalkeeper in his own right, but his supposedly better ability as a footballer made him the preferred option. It was a curious decision but one which helped to paint the narrative in the press, who had been gushing in their praise of the Spaniard, and, in particular, his apparent reinvention of the defenders Pablo Zabaleta and Gael Clichy, who were playing as narrower full-backs. City, like United, had enjoyed a perfect start to the season and this head-to-head was an early test of two title favourites.

From a United perspective, it would be interesting to see how Mourinho would play the game. Following the almost soulless defeats in big games under Moyes, there had been a recovery of sorts in most of the big encounters under Louis van Gaal, although these were more battles of attrition than examples of true quality. Ironically, the better football under the Dutchman had seemed to come in the bigger games, though it would be a stretch to say United were ever truly imposing in the way supporters were used to. It would even be fair to describe the last few years of Sir Alex Ferguson's reign like that; the gap had certainly closed in terms of quality between the top four or five sides and not since United boasted a talent like Cristiano Ronaldo had they truly gone into a big game and bossed it with their own style.

Under Jose Mourinho, it still wasn't entirely clear what that style would be. The first-choice midfield pair seemed to be Pogba and Marouane Fellaini, with Juan Mata, Wayne Rooney and Martial playing as a three behind Ibrahimovic. Although they had Michael Carrick in reserve, United apparently lacked a midfielder with the holding ability traditionally found in Mourinho teams, be it Claude Makelele in the early Chelsea years or Nemanja Matic in the latter spell. To most, Morgan Schneiderlin was an obvious candidate for this role but, for whatever reason, was not among the manager's first choices. Fellaini was not without his own qualities but describing him as a midfielder of that ilk was not accurate, nor was it fair to expect that kind of performance from him. Bastian Schweinsteiger was possibly experienced enough to have dealt with the responsibility but had hardly been the most reliable in terms of fitness. While clearly still a matter to be addressed, Mourinho had addressed other areas of the team he felt were more in need of immediate critical surgery. In front of the midfield, United had a fair few players who could operate in the 'number-ten' role. If it was accepted that Martial and Rashford would duel for a place on the left (with Memphis Depay also an out-of-favour Louis van Gaal alternative) or as back up for Ibrahimovic, then that left four spots for Rooney, Mata, Mkhitaryan and Lingard to compete for. Currently they were being occupied by Rooney and Mata; while supporters were sure it was only a matter of time until Rooney would be forced into the sidelines, Mata remained a favourite, and Mkhitaryan was the prime choice to partner him. Lingard was a divisive figure in the support; his inconsistency and concerns about his ability to influence in big games was often called into question even though he had proven himself as a player with a knack of making an impact on the big stage. This was a player, after all, whose stunning goal had won the club its first FA Cup for 12 years. The truth was that none of the four were cast-iron certainties in the way that they had made themselves undroppable and there was enough evidence to suggest that finding the right solution was an ongoing process for the new manager.

It was this area which proved to be key against City. Mourinho chose to give Lingard and Mkhitaryan their first starts of the season, with the idea being that they would work hard against City's defenders and push them higher up the pitch. Rooney retained his position in the team. It was a bold approach but fundamentally flawed; City flooded the midfield early on to seize control of the game and looked good with their quick movement. It was, however, a long ball which proved United's undoing; young City forward Iheanacho, in for the suspended Aguero, rose unchallenged to head on. Eric Bailly had been marking him and perhaps the position of the forward, close to the centre circle, made Bailly believe it was a challenge not worth contesting as he would perhaps clean up the second ball. However, this much had not been communicated to Daley Blind; Kevin De Bruyne seized the loose ball and surged past Blind, beating him easily for pace before slotting home from the edge of the area. Miscommunication seemed to also be the cause of the second goal — De Bruyne's shot hit the post and Iheanacho converted the rebound. He looked offside; replays showed Blind, haplessly out of tune with his fellow defenders, keeping him on.

After 36 minutes Mourinho's approach seemed foolish; Guardiola's City team looked as if they were running rings around United, even if the goals had come from mistakes. Lingard and Mkhitaryan had been deployed as runners but were ineffectual both defensively and offensively, and the choice of a two-man midfield was proving to be costly. So poor was the performance of United's three 'schemers' that it wouldn't have been a surprise to see Mourinho make changes while the first half was still going on. He didn't, instead waiting for the break, by which time he had seen his side get an unlikely lifeline. Bravo came flapping for a free kick and Ibrahimovic showed tremendous composure to finish in a difficult position. There was still time for the Swede to somehow miss two opportunities which were arguably easier to score than the goal, but at least United had got themselves back into the game. It was a goal that breathed a new confidence in the hosts and after the changes were made — Lingard and Mkhitaryan off, Herrera and Rashford on — United looked much more balanced. Their second-half performance was stirring; in the 56th minute Bravo took a risk too many by playing with the ball and hit it too heavily inside his own box. Rooney charged it down and looked to be in control of the situation, but Bravo lunged in with a two-footed challenge; it was clear for all to see that it should have been a penalty and a red card, all that is except for Mark Clattenburg, the referee, who adjudged that there hadn't even been a foul. Despite the impressive showing of Marcus Rashford, United couldn't get an equaliser, and were left to pay the price.

'The two halves were completely different,' Mourinho insisted afterwards. 'In the first half we were below the level to play this match. You have to be completely ready in terms of the speed of your thinking and decision-making. The second half was completely different. We were a team that had the courage and honesty and dignity to chase with pride the result which I think we deserved — we deserved a goal in the second half.'

That was Mourinho's response to the narrow defeat, which arguably shouldn't have been a defeat by the letter of the law (assuming, of course, that United would have scored the penalty they should have been awarded), but the reaction from the press was to instead focus on quality shown by City in the first half when they were winning the numbers game in midfield. If the reaction to that defeat in isolation was over the top then the critics were given more ammunition when United lost their next two games — the 1-0 defeat in Feyenoord in the first Europa League game was an underwhelming start to continental competition but not as embarrassing as the 3-1 capitulation to Watford in the next league game. In Europe, Mourinho had rotated heavily, but against Watford it was clear that there had been casualties from the City game. Mkhitaryan was out, and Blind was the defender dropped, with Chris Smalling called up. The imbalance in midfield was clear; all could see that Fellaini and Pogba were incompatible as a pair, with Pogba at his best going forward but Fellaini not having the positional discipline to allow the French player the freedom to influence the game in the area he was best. A 4-1 win over Leicester City, with Herrera alongside Pogba and Carrick coming on as a substitute (and Pogba putting in his most impressive performance yet), suggested that a corner had been turned. By far the biggest newsworthy item from the selection for that game was the dropping of Wayne Rooney. Rooney was on the bench and so couldn't be described as unfit — and, with the game being the first home game following two consecutive defeats in the league, the pressure was on for Mourinho to pick a side to win. Out too went Luke Shaw, with Blind in at left-back.

It was a selection the manager went with again the next week, with Stoke City the visitors to Old Trafford (in between, another rotated side won in the Europa League). This time, however, United came up against a new problem which was set to become a repeated one. Stoke, almost unapologetically, came for a draw, but since goalkeeper Jack Butland's ankle injury the preceding March, they had conceded 33 goals in just 13 games. However, Butland's replacement, the veteran on-loan stopper Lee Grant, put in an inspired performance, and Stoke were disciplined enough to not give anything away. United's issues with their dependency on Ibrahimovic were exploited as early on as this fixture. As brilliant as he was at finishing and as a penalty-box threat, his lack of pace meant that United generally only stretched defences down the left-hand side through Martial or, as in this instance, Rashford. Opponents learned to double up in that area and so, at Old Trafford in particular, where visitors could come and play just for a point and escape widespread criticism, it made for a potentially difficult afternoon or evening. Jesse Lingard, if on form, could provide penetration on the other side, but hoping for Juan Mata to provide the explosive burst of pace to get behind the defenders was hoping that he was a different player. Mourinho's reticence to use Shaw was arguably down to issues with the player's personal and professional discipline, and what the left-back's absence left United with was that attacking thrust which would occasionally free up space for the left-sided forward. With no threat from that area, the opponent could — if organised well enough — have the game played in front of them, and so long as they had tall defenders or a goalkeeper in form (and Stoke had both), they could pretty much see out the game comfortably. Two minutes after bringing on Anthony Martial to play on the left and moving Rashford on to the right, Martial took advantage of Stoke's reorganisation to curl home a stunning effort.

Mark Hughes, the Stoke manager, was forced to make attacking changes and bring his team out. Frustratingly for Mourinho, De Gea made a rare gaff when spilling a shot from Glen Johnson, allowing Joe Allen to pounce on the rebound with just eight minutes left. United threw everything at the Stoke goal and Paul Pogba hit the bar but, as Hughes famously once said, United simply ran out of time and couldn't get the second. Pogba's miss was highlighted afterwards as the midfielder had gone close with a number of speculative long-range efforts.

Far from it being indicative of United's issues, Mourinho insisted it was the best performance of the season so far. 'It could have been one of these fat results,' he told the BBC. 'It could have been 5-0 or 6-0. We had big chances, with amazing saves and big misses. We will play worse and win games for sure. You can have sometimes draws where what you do does nothing to change the result. The players and I did everything. I made changes, everyone was giving more and more but we could be here all day without winning the game. We had 90 minutes of control, we had 90 minutes of ambition. We played really well and it was a good home performance and we created lots of chances. In the first minute, their goalkeeper made an unbelievable save and he kept doing that until the end of the game. Stoke fought like they do every game. They came for a draw. They were lucky but luck is part of football and my tribute to them is that they're not guilty of our bad luck.'

'Guilty' was an interesting turn of phrase considering that Mourinho was effectively accused of crimes against football in United's next game. They travelled to Anfield after the October international break and, indicating the manager's learning curve, this time he went for a three-man midfield of Fellaini, Herrera and Pogba. Pogba's position was slightly more advanced, while Ashley Young and Marcus Rashford were chosen to provide the energetic legs down the flanks. Liverpool, meanwhile, played with three midfielders of their own, with Emre Can, Jordan Henderson and Philippe Coutinho protecting a shaky defence. The result was a game which was difficult to watch, and there were plenty of United supporters frustrated with their team's performance, but in the context of a) the way they had been cut apart in the first half against City and b) this particular fixture it was an almost understandable approach. It may have been jarring, but this was Mourinho and this was what he did everywhere, mostly with success. It was obvious that he was waiting on a slip from Liverpool or a change from Jurgen Klopp to stretch the game. When the change did finally come, it did nothing to help, with Klopp withdrawing a forward, Sturridge, for another midfielder, Lallana. United surrendered the majority of the ball — recording their lowest possession stats since Opta began recording such data in 2003, 35 per cent — but Liverpool did nothing with it.

Afterwards, Mourinho was bullish when presented with that stat on Sky Sports. 'That was the game that we played — we don't control the game by having the ball all the time,' he said. 'Two shots on target with 65 per cent of possession. You have to be critical of Liverpool. It is their problem, not our problem. It is not the result we wanted but it is a positive result. It is a result that stops a direct opponent getting three points at home, so not a bad result. The game was difficult for both teams but for longer periods it was more difficult for them than us. We controlled the game not just tactically but the emotion of the game. That was probably the quietest Anfield I had and I was expecting it to be the other way. The reaction from their crowd was permanent disappointment. People expected us to come here and be really in trouble, which we were not. Other candidates for the title have easier fixtures at the moment and it is important to keep close to them. Our moment to win four or five matches in a row will come and we'll be there.'

The perception of the game, not for the last time, was distorted into one where Liverpool were seen as the team who had tried to play football and United had played negatively and for a draw. When you look at Mourinho's comments about preventing a 'direct opponent' getting a home win it's almost impossible to argue with that perception, but perception is not fact; even if it takes analysing the finer details to emphasise the difference between playing for a draw and playing to ensure your team doesn't lose. In the bigger games, the latter quality is often unappreciated because it doesn't lend itself to a spectacle, but it is a strategy that requires planning on an almost meticulous level. The planning centres on intensive study of the opposition and the idea that victory can be achieved through concentration and application, focussing on errors of the opposition, or changes made by the opposing manager to their normal shape.

At Anfield, such intricate planning wasn't necessary because Liverpool's own team wasn't so unstoppable, and it was this point when United's supporters own frustrations emanated. It, apparently, wasn't befitting of a United team to go to Anfield and play that way. A more positive result could possibly have been accomplished with a more positive game plan, but expecting that from Mourinho was, again, expecting a different manager. Does this mean that the approach was negative? No, it means it was somewhere in the middle ground, but the football media and generally the football supporting public don't deal in the middle ground, they deal in the spectacular opposite ends of the spectrum where it is easier to digest sensationalised opinions. Mourinho was deploying the sort of game plan he has used at Anfield in the past, probably most famously in 2014, when Liverpool were chasing the title. Mourinho even gambled with using a below-full-strength Chelsea team and his game plan was hugely successful when then-Liverpool manager Brendan Rodgers was forced to gamble to try and win the game. It opened the game up and Chelsea won with two counter-attack goals. In October 2016 Jurgen Klopp was not so ambitious, despite playing at home, and yet it was his rival manager who was levelled with the criticism.

Press attacks rained in on United's players, too. Chief target was Paul Pogba. Pogba's arrival as a world-record transfer fee had set tongues wagging amongst Premier League managers, one of them Jurgen Klopp, who questioned the fee: 'The day that this is football I'm not in a job any more, because the game is about playing together,' Klopp said. 'I want to do it differently. I would even do it differently if I could spend that money.' Following similar comments from Arsene Wenger, Mourinho bit back. 'When I heard some of the comments and some of the managers criticising that, I don't think they ever have this problem because, to have this problem, you need to be at one of the top clubs in the world,' Mourinho said. 'So at Man United it can happen.' Mourinho had also reflected on the fee and suggested, with some accuracy, that soon enough Pogba's fee would be seen as a fair price in a quickly escalating market, but in the aftermath of the draw at Anfield, the Frenchman's form was heavily criticised. Graeme Souness, working on the game as a pundit for Sky Sports, laid into the midfielder. 'Pogba may eventually be £100m worth, but right now I don't see him anywhere near that,' he said. 'I see a young man who's struggling to find his best position and best form in a team that's struggling to find their best form. I don't see him having a great understanding of the game.'

Mourinho, while defensive of the way his team had played, did at least admit that they might have played better. 'We should have had a little bit more,' he said. 'I think we missed a little bit of sharpness through the middle between the positions where Pogba was.' Pogba shouldn't escape all the blame, as shouldn't Mourinho, but the context and the extenuating circumstances did make it all seem as if it was being blown out of proportion. Playing as a number ten, he had the responsibility of bringing Zlatan Ibrahimovic into the game, as well as the general level of expectancy for his normal contribution, to deal with.

So, if there are those mitigating details to relieve Mourinho and Pogba of some of the criticism for why United's performance was relatively poor even if the game plan was somewhat effective, what are they? Firstly, nobody could argue that United's defensive performance was out of tune. In midfield they rarely looked in threat of being overrun and even had a couple of good first-half chances through Zlatan Ibrahimovic and Pogba. It's easy to point the finger at the manager and the big-name players, but even if we discount Klopp's own approach and credit him with not wishing to lose just as we are with Mourinho, there still must be something in the small print which meant the players on the pitch were expected to have done better against a Liverpool team there for the taking. Pogba's repositioning didn't help, for starters. Herrera had done well since coming back into the side but he and Fellaini hardly screamed a midfield pair that had the necessary solidity to easily compete against a midfield three by themselves. While Eric Bailly and Chris Smalling earned rave reviews for their own performances, and Smalling was named man of the match by many, there was something to be said about the eye-catching nature of his defensive work. At Manchester United, as at most big clubs, there is an added responsibility and standard demanded of players. It isn't just enough to be able to continuously head balls out of the box; even as a centre-half, you have to be aware enough of where you are heading the ball and where it is likely to land. Too often, United's clearances landed at Liverpool feet, inviting more pressure and causing the defence to drop deeper. The spaces between the back and the front became more vast and Pogba and Ibrahimovic subsequently were made into the isolated figures that they undoubtedly were.

Pogba kept his place in a much-changed team against Fenerbahce three days later and provided an emphatic response, scoring twice in a 4-1 win; one of them a stunning long-range effort. Afterwards, his manager was quick to give his under-fire player some praise. 'First of all, in some of your mouths, he goes from the worst player in the Premier League to a great player in 48 hours,' said Mourinho. 'I am not specifically saying it is you. I say media, especially the Einsteins. We know he is a very good player. We know he needs some time to show his potential. I know Italian football very well. I know teams play completely different from the Premier League. I am not saying we are better but we are different. Different in the intensity, the number of touches on the ball, everything is different and he needs time to adapt. He is a self-confident boy. He was not depressed because some people said he was a bad player. He was calm. It is always nice for a player to score, to score at home and especially to score such a beautiful goal.'

The four-goal haul only strengthened criticism about United's pragmatism at Anfield. With this firepower in their locker, why didn't they use it? 'The situation is that we played with Lingard, with Mata and Martial,' Mourinho said. 'I am not an Einstein. I don't know a tactical system that can play with four wingers at the same time. Mkhitaryan has to work more to get the intensity and fitness to play at a high level. To have him on the bench and give him 15 or 20 minutes like I did to Memphis, I think it is much better for him to work yesterday much harder and he did today in a specific session and wait for his chance, but he is ready very soon.'

It would be a month before Mkhitaryan was in fact back in the team, and by that time the Armenian's absence was one of a few concerns United supporters were beginning to voice about their manager. By and large, he had been given a pass for the Anfield draw, thanks in no small part to the fact that a result against your most vicious rivals will always provoke a tribal bias; a bias which, at all other times, may seem thoroughly unreasonable. Most supporters would have taken a repeat of that Liverpool result in the next league game at Stamford Bridge but those hopes were undone in the first minute when Pedro scored before United had even touched the ball. It went from bad to worse when Gary Cahill scored in the 21st minute and the visitors, whose only change from their resolute display six days earlier was Lingard in for Young, were even more calamitous in defence in the second half, conceding two horrendous goals.

'I'm not disappointed with the performance, but with the mistakes,' Mourinho said. 'If we could delete the defensive mistakes, the performance was good. But when my teams have perfection in their defensive performances, people say that is not important. But the reality is that it is important. We made an incredible defensive mistake, I say incredible in capitals, in the first minute and then the game is different. It is one of those days when you give the advantage to opponents by doing nothing. We put ourselves in a situation where we gave Chelsea the game they wanted to play: the block compact and low, as it was in the second half, and wait for the chances on the counter-attack. Football matches start at 0-0, this match started 1-0. In terms of points, we got zero points, we lose three points. We are six points from the top, three from the top four, we now need to win matches. We need to win our matches now, which are not easy. We need to win to close that gap — after these last three matches, we made two out of nine. We now need points.'

Mourinho, who had said before the game that he would not 'celebrate like a crazy kid' if his new team scored against his old one, confronted Chelsea boss Antonio Conte on the touchline after the Italian celebrated his team's fourth goal as it was a last-minute winner. 'You know me: I spoke to Conte, not to you,' the United manager said when asked about the incident. 'I'm not the kind of guy to come here and share with you things I don't want to share. What is between me and Antonio is for us ... or up to him to talk if he wants to. That is his problem. I have no comment.'

Conte defended his actions afterwards, while Mourinho's grumbles continued into the week, ahead of a League Cup game with Manchester City. What would normally have been a low-key affair had been elevated into an important fixture for the United boss, who admitted to Sky Sports that he had yet to settle into life in the north; he had not yet bought a house and was residing in the Lowry Hotel in the centre of Manchester. 'For me it's a bit of a disaster because I want sometimes to walk a little bit and I can't,' Jose said, providing headline writers with their dream. 'I just want to cross the bridge and go to a restaurant. I can't, so it is really bad. Buy a house? I do not know, I do not know. The reality is that my daughter will be 20 next week, my son will be 17 in a couple of months. They are very stable. University in London. Football in London. Friends. So they are in an age where they can't chase me like they did before. So for the first time the family lives in a different way. We try to feel it, we try to see the evolution of our feelings and see how we cope with the situation. But I have my apps and I can ask for food to also be delivered, which I do sometimes. You know the history of the paparazzi, for the hotel and the brand that sponsors me, the clothes brand, is amazing because they are there every day. Everybody knows the name of the hotel! Everybody knows the last arrivals of that brand! So for them, it is amazing.'

Ahead of the game, *The Times* reported that some United players were surprised and disgruntled with Mourinho's approach to training and one-to-one interactions. *The Independent* reported that some members of the squad had hoped he would be more personal as his reputation had suggested he might be: 'It's created an isolated feeling between the squad and the manager, and could be one of the major factors behind Sunday's capitulation at Stamford Bridge.'

There was no suggestion that Mourinho's job was at risk but it was widely being presented by areas of the press that the Portuguese manager was yesterday's man, a coach unable to keep pace with the likes of today's stylish bosses like Guardiola, Klopp and Conte. He needed a result and a performance and he was rewarded with a 1-0 victory in the cup. It was Mourinho's strongest team and he had clearly learned lessons from the league fixture against City, and his team's capabilities. Eric Bailly had picked up an injury at Chelsea — his exit from the field promoted United's complete fold — so he was unavailable, and Mourinho chose Marcos Rojo to play alongside Daley Blind. Carrick and Herrera were selected to play in midfield with Pogba, while Juan Mata was picked to play from the right. Matching City for numbers worked a treat; Guardiola's side were not able to impose themselves on the game and United's victory, earned through a Mata goal, was well earned.

The reaction to the Chelsea defeat was what the manager wanted. 'We were on a good run of results but it was a big defeat — numbers that the history of this club doesn't deserve,' Mourinho said after watching his side qualify for the quarter-final. 'When I'm in a club my heart belongs to the fans and I felt deeply for them. The reality is that I never had people like these ones. We lost 4-0 and they were supportive. Today the stadium was full of real support and it looks like the love people have for the club is bigger than bad results, bigger than three bad seasons. We must give something back.'

Hopes that the result would kick start some form did not bear fruit; United then drew 0-0 at home to Burnley, who had ex-Red Tom Heaton to thank for an outstanding performance in goal. The hosts had 72 per cent of the ball and an incredible 38 shots, though only 11 of those were on target. Frustration was already setting in before half-time; Mourinho was incensed when referee Mark Clattenburg failed to award a penalty for a blatant foul on Matteo Darmian. He made his comments clear at half-time and when he emerged for the second half, it transpired he had been sent to the stand. In the 68th minute, Herrera was sent off. United reacted by sending on Rooney and Fellaini but their pedestrian and obvious line of attack was dealt with by Burnley; when Heaton was beaten, the woodwork wasn't, with Mata and Ibrahimovic both being denied by the frame of the goal. It was a repeat of the Stoke game; the organisation of the opponents and United's lack of penetration were becoming regular themes in these games where a 'smaller' opponent would come to Old Trafford.

However, Mourinho found that instead of criticism, Burnley's rearguard effort was applauded and the United boss was again under pressure, this time for his team's failure to find a way to win the game. The general consensus was that a team with United's resources should be able to win these games without breaking a sweat, and while that is a fairly rudimentary argument which ignores the golden rule of football, that anything can happen (as indeed Burnley had proven), it was a fairly straightforward argument which had some truth to it. Of course, if you spend more money assembling your squad, inevitably it stands to reason you will have better players and should therefore stand a better chance of winning. So, when it was being printed that United's team which cost anywhere between £200m and £350m, depending on who played and which inflated transfer fee was being counted, had failed, it was technically true, and when it was being printed that it was Jose's failure, again, it was technically true.

Still, using that argument was a tremendously flawed one. It first of all suggested that the squad, as expensively assembled as it was, was full of no-hopers, which was blatantly untrue. In an hyper-inflated market, transfer fees can make your eyes water, but United were hardly the most obscene offenders in that regard, even if their acquisition of Pogba had set a new record. It was true that a number of players in the squad were purchased for fees that seemed unreasonably high, but those fees were determined by a number of factors. The first is one which has applied to United for at least 25 years, and that is that whenever they are interested in a player, the selling club will immediately raise their asking price by a considerable amount. This does cause some inflation as a ripple effect but Wayne Rooney works as a perfect example of the point at its most explained. When it was clear that Everton couldn't keep him after his stunning Euro 2004 performance, Newcastle United were in talks to sign him for £20m. When Manchester United entered negotiations, the price became almost £30m, and Rooney hadn't even played another game due to him being out with an injury. The cause for the premium? Simply, *being* Manchester United.

By October 2016 Rooney had broken Sir Bobby Charlton's international goalscoring record and was closing in on his United record too. He had won a number of trophies and played such a major part in those successes that nobody could deny he had been worth every penny paid for him, even the large section of support who had grown disillusioned with the striker after his transfer request in 2010. Labelling him as an overrated £30m player in 2016 was disingenuous at best, as explained earlier.

There were plenty of cases where United could be said to have overspent. Luke Shaw had potential but hadn't really justified the investment as yet; Juan Mata was a fan favourite but the then-record fee still seemed steep for a player who Mourinho was happy to let leave Chelsea. Most United fans at the time would have thought the £23m release clause for Marouane Fellaini was excessive before that expired and the club had to fork out another £5m. The fees for other first-team players like Darmian, Blind, and Rojo did seem very high considering their performance levels and that was before even considering the likes of Memphis Depay and Morgan Schneiderlin, who clearly seemed to not be in the manager's plans and had cost a combined £60m. All that being said and admitted, was Mourinho to blame for the overspending of previous managers on players who were either overpriced or simply incompatible? He was charged with resolving the issues created by those management periods, and clearly that was a scenario which would take some time, but he was not responsible for it.

Another element at play which Mourinho may not have been prepared for was what could be described as the Leeds United factor. In 1996 Alex Ferguson was heavily critical of the Leeds players who had put in two energetic efforts against his own team in a season where their form had been questionable at best. Ferguson suggested that the Leeds players were cheating their manager Howard Wilkinson and that they may be much higher in the table if they showed that level of commitment every week. When Jose Mourinho had been to United as a visiting manager he had always used the same approach — the approach which was now being regarded as too defensive — and he had generally had good success with it, with wins for Chelsea and Real Madrid at Old Trafford as well as that infamous draw with Porto which more or less announced him to the world stage. He was not a manager who had ever taken a team to United without the idea of getting a positive result and now he was confronted with the situation that most teams were happy to go to Old Trafford just for a point. In recent years that had proved a very achievable target for many visiting teams, many of whom earned their draw with some degree of comfort. With penetration coming, generally, from just one area of the pitch, and opponents being able to deal with United's general lack of pace and thrust through the middle, Mourinho was discovering that the formula for winning home games was much more complex than he might have originally thought. It didn't matter if the reaction of the press was over the top, that was the pressure cooker that came with being in charge of Manchester United, and regardless of any of the contributing factors, at United's level results come first, and so long as opponents could get a point from their game at Old Trafford, it was justification for their approach.

Again, though, this is not to absolve Mourinho completely. What he was responsible for and was accountable for was the success of his own signings (though that is not to say he wasn't accountable for the entire squad, just that he shouldn't have been judged on their fees three months into his management reign), and though Bailly and Ibrahimovic had been successes, Pogba's stuttering influence had most at least saying he was overpriced, while Mkhitaryan's absence from the squad was even more bewildering to those who identified him as the perfect player to have provided the creativity required to have broken down Burnley. The fact that the former Dortmund player had been so publicly shelved after the City league game had many concerned that Mourinho's explosive bust-ups, normally the first indication of the cracks in the foundation, had already begun.

The manager was also responsible for finding that winning formula, particularly in home games, and fast. Two more home games, against Arsenal and West Ham, were set to come in quick succession in the league, and with United sitting eight points behind leaders City in eighth place, they needed to get some victories strung together quickly if they wanted to launch a genuine title challenge. After a defeat in Turkey in the return against Fenerbahce put United's Europa League status at risk, the game against Swansea City took on extra significance. No win in four league games and three defeats in nine, already mischief makers were pulling out statistical references to David Moyes and Louis van Gaal and saying that United were regressing further still. A 3-1 win in South Wales, with all the goals coming in a storming first 33 minutes, was a convincing response, but United then drew their next three league games after the international break — the home games with Arsenal and West Ham and then the away game with Everton. Despite dominating all of those games, United were profligate in front of goal, and against Arsenal and Everton they succumbed to last-minute equalisers. The Everton game was particularly galling; with five minutes to go, Mourinho brought on Fellaini with the idea that the Belgian's physically disturbing presence would disrupt the host's search for an equaliser. Instead, Fellaini got involved where he didn't need to, clumsily fouling Idrissa Gueye in the box and conceding a penalty, which Leighton Baines smashed away. Gueye was lucky to still be playing after Marcos Rojo's awful challenge in the 15th minute, which should have seen the United defender sent off.

With the decision of the boss having a direct impact on the result, he was naturally questioned about it afterwards. 'I thought you would know more about football than you do,' the United boss told reporters who were questioning him about the Fellaini substitution. 'Everton is not a passing team any more like they were in the past. Everton is a team that plays direct: goalkeeper direct, Ashley Williams direct, Ramiro Funes Mori direct. Everything direct. When you have on the bench a player with two metres you play the player in front of the defensive line to help the team to win the match. We are not getting the results we deserve. We are getting draws but deserving victory. Opposition are leaving the stadium super happy with points they don't deserve and we are leaving the stadium with a feeling we deserved more. When my teams [at Chelsea] are playing pragmatic football and winning matches and winning titles you say that is not nice and not right. Then my team play very well — and is a huge change to the last two or three years [at United] — now you say what matters is to get the result no matter what. In this moment we have teams getting results that defend with 11, kick ball and attack the space on the counter-attack ... it is phenomenal, it's beautiful. You have to make a decision.'

The draw left United in sixth place on 21 points. Manchester City, whose form had also stuttered, were nine points ahead but were in fourth place, while leaders Chelsea were sitting pretty on 34 points. The critics had a field day with the numbers. That 21-point tally was lower than David Moyes (22 points) and Louis van Gaal (25 points) had accumulated after the same number of games. Including the latter end of his period at Chelsea, Mourinho's last 30 Premier League games had yielded a return of 1.2 points per game, as opposed to the average of 2.29 points per game in the 196 Premier League games before that. It was enough to have a BBC website column stating, 'Jose Mourinho's aura is well and truly gone after a sorry end to his Chelsea reign, and a shaky start to his Manchester United one.'

It may have been a premature obituary for the boss, but United's reputation for dispensing of their managers had essentially followed a similar pattern; as soon as it was mathematically impossible for either to get the club in the Champions League, they were fired. The pre-season spending and the identity of the players brought in had supporters dreaming of a title challenge. Whilst they were not exactly on the manager's back for not providing that — most recognised that the issues in the squad ran deeper — being so far off a Champions League place in the league was a definite worry. It placed extra importance on the visit to the Ukraine to take on Zorya Luhansk in the final Europa League game, with qualification to the Champions League the prize on offer to the winners of the competition. United needed to win to qualify for the knock-out stages, but despite having more than three quarters of the ball in the first half they found themselves frustrated. Straight after the break, however, United found a breakthrough; Henrikh Mkhitaryan, who had found himself back in favour, scored his first goal for the club, a fine solo effort after running from the half-way line. He then created a second for Ibrahimovic, whose goal was his sixth in seven matches after a run of seven games without one. The Swede, like the Armenian, and like so many others at Old Trafford, provided the perfect response to criticism. Eric Bailly's return from injury went well, and the defender put in a good showing on his first game since limping off against Chelsea. Mourinho even brought on Fellaini with 20 minutes to go, a decision which seemed like a defiant two-finger salute to those who thought the midfielder might not play for the club again after what happened at Goodison. As notable as those who were playing was who wasn't; Schneiderlin and Depay had found themselves playing in Europa League games, but now, when it came to the crunch, they were not even in the squad, fuelling rumours of a January transfer for both.

Maybe qualification liberated United or eased some of the pressure on some of the players. Maybe their bad luck simply turned. Either way, they successfully navigated a tricky winter period, winning six league games on the bounce. It was a run which seemed to suggest United had come on leaps and bounds, showcasing a variety of styles; starting with a well-contested game against Tottenham, United were also required to demonstrate patience to win games late on against defensive opponents, with Paul Pogba playing a prominent part. It was Pogba who opened the scoring and then provided a magnificent assist for Ibrahimovic to score in the last couple of minutes at Crystal Palace. Pogba then scored his own late winner against Middlesbrough; Boro had taken a shock lead despite their own rearguard approach and United threw everything at their opponents, scoring in the 85th minute through Martial and then a minute later through his compatriot. Mourinho praised the supporters afterwards. 'My players were phenomenal,' he said. 'We managed to do something I love — bring the fans to the pitch. The last 15 minutes were 70,000 on the pitch against 11.'

On 2 January United played at West Ham's Olympic Stadium for the first time. The Hammers were cautious after Sofiane Feghouli was sent off in the 15th minute; at half-time Mourinho made the bold move of bringing on Juan Mata for Matteo Darmian and moved Michael Carrick into defence, adding an extra man into his team's attacking arsenal. It was a move which took 18 minutes to work, and Mata himself was the goalscorer. As soon as the breakthrough had been achieved, Mkhitaryan was withdrawn for Smalling. This sixth win on the bounce (ninth in all competitions) had, frustratingly, not improved United's league position, to the delight of rival fans and meme makers everywhere. They were sixth at the start of the run and sixth at the end even if now they were much closer to Tottenham, Arsenal and City than they had been. A little higher in the table lay Liverpool, who were the next visitors to Old Trafford in the league. Before that, Reading and Hull City came to Manchester for FA Cup and League Cup ties respectively, and both were beaten. These routine victories were most noteworthy for the return of Wayne Rooney to the first team, having been missing over the festive period. Rooney played well and was back in the squad to play Liverpool, where the pre-match talk centred around the style of football of both sides and whether they would produce another dull affair between them.

United's performance indicated that they had something to prove after how heavily criticised they had been in October, and Liverpool goalkeeper Simon Mignolet was the latest visiting keeper to put in a stellar performance. When the visitors made a rare foray forward and won a corner, Paul Pogba handled the ball in a decision which was described as inexplicable by almost every reporter. He didn't seem under any intense pressure, and neither did his team, but when James Milner converted the penalty the entire context of the game changed. Liverpool's conservative midfield of Henderson, Can and Wijnaldum became even more compact and United struggled to try and penetrate a seven-man defence. At half time, Rooney was brought on for Carrick, and with 25 minutes to go Mata was brought on for the ineffectual Martial; the move was symbolic, with Mata's delivery seen as the key as opposed to Martial's direct running. When that didn't work, Fellaini was brought on for Darmian, and United went direct — the approach finally paid off in the 84th minute when Fellaini's header hit the bar and Ibrahimovic converted the rebound. It was the Swede's 14th goal in 20 league games.

United were certainly deserving of a point, if not all three, considering that they had been the more ambitious team throughout the 90 minutes. Mourinho openly confessed that he was looking forward to the perception of this game: 'I didn't think the game had super quality,' the United manager said. 'We didn't reflect the qualities we have and Liverpool have — but it was very emotional, intense, aggressive. We fought until the last second. They were clever. They took their time, they know how to play football and control the emotions of the game. They knew they would be in trouble in the final few minutes. I have a problem with my neck because I was always looking to the left in the second half and I saw so many yellow shirts in front of me I thought "let's go for it". We lost two points when we wanted all three. The people need to know what Marouane Fellaini is great at and what he is not so good at. Marouane is very good in some aspects. We were the team that attacked and Liverpool were the team that defended — let's see if the critics are fair. I enjoyed it but I will obviously be disappointed we didn't get the three points.'

Afterwards, however, Jurgen Klopp once more attempted to pour scorn on United's approach, labelling them a long-ball team: 'In the end period of the game when United started playing long balls after 80 minutes of high intense football it is really hard,' the Liverpool boss said. 'I hoped we would have a bit of luck, unfortunately not, but all good. Tomorrow I can enjoy the result, but tonight only the performance. It is so intense. They play long balls, it was a wild game. There was a lot of action in the last few minutes. We were here to win the game, which is why we are not 100 per cent satisfied.' Those agreeing with Klopp's version of the narrative pointed to the shot tally — in Liverpool's favour by 13 to 9 — though this didn't take into account United's gambles and Liverpool getting shots in on the counter-attack. The long-ball stats also appeared to support the accusation, as United played 53 to Liverpool's 35. Over the season to date United had played 510 as opposed to Liverpool's 478; in the 'long-ball' league table, United were 12th and Liverpool 16th. This game aside, United had only played a dozen or more long balls over the season, and the reason why there were so many could be perfectly described by the events of games like these, where the opponent abandons their natural shape and condenses the space in front of goal. With all alternative options exhausted, United then deployed Fellaini and pumped balls into the box.

The difference on the spreadsheet, therefore, was more reflective of a negative approach from Liverpool than from United, regardless of Klopp's protestations. The attempt to suggest otherwise was symbolic of the growing trend in football; to refer to statistics which, when presented in isolation and out of context, support one argument. If it proved anything at all, it was simply that statistics in football games should only be used by people who completely understand the various complexities and circumstances. When spread out over the season and taking into account the number of late goals and home draws (now five), it really wasn't that sensational a number, and certainly not definitive enough to suggest that it represented United's style of football.

The counter-point to this arrives back at one of the initial concerns about Mourinho — that he wouldn't bring good football to United.

There had been enough entertainment over the past few weeks to dispel that, with the likes of Pogba and Mkhitaryan playing some good football, and there had been enough of that 'resolve' supporters were used to seeing with the late wins. It was different to the Ferguson era, of course it was, but it was a more familiar looking United side than supporters had seen for the previous three years. Describing a team as 'long ball' is to tag them with the label associated with the Wimbledon team of the late 80s and 90s, and when used in the context as Klopp was using it, it becomes a derogatory and almost defamatory statement, considering that style of football is 'beneath' what Mourinho described as the 'Einsteins'. It was as if it was almost against the rules; that in bringing on Fellaini, the United manager had broken some gentleman's agreement amongst the football purists who have all agreed that hitting a ball into the box in a certain way that the opponent doesn't like or isn't able to defend should be illegal. Where there can be some truth drawn from it — insomuch as United's brand of 'entertaining football' does not include the long ball as a staple, nor does that of most top teams — it's also dismissive to suggest the long pass can't be an art in itself. David Beckham, Paul Scholes and Juan Sebastian Veron were three magnificent passers of the ball over long distances, and Steven Gerrard was so revered for it on Merseyside that his passes were deemed 'Hollywood' (though this term was applied derisively and sarcastically by rival fans as he wasn't quite as gifted in this department as the aforementioned players). So, when does Hollywood become less glamorous, or a long pass become a long ball? One might suggest it depends on the shade of red of your football shirt. (Incidentally, little over a year later, Manchester City's Fernandinho and Roma's Daniele De Rossi described Liverpool as a 'long-ball' team, comments which were effectively two trees falling in empty forests in comparison to how Klopp's words were treated with validity by the press.)

Despite a draw at Stoke in the next game — earned by an equaliser from Wayne Rooney with the last kick of the game, which perhaps even more significantly was his 250th Manchester United goal, breaking the club record — and despite a defeat at Hull, by the time the January transfer window closed United fans were optimistic about their team's chances in the second half of the season. A title push looked unrealistic but the Hull loss was only by a single goal and was in the second leg of the League Cup semi-final so United were in the final by virtue of their 2-0 first-leg win. There had been progress in the FA Cup too, with a 4-0 win over Wigan which seemed more like a testimonial for Bastian Schweinsteiger. The German actually scored the fourth goal in what would be his penultimate game for the club, ahead of his move to Chicago Fire. By this time, Schneiderlin and Depay had indeed both been allowed to leave, to Everton and Lyon respectively, as Mourinho pruned his squad.

There was a sense of regret with all three departures and yet an almost universal backing of the manager with these tough decisions. Schweinsteiger had been a bit of a fans' favourite, thanks in part to his brother's social media postings which seemed to show that there was a genuine affection for the club. However, the German legend had divided some in the support due to his time out injured — not in itself a crime, though after he was spotted supporting tennis player partner Ana Ivanovic, when some felt he should be back in Manchester continuing his rehabilitation, patience wore thin. Patience had almost certainly been tested with Memphis Depay, whose level of consistency made some yearn for Nani; the winger's best form had been saved almost exclusively for Europe, and, even then, against some of the poorer teams. There was the concern that he had been let go prematurely, as there was too in the case of Schneiderlin. While Mourinho persisted with Marouane Fellaini (who had even been booed by some fans after that Everton disaster) it seemed baffling that Schneiderlin remained underused, particularly as he seemed to possess everything the manager normally liked in a holding midfielder. Still, the supporters were willing to accept that the experienced manager had seen something at closer quarters which meant this was not the case, and at least when Everton signed him United recouped what they had paid Southampton in the first place.

Following the ostensible marginalisation of Mkhitaryan which had eventually resulted in a recall where the playmaker was proving instrumental, Mourinho had, in this short space of time, earned the trust of the support who were probably on the fence. There was, then, at least a sense of togetherness and a support of the manager which may prove to be crucial with the business end of the season awaiting.

In His Own Mould

Manchester United went unbeaten for the following 11 league matches, to extend their run to a stunning 25 since they tasted defeat at Chelsea. Stunning, as a description, applies in this case only to the achievement; as commendable as it was, Jose Mourinho's team were hardly convincing. Those 11 matches after the closure of the January transfer window included five more home draws, against — consecutively — Hull City, Bournemouth, West Brom, Everton and Swansea City.

Without a shadow of a doubt, United's inability to find a way past the so-called lesser lights of the league had significantly undermined their title challenge and yet, despite the last of those draws against Swansea being as disappointing as it was, United were somehow still in with a shout of fourth place. The result put them in fifth, one point behind Manchester City and Liverpool ahead of them. Summing up the season very nicely indeed, the result came three days after United achieved a commendable 0-0 draw at neighbours City, despite suffering with an injury list which just kept growing relentlessly.

United had won the League Cup in February — thanks to a late winner from Zlatan Ibrahimovic — but even Mourinho's status as the first-ever manager of the club to win a major trophy in his first season wouldn't necessarily be enough to see that campaign described as a success if he was unable to qualify for the Champions League. Fortunately, as the season came into its final month, United had two chances at this, thanks to their continued progression in the Europa League.

The schedule had been punishing. United needed extra time to overcome Belgian side Anderlecht in the quarter-finals and that victory had come at a significant cost. Marcos Rojo, the defender who had overcome that potential black mark against his name following the reckless challenge against Everton, had more or less made the position alongside Eric Bailly his own, but after 23 minutes he pulled up and had to be replaced by Daley Blind. Just before full time, Ibrahimovic landed awkwardly and had to be taken off. After a season where he had defied all expectations to score 28 goals, he would now be missing for the climax — and worse still, it was feared that the legendary forward's career would be completely over — as it was confirmed he had suffered serious ligament damage. Pogba too picked up a knock and, against Swansea, Bailly and Luke Shaw both had to be substituted, and with Jones and Smalling both out of action, United were desperately short of defenders ahead of their semi-final tie with Celta Vigo. Mourinho admitted that he had been disappointed with the England centre-halves, believing that they should be able to play through the pain barrier. 'It's not just about them,' he said. 'It's about the philosophy and mentality around them. It's not just about them and you know we go with the players we have. [Smalling and Jones are] cautious. Cautious. Cautious. Just a cautious approach. It's a profile. It's the philosophy of work. Just that.'

Bailly battled through the pain barrier to play against Celta Vigo; a game decided by a magnificent free kick from Marcus Rashford. The tie sandwiched a league game at Arsenal, and with United still to visit Tottenham, Mourinho took a significant gamble when he heavily rotated his team. Axel Tuanzebe, a player many had wanted to see being given regular game time earlier in the season, was given his first start at the Emirates. Jones and Smalling were selected to play (Bailly and Blind had played in Spain, a clear sign of who the manager felt were first choice) and so too were Juan Mata, Wayne Rooney and Anthony Martial. The game was closer than it had any right to be, going into half-time level as it did, before Arsenal scored two goals early in the second half to put it in their favour. It was far from a vintage game and the relatively poor Arsenal team made it easy to suggest that Mourinho could have got a better result here had he picked a full-strength team. With fourth place achievable, it seemed inconceivable that a Manchester United manager would clearly disregard it; but the post-match comments from Mourinho showed a man who was happy to defend his decisions. 'We made eight changes. Of course, we knew we were not coming in our maximum power. That's a decision. We want to try to win the Europa League — it's more important than finishing fourth,' he admitted. 'The last trophy I won was three months ago. I didn't care about that. Thursday is the match of the season. I hope Old Trafford feels the same, because we need Old Trafford.'

Seventeen minutes into the second leg, Marouane Fellaini headed in Marcus Rashford's cross to give United a distinct advantage in the tie — 2-0 up, and with home advantage, it should have been a formality; however, staying true to the narrative that Old Trafford had become something of a Theatre of Frustration, United failed to put this game away and the visitors grew in confidence. United had been involved in some great semi-final performances, and atmospheres, in Europe over the years; this was not one of those occasions. Despite Celta residing in 12th place in La Liga and despite having lost their last five matches, the visitors bossed possession — having almost two thirds of the ball — and had begun to realise their only hope was to go for broke.

Having put all of the proverbial eggs in this basket, United's players resembled a team disconcertingly aware of the fragility of the eggs — Roncaglia equalised in the 85th minute and the prospect of a humiliating turnaround seemed close to reality. Two minutes later the tension boiled over and, after a heavy challenge, Bailly took a swing at former City striker John Guidetti. Roncaglia then swung for Bailly, and the referee sent both off. Guidetti's involvement in the tie, however, was not yet over, and in the six minutes of added time he was presented with an easy chance to win the game for his side, but fired wide of the goal.

By the skin of their teeth, United were through, with Ajax the opponents in the final where the value of Mourinho's gamble would be determined. 'We were the best team in the first leg but we never kill, we never score goals related to the chances we have,' the United manager said of his side's performance. 'It was an open game at home, all the pressure on our side. They were completely free of responsibility and gave us a very hard match. We suffered until the end and it was open until the last second. The boys gave everything they had. I'm really pleased for them. After 14 matches, we are in the final. If we win the Europa League, I am more than happy. It would be amazing.'

For better or for worse the United boss had personally taken the risk on, and when he rotated again for the game at White Hart Lane — effectively handing a very strong Tottenham side the three points — it seemed as if the manager had given up on fourth place in the league completely, therefore surely increasing the scale of the gamble. It would have been a decision that was more palatable if the games were simply games United were not going to win; the swing in points in these crucial encounters effectively ruled the club out of the running for that last Champions League place in the league, and their following game, a 0-0 draw at Southampton (which was only a draw thanks to an early penalty save from Sergio Romero), confirmed it.

Mourinho's heavy rotation went a step further for the final league game of the season. Paul Pogba was selected in the starting line-up only because he had recently missed some games due to the death of his father, and so the decision was taken by the player to play and get some minutes under his belt. Eric Bailly, suspended for the final, and Phil Jones, who wouldn't be selected, were both picked. Jesse Lingard was also picked, and the player who had scored the winning goal in the previous season's FA Cup Final hoped to do enough in this performance to force his way into contention for selection against Ajax, even though it seemed as if he would have to make do with a place on the bench. This was the same situation that Wayne Rooney found himself in, too, though the legendary striker's marginalisation in the second half of the season meant his selection here was more likely to be the opportunity for a goodbye. Mourinho had managed the Rooney situation magnificently, giving the player all of the respect that his achievements at the club had earned, but also moving forward with the players in form. So the remainder of the team against Palace — goalkeeper Joel Pereira, Tim

Fosu-Mensah, Axel Tuanzebe, Scott McTominay, Josh Harrop and Demitri Mitchell (four of whom were getting their first starts) — gave the side more of an 'under-23' look, and was indeed the youngest line-up the club had ever fielded in Premier League history. Fears of a heavy defeat were real but unfounded; United's young stars put on a magnificent display that was reminiscent of the 4-0 win over Galatasaray in 1994. Josh Harrop scored a superb goal and Pogba added a smart second before being withdrawn for Carrick. With two minutes to go, Rooney was taken off to a standing ovation from the crowd and replaced by Angel Gomes.

This occasion, then, turned out to be slightly more memorable than it otherwise would have been. For a club who had drawn 11 of its home games, Mourinho might have learned a lesson from observing the way that the crowd got behind a team comprised of young players. It wasn't necessarily a reason to suggest that they should always play, of course, that's a stretch too far, but it was enough of a reminder that it could well prove to be a valuable galvanising tool. Even if Old Trafford can be apathetic, one thing it will always do as a collective is get behind a young player. For a manager still learning and coming to terms with working for Manchester United, he would do well not to discount the importance of this possible advantage. At the time, though, his concentration was fully on the Europa League Final. He purposefully attended his post-match interview while the players were giving their end-of-season lap of honour so that he could avoid speaking to journalists.

Football, however, took a back step from the headlines the day after the Premier League season ended when a terrorist attack at the Manchester Arena killed 22 people who were attending popstar Ariana Grande's concert. The news shook the entire city, particularly as young children were amongst the dead, and it was suggested that the Europa League Final would be postponed. With United scheduled to travel to Stockholm (a city that had suffered its own terrorist attack the previous month) on the Tuesday afternoon, UEFA issued a statement that morning saying that the game would go ahead and attempted to reassure travelling fans that extra security measures were in place.

Despite all the pressure about the ramifications of winning or losing, the major concerns were whether or not recent events would prove to be overwhelming for United's players; in this context, victory or defeat barely mattered, as supporters would have forgiven their players for their minds being elsewhere. It made for an incredibly emotional evening and the United stars instead put on a spirited display; in the 18th minute their bright start was rewarded when Paul Pogba's deflected effort went in. From then on, it felt like a classic Mourinho affair, as much as it could in the circumstances. United were occasionally edgy in the first half but once they scored a second just after the break — Mkhitaryan cleverly flicking in a Smalling header — they were able to see the game out. It was possibly the least eventful of any European final United had won and definitely the most comfortable. After a year of ups and downs and some uncertainty about the way he had gone about things, this was certainly a trademark of Mourinho that United supporters could easily become accustomed to.

Mourinho himself had gone through a period of adjustment. He had learned that at Manchester United the scrutiny that accompanied performances as well as results was quite unlike anywhere he'd known before, even at Real Madrid. The sensationalist and instantaneous way football media had evolved meant conclusions were now being reached every week, and at Old Trafford those reactions were magnified more than anywhere else in the country. That climate, in English football especially, creates a situation where perception is quite often king. There promised to be a significant swing on the perception of how successful Mourinho's first season in Manchester had been depending on the result in Sweden. Lose and it would undoubtedly have been seen as a disaster, even with the League Cup.

Even if his position hadn't been untenable, those late-season team selections would have had United supporters questioning his judgement. What a difference one win makes. Instead, Mourinho had delivered one of the club's greatest triumphs, with its best-ever season outside of Busby and Ferguson. There were still questions to be asked and there was still progress to be made — the biggest question that is relevant to this book is just how close was Jose Mourinho to what constitutes a true Manchester United team, and how much of the success of the 2016/17 season was borne out of the manager's own tried and trusted methods?

A case for the defence

One must answer the last question of the last chapter in multiple ways. The first of which is how that relates to the club, which is the point of this book, the second, how it relates to the manager, and the third, how that success was built upon in the future.

Within each of those answers there are various strands and so to start at the beginning we need to consider the core identity of Manchester United. Ask anyone and they'll give you different answers — they'll tell you about tough-tackling midfielders, flying wingers, and outrageously gifted showmen. They will tell you about a traditional 4-4-2 or about late goals. All of these play a part but there are fundamental values at the root of all of this which were the mandate given to Matt Busby and Jimmy Murphy back in the 40s, when it is relatively safe to say the true identity of Manchester United was born. The first was that the people of Manchester should be entertained on a Saturday; the second was that the team should be populated with young players. These are the core philosophies of the club — of course, a third must be added, because with these values, success was achieved, and United's status as England's most successful club means that success is essentially the primary barometer of judgement. If it can be achieved with the implementation of the holistic values then all the better, but so long as a manager is successful, he could probably get away with not concentrating so heavily on young players getting a chance, and, really — at least for a certain period of time, until it became intolerable — he could probably get away with not playing a magnificent brand of football. Without success, however, even if the manager was the nicest guy in the world, it is difficult to imagine that just playing attractive football, even with a team of young local players, would be enough for a manager of Manchester United to remain employed for many seasons. That is, of course, the cause of modern football, and this evolution means values and the application of them must be adjusted accordingly. It means that we must consider how practical it is, in this post-Bosman, oil-money-infused era, what constitutes success and how practical and reasonable expectations are.

If United's recruitment of the Busby Babes was a lottery win then just how fortunate was their class of 1992? This isn't to say one was better than the other, but consider the star names from the 50s, Bobby Charlton and Duncan Edwards. One from the North East and the other from the Midlands. United's success in the 1990s was based on the likes of Giggs, Scholes, Butt and the Nevilles, all of whom were local lads. That kind of fortune has only happened once ever in British football, and that was then. If that sort of breakthrough happens only once every 100 years, well, even if it happened in the next ten, are the conditions of British football conducive to the development of those players so that they all play at the top level, let alone at the same club? The odds are high.

What of the manager? History tells us that it requires a certain character to oversee transition, someone strong enough to deal with the change, particularly if that change involves — as it has twice in United's history — the phasing out of successful players by new managers. Could Jose Mourinho have had the success he had in his first season, or could he have done even better, if he had been the one chosen to succeed Sir Alex Ferguson in 2013? It's a great hypothetical and one most people would presume to be the case; however, it should not just be taken for granted that he would have been able to walk into Old Trafford and everything would go as swimmingly as we expect. He would still have probably made the same judgement calls as David Moyes did, which were described earlier in this book as understandable errors in judgement. Of course, what Mourinho had in his favour was a track record of winning, but even then, imposing change on an experienced dressing room? And then having to tell some of those players that their time was coming to an end? Players who were every bit the winner that Mourinho was? It is not inconceivable to hypothesise that it could have all gone very wrong very quickly.

At the end of October 2017 Manchester United had enjoyed their equal best start to a Premier League season ever, but you wouldn't know it from the reaction. United's season had got underway with a little bit of an education. After a pre-season in North America which was much more to Jose Mourinho's liking than his first one, the first competitive game was the European Super Cup with Real Madrid. The build-up to the game focussed around the possible transfer of Gareth Bale.

Real were adjusting to life in the transfer market as the club who were no longer the big dog; in some respects, just like United had to, they relied on their historical lure. In the summer of 2017 it's fair to say that money trumped romance. In a move which escalated quickly from 'that can't be true' to a stadium unveiling, Neymar went from Barcelona to Paris after the French club activated his buyout clause of €222 million. This major transfer was undoubtedly going to have a huge ripple effect and Real felt their chances of securing Kylian Mbappe, the Monaco prodigy, would be dealt a blow due to Barcelona's requirement for a replacement.

It had been another frustrating summer for Madrid, who had started it expecting to sign David de Gea again. Most United fans had accepted it and had supported Jose Mourinho's decision to play Sergio Romero in the Europa League just about all the way throughout the competition. There was some suggestion that Romero deserved his shot at the number-one jersey, while others speculated United may move for a goalkeeper, with Atletico Madrid's Jan Oblak one of the prominent names mentioned. Real Madrid were celebrating being the first club to win the Champions League (under its current guise) in back-to-back years though it quickly became apparent that they would be priced out of any realistic move for De Gea. On 15 June

Sunderland goalkeeper Jordan Pickford signed for Everton for a deal worth around £30m; Pickford was undoubtedly a fine prospect but Sunderland had been relegated and it was certainly an eye-catching sum of money. That was followed a few weeks later by Kyle Walker's move from Tottenham to Man City — the right-back cost £50m. It made United's £30m move for Victor Lindelof — the Swedish defender who might have come in in January — look reasonable, but also demonstrated how difficult business might be in this hyper-inflated market.

As always, United had been linked to a plethora of names, with Eric Dier of Spurs and Alvaro Morata of Real Madrid the two most mentioned. Madrid were spending their summer trying to offload Morata and James Rodriguez to raise funds for their chase of Mbappe; though United had been linked with both of those players, as well as the utility man Fabinho from Monaco, it was clear that their number-one target in the summer had been Antoine Griezmann. Ahead of the Europa League Final, Griezmann had gone as far as to state on television that his chances of joining United were '6/10', a reference to whether or not they would qualify for the Champions League. United, however, were reluctant to activate the reported £87m buyout clause in the player's contract (you would have imagined that would have been less of an issue in August as opposed to June, with the nature of how quickly transfer fees went through the roof) and, with the deal dragging on, Atletico were hit by a transfer ban, which meant they would be unable to register any players until January. It meant that their own move to sign Diego Costa from Chelsea was put on hold and Griezmann released a statement saying he would stay at Atletico.

It was a blow to United, whose front line was looking rather threadbare. Captain Wayne Rooney had been allowed to return to Everton on a free transfer and the club's 'retained' list did not include Zlatan Ibrahimovic, whose contract had expired. With the severity of his injury, United opted to wait and see how the player's recovery went through the summer before offering a new deal. With mounting speculation that they would move for Morata, all sorts of permutations were presented again — that De Gea would go the other way in a straight swap, or that United might still try and use it as some sort of leverage to get Bale.

Just after 8am on Saturday, 8 July, United caught the football world by surprise by announcing that they had in fact agreed a deal with Everton for their striker Romelu Lukaku. This transfer by itself sparked a chain reaction; Lukaku had been the primary target for new champions Chelsea and the Blues submitted a bid to match United's, but Lukaku wanted to move to Old Trafford. Chelsea then moved for Alvaro Morata; the Spaniard had dyed his hair red in one of the more obvious 'come and get me' pleas, but was forced to accept the move to Stamford Bridge.

Chelsea were quietly the chief protagonists in United's most important transfer business of the summer; the Lukaku move had apparently upset Chelsea officials so much that it was said there was no way that they would allow Nemanja Matic to move to United. This was an area of the side Mourinho seemed keenest to address. While Paul Pogba had impressed those who had watched him first hand — the number of times he hit the woodwork and the amount of chances he created which were spurned by team-mates almost had to be seen to be believed — the jury at large was still out on him and there was no doubting that the addition of a screening midfielder would be crucial to the next stage of his, and United's, progression. With Matic an unlikely target, United were instead linked with Dier of Spurs. There were rumoured bids for Dier, supposedly a United fan, which were of course dismissed. Perhaps Jose Mourinho had not yet been sent the memo about Daniel Levy's infamous reluctance to deal with United over transfers. Speaking of memos, Mourinho cut a frustrated figure on the America tour, leading to suggestions he was unhappy that Ed Woodward had yet to secure the final two transfers that he wanted. One was that holding midfielder, and the other was a wide man, widely thought to be Ivan Perisic, the left-sided Inter Milan player.

Almost as soon as United arrived back in Europe, news began to break that they were making a serious move to sign Matic. Chelsea's position had weakened due to their own acquisition of Monaco midfielder Tiemoue Bakayoko. With him and N'Golo Kante, there was no reasonable place for Matic in the squad. Chelsea had accepted that they would have to sell the Serbian international and had tried, without success, to negotiate his transfer to clubs overseas. Juventus were the most serious bidders but they were unwilling to participate in the inflated market — the move was dead in the water when Matic informed his club he wanted to move to Manchester, not to Turin. On the last day of July it was announced that United and Chelsea had agreed terms; soon after that, Matic was a United player.

It left the Perisic deal as the remaining piece of business — at 29, United were not willing to pay over the odds for a player who would probably have no real resale value, while Inter, understandably, didn't want to lose a star player on the cheap. So, with the club in Macedonia for the Super Cup, the talk was on United going for Bale as an alternative. Mourinho was happy to say as much in his pre-match press conference. 'Well if he's playing tomorrow, no. It's because he's in the coach's plans and because he also has that motivation to continue at Real,' he said. 'If he is not in the club's plans, that with the arrival of another player would mean he was on his way out, I will try to be waiting for him on the other side and fight with other coaches that would want him. But if he plays tomorrow, that is the best confirmation he is wanted by the team.'

Bale did play — and Mourinho described the prospective transfer as 'game over' — as Madrid gave United a bit of a lesson in their 2-1 win. In the first half, Zidane's side played with the quality everyone knew they had, and it took United some time to come to terms with it. When Isco made it 2-0 in the 52nd minute (adding to Casemiro's first-half goal) it was no less than the European Cup holders deserved. Mourinho then made a few changes which would come to define his early teams of the season. First of all, Rashford was brought on for Lingard, and then Fellaini was brought on for Herrera. United became much more combative as a force and much more threatening as an attacking team — Romelu Lukaku missed a great chance even before he pulled a goal back on his competitive debut in the 62nd minute. Madrid, the clear favourites before the game, held on, and United's frustration with not being able to get anything from the game was a reflection of how close it had been, and what a good account they had given of themselves.

United didn't sign Bale and couldn't get Perisic; they also had little trouble keeping hold of De Gea, and Madrid were left completely frustrated when Paris, having already signed Neymar, then signed Mbappe. Whilst almost every reaction to the news was 'What about Financial Fair Play?!', Paris announced that in fact the deal was only a loan deal, and that the £150m fee to make the transfer permanent would be paid in 2018, making the news *much* more palatable.

Back in England, Manchester City were the country's big spenders again, splurging over £215m on Walker, Monaco pair Benjamin Mendy and Bernardo Silva, and Brazilian duo Danilo and Ederson. It was a major injection of cash, mostly to address defensive issues, but when City started the season with the kind of form you would imagine from a club who had enjoyed well over £1 billion of investment on its playing staff from scratch, they were inevitably heralded as the choice of the purists. The level of expenditure between the clubs in Manchester, and then again with the rest of the league, highlighted the contrast in resources. Chelsea spent almost £200m strengthening their title-winning squad, whereas City's investment under Guardiola had allowed the manager to address all of his concerns and all of the team's weaknesses in one fell swoop. Mourinho wasn't quite so fortunate in that he had to prioritise, meaning that the critical areas of attack and midfield were concentrated upon more than the defence. Nonetheless, United's own flash summer meant that they would be expected to compete.

Their own start to the season had been impressive. Their perfect start in August — two 4-0 wins over West Ham and at Swansea respectively, and a 2-0 win over Leicester — was impressive enough, though the minor details seemed to make it even more so. These were the sort of games United had struggled with the previous year, but with Romelu Lukaku as a mobile front man who would cause defenders more problems with his movement as opposed to the less mobile Ibrahimovic, and with Nemanja Matic providing the solid midfield defensive screen which enabled Paul Pogba to solely concentrate on influencing the game where he caused most damage, United were much more well equipped to deal with teams who arrived at Old Trafford with the intention of nicking a point. It was a significant advancement which the players deserved credit for, and so too did the manager, who had identified how to resolve the issue and had done so with comprehension. There was a bonus counter-point. With teams now having to put in the extra effort to chase United and then chase the result, it meant Mourinho's late changes were punishing for opponents. The fresh legs of the likes of Jesse Lingard, or, in particular in the first two games, Anthony Martial, were absolutely devastating for defences to deal with, and routine 2-0 wins became impressive 4-0 destructions.

The clamour was for Martial to start and so that call was answered against Leicester. The former champions were far more difficult to break down — Mourinho brought on Rashford, the forward whose place was taken by Martial, and the keen young England forward made his own impression within five minutes by volleying in from a Mkhitaryan corner. Despite drawing at Stoke, United's fine form continued, with 4-0 wins over Everton and Crystal Palace sandwiching a less-than-convincing 1-0 win at Southampton.

The perception of United's September was less flattering than how most had reacted to their August form. The size of the bigger scorelines had apparently flattered them and Man City's run — where they had defeated Liverpool and Crystal Palace 5-0, and won at Watford by six before a very impressive schooling of Chelsea in a 1-0 win at Stamford Bridge — meant Guardiola's team were most definitely the one in favour with journalists.

City enjoyed another perfect month in October, winning 7-2 against a Stoke side with decidedly less fight than the one who had played against United, 3-0 against Burnley and then 3-2 at West Brom. The Stoke result in particular was one enjoyed by reporters, with *The Telegraph* describing it as 'the Guardiola blueprint being executed in vivid Technicolor … a victory for the purists' and Stuart Brennan, Manchester City reporter for the *Manchester Evening News*, tweeting 'MCFC need to win the title for the sake of football'.

The hyperbole was prompted in part by United's dour 0-0 draw at Anfield earlier in the day. Just as it had in both previous encounters, the blame for the poor match was put squarely at Mourinho's door. Without question, there was a selection of the United support left frustrated once more. The same issues with defence had been exposed numerous times already throughout the season, and even though United were missing Paul Pogba — who had been in inspired form, but had picked up a hamstring injury in the first Champions League game — and Marouane Fellaini, who, alongside Matic, had transformed his game as a dependable and even valuable member of the team, supporters still hoped that Mourinho would set his team out to earn a comprehensive victory.

Before the game United were dealt a further blow when it transpired Eric Bailly had been injured on international duty and so Mourinho had to play Smalling and Jones at the back. Ironically, the injuries meant that his side was more offensive in formation than the team which had played this fixture almost exactly a year prior; the irony is because despite the result being exactly the same, so was the reaction, with Mourinho being perceived as the spoiler.

Anthony Martial and Henrikh Mkhitaryan didn't enjoy their best games and it meant Lukaku was isolated up front for most of the game; barring a moment of quality where Martial flashed into life and played in Lukaku, only for the Belgian striker's effort to be saved. Liverpool had their own chance when Joel Matip was denied by a brilliant instinctive save from David de Gea. Mourinho, again hoping that Klopp would gamble so that his game plan would pay off in victory, was again left frustrated by the German's own pragmatism, though afterwards Klopp once more attempted to change the narrative.

'I'm sure if we played like this, you could not do this at Liverpool. Obviously for United it is OK,' the Liverpool manager sneered. 'It's quite difficult when a top-class team like United has that defensive approach. I think United came here for the point and they got it. We wanted three points and didn't get it. We were dominant, it is a home game for us so we should be dominant. I am okay with the performance — it is not my job to judge the United performance. For me today, one team who can become champion this year was in our stadium and is not a world apart from us. It's not that we are playing different planets and they are really good and we do not find the entrance to the stadium.'

Instead of pointing out that United had in fact scored eight more goals than Liverpool in just eight games, or indeed that he had set up his team far more positive than Klopp had done at Old Trafford, Mourinho concentrated instead on the events of the game, saying he was reasonably happy and pointed out that Liverpool's best chance came from a set play: 'In the second half I was expecting more but what I was fearing happened,' the United boss said. 'They play with a very strong midfield, with three real midfield players, we only had two. I was waiting for them to make an offensive change, to try more, but he never did it. He was "very offensive, very offensive, very offensive" but 90 minutes with the same players? He didn't try anything. He was afraid of our counter-attack and I tried that with Lingard and Rashford because I had no way to improve my midfield.'

Klopp's withering and derisory put-downs were repeated in paraphrase and at length by some sports writers, presenting the inflated impression that Liverpool had actually been impressive themselves, and completely missing the fact that Mourinho had already won two trophies in his supposedly 'unacceptable' way. Taken in the context of it being an admittedly poor performance in arguably the biggest fixture of the season, some criticism of the manager had to be fair. Many defended Mourinho, saying the result was hardly a disaster, and the performance was hardly worse than some others from other managers in recent years, even Sir Alex himself.

It was a pragmatic approach and, although the grey area between setting a team out not to lose and setting one out without a real intention of winning meant that too many people confused the former for the latter, there was no doubting that with Mourinho's reputation *for* pragmatic football, and the tendency of the football media to reach constant, definite conclusions in all matters relating to Manchester United on a game-by-game basis, a) the manager would have known what to expect from the post-match reaction and b) the perception therefore barely mattered. It became a subplot that, in earning a draw, United had matched their best-ever start to a Premier League season; it was perceived as the closest thing to a defeat a genuine United first team had tasted in the league since the 4-0 humbling at the hands of Chelsea almost a year before, and so it was treated as such.

Thankfully for the press they didn't have to wait too long until the real thing — seven days later, United lost to newly promoted Huddersfield Town, and, the climate being what it was, a blip was turned into a crisis, turning what was already one of the most embarrassing results in the Premier League era into a real problem for Jose Mourinho.

The most prominent feature of that Huddersfield defeat was the performance of the ring-rusty Victor Lindelof. Midway through the first half, Phil Jones did as he often had in the past, and pulled up injured. Jones, to that point, had arguably even outperformed Eric Bailly in general over the season, certainly establishing himself as the first choice to pair alongside the Ivorian. There were some concerns — outlined by the goals conceded in the 2-2 draw at Stoke, where both central defenders might have done better for each goal, though Jones's lapse of concentration from a corner for one of them certainly the less expected from a defender at the top level — but it was worth pointing out that until this game those were the only goals United had conceded in the league. Within ten minutes of his introduction, Lindelof found himself taking the lion's share of the blame for the hosts taking a two-goal lead. The Swede's positioning was off, and yet one might attribute that to his lack of familiarity with his team-mates in senior games to that point. It didn't reflect well on Jose Mourinho, whose choice to integrate the defender into first-team action on a gradual basis appeared to have backfired, at least as far as this result was concerned.

To chase the game, Mourinho brought on Mkhitaryan; here was a player whose own assimilation to the first team had followed a similar path to Lindelof's, and it could be said that by and large the Armenian had been a success so far, although the margin of that opinion was narrow and determined by his goal in the Europa League Final. Ahead of this game, the playmaker's form had been called into question, and he had been dropped to the bench because Mourinho had wanted more urgency. Bringing the player on when United's need was even more urgent? If it was a prompt for him to show he could be relied upon then it was a gamble that didn't work, on a day when little else did.

United won against Swansea to continue their defence of the League Cup, but all eyes were on their game against Tottenham on the last weekend of the month to see if the team could respond to their poor recent form. With Spurs travelling to Old Trafford on equal points with United, and both sides five points behind City, it was a day when a draw would suit neither team. Mourinho wasn't exactly able to answer his critics with the performance; he did a 'shushing' gesture to the television camera which predictably became the image of choice for most media outlets, but it was the result — a narrow 1-0 win, earned by an 81st-minute Martial goal — rather than the display which gave the boss some vindication. Spurs had been missing Harry Kane and their manager Mauricio Pochettino decided to play Son up front instead of Fernando Llorente, a more orthodox striker who came on as a substitute. Their approach was not dissimilar to United's own at Anfield, but the relentless driving rain made it impossible for either team to really showcase their footballing ability.

The victory meant United were still on track in equalling their best-ever Premier League start. Their first ten results read: P10, W7, D2, L1, F23 A4, Points 23.

Compare that to their first ten results of the previous season: P10, W4, D3, L3, F13 A12, Points 15.

Add into this United's perfect Champions League record, which had seen them win 3-0 at home to Basel, 4-1 at CSKA Moscow and 1-0 in Benfica, then there was almost little room to complain about how Mourinho's second season was going. In comparison with the competition, then only City could boast a better start to the season, and if Mourinho was truly being judged by comparison to City's results with the investment they had enjoyed, then the issue surely rests with the parameters. (In the interest of fairness, it's worth pointing out that the performance of Mourinho and United should, too, be evaluated on their respective resources against other clubs) City had spent over £100m in the summer of 2017 on full-backs alone — they were in need of regeneration in that area, but it's worth pointing out that, in the likes of Bacary Sagna and Gael Clichy, they had already used their new-found status to poach some of the star names from rival teams in the league. The point, however, is that in comparison with their own performance, instead of comparison with their rivals, United had most definitely progressed (though even the latter point could be argued too, in general). This does not mean United were absolved of responsibility to compete. The club had been in a similar position a couple of times before in the Premier League era, against Blackburn Rovers and especially Chelsea, and had developed a team that was worthy of defeating their domestic rivals.

After winning against Tottenham, Mourinho used his post-match press conference to address the seemingly constant stream of hyper-analysing. 'Some people speak too much,' said the United boss. 'You know, calm down, relax. Relax a little bit. Don't speak too much — speak, speak, speak. You know, relax … relax a little bit. Don't be so nervous, don't be so excited. Calm down a little bit.'

Speaking in his position as a pundit for Sky Sport's *Monday Night Football* show, Gary Neville offered the suggestion that Mourinho was similar to another legend of the sporting world. 'I would say Pochettino and Klopp have reputations for being wonderful attacking coaches, but Mourinho is a bit like [Floyd] Mayweather,' Neville said. 'Mayweather was called boring at times where he used defence as a weapon and let others tire themselves out. Klopp in that game the other week didn't feel like he could fully go for it because he thought Mourinho could do him with a Mourinho masterclass. Tottenham lacked the belief to really go for it because I think it gets into their heads. "I can't get done on the counter-attack, he'll do me." He deserves more respect. That little shush was "be quiet, I'm going to do it my way and we are going to win my way."'

United's supporters generally lapped up Mourinho's gesture, but they weren't so enamoured with his comments in the match programme ahead of the next game against Benfica in the Champions League. 'I hope you enjoy the game more than some of you did against Tottenham,' Mourinho wrote, in an oddly-timed swipe at the fans. Old Trafford was not quite its most boisterous against Spurs, though there were the odd intermittent periods where the volume was louder than usual. It was thought to be a reaction to United supporters booing when Marcus Rashford was substituted for Martial against Spurs; but Mourinho's own response seemed over the top considering these are the sort of innocuous events which occur in many football matches. For the manager to apparently have taken it personally when the reality was that it was simply a show of support for the withdrawn player seemed to be creating an issue where there wasn't one. The sign of a manager feeling the strain of leading the premier club in the country? Or the frustration of a coach who felt he was being unfairly criticised?

Smoke and Mirrors

Manchester United won 2-0 against Benfica to all but rubber stamp their qualification to the knock-out stages for the first team since they were reigning champions of England. One more point was needed from two games to make it mathematically certain.

However, this progress was undermined by another league defeat. United were still without Paul Pogba but there was no place for sympathy or mitigating circumstances as far as the press were concerned. Manchester City's 3-1 win against Arsenal had put them eight points clear at the top, and despite Chelsea's awful defence as champions seeing them a further four points behind United who were in second, the general perception was that it was seemingly Manchester United's responsibility, on behalf of the country, to challenge City for the title. Jose Mourinho may have already sniffed the change of mood, and to that end he seemed to at least attempt to address the criticism which had come his way, by lining up with a 3-4-3 formation. It was, on the face of it, a bolder approach than he had tried at Anfield, no doubt based on the knowledge that Antonio Conte was under some pressure to win the game himself, so he was more likely to take a gamble than Jurgen Klopp had been.

Despite a more encouraging approach from the boss, United's players instead put in a flat performance, and were punished for their defensive frailty when neither Phil Jones nor Chris Smalling were within the proximity of Alvaro Morata, who rose unchallenged to head in from the edge of the area. It was, again, the kind of defensive mishap which undermined any real ambition of winning the league. In normal circumstances, these sort of incidents over the course of a season could hopefully be learned from and not become too costly. With the Manchester derby looming on 10 December, United knew that it was crucial that they win every game up until that point.

They did so — Pogba's return inspired a 4-1 win over Newcastle United, but United were anything but inspiring in a 1-0 win over Brighton. With the impressive Watford, and Arsenal, to come in consecutive away games before the derby, there was no room or margin for error. At Vicarage Road United put in one of their finest displays of the season, scoring four stunning goals to win 4-2. That was matched by a blistering start to the game at Arsenal, where the hosts' own generosity helped United establish a two-goal lead in the first ten minutes.

A compelling game unfolded as Arsenal poured everything forward in search of rescuing a result — United were inspired by Paul Pogba, who was the dominant figure, orchestrating counter-attack after counter-attack. Mourinho's team were also grateful to David de Gea in goal who had a fine display, but it was Pogba's performance which left a lasting impression. The Frenchman had faced criticism for his performances in his games but his absence had been badly felt in United's trips to Anfield and Stamford Bridge. Now the team had Nemanja Matic to shoulder some of that discipline, Pogba had the space to control and dictate the game, and the way he did so against Arsenal only gave further cause to lament his injury-enforced absence earlier on in the season. Pogba gave a highlight-worthy clip to summarise his influence on the game by turning his compatriot Laurent Koscielny inside out in the Arsenal box before laying the ball off to a grateful Jesse Lingard. United won 3-1, but that wasn't Pogba's final act of the game — he was dismissed for a bizarre challenge on Hector Bellerin. The defender's own body shape looked unnatural and Pogba almost had little option but to collide with the Spaniard; still, an outstretched leg certainly made the challenge look very ugly and a red card was inevitable. It was a crushing blow, as Pogba would now miss the Manchester derby. There was the quietest talk of an appeal, and technically United may have had a case, but there was a greater probability of an appeal actually increasing the suspension.

Qualification to the knock-out stages of the Champions League was belatedly assured with the sort of routine win over CSKA Moscow which had become notable by its own absence over the preceding years. Romelu Lukaku scored in a 2-1 win, only his second goal in two months, which would hopefully provide a much-needed boost of confidence ahead of the derby. Lukaku's build-up play had been quite impressive at Arsenal and there was no chance of the forward being dropped, but there was now, nonetheless, the rumbling that a bad run of form was all well and good, but the player needed to regain his confidence and quickly. If Lukaku had answered some critics by making the step up to Champions League level with apparent ease, then there was still some valid judgement being considered about the Belgian's capability to score in the truly big games.

The level of concentration on Lukaku's performance had nothing on the spotlight which was being focussed on Jose Mourinho; the United boss might have felt suitably prepared with a) previous experience of the British press and b) a hostile relationship with the media as Real Madrid manager, but even he would have had his eyes opened over the winter of the 2017/18 season.

Memories appeared even shorter than the list of mitigating circumstances which were attached to United's dismal derby defeat to City on 10 December. The two trophies won in Mourinho's first season were apparently erased from comprehension as City continued to plough their way through opposition and looked set for a record-breaking season, with many who claim to be neutral already set to proclaim Pep Guardiola's team as the greatest in Premier League history before the turn of the year. As early as October, that question had been posed on Sky Sports' *Sunday Supplement*. Liverpool-supporting journalist Tony Evans suggested in a column for *ESPN online* that the only team to compare with them were Arsenal's 2004 team: 'They are arguably the most exciting side to watch in Premier League history,' Evans wrote, in the wake of City's 2-1 win at Old Trafford. There were narrow margins — City's goals came from defensive errors by Lukaku, of all people, who then missed a gilt-edged chance at the other end. Mourinho complained about a penalty claim on Ander Herrera in the last minute, but it appeared to most as if the Spaniard had dived. In truth, the difference between the sides seemed much greater than the single goal and probably greater than the 65 per cent possession City had, and probably greater still than the Paul Pogba-shaped hole in United's midfield. It could be claimed that Mourinho got his selection wrong but he had only the rookie McTominay on the bench in terms of midfield numbers — with Matic and Herrera the only senior players in that area, it was always an area of the pitch and game United were going to be conceding from the off.

It was a game where the reality of the resources available to either manager exposed themselves bare for all to see.

The difference between United and City could roughly be summarised by their right-back situation; Mourinho had a 32-year-old converted right-winger there, Antonio Valencia, who cost £16m when he arrived from Wigan Athletic in 2009, ostensibly then as a replacement for the recently departed best player in the world. Valencia had been moved back into that area due to his inability to command a place on the right wing, his natural position. He had made that position more or less his own since David Moyes lost faith in Rafael, the low-cost Brazilian who had impressed so much in Sir Alex Ferguson's last year.

By comparison, Pablo Zabaleta was one of City's first post-takeover signings, a player fit for purpose at right-back at £6.5m in 2008. The Brazilian Maicon was bought for £3m but failed to make an impression; City then used their financial leverage to convince another player to leave Arsenal, acquiring Bacary Sagna, one of the league's most in-form right-backs, in 2014, adding to their title-winning squad of that season.

Post-takeover, and prior to Pep Guardiola's arrival, Manchester City's spend on their defence had clocked in at approximately £275m. The senior defence (including goalkeepers) in the squad he inherited collectively cost £120m. One of his first actions was to replace the England international goalkeeper for another goalkeeper, Claudio Bravo, who cost approximately £20m, and then bring in the most highly rated English defender, John Stones, for almost £50m from Everton. Almost exactly a year prior to the Manchester derby in the 2017/18 season, Guardiola's City team had been beaten 4-2 at Leicester City. Their defensive performance was widely criticised after conceding two goals in the first five minutes, prompting Guardiola to come out after the game and insist, 'I am not a coach for the tackles so I don't train the tackles. What I want is to try and play good and score goals … What's tackles?'

City were good enough to finish third, and their defence good enough to concede 'just' 39 goals, but Guardiola sought to eradicate the problem entirely by launching an unprecedented transfer splurge on his defence. First of all he signed Benfica goalkeeper Ederson for a record £35m, rendering Bravo a £20m aberration. Then Kyle Walker, the best right-back in the league, was prised from Spurs in a stunning £50m transfer. Monaco's Benjamin Mendy, the most impressive left-back from the previous season on the continent, followed for £52m, while Real Madrid full-back Danilo arrived for £26.5m to act as cover. It took Guardiola's own spending in defence alone, in just over one year, to £233.5m.

United's defence against City had been the £16m Valencia, £10m Chris Smalling, £16m Marcos Rojo and £18m Ashley Young, signed in 2009, 2010, 2014 and 2011 respectively, with the first and last on that list being converted wingers. This presents an admittedly skewed look but goes some way to explaining the level, scale and speed of regeneration City's resources afforded them as opposed to those available to Mourinho. Of course, the United manager had money to spend; £61m had been spent on centre-halves Eric Bailly and Victor Lindelof. But even accounting for that, and the fact that there was the £27m Luke Shaw, £17m Phil Jones, £14m Daley Blind, and £13m Matteo Darmian who were also inherited, the difference in what was available was plain to see.

As if to hammer home the point, United were defensively all over the place in consecutive 2-2 draws, first at Leicester City and then at home to Burnley, either side of Christmas. After the latter result, it was suggested to Mourinho that United's run of poor form was 'unacceptable'. 'One thing is a big club and another thing is a big football team. They are two different things,' Mourinho responded, after bemoaning the concession of more, as he described, 's' goals. 'We are in the second year of trying to rebuild a football team that is not one of the best teams in the world. Manchester City buy full-backs for the price of strikers. When you speak about big football clubs, you are speaking about the history of the club.'

It was then put to Mourinho that more should be expected considering he had spent 'around £300m' (the real figure was around £261m). 'It is not enough,' he said, to the delight of mischief-making headline writers across the country. 'And the price for the big clubs, the price for the big clubs is different from the other clubs. So the big, historical clubs are normally punished in the market for that history.'

Predictably, Mourinho's comments were treated as laughable by the press, who concentrated more on the headline than the context. In a straight comparison, Guardiola had spent 'only' £100m more than Mourinho in 18 months, and, according to most observers, that meant that the difference in class should not be as evident as it seemed to be in their most recent head-to-head, even accounting for Pogba's absence. Some thought Mourinho's comments suggested problems were deeper, that he was getting his excuses in early, lining up for a supposed exit.

The issues at United were more complex, however. While a generous percentage of the support were willing to still consider that United were a work in progress and also accept that City's comparative resources meant that competing with them in the short term was unrealistic, there were others who were not quite so content. In some ways Mourinho was a victim of his own success. His double cup win, having been achieved with four of his own signings in addition to the composite squad, had suggested more success was to follow. It was, however, achieved in typical Mourinho fashion; the 2016/17 season had started with the team playing pretty good football, and then, as the business end approached, the pursuit of winning became the priority, so much so that it wasn't only aesthetically pleasing football that was sacrificed, but the league too. This was anathema to United supporters in general, and especially those who had harboured concern about hiring Mourinho for precisely these reasons.

In the wake of the 'not enough spent' comments, there was a fascinating subplot in the January transfer window in the shape of Alexis Sanchez. The Chile international striker was set to leave Arsenal at the end of the season as his contract expired. He had been widely tipped to join Manchester City, with Guardiola making a £60m bid to sign him on deadline day in August 2017. The move was apparently so close to being done that the *Manchester Evening News* had reported that the player had already been allocated the number-nine shirt.

Arsenal, though, refused to play ball unless they secured a replacement, and were none-too-pleased by City's bullying tactics. Despite most feeling they should just cut their losses, they sent a message to City by keeping hold of their player. It had the expected effect, and Sanchez's form was nowhere near as prolific as it had been the previous season. When January rolled around, Gabriel Jesus picked up a short-term injury. Instead of making do, Guardiola again flexed his club's financial muscles by advancing the move for Sanchez. Instead of waiting for the summer, when they would have got him for nothing, City made a £20m offer. Arsenal, still incensed, but now realising they had little option but to sell, agreed to let him go for £35m — a fee City would not agree to, as they believed they had everything in place with the deal.

Perhaps sensing they could benefit from the frostiness of the relations, United then made their own enquiry for Sanchez, suggesting to Arsenal that they would offer £25m. It opened the pathway of communication and it quickly became apparent that Arsene Wenger was interested in Henrikh Mkhitaryan. The Armenian's inconsistent form at Old Trafford was currently in one of its deep dips, and so Mourinho agreed. It was, however, the former Dortmund schemer whose deliberation over a move to London caused a lengthy delay to the transfer. In the time between the speculation breaking and the confirmation of the transfer, reports of Sanchez's potential wage at Old Trafford went anywhere from £275,000 to £600,000 a week. While Mkhitaryan took his time to decide, Manchester City boss Pep Guardiola announced that they were withdrawing from negotiations, with most sources citing it as a 'matter of principle', despite City never having reached an agreement with Arsenal in order to hold negotiations with the player.

Amusingly, this was all played out against the backdrop of United's desperation — they were presented as a team hugely over-paying for an ageing player who was due to be out of contract, while City had achieved some form of moral success for refusing to pay around £10m more for a temporary replacement for an injured striker. There was also apparently a message sent out by the champions-elect

— you don't mess us around and expect to get another chance to sign.

'Normally we try to be stable with the wages of the players because I think it is good for the team and stability of the club,' Guardiola told the press. 'In the past, what the club did, was at that price. What happened last summer, everything increased amazingly. You have to adapt to that. I think the price in the summertime will be higher than this winter. Sometimes you have to anticipate that. We've spent a lot of money, we can't deny that, but I've never put pressure on a club when they believe it is too much. Immediately I accept that decision and move forward to find another solution. The stability of the club is the most important thing.'

For United fans there was something especially poetic about City's behaviour during the rest of January. First of all, Gabriel Jesus recovered to play again within the month, and then after suffering another short-term injury, this time to Leroy Sané, Guardiola's response was to again dip into the transfer market. City's 'informal' offer for Leicester City's Riyad Mahrez was a stunning £60m; Leicester's chief executive, Susan Whelan, followed the first rule of negotiations — never accept the first offer — and instead suggested what *The Guardian* reported as a 'package' of £95m, which would include a player. If we are to hypothetically suggest that the unnamed player may have been valued at £20m, the idea of another £15m being added by Leicester — all things considered in the present market — didn't seem so absurd. Manchester City, however, felt they could force the issue, and refused to budge. They didn't sign Mahrez (until the summer, when they reneged on that 'second-chance' policy when their repeated £60m move was successful), and Sané was soon back from injury. City did make their own move in January, spending a huge £57m on the uncapped but highly rated young French defender Aymeric Laporte from Athletic Bilbao.

Sky Sports' Guillem Balague had tweeted in reference to the Sanchez transfer that it was a choice of 'Pep or money' for the striker — this followed the commonly accepted narrative that a footballer interested in playing in the right way would — could, even — only be interested in furthering his footballing education under Guardiola, while a move to United and Mourinho could only be about money. Wherever you stand on the comparison, there is no doubting that

Guardiola's style of play is expansive and expressive. He likes his teams to be dominant and to control the game. At Barcelona one could argue that he was fortunate to inherit three of the best players of all time — Lionel Messi, Andres Iniesta and Xavi — and at Bayern Munich the team he took over were European Champions, while the point about the resources he has at City has already been made, so it's a straightforward and fair point to suggest he has been hugely blessed with the jobs he has had. One could look at the job he did at Bayern and argue that as a club they regressed from the situation they were in compared to when he arrived, and, equally, look at that largely unimpressive first year in England and reason that Guardiola is a great coach of great players, rather than a specialised improver, as his generous reputation perhaps suggests.

Raheem Sterling is a case in point — his poor 2016/17 season seemed a distant memory compared to how he played for most of 2017/18. Guardiola was heralded as having got the best out of the winger, but could it really be said that Sterling was a true beneficiary of specialised coaching more than following his own lofty career trajectory and potential as suggested by the big fee City had paid for him?

Regardless of how true and accurate the praise for his rival is and was, it was just another issue for Mourinho to handle. It was an issue exacerbated by United's own poor form in the games after Sanchez arrived. The idea of signing one of the league's best strikers seemed a great one on paper. Lukaku had filled a void, temporarily at least, in that he was able to score against the so-called smaller sides, a problem for United the previous season, but the team still seemed to be lacking a real consistency up front. It wasn't a case of Sanchez arriving in Mkhitaryan's place; these were not like-for-like players.

The issues caused by Sanchez's arrival were apparent on his league debut at Tottenham Hotspur. The brightest spark of United's stuttering winter form had been their away game displays. With Paul Pogba, Jesse Lingard and Juan Mata ably assisted usually by the in-form Anthony Martial on the left, United had stumbled on a combination of players who were playing football which was far more attractive than the reputation they were getting in the press. In games at West Brom, Leicester, Everton and Burnley, that quartet (save for Pogba who was suspended at the Hawthorns) created a plethora of opportunities. It was clear that something would have to give because the numbers didn't add up; additionally, Sanchez's favourite area on the pitch was the area where Martial and Rashford had combined to largely successful effect so far during the season.

What gave was Juan Mata — and also the shape of the team. Having been given pelters for his pragmatism at Anfield and Stamford Bridge, Mourinho lined up with a two-man midfield of Pogba and Matic and an ambitious four-man attack of Martial (from the right), Lingard through the middle, Sanchez on the left and Lukaku through the middle. There was little chance to see how effective this combination might be because Spurs scored within 15 seconds, catching United's left-hand side cold. Young, Smalling and Jones did not cover themselves in glory and exposed United's greater issues. Despite their attacking riches, Mourinho's side could not impose themselves on the game. The two-man midfield was overrun and Spurs could have won by a more handsome scoreline than the 2-0 they eventually achieved. Inevitably, Mourinho was criticised for supposed naivety; that criticism was intensified less than two weeks later when exactly the same team lost at relegation-threatened Newcastle United by a single, farcical goal. Chris Smalling dived near the halfway line and from the resultant free kick United's defence was stationary as the Magpies scored.

Their defensive issues were well documented, well documented enough for it to be as much an issue caused by the current manager as the previous ones. Valencia, Smalling, Jones and Young — and David de Gea in goal, too — were all brought in by Sir Alex Ferguson and have survived three changes of manager. Valencia and Young can, to an extent, be given much praise for their reinvention. And, when errors occur, they can be understandable. By the same token, it is also understandable that, despite lofty predictions, Smalling and Jones were not the next Ferdinand and Vidic. Louis van Gaal deserves credit for the improvement of those players as individuals and a collective, and so does Jose Mourinho, and in normal circumstances one could easily contend that United's unarguable progress under Mourinho would be enough to have them identified as contenders. There was, however, a much harsher spotlight now, and a narrower allowance for errors. Points had been dropped at Stoke City, Huddersfield, Chelsea, Leicester City, Tottenham Hotspur and Newcastle due to defensive errors. Supporters perhaps had every right to question the manager considering the form of Luke Shaw had been more impressive than Young, and the fact that there were two centre-halves signed by the manager who were not playing (though, admittedly, Eric Bailly was out injured). It was against the manager's track record — against most top-level manager's, to be truthful — to throw in the rookies Axel Tuanzebe and Timothy Fosu-Mensah, so both were out on loan. Nonetheless, the point is that there were theoretically huge improvements to United's defence that could be made in-house without the need for further expenditure.

Some, however, attribute United's failure to muster a proper league challenge down to the more traditional criticisms levelled at Mourinho. After all, despite the league race being all but over by the end of February, both City and United had conceded just 20 goals with ten games left to play. The difference was at the other end — City had scored 79 goals by the same point, compared to United's 53. It didn't matter that United's record was the same as the much-celebrated 'free-scoring' Spurs side, or that it marked a second consecutive year of improvement in front of goal, and, to be fair, the criticism was not unwarranted.

The arrival of Alexis Sanchez had brought United's attacking play into sharp focus and it seemed that the signing was more opportunistic than carefully planned, due to the subsequent issues and teething problems. In fact, it was suggested that Mourinho had assembled his attackers with little care or consideration, hoping instead for individual brilliance rather than setting out a tactical blueprint. It seemed a fair suggestion to at least ponder, considering the conflicting styles of some of the forwards compared to the fluency which had been developing prior to Sanchez's arrival. As United laboured to that defeat at St James' Park, it became a fair assessment to suggest there could even have been regression in Mourinho's short reign, at least from May 2017 to February 2018. At the end of the 2016/17 season, United, for better or worse, were starting to resemble something which looked like a Mourinho outfit, what with its solidity and strong, physical spine. Despite having all of those components in February 2018, the cohesion of the side did not seem as well structured as it had in the Europa League Final.

The overriding point, and to return to the central theme of this book, was whether or not Mourinho's game plan, 18 months in, was compatible with something that was recognised as the *Manchester United way*. Or, equally, whether it contradicted it.

The first thing to say is that the progress, in whichever way you wish to summarise it, from the David Moyes era was measurable by whatever means you choose. In the league you can choose games won, goals scored, goals conceded or final position. In the cup competitions the progress is there for all to see, as is United's return to the Champions League. Visually, they were more appealing in the 2017/18 season than at any point under David Moyes, and more difficult to beat in general, more difficult to beat at Old Trafford, and more fluent and varied in attack (and this despite Moyes taking over the champions).

Louis van Gaal's era was remembered for dull, slow football — ironic, given that his first pre-season seemed to promise so much by way of the opposite. In those admittedly very early days, it's fair to say that Manchester United supporters were all for embracing a new 'philosophy', even if it meant a change in formation. Seeing how aesthetically pleasing it could be when executed well, should the blame rest with the players or with the manager? And, more pertinently, considering that United's own fans were more than happy to adopt a different style of play, it's worth returning to the issue of what is fundamentally important about the club's identity that is a) worth preserving and b) worth mentioning when referring to managers' adherence to it.

All of Ferguson's successors have remained faithful to the club's record of bringing through young players. Mourinho's list of almost 50 players at his unveiling might well have been stage-managed fun, but it was serious business in February 2018 and no token gesture when Scott McTominay was selected to play against Chelsea at Old Trafford. It was only his tenth league appearance and so clearly a considerable ask, and yet not a selection made out of desperation. Ander Herrera was injured but McTominay's form had impressed Mourinho so much that there is every reason to believe the youngster would have been given the nod anyway. He was impressive in helping to control the midfield as United won 2-1 — a victory earned by a header from Jesse Lingard, another youth product enjoying the best time of his career under Mourinho.

It was another local lad, Marcus Rashford, whose brace defeated Liverpool a couple of weeks later. Liverpool's own progression under German manager Jurgen Klopp had also been heralded in the press, with former Chelsea and Roma forward Mo Salah having a fantastic season. Liverpool would finish the season in fourth place and one point worse off than the prior season, although the general perception of anyone who had cause to harbour any fondness for the team from Anfield was that they were the second-best team in the league and best placed to challenge City.

Against United, however, Salah was anonymous, and Mourinho's game plan — surprisingly simple — worked a treat. Klopp had £100m worth of centre-half on the pitch in former Southampton pair Virgil van Dijk and Dejan Lovren, yet it was precisely this area Mourinho exposed to win the game. Twice, Romelu Lukaku won headers against Lovren, and from the resultant knock-downs, Rashford scored to settle the game in the first half.

The wins against these famous rivals had been achieved in the manner which suggested there could well be a compromise in styles that was faithful to United's own identity and wouldn't require such a shift in Mourinho's. So when the manager said, 'Sevilla and Brighton are more important games than Liverpool' after the game, with a reference to those games being in cup competitions, there was an acceptance rather than an objection. Having faced much criticism for his record against the better teams at United, Mourinho now could point to recent victories over Spurs, Arsenal, Chelsea and Liverpool, but was quick to put things in perspective: 'It says nothing,' he declared. 'In modern football you have to live day by day, week by week and match by match. We have a match in two days and I can imagine that if we lose against Sevilla on Tuesday everyone will have forgotten what we did in the last couple of weeks.'

Which was all well and good, only, not only did United lose to Sevilla in the Champions League, they went out with a whimper, and for the first time a large section of the fanbase expressed anger at the manager. His selection of Ashley Young against Liverpool had been a masterstroke; Young kept Salah quiet for the entire game. It seemed natural, therefore, that Luke Shaw would come back in to provide natural width on the left. He didn't. Elsewhere, Paul Pogba — who had missed the Liverpool game with an apparent injury —

was only named as a substitute, with Matic partnered by Marouane Fellaini to create a midfield which hardly screamed dynamism. And so it proved. The performance was controlled and uninspiring; as the game remained scoreless moving into the second half, the first-leg result of 0-0 looked every bit the deceptive scoreline they tend to be. Sevilla scored not once, but twice — and United's urgency arrived much too late, with Lukaku's goal not even a consolation.

Mourinho insisted that he didn't think his team had performed poorly. 'In the first half, I don't remember a dangerous situation for them,' he said. 'It was good control from them but without any kind of danger. We had again a good start in the second half and had chances to score.'

If eyebrows were raised by his insistence that the performance was acceptable, then ire was raised by his following remark about the club's historical standards. 'I sit in this chair twice in the Champions League and knock Manchester United out with Porto and Real Madrid so is not something new for the club,' he said. 'Of course, being Manchester United manager and losing a Champions League tie at home is a disappointment.'

Taken on face value, there was little wrong in what Mourinho said, and certainly nothing untruthful. Reading between the lines, the manager was downplaying the severity of the exit by suggesting the club's recent history did not justify such high expectations. With similar firefighting comments from the likes of David Moyes and Louis van Gaal still relatively fresh in the memory, it was not what supporters wanted to hear. It also sounded very much like self-preservation, defending his own record instead of — as, in fairness, he had in his first six months at the club — speaking up the club's expectation levels and the hopes of fans.

Gambles are part of sport, and generally speaking United supporters will forgive a risk chasing a reward, even if the gamble doesn't pay off, so long as the risk was a positive one. Mourinho had flirted with the wrong side of this theory when fielding weaker sides in the league when a Champions League place was still up for grabs towards the end of his first season. Choosing to bench Pogba was a pragmatic risk which backfired spectacularly.

A dull 2-0 win over Brighton in the FA Cup ensured progress to the semi-final, where they would face Tottenham at Wembley.

Following the international break, United then brushed aside Swansea City 2-0, scoring both goals early in the first half to provide a surprisingly warm flashback to the days when such routine victories were commonplace. The win set in place an occasion which had appeared to be an inevitability for a few weeks — the return Manchester derby at the Etihad Stadium on 7 April. United's run of four consecutive victories in the league meant that they had at least avoided the professional shame of giving their nearest rivals a guard of honour on to the pitch, but that was scant consolation for the few thousand reds who made their way across town to witness what would be a blue party in the event of a home win, which would seal the destination of the title, as predictable as the end to that particular race had become.

The build to the game had a slight twist through the behavioural quirks of Pep Guardiola. City were coming into the match having lost 3-0 in the first leg of their Champions League quarter-final with Liverpool at Anfield. They had won the League Cup but had suffered an embarrassing FA Cup exit to Wigan Athletic. Having been hailed as the best team in Europe prior to their short visit west, City were now faced with a rather different prospect of how this season would pan out. It was supposed to be unprecedented — City, with all of their fortune and all of their brilliance, would sweep all before them. And yet one by one those expectations were put into check. The 3-0 'European' scoreline put the United game in a different perspective. Here was a once-in-a-generation, once-in-a-lifetime even, opportunity to win the league against their nearest rivals. Of the few meaningful records there were left to set, winning the game and the league against United would also break United's own record of how early they'd won it back at the turn of the century.

For Guardiola it was about game management — he knew he could not field a weakened team against United in the remote hope that his team would score four goals without reply a few days later. There was rotation. In came £26m reserve defender Danilo, with Bernardo Silva (a player who cost more than £40m and had featured as many times as any other player that season) and Ilkay Gundogan (a player whose performance levels had been compared favourably and directly to Paul Pogba's on multiple occasions) the other 'reserves' brought in.

City would start the game as favourites regardless, and yet, in what was perhaps the first suggestion that Guardiola was not coping well with the scrutiny, the City boss launched an astonishing swipe designed to cause unrest the day before the game. Guardiola's relationship with agent Mino Raiola was well known to be difficult, Raiola seemingly holding a grudge against the former midfielder from their relationship at Barcelona, where the Spaniard had apparently mistreated Zlatan Ibrahimovic (who, by now, had moved on a free transfer to Los Angeles Galaxy). On 25 March Raiola had been quoted as describing Guardiola as a 'coward, a dog' of a man, despite being a 'fantastic coach'. Since then City had played against Everton and Liverpool but the City boss waited — perhaps with purpose — until the eve of the United game to claim he was offered the chance to sign Paul Pogba in January.

'I will answer him; I don't understand why I am,' Guardiola said. 'Finally, the people discover my secrets — a bad guy. I'm a coward. I don't understand why I am a bad guy. I never speak with him so his opinion about me, I don't know. But being a guy who two months ago offered me Mkhitaryan and Pogba to play with us — Why? Why the offer? He was interested in Mkhitaryan and Pogba to play with us? So he has to protect his players and has to know he cannot bring the players to a guy like me, like a dog. And comparing a dog is bad. It's not good. He has to respect the dogs ... I said no [to Pogba]. We don't have enough money to buy Pogba because he is so expensive. I'm surprised because I am a dog. He wants his players to come to here. So, no. No way. I am not a good guy. He deserves his players to play with better guys. But he knows as well I am a top manager. Thank you.'

It was unchartered territory for a manager to enter into in the British game. It was perhaps the last honourable boundary left to cross, one where managers had taken a silent vow with each other to protect one another. Players were difficult enough to control as it was, and their agents notoriously and increasingly difficult for managers to work with, without managers getting involved and talking about which opposition players they have been offered. It was a precedent, and a pretty ugly one, not befitting someone of the holy and dignified reputation the press had bestowed upon Guardiola. Mourinho's response, on this occasion — clueless, apparently, and dismissive

— was played perfectly. Nobody needed to debate whether or not Guardiola's comments were true or not. In a way, that was barely the point. It would not have been a surprise to any United fan to hear that Raiola had tried to elicit interest in his star players. It was his job to keep them in the news. The agent would have known that there was little chance of United selling their top star to City — and even less of it happening in January. Was it part of a negotiating tactic to get Pogba a new deal? Or the start of a machine to move Pogba on to another club? These kind of events happen so often in football that the only remaining surprise was Guardiola's apparent need to make it public. The motivation for doing so was obvious. If Mourinho was smarting from the comments, he did not show it. It is conceivable that in the context of a one-off game, he would have been pleased to see Guardiola resort to such desperate measures.

All things considered, United were on a hiding to nothing in the derby. Despite this, Mourinho selected a strong side, with the emphasis on work-rate. A three-man midfield was picked, with Jesse Lingard and Alexis Sanchez providing support for Lukaku. It was a game plan that seemed to work; more than half of the first half went by with the visitors comfortably dealing with the champions-elect. Perhaps City fans were still reeling from the psychological blow of how heavily their team had been beaten, but the Etihad Stadium hardly felt as if it was hosting the most momentous day in the history of the club. Indeed, it seemed United's biggest danger was themselves, and so that proved in the 25th minute. Antonio Valencia sliced a clearance behind for a corner when one might have presumed a more natural right-back would have been able to deal with it more comfortably. From the resultant set play, Chris Smalling watched as the man he was supposed to be marking, Vincent Kompany, thundered in a header. Heads dropped in the United defence and five minutes later Gundogan toe-poked home a second goal. Raheem Sterling then made a mockery of just how highly Guardiola's work with him had been talked up, as the former Liverpool winger was guilty of missing a hat-trick of easy chances provided to him by a generous United defence whose positioning was all at sea.

Half-time couldn't come quickly enough, and 2-0 was flattering to United at the break. The most reasonable of high expectations in the second half would be to try and regain the composure showed for the first 25 minutes and to try to avoid an embarrassment. Prior to the interval one could sense the mood had changed in the stadium; the early anxiety had completely dissipated, giving way to a mood of collective jubilation and even baiting. Every simple pass was greeted with an 'Ole', as if this straightforward footballing act had been carved by Michelangelo. In many ways this very game had followed the pattern of the journey travelled by City and their supporters over the last decade; they had been the unexpected beneficiaries of lavish generosity, and, with victory in sight, were triumphantly crowing in the ways one would expect of a football crowd.

United had already enjoyed a comeback to win in this situation against Crystal Palace, but nobody would have predicted the same thing to happen here, much less the speed in which it occurred. Within ten minutes Paul Pogba — whose anonymity in the first half had some genuinely questioning his motivation — had scored two goals to level it up; two goals scored in the sort of positions United supporters had been crying out for him to occupy. City, who had apparently become complacent in preparation for the post-match celebrations which had been scheduled, could not rediscover their own flow and then United hit a third through Chris Smalling. Guardiola rung the changes, bringing Sergio Aguero, Kevin De Bruyne and Gabriel Jesus, but United stood firm to record a famous victory and put City's champagne — with corks already popped — back in the fridge.

'Our challenge is to finish second, but I want to congratulate City for the title — because they are going to win and deservedly,' Mourinho said afterwards. 'They gave no chance to the others because they had this season of not stopping winning. My objective here was to get points and not spoil any celebrations. The point is can we improve enough to catch them next season?'

Eight days later City were crowned champions. They had been beaten by Liverpool in the second leg to exit the Champions League but overcame Tottenham at Wembley to put themselves on the brink of the title again. It was expected that they would have to wait until facing relegation-threatened Swansea City, as United faced bottom club West Brom at Old Trafford and were duly expected to win. Except the Baggies — for whom relegation was a practical inevitably — upset the apple cart and won 1-0 against Mourinho's team, handing the title to City somewhat prematurely. Having asked the question about improvement, the manager must have had a few answers given to him in a performance which was reminiscent of many of the worst days under Moyes and Van Gaal, and, fittingly so against West Brom, whose post-Sir Alex Ferguson record at Old Trafford now read three wins, one draw and one defeat, having not previously won there since 1978. How could the players show such commitment one week and seem so lethargic the next? For many, the buck stopped with the manager, though the trend of not just the results but the nature of them seemed to indicate the problems ran deeper.

After the result against West Brom, it was again suggested that Mourinho, a man who had built a reputation on his tactical nous, was out of touch with both the game and his squad. As the 2017/18 season drew to a close and we reached a half-decade since Sir Alex Ferguson, it is an appropriate time to discuss the significant tactical evolution that had been experienced at Old Trafford since May 2013.

It is widely accepted that a typical Sir Alex Ferguson team at Manchester United would play 4-4-2. When this writer thinks about the quintessential 'Fergie' team it is difficult not to automatically think of the 1994 or 1999 sides. There are slight variations between the two, but let us first consider the common ground — a goalkeeper who has good distribution; dependable full-backs who have to be able to join in the attack; a ball-playing centre-half and a rough and ready centre-half; midfielders who could feasibly and fairly be described as 'box-to-box'; wingers, and a strike partnership.

Of course, some of the players in the 1994 and 1999 sides were the same. Peter Schmeichel, Denis Irwin, Ryan Giggs, Roy Keane, too, while Nicky Butt and Gary Neville were breaking through. The differences between, say, Paul Ince and Bryan Robson or Keane, or Keane and Nicky Butt or Paul Scholes were not so pronounced; neither were the differences between Steve Bruce and Gary Pallister or Jaap Stam and Ronny Johnsen. David Beckham was a departure from Andrei Kanchelskis, the former relying more on his industry and delivery of crosses as opposed to the latter's tendency to dribble and penetrate defences with speed. The Eric Cantona and Mark Hughes partnership was also different to Andy Cole and Dwight Yorke; Cantona would drop deeper and even Hughes was barely considered a prolific striker. Both would bring others in to play. Yorke and Cole had a wonderful period where they not only benefitted from the service provided by others, but also each other, and both based their games predominantly around goals.

The style of football in both sides could be easily described as multidimensional. Both teams had enough aggression and physicality to not be bullied off the ball, and enough pace to devastate opponents on the counter. The quality talismanic footballers of the likes of Robson and Cantona were somewhat replaced by a natural fluency with the 'Class of 92' whose youth and familiarity with each other helped them dominate English football for years.

Even Ferguson's third great United side, from 2007 to 2009, more or less played 4-4-2. There were experimentations over the years. Brief dalliances with a 3-5-2 which barely lasted longer than 45 minutes occasionally occurred — in the 1996/97 campaign, the manager trialled a 4-3-3 system which lasted most of the Champions League campaign.

It didn't start well; Eric Cantona was lost as the uncomfortable spearhead of the attack and *The Guardian* reported he 'spent much of [the game] with his back to goal gazing down the pitch at what Juventus were doing to Ferguson's tactical plan'. A few months later, the same system was spectacularly effective, though the forward 'three' against Porto was a more conventional front line of Cole and Ole Gunnar Solskjaer in front of Cantona. *The Mirror* described United's 4-0 win as 'breathtaking' and described it as a 'renaissance of English club football led by a French captain and Scottish manager'. Cantona's retirement that May prompted further changes. Perhaps it was no coincidence that improvement came when United had to play their traditional 4-4-2 system against Juventus in October 1997. Even if it was a coincidence on that occasion, it was most certainly a deliberate 4-4-2 which played throughout the 1998/99 European campaign, as United and Ferguson concentrated more on their own strengths than any special requirements the continent may have.

So it was perhaps no surprise that further interference to try and follow the European trend again disrupted United's natural chemistry; Juan Sebastian Veron and Ruud van Nistelrooy were two of European football's absolute best, and while the latter smashed in a staggering 150 goals in five years, the former — whilst extravagantly gifted and enjoying his best form in continental competition — never really fit perfectly.

The team that won the Champions League in 2008 lined up in a 4-4-2, though the fluidity of Cristiano Ronaldo, Carlos Tevez and Wayne Rooney made the system of that team just as easily a 4-3-3 (in Moscow, it was a deliberate move to have Ronaldo from the left to try and expose — as he did — Michael Essien's height). On the night of the final, Owen Hargreaves played as a right-sided midfielder; this had been Ronaldo's default position, with Ryan Giggs the usual left-sided player. Giggs was no slowcoach but years of hamstring injuries had seen him develop and refine his style of play into a cultured play-maker from wide as opposed to the flying winger he once was. Paul Scholes was almost completely changed from the box-to-box scorer he had been nine years before; now he operated as a deep-lying dictator of the pace of games alongside Michael Carrick. Rooney and Tevez harried and harassed from the front.

One year before, in April 2007, Ferguson had stumbled across a system which seemed as if it would become his next tactical evolution, when he played a 4-2-3-1 against Roma. This featured Carrick and Darren Fletcher as midfielders behind a floating 'three' of Ronaldo, Rooney and Giggs. This central area was exposed to magnificent effect as United scored seven in what was arguably their greatest-ever European night (aside from the final victories). This system, alas, was rarely used again. There were variations of a 4-3-3 system used at various times; for example, at Arsenal and AC Milan in Champions League games. In the latter in 2010, Ji-sung Park was deployed as a 'reducer' on Andrea Pirlo. These were generally one-offs, dependent on the opposition, and even in his last season Sir Alex played — mostly — a traditional 4-4-2 with Wayne Rooney and Robin van Persie as his strikers.

David Moyes had barely enough time to establish any notable tactical shift, and even though he played the generic and straightforward 4-4-2 it has to be said that his two signings were players who arguably thrived in other systems, or at least roles better defined in other systems. Marouane Fellaini arrived as a midfielder who had caused more problems as a physical number ten; the tall Belgian wasn't notable for his fancy footwork. Juan Mata signed from Chelsea for a club-record fee of around £38m and he too was, by reputation, a number ten. Fellaini was played mostly as a conventional midfielder and Mata was tried in a number of different positions, though mostly from the right. At the time nobody could argue that United didn't need a more dominant midfielder or that they weren't in need of some creativity, and yet neither of Moyes's signings seemed to fit the bill in a straightforward way. Without doubt, Mata had the creativity, but the fact he was left-footed and also not the quickest meant he was an ill-fitting right-winger. Whether or not there was a greater long-term plan in place in the mind of David Moyes is unknown, but, certainly going by the admittedly short period he had to spend with the players at Old Trafford, the results were far from convincing.

It wasn't, then, until the arrival of Louis van Gaal that United supporters experienced their first real tactical revolution. A 3-5-2 system was used in pre-season, as earlier described. And it was quickly abandoned and then trialled again on further occasions throughout the season. Towards the end of his first season in charge, Van Gaal used a 4-3-3 system, with Fellaini effectively operating as a number ten. It was not pretty but it was pretty effective in helping United score four against Manchester City just a few weeks after hitting three past Spurs. These systems, and a 4-4-2, were used throughout Van Gaal's second year in charge. In the summer of 2015 Bastian Schweinsteiger and Morgan Schneiderlin were signed with the idea of giving the team a greater presence in midfield. It didn't work. Neither player impressed in their short spells at the club, Marouane Fellaini never really improved in terms of being the central midfielder United needed, and Ander Herrera, without a regular partner, could not settle down. Michael Carrick, now a veteran with increasing injury-related absences, remained the most reliable member of United's central midfield and that did not bode well for their chances of success.

The enthusiasm that surrounded the final three or four months of Van Gaal's reign laid almost exclusively at the feet of three players — Anthony Martial, who had started life at the club in impressive fashion, Marcus Rashford and Timothy Fosu-Mensah, who had stepped into the first team in an injury crisis and had played their way into actual contention for the rest of the season.

There was no recognised senior system for a prolonged period of time, nor were there any real areas of the team where players had made positions their own. In some cases, players were playing in different positions from one week to the next. Fosu-Mensah was indeed a case in point; the teenager was asked to play right-back, centre-half and defensive midfielder and performed admirably in all three roles. Marcos Rojo played at left-back and centre-half, as did Daley Blind, who would also occasionally moonlight in defensive midfield. Wayne Rooney, with his 'special privileges', moved between striker and midfield, as did Fellaini. Ashley Young played on both wings and in both full-back positions. Defensively and offensively there was no cohesion as no areas of the team had any real game time to establish any rhythm. Unsurprisingly, the results were inconsistent. While the deeper issues have been considered in depth much earlier in this book, it's worth at least revisiting the idea of Manchester United's 'tactical evolution' up until and including the Van Gaal era to consider its success, or, more accurately, the lack of it.

What went wrong? The first thing to say is that no system was ever pushed for a long enough period that it was deemed the manager's default formation. And so, with that lack of familiarity, perhaps judging the players is a little harsh. Had Van Gaal stuck with a three-man defence for 40 games — or, well, even 40 days — instead of 40 minutes, and had clearly defined roles and expectations for players within that system, perhaps it would be fairer to evaluate the tactical intelligence of the players and whether or not Old Trafford was receptive to it. Generally, Van Gaal favoured a possession-based game. During his reign, it seemed Van Gaal's demands were suited for more technically capable players than the ones he had; it often led to ponderous, difficult-to-watch games. The defence had improved and the midfield could hold on to the ball but these seemed like two different units, with the attack a separate entity of itself. United 's supporters were all too ready to embrace the idea and bought into the concept of a new philosophy; that word, however, became a punchline in the last four or five months of Van Gaal's tenure. While it's certainly a fair question to ask if United's players had the technical nous and intelligence to play in Van Gaal's style in a more aesthetically pleasing way, surely any reasonable study would conclude that the directive was never clear or convincing enough, even under a manager who was renowned for being autocratic. Critically, Van Gaal's prolific changing of systems would have surely given the squad less cause to trust his direction. And by the time that a system was used which seemed to show signs of success — the 4-3-3 in the early spring of 2015, for example — Van Gaal had already alienated members of the squad. For a coach so experienced and so reputed to be steadfast in his ways, it appeared he led by example instead with his own uncertainty. It wouldn't be the last time this charge could be levied at a United manager.

Lost in the relative failings of the manager or the players is the relative willingness of supporters to embrace a style of play that was so different to what they were used to seeing at United. As traditional wingers had become such a rarity, and possession-based football was all the rage, this departure from the familiar Manchester United way was significant enough in that it revealed that fans were happy so long as they were entertained. There were some who grumbled about the specifics, sure, but there was no specific loyalty to a formation or even, when it came down to it, specific roles such as wingers, as synonymous as they had previously been with the identity of Old Trafford's best teams. When it boiled down to it, there were three principles, two of them fundamental — to win, and to do so playing attractive football. If those objectives could be met playing 'homegrown' players (that is to say, players developed through the club, regardless of nationality in the modern age) then all the better.

How supporters rejoiced, then, to hear Jose Mourinho speak about 'specialists' for positions soon after he arrived. The success which was most familiar to United fans was his work at Chelsea, with a strong spine. Considering how weak and unpredictable their defence had been, relatively speaking, having this area addressed was a welcome prospect. Mourinho's first Chelsea team had been defined by a physically strong spine — John Terry at centre-half and Didier Drogba up front, with Frank Lampard picking up the pieces as the most advanced midfielder of a three in a 4-3-3 system. The players identified by Mourinho gave United fans cause to believe there could be a reproduction of that formation and style. Zlatan Ibrahimovic, Paul Pogba and Eric Bailly were certainly players of stature to provide missing physicality and presence, while there were enough supplementary players at the club who might theoretically fill in the other gaps. United had quantity, if not quality, in their midfield selection. Michael Carrick, Ander Herrera, Bastian Schweinsteiger, Marouane Fellaini, Morgan Schneiderlin — five players of differing qualities, with surely two of them capable of fulfilling Mourinho's requirements alongside Pogba. They had quantity, if not quality, in their centre-half area too.

The manager's track record of bringing through young players raised some concern, but only from those with a hyper-critical oversensitivity to it; the loudest voices on this score seemed to be those with an anti-Mourinho stance rather than genuinely proactive campaigners for young players. He had to at least be given a chance.

The one thing Mourinho was expected to do was shore up the defence. It transpired that this would be a much more difficult job than expected. The defence which won the title was Rafael, Rio Ferdinand, Nemanja Vidic and Patrice Evra. Only Rafael survived the Moyes era and his stock had fallen so badly that he was completely out of favour. Moyes's attempt to revolutionise and reinvigorate the back-line was done with internal players. For the biggest game of his reign, Bayern Munich at Old Trafford, Phil Jones and Alex Buttner were used as the full-backs. Jones had been the starting full-back alongside Ferdinand, Vidic and Evra for the first three league games of Moyes's reign. From that point, for the next five years, it would never be clear what United's first-choice, and therefore strongest, defence was. The earliest occasion where Valencia and Young were both used as full-backs was in a game against Hull City in November 2014. They flanked combinations of Chris Smalling, Marcos Rojo, Phil Jones, Jonny Evans and Paddy McNair.

Given time, and despite no distinguishable upgrades, Van Gaal's coaching most definitely brought the defenders on as a collective. From August to the end of November 2015, United's 23 games included ten clean sheets. That was the pinnacle. Van Gaal's last game, the 2016 FA Cup Final, had a defence of Valencia, Smalling, Blind and Rojo. That combination had played together in the calamitous 3-2 defeat at Upton Park 11 days prior to the final. They had also played together in the 1-0 win over Aston Villa on 16 April. Those 180 minutes were the sum total of their experience together, and although a long-term injury to Valencia that season hardly helped matters, it was hardly a ringing endorsement for the settlement of a defence, though it did at least seem that Van Gaal favoured Smalling and Blind in the centre, considering they had started the first eight league games of that season together.

With just 23 appearances in the league, nobody could say Daley Blind was first-choice centre-half under Mourinho, even if 39 appearances in all competitions meant that he was not exactly an alien either. It is somewhat surprising, nonetheless, that Blind was also selected from the start against Ajax in the Europa League Final of 2017; in fact, the only change to the defence who had faced Crystal Palace was Darmian in for Rojo. Two Van Gaal signings and two players who had been at the club since well before Sir Alex Ferguson retired (one of those, Valencia, had of course been repositioned in the Van Gaal era). With the pressure on in April 2018's FA Cup semi-final, Mourinho selected an entire defence from the Ferguson era — with Phil Jones and Ashley Young picked alongside Valencia and Smalling. It was the same four that started the final. They admirably stood firm in the semi-final, while a defensive error led to defeat in the final.

United's league finishes since Ferguson's retirement weren't false indicators, nor were the defensive records in that period. Even at their worst, United had never been heavy shippers of goals in the Premier League, the worst being 45 in 2002 and also 2000 (a season where they set a record for winning the league so early!). But there was nonetheless a consistent pattern of conceding almost a goal a game. Despite Van Gaal's excellent start in the 2015/16 season in this respect, United still conceded 35 goals. Mourinho took that number below 30 (just, with 29) for the first time since 2010, when the club's defence was arguably at its collective peak.

In the 2017/18 campaign, though many poor results could be dissected and attributed to individual defensive errors, it continued to be mean, with 28 conceded. United were, initially, as difficult to beat as they had been under Sir Alex Ferguson, with numbers in the 'loss' column beginning to resemble something supporters were more familiar with.

There could be no question that Mourinho's work had helped the club progress. His tactical approach had irrefutably improved the club's organisation from a defensive standpoint. The room for improvement, which could be made, represented some of the distance between United and City. However, this is a scale of improvement that would further be Mourinho's trademark; it would move United closer still to a typical Mourinho side.

If defensive errors accounted for the results at Stoke City, Huddersfield Town, Leicester City, at home to Burnley and at Tottenham and Newcastle, then we are suggesting that United could have conceded around seven fewer goals and picked up between ten and 13 extra points. It would still not have been quite enough to match Manchester City, but it would be somewhere approaching the miserly peak of Mourinho's first Chelsea team. To do that with a defence he largely inherited speaks volumes about his capability as a coach. The propensity for individual errors can be tackled and compensated with successful systems, but it can never be completely eliminated. United's league finishes since Ferguson retired *haven't* been false. Their improvement from seventh, fourth, fifth and sixth, to second, with a points tally which would have won them the title in some years, has to be attributed to the coach as well as the players.

It was a relative success, which also suggests that there was not the fundamental incompatibility between Mourinho's style and something which can pass as entertaining football. The goals-for column still read a little too low but it was nonetheless comparable with some of United's Premier League-winning sides. The return for the 2017/18 season was almost identical to the 2008/09 side which boasted Rooney, Ronaldo, Tevez and Berbatov. This is not to suggest that the United side in 2018 compares to those European Cup winners — that is clearly not the case. But it did suggest they were not as poor as Mourinho's reputation has been portrayed at Old Trafford. Certainly, their wins and performances in the bigger games in the latter half of the 2017/18 campaign were quite easily the best and most entertaining since the retirement of the greatest manager of all time.

Arguably the greatest catalyst for the short-term improvement in United's team under Mourinho was Nemanja Matic. Matic arrived as automatic first choice in the middle of the team, whether he was accompanied by one or two players. The changing of those systems on a weekly basis indicates two things; the first is obvious, and that is to say it is clear Jose Mourinho still hadn't settled on a first 11 which was an automatic choice. The second was that it was clear the manager hadn't settled on a *system* which was an automatic choice, although, as the 2017/18 campaign drew to its close, it did seem apparent that, at least for bigger games, the manager had decided that a 4-3-3 formation would give the best balance of protection and expression. However, this in itself revealed something of a major flaw in the transfer strategy. Matic's positive influence was only temporary, with many supporters feeling his presence was obtrusive as early as the end of his first season. The Serbian was 29. He was not a signing for the long term in any event, much less one that a team could be built around for the future.

The arrival of Alexis Sanchez from Arsenal was a pivotal moment as it revealed much about the manager's uncertainty about the balance of his side. Sanchez made his league debut at Spurs on the left-hand side of the 'three' in a 4-2-3-1; this was an uncharacteristically bold formation from Mourinho, who had faced heavy criticism for alleged conservatism earlier in the campaign. When United capitulated at Wembley, conceding in the first 15 seconds, Mourinho was criticised for not selecting a team with the necessary balance.

It was a tough call for the manager. The most vociferous of calls was to play a 4-3-3 system as this appeared to get the best out of Paul Pogba. But that meant a big selection headache up front. Zlatan Ibrahimovic had left for MLS, but Romelu Lukaku was an automatic choice up front. Sanchez's recent arrival meant he was always likely to be a prominent choice, which left one place in that forward line of three to be contested by Jesse Lingard, Anthony Martial, Juan Mata and Marcus Rashford. Mata was a favourite, while Rashford and Martial had endured similar seasons, starting well in competition with each other before struggling since Sanchez came in. Rashford, of the pair, had responded best to the challenge, as his double against Liverpool showed. Neither had shown the level of consistency of Lingard, who got the nod in all of the important games as he had deserved.

So, as the 2017/18 season ended, how far apart was the ideology of Manchester United from its current identity? And how close were they compared to any other time since Sir Alex Ferguson's retirement? Well, though Ferguson had tinkered with variations of different formations, he essentially started and ended with a 4-4-2 system. David Moyes never really strayed from that. Van Gaal did, to limited effect, though it was almost certainly established during this period that formations were the least important factor as far as supporters were concerned.

Antonio Conte's arrival at Chelsea saw him introduce a successful 3-4-3 system, which was also adopted by Arsenal for the latter part of the 2016/17 campaign as Arsene Wenger saw his city rivals win the league. Mourinho himself used a similar shape to take on Arsenal at the Emirates in December 2017, coming out successful in a 3-1 win, but his most commonly used shapes at United were 4-2-3-1 and 4-3-3. Again, there was no resistance, generally speaking, to using formations other than 4-4-2, though there were inevitably objections which occurred along the way when it came to a certain system not helping one player or not providing a place for another. This was, to be clear, never an issue of conflict with Manchester United's ideals, rather the perennial and never-ending grumbles from the stands, newspapers and television pundits. It may have occasionally been projected as an issue about United's historical standards, but the argument appeared weak on the basis of evidence of the previous half-decade.

Initial fears that Mourinho would completely disregard the tradition of youth players seemed unfounded a couple of years in. Taking aside the last day of the 2016/17 season, when a bunch of young players made what were effectively token appearances with some being moved on before the next season, Mourinho, on the balance of things, was probably more proactive with this aspect of the job than many would give him credit for. One could argue that he did not place as much faith in young players as Van Gaal did in times of injury worries, but such an argument could fairly be rejected with the reference to Scott McTominay's inclusion in important games.

The strongest concern, and by far the most valid, was the idea of entertaining football being played, or lack of it. For this point it is worth pointing out that entertaining football and 'goals scored' are not mutually inclusive or exclusive terms that definitively prove anything, as the reference to United's 2008/09 season illustrates.

The summary point is that United's 4-4-2 system had gone, and their first team now played a 4-3-3. The criticism wasn't about the system, rather the effectiveness of it. It was a fairly straightforward 4-3-3, used in some respect to public demand to try and get the best out of Paul Pogba. It was not a system that was counter-productive to good football and indeed it had featured in most of United's best performances in the latter half of the 2017/18 season. It would be a stretch to consider that this 4-3-3 system was the permanent representation of United in the same way that it was the hallmark of Mourinho's Chelsea teams. And, in that regard, United could be considered the closest they had ever been to a new permanent system, but not quite there yet. As close as they had been to a system, but as far away as they had been from their 'ideological' identity.

* * * *

Some would fairly have said Mourinho played a 4-3-3 which was too pragmatic to play against West Brom at home. On this occasion, having seen Pogba flourish in the same role previously, the selection could not be questioned. Victor Lindelof had been selected ahead of Eric Bailly, and Juan Mata had been chosen instead of Jesse Lingard, because Mourinho anticipated that his team would need patience and spend a lot of time on the ball. Patience became sluggishness and the familiar problem of an inability to impose themselves, or galvanise themselves, to show the requisite commitment levels to win a game where they were heavy favourites to. Without question this is an issue that is the responsibility of the manager; however, it was an issue he inherited, not one he caused, and, having seen the dichotomy and polarisation in performance from one week to the next, even a manager as experienced as Jose Mourinho should be entitled to scratch his head like the 75,000 in attendance at Old Trafford.

If it is fair to say it is a problem he inherited, then the matter only becomes further complicated by the fair acknowledgement that it is not a problem inherently held by each and every player that was at the club prior to his arrival — even those who come in for the most amount of criticism. Chris Smalling serves as a perfect example. In November 2017 he was left out of the England squad, with manager Gareth Southgate questioning his ability to play out from the back. Smalling was eventually left out of England's World Cup squad for Russia 2018. And, of course, there had been errors — notably at Newcastle, and again the lapse of concentration at City — that led to the concession of goals. But Smalling's own recovery and his commitment levels in helping his team turn around difficult situations could not be questioned. The goal United conceded against

West Brom was from a corner where it seemed the hosts had no plan on how to set up at a set piece; three days later, Smalling scored in a good performance at Bournemouth, and then was one of the best performers as United won against Tottenham in the FA Cup semi-final (his performance typical again — recovering from the setback of an early goal conceded to help United win).

One criticism that must be fair, of United as a collective unit, was that from the early days under David Moyes from when he dropped Rio Ferdinand, and for the following five years, there had never at any point been a defence where four names were picked consistently. It therefore stands to reason that it is undermining the collective strength of a team, and also the strength and potential of the individuals in the defence, to have such a restriction, whether that has been caused by form or injury, or otherwise unavailability. It is not just a Jose Mourinho thing; any team with serious ambitions of consistently challenging for the biggest honours usually has a settled defence.

United's 2-1 win in the FA Cup semi-final, over Tottenham at Wembley, was achieved with the sort of good football that is associated with the club. It was not, for example, the peak of United against Arsenal in the 1999 FA Cup semi-final replay (then again, it would be ridiculously unfair to criticise a game at the side of that one), but it was at least a strong enough example to place alongside recent big-game wins over Manchester City, Chelsea and Liverpool to demonstrate that criticism about Mourinho's style of football has been hugely exaggerated. In fact, there was even the suggestion that Mourinho's own style was necessary for United to succeed. The pragmatism which was the foundation of Van Gaal's FA Cup success now seemed an important feature.

In their league visit to Wembley, United had come undone inside the first 20 seconds. Their entire game plan had been undermined by the forward-heavy formation Mourinho had fielded. The only change Mourinho made was to select Ander Herrera in place of Anthony Martial (a relevant point to make, considering the vociferous support the French youngster has received in direct reflection of Mourinho's apparent defensive nature). It was a sensible defensive choice; Herrera, after a season when his performance levels had dipped from the previous campaign's player of the year-worthy displays, was outstanding, and seemed to breathe new life into his career at the club. Furthermore, despite conceding early on, the players collectively had enough to rally and respond in the first half, a critical point to make when considering their turnarounds had previously come after the interval and the manager's intervention. The more conservative approach not only helped United control the majority of the game but was also conducive to some entertaining football.

On the same weekend, Liverpool surrendered a 2-0 lead against doomed West Bromwich Albion to give United a strong advantage in the 'race' for second place. It was an advantage United did not relinquish and, while the strength (and proximity, and press perception) of City's success shone a harsher perspective on the club's progression under Jose Mourinho, nobody could deny it. (Indeed, Mourinho reacted to United's qualification for the final by saying the press would 'kill him' if he didn't win it.)

Certainly, the season had endured bumps, particularly as the assimilation of Alexis Sanchez into the side proved difficult, but suggestions of regression were rendered just that, as United came through and showed promising signs of cohesion. The cost, the collateral damage, was speculation over the futures of younger players like Marcus Rashford or, more specifically, Anthony Martial.

The more things change ...

The win that did the most to settle second place was achieved against Arsenal; a last-minute winner in outgoing, opposing manager Arsene Wenger's last visit to Old Trafford was enough to settle any nerves, but it came at a cost as Romelu Lukaku was injured, becoming a doubt for the Cup Final.

It meant the last three league games suddenly became opportunities for players to impress. For both Anthony Martial and Marcus Rashford, it meant a start against Brighton. Peculiarly, Marcos Rojo was selected to play in defence when it seemed to most that he was around fifth choice in that position — Eric Bailly, judged by most to be the best defender at the club, was left on the sidelines. Jose Mourinho's explanation the previous day only served to confuse matters.

'There's no situation,' he said. 'He [Bailly] is fine, no injury, he is one of our five central defenders and honestly my work is not about World Cups and preparing players for the World Cup or giving chances to players at the World Cup. But he's the only central defender whose country is not in the World Cup, so if I have to make a kind of more emotional effective choice to help my players he's the one I'm not going to help. Rojo, Lindelof, Jones, Smalling, all of them are wishing to make the squad for the World Cup and Eric is not under that pressure. I try not to [make sentimental decisions], I try to be a good team manager and that means being a bit cold, a bit selfish but I'm not as bad as that and I still have space for a little bit of feelings. So when I look to the other four central defenders fighting for a position in the World Cup, I'm giving less to Eric.'

There was the recurring idea that Mourinho felt he was not getting the credit he deserved for leading this particular squad to second place and a cup final, and if he had a point (and he surely did) then he must have noticed the disparity in the options available to him in defence, not only compared to other managers but also within his own squad. With second place effectively secured, perhaps it was a calculated gamble that others perceived to be slightly mischief-making, with the manager highlighting the paucity of his options. United lost 1-0 and struggled to create anything of note, which was a damning blow for fans of Martial. Just in case supporters hadn't got the message from the performance, Mourinho all but spelled it out for them after the loss.

'It was not good enough,' he told Sky Sports. 'The players that replaced others did not perform at a good level and when individuals do that it is difficult for the team to play well. Maybe now you will not ask me why A, B and C do not play so much. I knew what was going to happen and I told them, but that is what we got. What happened in the last 20 minutes is normal. The attitude from the first minute and especially in the first half, they had more appetite. I did not succeed in persuading my players that getting four more points is important. It is for me, but perhaps not for them. I wouldn't say disappointed. I know them. I thought that the possibility to start the game and give reason would give them something. You have the answer now when you ask "why always Lukaku?" We are probably not as good as people think we are individually.'

Rashford and Martial were both dropped for the following game against West Ham, where United achieved the necessary point to guarantee second place. Mourinho played a three-man defence, but the game seemed destined for a goalless draw the second it kicked off. Two games without a goal, and United were far from inspiring in their last league game of the season, a 1-0 win over Watford, which was achieved thanks to a first-half tap-in for Rashford. The contribution was enough to edge him into the primary position should Lukaku not make it for the FA Cup Final.

It could fairly be said that if Mourinho had been giving his players a chance to shine for their international bosses, then the prospect of them impressing him enough to get into his FA Cup Final team was remote, and, in any event, there could not be a convincing argument for any place to be challenged. Scott McTominay had played so well against Chelsea in the league and had featured in those last two league games, but he would have had to have been outstanding to push his way in front of the apparently rejuvenated Ander Herrera, who was destined for the role of picking up Eden Hazard. Rashford was ready as a reserve for Lukaku, meaning that there was one place left, alongside Chris Smalling, that was still unaccounted for. The logic for the dropping of Eric Bailly had been stomached against the belief that he would be preserved for the Cup Final. If not him, then Victor Lindelof had played well enough against this same team in the league to justify his own place. Phil Jones had recovered from early nervous moments in the semi-final to play pretty well, but his wayward positioning at Stamford Bridge, which was partly accountable for Alvaro Morata's header, would have been in the manager's thoughts.

Selections for cup finals — particularly for this modern Manchester United side — were the most telling selections from managers. These were the crunch games where the manager's reputation would be enhanced or damaged, and thus he would choose the team and shape he was most hopeful of achieving victory. The biggest call, therefore, was the selection of Phil Jones. Herrera over McTominay was an expected and sensible move. Rashford had earned his place more than Martial had. United were playing 4-3-3, a formation designed to get the best out of Paul Pogba, so there could be no criticism of the manager on that score. Jesse Lingard, too, had earned his place in this team ahead of Juan Mata. And maybe Jones's own form did justify his inclusion — but picking him meant that in the crunch game Mourinho trusted neither of the centre-halves he had brought to the club at a combined cost of around £65m. The defence and the goalkeeper were all brought to the club by Sir Alex

Ferguson; while De Gea's status as best in the world was widely agreed, the same couldn't be said of the others. Louis van Gaal and Jose Mourinho had indulged in transfer activity which confirmed this; it was a defence which had required an upgrade for four years.

There was also the fair counter argument that suggested, two years in, Mourinho had not achieved the best results with the resources he had. The centre-half situation was the perfect example of that, and for a manager who is as unrivalled as he is in the art of defending, it had to be a criticism of him that was valid as soon as an hour before kick-off at Wembley because of everything that the selection represented. It said quite clearly that the players he had bought were not trusted to play in the biggest game of the season.

Those criticisms were only louder at half-time. United started nervously, though Chelsea, too, didn't appear completely comfortable. In the 21st minute Cesc Fabregas found Eden Hazard with a raking pass. Hazard, who was supposed to be tightly tracked by Herrera, was ten yards away from the Spaniard and had isolated Phil Jones. Jones backed off Hazard — possibly anticipating that Herrera would spring into action — and the Belgian's first touch was exquisite, taking both of them out of the game. The forward then drew a foul from Jones, tempting him in twice; with more than an hour to play, it seemed like Hazard was gambling that the referee Michael Oliver would send Jones off. Jones, however, made a concerted attempt to win the ball, so, even though Hazard did win a penalty, the England defender was only cautioned. Hazard scored the penalty with ease.

United's response was stuttering and laboured. So many times in the 2017/18 season they had improved in the second half and that was again the case in the final, but that improvement was scarce and Chelsea's hold on the lead was comfortably seen through to win them the trophy.

'I think we were the best team, but that is football,' Mourinho insisted afterwards. 'I am quite curious to know what you say or what people write because if my team plays like Chelsea did, I can imagine what people would say. I congratulate them but I don't think they deserved to win. I am Manchester United manager and I have to be respectful, not just because they are my previous club but because they are the opponents today and I think we deserved to win. It was a bit hard for us to play without Lukaku against a team that defends with nine players. You need that presence. Chelsea are not stupid. They know our team without Lukaku or Marouane Fellaini does not have a presence — so putting eight or nine players in front of the box, they knew they would be dominant in that direct football. Every defeat hurts but I go home with the feeling we gave everything. No regrets.'

Putting aside the simple argument of Chelsea deserving the win because they scored a goal and United didn't, Mourinho's assessment of the balance of the game was mostly fair, with one critical absence. Chelsea, on the balance of the game, may not have deserved to win, but United deserved to lose for committing the sort of error that had summed up their season.

Maybe, as well, Mourinho had a point about the reception of this victory. February's win over Liverpool had seen United exploit basic defensive naivety, punish it and hold on to the lead. Here, Chelsea had done exactly the same to his team. However, to complain about such a thing after losing a cup final was merely a deflection technique and one which was ill-timed and ineffective.

Without question, United's hopes of success in the 2017/18 season had been undermined by the defensive errors they had made. It is within this area of the pitch that the most perplexing dichotomy of Mourinho's first two years has taken place. The goals-against column in the league read 28, the lowest it had been since 2010. United's record low in the Premier League was 22 in 2008. Their average conceded per season in the Premier League was 33 and the average in the four seasons before Mourinho arrived was 39.5, the highest it had ever been over such a period. The manager's work must therefore be appropriately praised.

Many supporters felt that an entirely new defence was required and the consequential point to take from that is that it would be generally considered by most that the defence who played the 2018 FA Cup Final were an adequate reserve defence. Given that perspective, to have achieved similar goals-against columns to United's best-ever defence is a testament to the magnificent organisational skills in that area of the manager; notwithstanding the Bailly and Lindelof signings, for whom it must be said the jury was still out, it did suggest that given adequate resources to properly strengthen the defence United could theoretically do even better in that area. Individual errors, as mentioned earlier, accounted for goals and points lost at Stoke, Huddersfield, Leicester, Spurs, Newcastle and Brighton in away games alone.

Turning those dropped points into wins still wouldn't have been enough for United to have won the league, but it would have taken them close to a record-points haul and given them a far more respectable looking challenge. Questions about attacking style and invention are fair and justified, but considering the significant difference those individual errors made, which can only be put on the manager's shoulders in terms of selection (which, it should be said, should not be altogether discounted), the improvement cannot be ignored or dismissed as irrelevant.

Neither should the consequential effect. Mourinho's traditional style of play generally included a Matic-type player, but the natural ability of the defenders he worked with in his other roles was objectively far greater than that of the ones he inherited at Old Trafford. Protection of those players has necessitated a more pragmatic style. Wide players have been given even greater defensive responsibility than in previous Mourinho teams because United have played with veteran wingers at full-back. Furthermore, returning to that earlier point, for the majority of the five years since Sir Alex Ferguson retired, at no point has there been a four-man defence (or even five-man, in the various trials and tribulations) which picked itself in either form, or, it should be said, availability. For United in 2017/18, Antonio Valencia made 31 league starts and Ashley Young made 28. Chris Smalling, too, made 28, but the list of other defenders speaks for itself — Jones made 23, Lindelof 13, Bailly 11, Rojo 8, Shaw 8, Darmian 5 and Blind 4. Looking at these numbers it could be said that Mourinho, therefore, chose the most consistently available side to him for the cup final.

The fallout of a final defeat, particularly when it means you finish your season empty-handed, does nothing to inspire perspective. Therefore, there was a large section of the United support who questioned Mourinho and even a percentage that is too large to be dismissed who thought that the manager's time was up.

Among the things he had received criticism for were: poor man-management skills; too pragmatic and defensive with his selections; not attacking enough with his selections; not spending enough time coaching attacking, leading to ineffective forward combinations; throwing his players under the bus; never taking responsibility for defeats; making questionable team selections; not picking popular players; making mistakes in the transfer market both with players he did and didn't sign; marginalising and disrupting the careers of young, exciting players at the club; unpopular press conference comments; still living in the Lowry Hotel instead of committing to buying a house; favouring older players over young ones; his downbeat demeanour; and, finally, last but certainly not least, the summary point of this entire book, disregarding the Manchester United way.

How justified are those criticisms? What are the caveats in the manager's favour? There are many facets to each point without descending into an hypothetical argument, but it is worth saying that many, if not most, of these points are levelled at any manager of any football club who is deemed to be underachieving. Mourinho's abrasive personality means that when there is an element of underachievement to be suggested, he is there to be shot at.

Still, it was hard to shake the feeling that dispensing of Mourinho's services would set United far further back once more. Having allowed two managers such a relatively short amount of time, regardless of Mourinho having earned the right to have at least one more year, one would argue that he also had the right to oversee a complete transition in playing staff, or as complete as he would like, in the same manner that Tommy Docherty was permitted to in the mid-70s. Docherty was certainly not the most popular figure in Manchester at the time of the club's relegation and it could be argued he had as many enemies as admirers by the time of his sacking in 1977, but it could not be contested that he was ultimately vindicated for all of his football decisions because of how he turned the club around.

In March 1988, arguably the high point of the turbulent early-Ferguson era, the manager said this: 'Some [players] aren't hurt enough by defeat … they're too ready to shut up shop for the season. But some who thought there was no pressure know differently now.'

Having spent too long on the carousel of underachievement, when hopes of success were realistically gone, too often form dipped. The modern football set-up makes underachievement a staggered and complex theme. Arsenal's infamous grasp on fourth place for almost a decade (with the occasional flirtation with third) sums up neatly the point that qualification for Champions League football has become an objective that on a business level is probably more important than winning the league.

In a conference call to investors in the week before the Cup Final, Ed Woodward said, 'Playing performance doesn't really have a meaningful impact on what we can do on the commercial side of the business.' This is mostly true, although there are differing levels to that, as experienced with the Louis van Gaal sacking.

Amongst the support, though, and the press, there is a level of expectation that means the pressure on Mourinho to win the league could present an untenable situation in the event of failure. That level of expectation disregards all circumstances at other clubs; it ignores all perspective other than the insular demands at Old Trafford. The manager's own public comments made it clear that he felt recruitment on the squad that finished second in 2018 was necessary.

Whilst not quite as hysterical as it could be, there was still, in the summer of 2018, a defined hierarchy of those attributes, which have been explained and returned to, which are important to Manchester United.

The first is success. It is closely followed by playing entertaining football. That is closely followed by having young players in the team, and it would be a nice addition if those players were homegrown. It is clear that those attributes are ranked in that order by the scale of the criticism associated with each of them, and, as such, they help to determine what is expected of the modern Manchester United, regardless of who is manager.

It was the late Sir Matt Busby's first accomplishment as manager to create an entertaining team. But it was when his and Jimmy Murphy's work combined to create the Busby Babes, a team of homegrown stars, that United became the universally adored football team they were. That team were tragically frozen in time in February 1958, but ten years later, when Sir Matt's last great team followed up two league titles with a European Cup win, it was a legacy with a trinity of hallmarks that extended beyond Best, Charlton and Law; it was success, style and youth.

When Tommy Docherty brought some of the good days back to Old Trafford, he brought style and youth, on the precipice of success, as he was sacked. Dave Sexton's side lacked the style and success so the decent work he was doing with regards to the youth set-up at the club was deemed dispensable. Ron Atkinson had relative success and style; there were young players in there, and Atkinson was judged for selling the popular Mark Hughes, but it was clearly the third most important aspect.

Sir Alex Ferguson delivered all three in spectacular fashion, although it is romantic revisionism to suggest it was all flair. There were plenty of professional routine victories, particularly in the later years, though that is not to suggest anything served up under that glittering era ever reached a nadir that was comparable with the five years which immediately followed it.

Those who were most vociferously against Mourinho would argue that he had not accomplished any of the three principle objectives in keeping with the club's identity but that would be viewing things through an incredibly harsh perspective. Success is always relative to both the history of the club and the contemporary situation and should also be measured in progress. How much progress United made in 2017/18 was open to interpretation, but there is an argument for and against.

Were United playing with the style associated with great teams of the club's past? Well, on the balance of things, despite an increase in goals scored, and despite some wonderfully gifted attacking and creative players, it would have to be said 'no'. Was this due to the manager inhibiting his team, restricting their attacking ability? In the early weeks of the 2017/18 season, when it seemed United were scoring four goals every week, it is worth returning to the point that some still weren't convinced and some still weren't entertained. It is also worth adding as a caveat that those better performances came from a team and system which looked settled; so the suggestion that things could improve with a superior defence is sensible rather than outlandish. There was clearly a reason for the general underperformance of talented attacking players. The natural inhibition that comes as a consequence of the extra defensive responsibility would undoubtedly be a factor. It didn't seem, though, to be the only one.

Is it right to say Mourinho disregarded the youth heritage and legacy at the club? Surely the evidence is there to say this would be an unfair accusation. Jesse Lingard and Marcus Rashford played almost all of the season. Scott McTominay was entrusted with some big occasions. Had the manager's personality ruined two of the brightest talents at the club (Shaw and Martial)? Possibly, although there is an argument that suggests that the players weren't completely blameless. Could the manager have done more to embrace United's legacy in this regard? Of course, but as with everything, a sense of proportion needs to be exercised. As was mentioned earlier, it wasn't in Mourinho's track record to give, for example, a Fosu-Mensah or a Tuanzebe a chance when a senior defender wasn't doing well. Some might say that example is an explanation of an inherent incompatibility between Mourinho and the club's identity, but it is surely more logical to be a reasonable middle ground. After all, the selection of McTominay against Chelsea in itself rebuts that point. However, more *could* be done. It would take abandoning some of those sensibilities to take a risk, something Mourinho had never been renowned for, though of course it's worth asking the players — would Fosu-Mensah, for example, have preferred to have made the five league starts Matteo Darmian made at United as opposed to the 21 he made at Crystal Palace on loan? It is almost undeniable that United would have been better served, but it might not have been in the best interests of the player's own development. The point remains, though this delves into another political footballing territory, that it would be better for United, and more in keeping with their history, to give those chances to their own players rather than buying an expensive import just to play a handful of games.

The greatest and most valid criticism is that of United's style, as inconsistent as it had been. There was enough evidence in Mourinho's history — indeed, it's been a strength of his — to suggest he could have United functioning well as a team rather than a collection of individuals. And there were enough quality individuals at the club that sooner or later they would have to take some of the responsibility and burden for playing attractive and cohesive football too.

It was therefore encouraging to hear Alexis Sanchez speak so candidly in the days after the Cup Final defeat. 'I think that in every game I've played in I've maybe found it hard to adapt to the style of play and I've been getting to know my team-mates,' the striker said. 'I believe that United really is a very big club on a worldwide scale and even more so in England where it's the biggest. They always want to win and to be fighting on all fronts and that's the reason I wanted to come here. I also had some great players alongside me at Barcelona, some highly experienced guys who had great quality. I think that United are not too dissimilar as a club to them in their size and stature. However, we still have areas where we can improve, and we can do this day-to-day and a game-to-game basis. I believe we need to improve in all aspects.'

There were enough positive signs there for those who wished to see them; there were enough negative signs for those who retained their pessimism. Nothing is certain in sport, especially football, even if Manchester City's financial muscle means that they would remain a significant and formidable opponent. Jose Mourinho is a man whose career had previously been defined by greatness. The summer of 2018 was clearly a turning point, but even those who believed Mourinho was destined to fail at Old Trafford might not have believed how quickly and how spectacularly that downfall would come.

Third Season Syndrome

To disregard all of the previous noted concerns about the capability of the squad Jose Mourinho had at his disposal in the summer of 2018 for a moment — let us venture into the generally pointless tunnels of 'what would X' have done, and, to make it even more unfair, let us pretend that X was Sir Alex Ferguson, the greatest manager of them all.

At the same time, let us not project our own ideas because it would be sacrilege to assume knowledge and foresight on the same level as such a successful coach.

Let us instead travel back to the summers of 1995 and, more relevantly to this particular argument, 2006. Both times, Ferguson took a squad with relatively few changes and was able to inspire it to greater heights than the previous campaign. 2006 is a much more pertinent comparison to draw, because then, as Mourinho faced in 2018, United's biggest rivals were able to blow them out of the water when it came to paying for players. It was indeed Mourinho's Chelsea who bolstered their title-winning squad with the free transfer of Michael Ballack, the £10m signing of Salomon Kalou, the £5m-and-

William Gallas acquisition of Ashley Cole and the £30m capture of Andriy Shevchenko.

From the outside, it seemed that United did not have the quality to match Chelsea, even with the £18m signing of Michael Carrick. One of Ferguson's greatest triumphs was his motivation of this squad of players to treat every single game as just as much of a cup final as their opponents. He instilled in his players a confidence and attitude that they could win the league if they accumulated enough points from the other 36 games where Chelsea were not the opponent. This eventually encouraged the confidence that they were a match for their wealthy adversaries. It was the quality on which five further league titles were delivered.

Given Mourinho's history at Porto and Inter Milan, there was enough of a track record to inspire some hope that he could galvanise a squad to perform better than expected. It seemed a reasonable expectation that he would implement these management skills in order to improve upon the second place in 2017/18 that he would describe as his 'best' achievement in a storied career.

This hope would never bear any fruit. Before a ball had even been kicked in anger in United's season, there was a political situation brewing at the club which was intense enough that a description of it being in 'turmoil' wouldn't, for once, be hyperbole.

Mourinho had identified a wish list of players and, according to newspaper speculation, that list included Willian of Chelsea, Toby Alderweireld of Spurs, Fred of Shakhtar Donetsk, Alex Sandro of Juventus, Diogo Dalot of Porto and a reserve striker, who most sources identified as Marko Arnautovic of West Ham. What was clear from that list was major reinforcement in defence was a priority for Mourinho. The first player signed was Dalot. Though the full-back had a release clause of approximately £18m, his services were so highly sought that United paid extra to get the signing over the line. Fred — courted by Manchester City — was next, at a fee rumoured to be north of £50m. Lee Grant, the former Stoke City goalkeeper, was signed to provide senior cover as Sergio Romero had a knee injury.

Negotiations for Alderweireld seemed to be protracted. The Belgian had a year left on his contract but Spurs, with Daniel Levy, were not willing sellers and quoted a prohibitive price of £60m. When it seemed the laborious talks were going nowhere, Harry

Maguire of Leicester City emerged as a prominent name when his performances for England in the World Cup drew attention. The Foxes were similarly reluctant to cash in on their asset, though it was suggested a fee of £80m might tempt them. It was suggested that Mourinho was keen, though how much of any interest in any player was genuine remained unclear. What was obvious, at least, was Mourinho's wish for further players to follow the two senior players (excluding Grant) he had signed.

The fact that none did seemed to be a particular source of irritation to the United boss as the club went to the US on their pre-season tour. Premier League clubs had agreed to reschedule the closure of the transfer window to the Thursday before the season started, a passage of time further complicated by the World Cup. England's progress in the tournament — as well as Belgium's, and France's — meant the extended breaks for the players involved would rule them out of most of the pre-season.

The fourth game of the tour was against Liverpool in front of 101,000 in Michigan. The team that slumped to a 4-1 defeat against their bitter rivals read: Grant (J Pereira 46), Darmian, Fosu-Mensah, Bailly, Tuanzebe (Williams 81), Mitchell (Chong 71), McTominay, Herrera (Bohui 81), A Pereira, Mata (Fred 71), Sanchez (Gomes 81).

The loss increased concentration on United's pre-season stumble. The size of the scoreline, in addition to the fact that United had yet to win on tour, was enough to shape the perception of the club's preparations. It was a difficult time. Jose Mourinho's reaction to the defeat was so strong that it almost caught everyone off guard. 'The atmosphere is good but if I was them I wouldn't come,' he said in a strange reference to the record crowd. 'I wouldn't spend my money to see these teams. I was watching on television Chelsea against Inter and the people in Nice decided the beach was better. They didn't go to the game; the stadium was empty. I think the passion many Americans have for soccer deserves more. They deserve the best teams and invest to bring the best clubs to the US. But we, and some other clubs, were not able to give to the people the real quality football that can attract even more passion in this country.'

For someone with a reputation for making calculated remarks to the press, the intention didn't seem immediately obvious. Mourinho seemed to be complaining about the timing of the pre-season, but it wasn't as if United were the only club suffering this issue. The United manager was asked about the body language of Alexis Sanchez, one of the few senior forward players to spend a pre-season at the club: 'Do you want me to be very happy with the players he has around him?' Mourinho snapped. 'We are not playing here to improve the team, the dynamic or our routines. We are playing just to try to survive and not have some ugly results. Alexis is the only attacking player that we have. We don't have wingers, we don't have strikers. He is the only one who is here and the poor man is trying his best with the frustration of somebody who wants more. This is not our team, this is not our squad — not even 30 per cent of it. We start the game with almost half the players who are not even going to belong to our squad on 9 August [transfer deadline day]. So what did this game give me? Nothing. Nothing at all.'

The other main name United did have available, Anthony Martial, had been absent from France's World Cup squad. He was, however, also absent at that moment from United's squad, as he had flown back to Europe due to his partner giving birth. It was rumoured that the manager was not happy with his forward's decision to go home. 'Anthony Martial has the baby and after the baby is born — beautiful baby, full of health, thank God — he should be here and he is not here,' Mourinho said. 'We had four or five players today who care for the club and try to give everything. They even risked themselves because they don't want to let all the kids by themselves on the pitch against Milan, Liverpool, Real Madrid. As an example, Eric Bailly was not going to play and when he saw that Smalling in the warm-up was leaving, he decided that he didn't want another kid on the pitch. It is not fair for Alexis, Mata, Herrera and the guys that are there.'

This came against the backdrop of speculation about Martial's very future at the club. It was suggested that Ed Woodward was reluctant to let Martial, one of the club's best and most exciting players, leave. Mourinho might have felt some justification in his judgement because of the star turn of Ivan Perisic at the World Cup; the Croatian forward's stellar tournament was capped by a great goal in the final. Perisic was no longer on the table, but Mourinho might have felt it strengthened his own hand in the pursuit of Willian.

Mourinho told reporters later that day that he was hopeful of getting two more players in. Less than 48 hours later, the United boss had revised his expectations. 'I am confident I will get one, but I think two I am not going to get which is not a drama,' Mourinho told beIN SPORTS. 'In every pre-season it happens the same with every club, which is the manager wants more. It's our nature, you always want more for your team but then club decisions are different and normally you don't get what you want, which happened during all my career. So if I get one player until the end of the market, that's fine.'

The sullen figure of the manager was, according to new recruit Lee Grant, quite the opposite impression the players were getting. 'From what we're getting from the inside it [the atmosphere around the camp] has been nothing but positive,' Grant told Sky Sports. 'The messages we are getting from the manager are positive ones and that is important for us going forward. His attitude and demeanour around the place is great and that is helpful for us, especially when we are undermanned and we are working our hardest.'

It wasn't just the players within the pre-season squad who were getting messages from the manager. As United returned to the UK, speculation intensified that the major transfer activity before the deadline would actually involve someone leaving Old Trafford. Paul Pogba, who, like Perisic, had enjoyed a fantastic World Cup (Pogba going one better by not only scoring in the final, but lifting the trophy, too), was linked with a move to Barcelona. The midfielder's fantastic form in Russia restarted the conversation about the struggles to get the best out of him back in Manchester.

'I don't think it's about us getting the best out of him, it's about him giving the best he has to give,' Mourinho told ESPN in mid-July. 'I think the World Cup is the perfect habitat for a player like him to give their best. Why? Because it's closed for a month, where he can only think about football. Where he's with his team on the training camp, completely isolated from the external world, where they focus just on football, where the dimensions of the game can only motivate. During a season you can have a big match then a smaller match, then one even smaller, then you can lose your focus, you can lose your concentration, then comes a big match again. In the World Cup, the direction of the emotion, of the responsibility, of the big decisions is always growing up. You are in the group phase, you go to the last 16, to the quarter-finals, to the semi-finals, to the finals. This feeds the motivation. This feeds the concentration of a player. So I think it was the perfect environment for him.'

The comments were divisive, and almost certainly wouldn't be well received by the Pogba camp. Ultimately the proposition of selling their record signing in the last week of the transfer window was not one that was entertained by Manchester United. Instead, questions were asked of the manager's own capability to perform in unfamiliar surroundings. Two seasons in Manchester was enough time to dispel the locality as 'unfamiliar' but Mourinho was still heading into unchartered territory. In May 2018 it was announced that Rui Faria, the manager's loyal aide of 17 years, was to leave the club and take a break from football. Kieran McKenna and the recently retired Michael Carrick were promoted to Mourinho's senior coaching team.

Faria's departure, though unconnected, became part of a bigger conversation about the modern structure of the club. The autonomous days of Sir Alex Ferguson were over and even Jose Mourinho appeared to accept that, even if it seemed obvious enough that he relished that amount of control. For that control, you have to earn respect, and the respect ordinarily is earned from achievements. That much was true of Sir Alex, who commanded the respect by virtue of everything he had accomplished at Old Trafford. Mourinho did not have the longevity in Manchester but might have felt justified in feeling he was entitled to similar respect due to his own trophy haul. He was reluctant to work with a director of football, or a sporting director, or any other intermediary under a similar name. He would have been nonplussed at the constant speculation in the press about the identity of such a man. It appeared that the club were happy to allow Mourinho to work as he wished and so no appointment was forthcoming.

As it transpired, the manager might have been better off with a middle man. The theory of the benefit of hiring one would be someone to find a reasonable conclusion to the impasse United found themselves in in the transfer market. Despite the pragmatic revision of his own expectations, Mourinho did not welcome a further signing to the club before the transfer deadline. Back in Manchester, it seemed the politicking at the club went into overdrive in a hugely controversial week. Manchester United, notorious under the Ferguson era for being difficult with such information, were now an open book.

'The other clubs that compete with us are really strong or they have already fantastic squads like Chelsea, Spurs, City, or they are investing massively like for example Liverpool buying everything and everybody,' Mourinho told MUTV after the final pre-season friendly, a 1-0 defeat to Bayern Munich. 'If we don't make our team better it will be a difficult season for us. My CEO knows what I want for quite a long time, I know he tries to do the best for me and I still have a few days to wait to see what happens.'

And so started a week of intense speculation. Despite Toby Alderweireld and Harry Maguire being the prominent names mentioned, others inevitably followed. Barcelona were hoping to cash in on Yerry Mina's decent World Cup showing, while a deadline-day rumour linked Atletico's veteran star Diego Godin with a loan or a permanent move to Old Trafford. Even Jerome Boateng, the former City defender and current Bayern defender, was mentioned. None came in. The acquisitions of Dalot and Fred did not seem as if they would help facilitate the necessary improvement to match Manchester City, or even Liverpool, whose 2018 improvement had been helped by large investments in Virgil van Dijk, Fabinho and Naby Keita. Tottenham Hotspur, who hadn't made a single signing, had a potential and a togetherness that suggested there was much more to come from them, while management changes at Chelsea and Arsenal made them relatively unknown quantities but very real threats.

When Mourinho faced the press on the Thursday before Friday, 10 August's season opener against Leicester City, he was already feeling the need to be protective of his work at the club: 'My view is that first of all is difficult for me to believe we finished second when I listen, when I read, not much but sometimes I do, it is difficult to believe that we finished second because you are capable of making people that finish second look like they were relegated, and people who win nothing, finish below us, and you make them look like serial winners,' he told reporters at Carrington. 'It is difficult for me to understand, we finish second which I keep saying, that I won eight championships and three Premier Leagues but I keep feeling the second last season was one of my biggest achievements in the game.'

When asked what his target for the forthcoming season was, then, Mourinho insisted the World Cup had caused him to concentrate on the short term. 'The target is the Leicester match,' he said. 'In football you need time to work and players on the pitch to work and we didn't have until now. I said that during pre-season, and it looked like I was saying something absolutely out of order, something crazy; I repeat — pre-season is difficult when you don't have your players to work, that's as simple as that … I have my players and I like my players. I like to work with my players, one lie repeated 1,000 times is still a lie, but the perception of people is that it's true. When you repeat 1,000 times that my relationship with my players is not good, a lie repeated 1,000 times is still a lie. I like my players and my group. I enjoyed last season, the fight to finish where we finished and to manage the best position this club has had in five years. I'm going to enjoy this season. I know the words you want me to say or not to say. It depends on the music, but words don't come easy. By the end of November or December you don't need words, you'll see by then which teams are candidates to win the Premier League.'

If those words were a facade, then they were at least diplomatic, which is more than could be said for the reports on the morning of the game. It was reported by *The Guardian* that Ed Woodward had specifically vetoed numerous transfer suggestions, among them the signings of Alderweireld and Willian. Two key lines stood out from the report. The first, the decision from the 'top of the club' that Mourinho 'should not be allowed to get his way if it meant potentially wasting tens of millions of pounds on a short-term fix', and the second, 'To Mourinho's intense irritation, United's conclusion was that in most cases he had targeted defenders who were no better than those they already had and who, in today's inflated market, could conceivably have cost upwards of £70m without vastly improving the team.'

The report cited the disagreement between Woodward and Mourinho over Martial's future and also said that Woodward had enjoyed breakfast with Real Madrid president Florentino Pérez over the summer with a view to discussing a £100m-plus transfer for Raphaël Varane. The conversation went nowhere, but the briefing to the newspaper made a significant statement.

Again, the fallout was divisive. Supporters who were not in favour of Mourinho's appointment in the first place, and those who had perceived the second half of the 2017/18 campaign as regression, were beginning to feel that Mourinho's comments over the course of the summer were not only counter-productive, but symptomatic of the kind of statements he would make in the build-up to him leaving other high-profile jobs. There were those who felt it was obvious that the squad needed further investment if it was to challenge, with the defence in particular being a key area. Mourinho, who had initially wanted five players, and had reluctantly accepted he might get just one, found his judgement on that 'one' called into particular scrutiny considering he had spent £60m on two defenders and neither of them had started the FA Cup Final.

Regardless of where your opinion lay on the above, one thing could be universally agreed — it was abysmal preparation for the opening day of the season.

United won 2-1 against Leicester. They were able to call upon Victor Lindelof, Marcus Rashford and Paul Pogba, all of whom made it right to the end of the tournament in Russia. Pogba scored the opening goal after a few minutes. Luke Shaw — one player whose days at the club would undoubtedly have been numbered if Mourinho had managed to sign Sandro — scored his first-ever United goal to secure the win, and top off a very encouraging performance.

'Pogba was a monster,' Mourinho said after the game. 'We thought maximum 60 minutes but he managed over 80. The decision belonged to Paul. I asked him and he made himself available and he was very good. Luke's game was very complete, even if I forget the goal. He made maybe one mistake defensively in the whole match and the linesman could have helped him with a free kick. He just has to keep going.'

It wasn't a brilliant display from United, who had less possession than their opponents, and also had fewer shots — never a brilliant thing, but especially not at Old Trafford. Those matters would have been the last thing on the mind of the manager as he went to bed that night, though. He would have been made aware of Pogba's comments to the press and on social media. He posted on Instagram: 'I'll always give my best for the fans and my team-mates no matter what's going on.'

He was asked by reporters if he was happy at the club as he left the stadium, and instead of giving a bland response he gave the cryptic statement 'There are things, and there are things that I cannot say, otherwise I will get fined.'

Nonetheless, a win was the most positive way to start a new season, and, with the exception of Spurs — who were the next visitors to Old Trafford — the fixture list had provided a fairly generous opening run for Mourinho's team. Their next game was at Brighton, and former United boss David Moyes believed the pessimism around the club would dissipate. 'If you were picking the fixtures for United in the first nine or ten games, you're not playing City, Liverpool, Chelsea … I wonder with Jose's words the other day — "let's wait until November" — I'd be very surprised if United weren't top of the league come the end of November,' Moyes told BBC Radio 5 Live.

The Leicester win may have papered over the cracks, but the trip to Brighton revealed them, warts and all. With Antonio Valencia — who had been named club captain in the pre-season — injured, as well as new recruit Dalot, Mourinho made one change in his defence from the Leicester game, with Ashley Young coming in at right-back to play alongside Bailly, Lindelof and Shaw. The manager's hopes of his own signings justifying the faith placed in them were extinguished as early as the 30th minute, as Brighton raced into a 2-0 lead. The visitors were at sixes and sevens and looked as if they might concede every time Brighton went forward. An unlikely goal against the run of play through Lukaku seemed as if it might spark some fight from United, but it was a red herring. Brighton did score a deserved third and even an injury-time goal from Pogba could not take the gloss away from their win, or provide any consolation for United fans. And they wouldn't find it in the post-match statements from anyone at the club.

'We were punished by the mistakes we made,' Mourinho said. 'For me that's the story of the game. We made incredible mistakes in some crucial moments. Mistakes that killed us.'

Much worse was to follow from Pogba, who, this time, wasn't afraid to talk: 'The attitude that we had was not like we wanted to beat them. They had more anger than us and that showed on the pitch,' the midfielder told Sky Sports. 'I put myself first. My attitude wasn't right enough. We'll keep trying and keep pushing and obviously it's a lesson for us.'

The game against Spurs, then, was already shaping up to be a huge one for United. A blip could be turned into a potential crisis. When the teams were announced an hour before the game, it was clear the manager was sending a message. At first it wasn't clear whether Ander Herrera had been selected at right-back, but it soon transpired that he was playing on the right-hand side of three. He was, in theory, the ball-playing defender Mourinho had wanted but not got. He was playing alongside Smalling and Jones, a damning verdict on the centre-halves the manager had himself brought to the club. Anthony Martial, who had played and looked poor against Brighton, was omitted from the squad altogether.

The experiment seemed to start well. United dominated the game and created some good chances, including one gilt-edged opportunity for Lukaku, who contrived to miss with the goal gaping. By full time the statistics looked much more favourable than they did after the Leicester game. United had 57 per cent possession and 23 efforts on goal. One problem, though — they lost the actual game 3-0. Having gone into the half-time break scoreless, there were a couple of hints that Spurs were beginning to become comfortable with their opponent's shape. Two goals in quick succession in the second half and United quickly unravelled; Lucas Moura, who had signed for Mauricio Pochettino's side in January (and had been a long-term rumoured target for United), was chief tormentor. Lucas added a third, singling out Chris Smalling and beating him. The misery of the night was compounded by the excellence of Alderweireld at the heart of the visitor's defence. At one point, after the Belgian had made a commanding slide tackle, supporters in the South Stand turned to the director's box and channelled their anger at Ed Woodward.

As far as the majority of the match-going fans were concerned (though the majority had emptied the stadium after the late third goal), Mourinho had their support, and the manager was keen to applaud the Stretford end before going down the tunnel. Gamesmanship; Mourinho's own performance kept going right into the press conference after the game.

It was the first thing he was asked about. 'My message was the same message as the supporters, the message that the supporters gave to the players was my message, it was the same,' he explained. 'When you play the way you play, when you create what you create, when we miss the chances that we missed, when at half-time everybody was frustrated but totally convinced that we were going to win the match. And even with the unexpected 2-0 result, the way the team kept playing until the third goal arrived, my message to the players has to be a positive message and I'm really happy, humbled by the way the supporters reacted to the boys, I think it was very much deserved, but sometimes players deserve and they don't get what they deserve, so we have to be humbled by the supporters' reactions.'

The face began to slip; first, he admitted he didn't know what his best defence was: 'Because in the first game Lindelof and Bailly, and today played Jones and Smalling, but now Jones is injured, and next match it will be Smalling, with another one, and when Marcos Rojo comes he will be an option, and no, I don't know my best back four.'

He was then asked whether the changes were affecting the confidence of the players, such as playing Herrera instead of Lindelof. 'You want to make the miracle of my team played so well and strategically we were so so good and you want to try and transform this press conference into "let's blame the guy". You have to tell me what is the most important thing,' the United boss replied.

'When I win matches I come here many times and you are not happy that I won matches, and you say the most important thing is the way of playing.'

When the journalist insisted he was just asking about the defenders, Mourinho bit back: 'No, no, no, you have to make a decision in relation to that, because I need to know what is the most important thing,' he said. 'If it is to play well or if it is to win matches? Is it to play offensively, or is it to play for a certain result? Today we were aggressive, we press high, Tottenham couldn't make two passes coming from the back, they made lots of mistakes because of our high pressure, we project the full-backs, we had Valencia and Luke Shaw arriving in dangerous positions, we miss goals with an open goal, we missed chances, we were unlucky in rebounds in both goals, we lost a game because we conceded a goal from the first corner of the match against us on minute 50-something. In the first-half, zero free kicks, zero corners conceded, in minute 50-something they have one corner and score a goal, and you want, with that goal, you want to transform the story of your game. But don't lose your time, because today I had the proof that the best judge in football are the supporters, they are the best judge.'

It was put to Mourinho that the fans had judged his team by walking out before the end. 'We lost last season here against Sevilla and we were booed, because we deserved it, because we were not good, because we were not dangerous enough, because Sevilla deserved to win the match,' he said. 'We were booed, and deservedly. Today the players left the pitch after losing at home and they were applauded, because they deserved it, so keep trying, and trying, and trying, and keep trying. Just to finish, do you know what was the result?' Mourinho stood to leave and then held three fingers up. 'This. 3-0, 3-0. Do you know what this is? 3-0. But it also means three Premierships and I won more Premierships alone than the other 19 managers together. Three for me and two for them two. So respect man, respect, respect, respect.'

The squad were given Tuesday off but there was no respite for Mourinho, and now the speculation had cranked up so much that it was no longer a case of him being accused of underperforming. The *Daily Mail* carried the first serious suggestions that Mourinho would be sacked if United lost their next game, going so far as to speculate that the players had been discussing the possibility of Zinedine Zidane — who had recently quit as manager of Real Madrid after winning a third consecutive Champions League with them — succeeding him.

'They are saying Jose will be gone soon,' *The Mail* claimed a source told them. 'Some think he'll be out if they lose at Burnley. Others can't see him lasting beyond September. We've seen this before and it just feels the same. The club will say it's supporting Jose but we all saw what happened with Louis. The players are already talking about the possibility of Zidane coming in.'

Mourinho might have felt some support by the news there was to be a banner flown by a plane at Turf Moor, paid for by United fans. It would reportedly bear the message 'Ed Woodward: A Specialist In Failure'.

United won the game 2-0, with two first-half goals from Romelu Lukaku. Lukaku missed opportunities to possibly double that tally; Paul Pogba missed a penalty. Even Marcus Rashford's red card couldn't take the gloss from a dominating performance. It calmed the storm ahead of the international break, but United's game after it was against high-flying Watford at Vicarage Road. The Hornets had won their first four league games and would provide a stern test. United put in their best display of the season, in the first half at least, to take a 2-0 lead into the interval. Paul Pogba was the heartbeat of a fantastic half-hour of football, and, even though Watford grabbed a goal back, Mourinho's team held on to win. Nemanja Matic's red card in injury time did not affect the result.

Pogba was outstanding once more as United won 3-0 at Young Boys to kick off their Champions League campaign with a comprehensive victory. Perhaps most impressive was an assured debut from Dalot at right-back, who Mourinho predicted afterwards could 'play for the club for the next ten years'. The manager was pleased with the result. 'Job done,' he told BT Sport. 'Not phenomenal but good enough. They were intense, compact and had self-esteem. Then after the first goal, the game was under control. We tried to score the goals that gave us the stability for the second half. It is important for us to win because probably every team is going to get six points against Young Boys. Now we have two important matches against Valencia and Juventus. They are very good opponents.'

Newly promoted Wolves were the next visitors to Old Trafford. Also visiting for the first time in a while was Sir Alex Ferguson; the legendary coach had undergone emergency brain surgery in May, and his presence at the Theatre of Dreams was by far the most positive news of the weekend.

With Matic out, Mourinho was forced to select Fred, who hadn't featured since the capitulation to Spurs. It could have been just as fair to say that he was getting a gentler introduction to life in England and the Brazilian did justify his inclusion with an early goal. Wolves grew in confidence and grabbed a deserved equaliser early in the second half. Pogba had given away the ball in the build-up and Mourinho was furious on the sideline.

Mourinho brought on Mata and Martial but was left bemoaning his side's capability to create after a frustrating, if deserved, 1-1 draw. 'I was expecting more from my attacking players. There was not enough creativity, movement or dynamism,' he told reporters after the game. 'They started better and were more aggressive, had more intent and I don't know why but they were more motivated. We made it quite easy for them to cope with our supremacy in the last 20 minutes. Overall we don't deserve more than this ... we deserve the punishment of one point.'

It seemed that Paul Pogba agreed with the general idea, but the midfielder seemed to indicate that it was the manager and not the players who ought to shoulder the responsibility. 'I'm not the manager, I cannot, like, say that but ... obviously we should show more option of playing but I cannot say that because I'm a player,' Pogba said. 'That's my way of thinking — we should move better, we should move more, yeah. We are at home and we should play much better against Wolves. When we are at home we should attack, attack, attack. That's Old Trafford. We are here to attack. I think teams are scared when they see Man United attacking and attacking. That was our mistake. I can't tell you [why] because I'm a player. It's not me.'

The midfielder seemed keen to ensure his comments were not misinterpreted. On the morning those remarks circulated through the press, he posted on Twitter: 'Some people make polemic even from "good morning" to create drama. Big Pogoodmorning everyone hope u get it twisted.'

Continuing in the theme of United's dirty laundry seemingly being aired for all to see, it just so happened that the following morning television cameras were present at United's training complex. They caught Mourinho and Pogba in an apparently confrontational exchange which was later reported to be the manager informing the player he was not only no longer vice-captain, but he would never captain the club again. *The Telegraph* reported a 'United source' as saying: 'Jose told the players that Pogba will not be the captain because he doesn't represent what a captain is and Manchester United is bigger than anyone. The players were happy with that decision and the reasons behind the manager's decision.'

How true that was remained to be seen. But Mourinho could at least feel grateful for the timing of United announcing their yearly profits for the 2017/18 season, where Woodward would be obliged to make statements which backed the under-fire boss in order to project the air of stability. 'Everyone at the club is working tirelessly to add to Manchester United's 66 and Jose's 25 trophies — that is what our passionate fans and our history demands,' Woodward said. 'It is easy to get caught up in the game-by-game fluctuations of our season or even the relatively minor pieces of business and industry news; I would like to take this opportunity to take a step back and look at the bigger picture. We are the biggest sports team in the world as measured by the number of fans. We know that position is one that requires continued effort and investment to maintain. Our board, our investors and everyone at the club are in line with the fans on what we need to do on the pitch and that is to win trophies. That is one of the reasons why we hired Jose Mourinho and we have already won three with him. Off the pitch it is clearly important to drive the business forward, giving us the financial muscle to compete in the highly competitive transfer market. This allows us to continue to blend world-class purchased talent with our continued development of top academy graduates. Our academy continues to be a huge source of pride in delivering talent for the first team with materially increased investment in recent years.'

Mourinho was in no mood to dampen any fires as he wrote his programme notes for the League Cup game against Derby County. 'An important lesson, a lesson I repeat week after week after week, a lesson some boys are not learning, every team that play Man Utd are playing the game of their lives,' Mourinho wrote. 'We need to match that aggression, motivation and desire. Ninety-five per cent isn't enough.'

Even a last-minute equaliser from Marouane Fellaini did not give the impression of United fighting in a way that their manager demanded. It only earned a 2-2 draw with the Championship side; Derby then won on penalties to send United out. In isolation it wasn't the most damning blow — embarrassments against York City, Coventry City and MK Dons are still fresh enough in the memory to tell us Manchester United can be comprehensively beaten by lower division sides and it not be the end of the world — but it was another addition to a rap sheet that was building against the manager.

Much worse was to come at the weekend. Having already seen his gamble with Herrera backfire against Spurs, Mourinho selected Scott McTominay in exactly the same position against West Ham. The big calls didn't stop there. Alexis Sanchez, poor for so long, was dropped, and Anthony Martial was brought in. Pogba, however, would play, despite the public showdown. 'Tomorrow he plays. He is a player like the others,' Mourinho said the day before the game.

'Manchester United is bigger than anyone. I have to defend that. No player is bigger than the club. If I am happy with his work he plays, if I am not he doesn't play. I am really happy with his work this week. He trained really well. The team needs good players. He is a good player. I explained in detail to the people that have to know, which is the squad and especially Paul. After weeks of analysing and changing opinions with my coaching staff, we made the decision that from now Paul is just a player and not a captain. Nobody trained better than Paul on Tuesday, Wednesday, Thursday. Some trained as well as, nobody better.'

Mourinho tried to downplay the fact everything had played out in front of cameras; within two hours, the footage had been viewed over a million times on social media alone. 'I don't care about the cameras. What confrontation? It's not a confrontation,' he insisted. 'You made a story — an incredible story — out of 15 minutes of training. Conversations with players I have many, many, many times. It was not the case but loud criticism, loud instruction, happens every day. Coaching is about that, but you make stories out of it, so I'm happy that the rules are only 15 minutes once a month, and with situations like that it is not going to change. There is no chance I am going to open the training session and let you watch a training session. No chance.'

He couldn't hide away from the fact he was making bold decisions and there was certainly no hiding place just five minutes into the game at West Ham. McTominay was caught out, as one might expect, on an offside trap, and the Hammers scored. A second followed just before half-time — Lindelof attempting to get in the way of a shot, only for it to deflect heavily off his leg and over De Gea. Though Marcus Rashford scored to try and get United back into the game, that hope was extinguished minutes later when the home side exposed the weak defence once again to easily score a third through Arnautovic.

Mourinho attempted to blame the officials for the defeat and if he had a point, marginally, on the decisions, he could have no complaint about the manner of the loss once again. 'The first was an offside goal,' he said. 'And the third was a refereeing mistake, although we were not very good in the transition. We are not a team that is very good when we lose possession and the other team counter-attacks ...

I want to play Martial — something that you are asking for a long, long time — and I left Alexis out. Martial is not a player very, very focussed on his defensive duties. To play him as a second striker and trying just to cover the area of Rice would be much easier for him. At the same time, I feel that we need quality on the ball building up from the back and Scott McTominay has that quality. Everything that left his foot was correct — a part of a special character; a special personality that the team in a negative moment needs. A team in a negative moment needs the kind of mentality Scott McTominay has.'

The praise for the youngster seemed peculiar if obvious; it was clearly the player's worst performance for the club, though he could not be blamed for it whatsoever. Mourinho was asked if he thought other players in the squad had the same mentality. 'Not all of them,' he replied. 'But every player is a different person. Scott McTominay is a kid with a special character.'

With defeat, United's start to the season matched the start made by David Moyes, with, as the former boss had indeed stated, a far kinder fixture list. If there were mitigating circumstances which would explain United's inability to challenge for the title — circumstances which could be discussed at the appropriate points — then there were none which explained the scale of the dreadful start United had made to their league campaign.

If Mourinho's hope was that the defensive horror shows which had featured so heavily in each of their league defeats to this point would vindicate his determination to sign defenders, he would only be partly right, and, still, that point would be entirely undermined by the decision to play midfielders in defence when there were perfectly capable defenders available. And because there was at least some culpability on Mourinho's part, then it was fair game to take a look at Manchester United now compared to where they were when he came in.

One can discuss the merits and responsibility for attacking football within the squad. The primary thing to consider is that Mourinho arrived with a reputation for pragmatic football and there was never any point that most United supporters expected that they would suddenly be thrilled by the brand offered by their manager. The second is that this would be tolerated so long as the winning accompanied it, as it usually did. Without the winning, then, what was the point? On this occasion, how much of that responsibility laid with Mourinho and how much of it laid with the players? United had been largely dour with Herrera, Mata, Rashford and Martial under Louis van Gaal, and with Pogba and Lukaku added to that list under Mourinho. Given the manager's reputation for risk-averse football, the buck stopped with him, although valid questions would be asked of players of such immense potential. It wasn't as if the Chelsea title-winning team of 2015 was devoid of attractive football; far from it, their first few months of that campaign featured probably the most attractive football a Chelsea team had played under Mourinho.

Still, in order to arrive at these conclusions, one then has to look back at the very construction of a team and the stability within it to allow creative players to express themselves. If we can deduce that Louis van Gaal decided early on that he would need to be pragmatic in order to protect the defence, some of those principles should be afforded to Mourinho too. At the start, at least. It was less understandable to still be at that point two years into his reign, and less understandable still that nobody, much less the manager, knew his best team or best formation from the players at his disposal.

The most damning conclusion to arrive at was the generally accepted notion that United had suffered a mini-regression under Mourinho, and if they were any further on from the squad that he inherited, then they were not far enough along in terms of what you might have expected to see, especially taking into account the investment. The more obvious and straightforward point was that United were regressing, the players no longer seemed motivated to play for the manager, they didn't seem to trust in a manager who had openly questioned their mentality, and there seemed to be only a remote possibility or likelihood of that turning around. Certainly, it was almost impossible to envisage the circumstances in which Mourinho could regain the sort of implicit trust his players needed to have in him in order for his prior successes to be repeated.

There was a prevailing wind of discontent, which had never really gone away, toward the owners and Ed Woodward. In times of difficulty, those frustrated with the top-level stewardship of the club make their voices known, as they had earlier in the season with the plane banner. Particularly since the 'sources' close to Woodward had told the press of the lack of confidence the board had in Mourinho's choice of transfer targets, some supporters voiced their disbelief that these decisions could be taken so soon after handing the manager a long-term contract. It seemed only logical that transfer targets would have been discussed at that point; what had changed in little over six months that such a mess now seemed irreparable under the current leadership?

After United laboured to a 0-0 draw with Valencia in the Champions League (a game which was followed by Pogba telling reporters he had 'been told he wasn't allowed to talk' to them, therefore saying everything he needed to), it wasn't a surprise that the idea of Jose Mourinho losing his job might be floated once more in the press. He would have felt let down by the speculation being fuelled by his captain of all people; Antonio Valencia 'liked' an Instagram post from a fan who demanded it was 'time for Mourinho to go'. Although Valencia subsequently apologised on Twitter, it was just another incident where the manager would have felt let down. *The Guardian* claimed that Mourinho believed 'the club should have backed him swiftly and publicly over the Paul Pogba situation and made it clear internally that player power will not be countenanced'.

Mourinho had stated after the Valencia draw: 'All my life I have followed certain golden rules. One of them is that a team can lose matches — that is just part of football — but it must never, ever lose its dignity. I also believe the team is always more important than the individual, and the crest on the chest is more important than the name on the back of the shirt. This is me. This is how I work. I want every player to be exhausted at the end of the game because of the hard work they have given for the club.'

Ahead of the next game, he attempted to put the travails of his side into perspective, whilst also admitting it was a collective responsibility to improve. 'This team can do much better than what it is doing,' he told the press. 'I said last season was a fantastic season for us and if you want something more, in pre-season I also said that this season was going to be very difficult. With all the respect, and I hope they don't interpret me in a negative way, if we are playing in a league like the Swiss league and we don't win that league, anything else apart from winning that league would be an awful season. In that season with the potential of our direct opposition, last season to finish second was a fantastic season for us. The same people that were to blame for the fantastic season of last season [are to blame now].'

That there was speculation was no surprise. The only shock — if it was, any more — was the boldness of the claim by the *Daily Mirror*, who ran the sensational story on the morning of the game that the manager would be dismissed whatever the result from the forthcoming game against struggling Newcastle.

Clockwise

Football is a peculiar sport; the team you support may win much more often than they lose, but the likelihood is, particularly in the more competitive countries, they will not win a majority of trophies they enter. This quirk allows supporters of even the biggest club to believe they are perennial victims of some banana-skin affliction, that it's 'typical' they will lose the biggest games. Perhaps it's a comfort thing, maybe even a British thing. That defeatist, deprecating sense of humour. In the 1986 movie *Clockwise* John Cleese's character utters a famous line which more or less sums it all up: 'It's not the despair, Laura. I can take the despair. It's the hope I can't stand.'

But we can stand the hope. We really can. In fact, more than that, we *live for* the hope. It's even worse than that for Manchester United supporters, who, more than most other clubs, have a history of success from a place where it seemed only hope *could* help them.

If the period after the Sir Alex Ferguson tenure has inflicted any terrible wound on Manchester United, it is the *normalising* which is greater than the others — the idea that United are not special, and will not conjure up something out of nothing, that a game won't magically transform after 60 minutes of monotonous, directionless football. Every now and then there is the odd comeback or last-

323

minute winner; these serve almost painfully as reminders of better days rather than indicators of a reborn philosophy.

And so it was after Alexis Sanchez's last-minute winner over Newcastle. There was no real hope for Jose Mourinho to save his job and the moment was not a spark of life in Sanchez's career at the club. Sanchez picked up a hamstring injury shortly afterwards. For Mourinho, though he had survived his execution date, a glance at the fixture list revealed the most likely reason why.

With a run of fixtures that included Chelsea, Manchester City, Arsenal and Liverpool in the league, as well as Juventus twice in the Champions League, it was easy to see why it would seem counter-productive to hire a new manager right away. So, if Mourinho had a couple of months' relief, what were the circumstances in which he might be able to convince Ed Woodward and the Glazers that he could still turn things around? Beyond the unrealistic suggestion of winning all of those games, perhaps going unbeaten in them might have been the slim hope the manager had. Supporters were just hoping they would avoid embarrassment. It did seem that the end game was here, and that it was a matter of when, and not if, Mourinho would be gone.

Against the Magpies, United had slumped to an early 2-0 deficit. They scored in the 70th, 76th and last minute to grab a 3-2 win and head in to the international break with some renewed optimism. Perhaps, if it had stayed at 2-0, it may have been the end. But even winning in such circumstances couldn't galvanise moods enough to think there was a corner being turned.

After the international break the Chelsea game, at Stamford Bridge, was also built up as a convenient setting for the manager's exit (Chelsea had sacked Antonio Conte despite May's FA Cup win and replaced him with Maurizio Sarri). That narrative was spoiled by one of the most impressive halves for a while; United turned around a half-time deficit to lead 2-1 with two Martial goals, but were denied what many felt was a deserved win when Ross Barkley equalised in the sixth minute of injury time. Chelsea technical assistant Marco Ianni celebrated in front of the United dugout, much to the chagrin of Mourinho, who jumped up but was restrained by staff and stewards. It was a flashpoint which seemed out of place even given the dramatic end; Chelsea's fans taunted their former boss, who held up three fingers to represent those three titles he had referenced against Tottenham earlier in the season. Even United fans were getting tired of the shtick, but had more or less universally defended Mourinho for his actions after the Ianni incident.

'A fantastic match, a very undeserved result for us but that is football,' Mourinho told the BBC. 'We were the best team, even in the first half when we were losing. We were in control, tactically — the result is really unfair for us. We conceded from two set pieces, but that is a way to score goals and you have to be able to defend against that. Anthony Martial is improving, he is doing different things than before. He is a more complete player than before — but he needs to improve. He has a huge talent and he wants it, which is a good thing. The team as a team was really good.'

He immediately diffused the incident with Ianni, saying: 'It is not my reaction, it is Sarri's assistant. He was very impolite but Sarri took care of the situation. They have both apologised to me. I accept. For me, the story is over. Don't do what everyone does and say: "It's Mourinho who does things." I don't know his name, I don't need to know. Everything is fine.'

A few days later, Juventus — with their new record signing, Cristiano Ronaldo — came to Old Trafford, and dominated in a 1-0 win which was much more comfortable than the scoreline suggested. Covering the game in the BT Sport studio were former United stars Rio Ferdinand and Paul Scholes. Ferdinand described it as 'men against boys' and Scholes's assessment was that Juventus were a 'class above'.

Mourinho was frank in agreeing. 'The other side was huge quality, and people look for Cristiano, Dybala, Pjanic, but in a top team you have to look for Chiellini, Bonucci, and Juventus is this kind of team when they are in front it's very difficult to get a goal,' he explained. 'Our attacking players were not, what I say in a funny way, with honey in their feet. Things were not coming. But everybody tried, everyone was strong, everyone tried until the end. In the second half Juve defended with an extra central defender to add to the amazing Chiellini and Bonucci. I thought we could take something from the game but it was not possible to score. We had the intention of being positive, so the boys had the feeling from the match we had at Stamford Bridge. But Juve is a different level, and if people don't want to accept that, it is their problem. I always try to be honest, they are a different level of quality and stability and experience and know-how, and at the base of their team they have Bonucci and Chiellini. That's the base that allows them to play with the freedom in attack. Lose the ball, no problem, we are here. We deserved a draw but it was not possible. I have no complaints.'

Perhaps such a schooling would have been a confidence hit for the United players, but they were able to turn in a decent performance to defeat Everton at Old Trafford, and then they snatched an injury-time win at Bournemouth. The manager was not as buoyant as the supporters were.

'We were defensively awful,' he complained. 'As a team we didn't press or do any of the work we did in the week. People watching this game will not believe how hard we worked this week. When we make a defensive mistake, instead of forgetting it and keeping playing, it triggers instability — like after a couple of minutes of the game with Ryan Fraser facing David de Gea, that triggered instability. It looked like we don't work tactically during the week, which is the worst thing for me as we work hard. But we have the faith that the game is not over, in the second half I could understand the frustration as we created chances but couldn't score.

It seemed as if the mood ahead of the crunch game in Juventus was very pessimistic indeed, and when Ronaldo scored a stunning volley midway through the second half, the match was panning out just as most expected. But Mourinho made changes, bringing on Rashford first, and then Mata and Fellaini. With four minutes to go, Mata scored a fine free kick. Just before the 90th minute, United were awarded another set piece in dangerous territory; Young curled in a dangerous ball, Fellaini made a nuisance of himself and Bonucci could only turn the ball into his own net. It was an exceptional win and result to boost what had been flagging hopes of qualification to the knock-out stages.

A polarising week, with dramatic highs, ended with a trip to Manchester City, who were coming into the game in more stable and imperious form, having scored a hatful of goals against Southampton and Shakhtar.

Paul Pogba was ruled out with injury and the trio of Herrera, Matic and Fellaini were no match for City's dominating midfield.

David Silva's early goal was added to by Aguero in the first three minutes of the second half. Anthony Martial scored a penalty but there was to be no comeback this time. Instead, there was only further emphasis of the gulf between the sides as Ilkay Gundogan scored a third to make it a big defeat.

'It's a heavy result for the effort of a team that had three away matches in the same week, with a super difficult match of a high, demanding level in Juventus against a team that had two friendly matches at home against Southampton and Shakhtar,' Mourinho said, while trying to insist that United were in the game until the third goal. 'One thinking is a bad performance and one thinking is a performance with mistakes. I think ours was a performance with mistakes. The physical fatigue and the mental fatigue leads to mistakes. They were tired physically and mentally. You need to be in football or another high-level sport to know what that is. The concentration of the big matches, they dry you. You are dry inside. To be ready again for another big match is not easy. We are outside the top four, how can we speak about the title? Let's fight to close the gap to jump into the top four. If we jump into the top four then let's see the difference.'

Perhaps he was managing expectations, or attempting to, but United did appear to be bumping from game to game, not knowing which team would be put out, not knowing which team would turn up. When Crystal Palace visited Old Trafford after the last international break of the year, Paul Pogba was back, and expectations were higher. Palace had lost on their previous 11 trips to Old Trafford and hadn't won in their last seven league games.

Mourinho had said on the eve of the game that he believed United could be back in the top four by the turn of the year. 'I know it's a big gap,' he said. 'But I also know until the end of December we have eight Premier League matches to play, and with eight matches we are speaking about 24 points.'

Two were dropped against Palace, as United laboured to a 0-0 draw. Mourinho seemed to make a point when bringing off Pogba for Sanchez with a quarter of the game to go; it made no difference to his team's flat performance. 'You must play with brain and also with heart and I think not enough heart,' he told reporters after. 'We didn't have that intensity that in my opinion is basically related with your brain, with your heart. There are games that are special games and not just one more, and this was a special game. It was the first of eight Premier League games until the end of December and a game we needed to win, and it was not enough from the heart. If we play with the same philosophy against Young Boys then we won't win.'

For that Champions League crunch game, Mourinho made perhaps his boldest selection yet. Romelu Lukaku was benched, as was Paul Pogba, for a game United needed to win.

A vibrant start from Lingard, Rashford and Martial quickly faded. When Rashford missed a one-on-one, Mourinho turned with his back to the pitch, folded his arms and shook his head. United's performance did not improve and in the 64th minute both of Mourinho's most expensive signings were brought on to the pitch. They didn't help matters. In fact, it was that familiar face, Marouane Fellaini, whose injury-time goal spared blushes, and fortunately ensured qualification from the group at the same time due to Juventus defeating Valencia in the other game. There was more than a touch of fortune, as Fellaini appeared to handle the ball on its route into the net.

At least there appeared to be an easier game next up; beleaguered Southampton had enough problems of their own, without a home win all season and with manager Mark Hughes the running favourite alongside Mourinho to become the first manager sacked in the Premier League during the season. Mourinho once more made a risky selection with his defence, this time putting not one but two midfielders in there; this time it was McTominay and Matic. The reason? Injuries were cited, but Marcos Rojo and Diogo Dalot sat on the bench. The Saints were inspired after seeing the recent issues United had endured with these defensive changes and flew out of the blocks, seizing on the inevitable mistakes and racing into a 2-0 lead. It was an incredibly embarrassing start for United and seemed to lump pressure on Mourinho.

Southampton had their own problems and United were eventually able to expose them, with Marcus Rashford the best player in United's fight back. Romelu Lukaku scored his first goal in 12 games before Ander Herrera equalised to get parity before the break. The second half was poor; the game finished 2-2.

'It doesn't matter the system we play,' Mourinho said. 'We lost so many balls in midfield, we lost so many balls in our transition to the last third, it was difficult to have that continuity. What we did so well in the last 15, 20 minutes of the first half, which was to connect with the attacking players by transporting the ball, leaving the ball in the right moment, the right choice of pass, playing simple, accelerate the game. In the second half we went back again to that dynamic where we lose too many balls midfield. And when the players don't understand that simplicity is genius, especially in some parts of the pitch, and they keep and keep and keep in going to complicated football it's difficult to have that continuity. It has to do with the characteristics of the players. With all due respect, we don't have many mad dogs that bite the ball and press all the time. We don't have many people with that spirit. I would say Marcus Rashford was a mad dog. He was, let's say, very, very tired with little problems. That appetite, that desire, that fire that you have, you need that to recover the ball faster and to recover the ball higher on the pitch, but these are just details. He was injured, he was asking to come off. Some players with that kind of injury do not play for two weeks, but Marcus no, Marcus I am pretty sure he will be fine for the next one. It is one kick here, one kick there, one fall here, one fall there, fatigue, lots of running, lots of movement, 75 minutes and he was done.'

It was, however, comments apparently behind closed doors which made bigger headlines after the game. Following another below-par display from Pogba, the midfielder was sensationally singled out in front of his team-mates. 'You don't play,' Mourinho said, according to *The Telegraph*. 'You don't respect players and supporters. And you kill the mentality of the good honest people around you. You are like a person with a flu, with a virus in a closed room — you pass that virus to the others.'

Before United's next game, against a rejuvenated Arsenal at Old Trafford, Hughes was sacked, spawning 1,000 memes about how failing to beat this Manchester United side was now a sackable offence. Mourinho again rang the changes against the Gunners and this time it appeared to be a very serious reaction to that Southampton performance. Lukaku and Pogba were again named among the substitutes. Twice United fell behind — once after De Gea effectively dropped the ball in his own net, and once after Rojo inadvertently directed a shot in; twice they equalised very quickly. Another 2-2 draw, this one decidedly more impressive than the last, considering the apprehensive way most United fans approached the match.

'As always we made mistakes and we paid for the mistakes,' said Mourinho. 'Today was more the same, but with great spirit and people ready to have a go and fight hard. It was a credit to the team. We scored four goals and drew 2-2! They went to the limit and were really tired. Some of them had not played all season, Chris Smalling playing in [a] very difficult condition, but Arsenal were only dangerous when we lost the ball in bad areas. Even from our bench you could feel the little panic when the ball comes to our defensive third. The spirit was Manchester United level but we miss certain qualities. I have to disagree with people who try to compare this to teams of Roy Keane, Ruud van Nistelrooy, Nemanja Vidic. Give us a break and time. I am happy with the soul and heart, but we are not consistent and uniform.'

Three days later, United put in their best display of the campaign, defeating Fulham 4-1 but playing some decent football in doing so. Paul Pogba was again on the bench but Romelu Lukaku — a Mourinho favourite — was back in the side and back in the goals.

On the day before the Fulham game, United, via *The Telegraph*, reportedly granted 'formal assurance' to Mourinho about the safety of his job. Mourinho's agent Jorge Mendes said: 'There have been more rumours of José Mourinho leaving Manchester United. It's totally untrue. José is very happy at the club and the club is very happy with him. He has a long-term contract with Manchester United and is fully committed to the club in building a solid winning project.'

Pogba was back in the team for the dead-rubber game against Valencia; dead rubber in the sense that United had already qualified, though it could have meant something, considering Juventus lost surprisingly against Young Boys. However, defeat in Spain meant Mourinho's team had to settle for the runners-up spot. Pogba was not particularly impressive but it remained to be seen how Mourinho would line up against Liverpool at Anfield. Could he afford to go without his best outfield player again? He certainly thought so.

In the press conference ahead of that game, he was asked how closely his United team resembled the image he wanted. 'Far,' he replied. 'A football team is not just about spending the money. A football team is like a house, too; a house is not just about buying the furniture. You have to do work in the house and when the house is ready, then you buy the furniture, you spend money on the best possible furniture and then you are ready to live in an amazing house.'

Earlier that week, it had been reported that Mourinho and Ed Woodward had met to discuss transfer targets for January, with the board prepared to bring in a defender. It was still suggested by some sections of the press that the manager had been advised that the board could still veto the choices made. Coming as those reports had at such a time, there was the acceptance that a change in management would not be made until the end of the season.

Just as they were at the Etihad, United were at the mercy of their hosts. Just as then, the game plan of the opponent was predictable, but Mourinho's team were simply willing prey. It seemed only a matter of time until the goal came, and when Sadio Mane reacted quicker than a prone United defence to a lofted ball in the 24th minute, it duly arrived. Nine minutes later and United had fortuitously equalised; goalkeeper Alisson fumbled a cross into the path of Jesse Lingard, who scored in front of the Kop.

At half-time, in need of some presence in the centre of the park, it was Fellaini and not Pogba who was brought on. In need of some unpredictability to stretch and test the home defence, Lukaku remained on the pitch while Anthony Martial sat on the bench until it was too late.

Liverpool won 3-1 but needed help from United's defence to achieve their further two goals, with defensive mistakes and deflections aplenty. Klopp's men were resorting to long-range efforts that were not troubling David de Gea; United sat further back still, inviting Liverpool closer to goal. The goals were made inevitable by Mourinho's decision to try and contain the opponent for the duration instead of giving them something to think about. Momentum being as key as it is in football, Liverpool — already in a rich vein of form and enjoying their football — were able to really enjoy the game, and United, who might have struggled to get something from the game even if they were at their strongest, were never able to make an imprint on the game even when changes were made.

The statistics after the game made grim reading. The 36 shots Liverpool had, which was the most a United team had faced since

Opta started recording such data in 2003, was not in itself an indictment, considering the hopeful and hopeless nature of at least half of those efforts. But it was the 19-point gap between Liverpool and United which hurt most, followed closely by the fact that the third goal became the 29th United had conceded in the league — that was one more than the entirety of the previous league campaign, 'achieved' in just 17 games. United were 11 points away from Chelsea, who had fourth spot.

For Mourinho, he had to confess that his team were second best. 'The strongest team won, but they won in the period when they were not stronger than us,' he claimed. 'In the first 20 minutes of the first half there was a huge distance. They were better and stronger, they did everything better than us. But in the moment when the game was going down, Liverpool's intensity was dying, the centre-backs were shooting from 30-40 metres because they could not find spaces in a dangerous area.'

At 9.45am on Tuesday, 18 December 2018, Manchester United issued a statement: 'Manchester United announces that manager Jose Mourinho has left the club with immediate effect. The club would like to thank Jose for his work during his time at Manchester United and to wish him success in the future. A new caretaker manager will be appointed until the end of the current season, while the club conducts a thorough recruitment process for a new, full-time manager.'

Timing

The only truly shocking thing about Jose Mourinho's departure from Manchester United, as it eventually transpired, was the timing of it. David Moyes and Louis van Gaal had only been dismissed after mathematical failure to qualify for the Champions League. It was suggested that would once more be the case, as United would stand to pay a much lower compensation sum if Mourinho failed to make the top four. To dismiss the manager in December was a statement in and of itself. It was an acceptance that it was a state of emergency at United. A look at the history of the timing of the mid-season post-war dismissals explains much. Wilf McGuinness and Frank O'Farrell were both dismissed in December; Ron Atkinson in November. Only David Moyes was given less than a year. In all of the above cases, it could be argued that United were not necessarily seeking to salvage something from the season. The problems at the club were far more grave than that; it was time for an emergency reset in order to concentrate on the most important thing.

That meant clinically cutting through that hierarchy and priority of the principles to get to the core of the matter; and it seemed to be that *the* most important quality had become the duty to entertain the supporters of Manchester United.

The toxicity at Old Trafford meant that comparisons between the Mourinho era and, for example, the Dave Sexton era were unfair to the latter even if the dull football was reminiscent. Sexton's only enemies, really, were those whose careers he had ended at the club, which is pretty much standard for any football manager. Mourinho didn't know who he could trust from players, to staff, to board level. Similarly, they didn't know if they could trust him.

In the difficult aftermath it was not straightforward to glean a positive perspective from Mourinho's reign. It was fair to say the club were no further advanced than the one he inherited, even if the journey they had been on in the duration could give the alternative argument. On one hand they had won trophies, one of them a European trophy, and had also achieved second place. Forget Mourinho's own protestations, there were enough bare facts to suggest, in his short reign, he could sit behind Busby and Ferguson as the club's most successful post-war coach. (This is not a statement of that fact, merely a suggestion that someone may hold that opinion.)

On the other hand, there was always the suggestion that United and Mourinho were oil and water, and that suggestion never went away. Mourinho, for his part, did not betray the youth policy at the club. He did not break the run of consecutive games going back before Busby where a young player developed by the club was part of the match-day squad, nor was his work on this front purely a token gesture. Marcus Rashford played more often for him than any other player. Jesse Lingard became a trusted player for the big occasion in a manner reminiscent of Darren Fletcher. Scott McTominay, despite the sour way it appeared that relationship ended, was promoted quicker than expected because of the raw qualities in his game that Mourinho liked in senior players. It's fair to say he might not have got those chances under another manager. He could have done more, but we would be dissecting a period of time which started with United finishing in second, barely strengthening in the summer and then struggling in the league just months later. If Mourinho had turned to youngsters en masse, it would have possibly been counter-productive to the development of those players anyway, and it would have felt like politicking at the worst possible time, just as it did with the repositioning of McTominay at centre-half.

The regression, and the scale of it, over the first half of the 2018/19 campaign was undoubtedly the major reason for Mourinho losing his job (as well as the negativity around the club). The likelihood of the form of the team turning around to such an extent that they could recover the 11-point gap between them and Chelsea in fourth place was clearly remote enough to justify the sacking.

United supporters might have grown frustrated and apathetic with the quality of football but it still seemed more a positive potential consequence of the change that they would see better football, rather than a terminal failure by which Mourinho was judged. Still — it was obvious that it was this basic principle the United fans were keen to see return to the club.

The favourite for the job at the time of the Newcastle game where it was first suggested that Mourinho's unemployment was imminent was Zinedine Zidane. The story went that he would be ably assisted by compatriot, and former United left-back, Patrice Evra, fuelled by the fact that Evra sat alongside Ed Woodward at several games. The fan's favourite was Mauricio Pochettino, the Tottenham manager who had seemingly excelled in most of the areas Mourinho had, objectively speaking, 'failed'.

Of course, speculation was raging about who would replace Mourinho within minutes of the news. In the first hour after news broke, United briefed that they would be making an imminent, interim appointment; that the caretaker manager would be someone who wasn't at the club, but was 'steeped in the history' of it.

By the end of the day it became clear that Ole Gunnar Solskjaer — the legendary striker who played for United between 1996 and 2008 — who was currently managing Norwegian side Molde, was the club's choice to steady the ship. Solskjaer had enjoyed a successful stint as reserve-team manager under Sir Alex Ferguson, but his only previous experience in the Premier League was with doomed Cardiff City. Cardiff were relegated under his watch. Manchester United had too much quality in their squad for the idea of a repeat of their own relegation in 1974 to be seriously entertained; the problem was that, after so many years of inconsistency, nobody was any the wiser of just how good the squad actually was.

When Skies
Are Grey...

The true test of how complex and political a mess the football operations of a club have become can be defined by the validity of the arguments on all sides. By May 2019 it was clear to see that amongst all the in-fighting between supporters who had been divided in their opinions about the merits of individual managers, all arguments had some merit and justification. If there is common ground to be found in these arguments then it is in grumbles about how the club has been run in the post-Sir Alex Ferguson era, be it by the Glazer family, Ed Woodward, or by a particular manager, or a combination thereof.

This book was written to analyse the footballing decisions more than it was to serve as a modern equivalent of Smith and Crick's important *Betrayal of a Legend*, though it has to be said there has to be some crossover; you cannot avoid the influence of the ownership on United's modern travails.

Their issues were given a harsher spotlight still by Manchester City's domestic treble success at the end of the 2018/19 season, while United limped to a sixth-place finish in the Premier League when it seemed Ole Gunnar Solskjaer had recovered the situation to make Champions League qualification a realistic goal.

Not winning the league can be explained away quickly by the financial muscle flexed by Manchester City, but Liverpool's own success (relatively speaking) in competing with them demonstrates what United were in prime position to do in the summer of 2018. Considering the resources available at Old Trafford, regardless of those that have been drained away out of the club, better could have been expected.

Solskjaer first faced the press on Friday, 21 December 2018, with the message very much one of the squad being much better than the league position, results and performances all suggested. Asked if he had any doubts when he was offered the job, the club legend smiled and insisted that was not the case. 'No, of course not, I didn't think twice when they called me to sign me as a player and this is more of an honour and privilege to be helping the club for a few months,' he said. 'It's until the summer now, five or six months to just help out in the meantime while the club does the process to get the next manager … When you get a job like this and they ask you to sign for six months you say "yeah, I'm happy to help out" and my job is to do as well as I can and they understand there are so many managers who would love to be manager of Manchester United. I'm one of them but it's not something we've talked about, they'll do a process for the next six months.'

Solskjaer had brought in Mike Phelan as his assistant alongside Michael Carrick and Kieran McKenna. When asked what his first impressions were of the squad he had inherited, he said the mood was good, and when asked about Paul Pogba in particular, he responded, 'It's about getting every player to the best, speaking to them on the training ground, philosophy, principles, how we want to play, it's not a matter of what team you're coaching, they all want to have a picture of how you want to play, they are quality players so it will be easier to get players expressing themselves.'

Solskjaer was asked about getting the club in to the top four and the style of play he would bring to the club. 'I think the first thing is the first game, think about getting my principles into the boys, get the players to understand how I want them to play and let's take the results later on to see how many points we can gather, but this club has made many, many points before but I'm not going to set that target now,' he said. 'You play with courage, go out there and express your skills, he said go out and express, take risks. The last game he [Sir Alex Ferguson] had as a manager was 5-5, that was almost the perfect end to him as a manager and I want the players to be similar, be the kids that love to play football and go out in front of the best fans in the world.'

Solskjaer's reign began with games against Cardiff City, Huddersfield Town and Bournemouth to see out 2018. There could barely have been three more accommodating fixtures, and yet United's form had been so erratic that you could not predict how it would go.

The first game at least went true to how you would normally expect a Cardiff City and Manchester United game to go, though for the travelling fans it had been a long time since they had witnessed something that was ostensibly so familiar. Marcus Rashford and Ander Herrera scored fantastic long-range goals but the most thrilling moment came when Anthony Martial, Paul Pogba and Jesse Lingard all combined in a fantastic move for Martial to score. United went on to score five times, the first time they had done so in the league for five and a half years (since Ferguson's last game!), but the style of football in the first half in particular was reminiscent of the early days of the 2011/12 season when Tom Cleverley, Anderson and Nani were all in such imperious form (indeed, Martial's goal was close in style to Nani's in the Community Shield of 2011). That such potential was capable was never in doubt; that it rarely showed itself gave cause for concern about a prevailing comparison of the respective trios in the inability to genuinely establish themselves as first-team players in a competitive squad.

Comprehensive wins over Huddersfield and Bournemouth followed. In terms of a run of good performances, this was as good as it would get for Solskjaer as the problems began to unravel themselves. For a while, results masked them. United won their first eight games under their interim boss, including a victory at Spurs in the league and Arsenal in the cup. The Spurs win was fortuitous. Solskjaer had seemingly got everything right on the night. He had appeared to settle on a defence of Young, Lindelof, Jones and Shaw and their consistency of form was reflective of their consistency of selection.

The midfield trio of Matic, Herrera and Pogba was combining to good effect. Solskjaer had boldly decided on the forward line of Lingard, Martial and Rashford, with the latter playing through the middle. Sanchez and Lukaku would have to be content with spots on the bench. At Wembley, though, Solskjaer played Lingard through the middle, confusing the Spurs defence, a tactic which worked when Paul Pogba's marvellous long pass was finished in style by Rashford, who had found space in the channel between centre-half and full-back. Despite Spurs battering United in the second half, De Gea was marvellous and kept a clean sheet.

A similar tactic worked at Arsenal in the cup with Lukaku seizing his chance from the right wing and Alexis Sanchez even getting on the scoresheet. It would be the Chilean's last goal of the season, but a 3-1 win suggested everything at the time was going in the right direction.

Though the transfer window was open, Solskjaer had expressed his intention to work with what he had; except, that is, for Marouane Fellaini, who was sold to Chinese club Shandong Luneng Taishan. The departure of the abrasive midfielder was seen as a momentous, overdue shift in direction in style at the club.

The run of wins ended with a 2-2 draw at home to Burnley. Even that had some positivity coming from it — United were 2-0 down in the 86th minute and still got a draw. Solskjaer had come in for criticism for playing Pereira and Mata, as if he was taking a good Burnley team lightly, but the 28 shots on goal and 75 per cent possession suggested the United boss hadn't got it wrong.

The first mumblings of discontent came against Paris in the Champions League. The build-up to the game had seen speculation that Solskjaer's very future depended on the outcome of the tie. The French side were shorn of their star man Neymar, but in Kylian Mbappe they possessed the player tipped by most to be the next generation's Ronaldo or Messi. United would be up against it even at full strength but had to play Bailly instead of Jones (not necessarily the worst swap, but, considering Jones's recent form and Bailly's relative ring-rust, hardly ideal) and were hampered further when Lingard and Martial were both injured in the latter stages of a competitive first half. It was a tough experience for Solskjaer, whose entire game plan depended on those two players doing some hard running in a style one wouldn't expect of the replacements Lukaku and Mata. The truth was that United were struggling anyway, but the changes really ruined any chances of getting a positive result. First of all, Presnel Kimpembe (who was fortunate to be on the pitch after a number of yellow card-worthy challenges) scored with a header, before Mbappe got in front of Bailly to make it two. A bad night became much worse when Pogba was dismissed late on.

'Today is a reality check for us,' admitted Solskjaer. 'They had the momentum after the first goal and controlled the game. You could see that we hadn't played at this level for a while and we will have to learn from this. It was an experience that can go either way, it's not going to be a season-defining one, it's one we have to learn from. First half there was nothing in it, but once they scored, they had the experience to play it out. We have not played games at this level for a while and that was clear to see.'

The Norwegian refused to admit total defeat just yet: 'Mountains are there to be climbed,' he declared. 'Just because you are down, you can't say it is over. We have to go down there and play a good game. It was a reality check from the top teams.'

Martial and Lingard were missing for the fifth-round FA Cup clash at Stamford Bridge against Chelsea but once more Solskjaer's tactical shift — playing Mata in a midfield diamond on a tight pitch — worked wonders, with United winning at the Blues for the first time since Ferguson's tenure.

The next test would be Liverpool, high-flying and in great form, with only one defeat all season. Nemanja Matic was injured in training the day before the game so Solskjaer called upon Scott McTominay. Jesse Lingard was rushed back from his hamstring injury for a place on the bench.

In the opening three minutes of the match Marcus Rashford pulled up with a muscle injury but stayed on. In the 21st minute, Herrera had to come off for Pereira, and four minutes later Juan Mata was hurt by Mohamed Salah and had to be withdrawn. Solskjaer gambled and put on Lingard instead of Sanchez. It almost worked — Lingard had United's best chance, but, when trying to snatch at the rebound of it, tweaked his hamstring and he had to be brought off just 22 minutes after coming on. United remarkably not only held on for a goalless draw, but looked the more likely to win the game with the better chances.

With the return leg against Paris approaching, Solskjaer had to use the game against Southampton to give some chances to players who would be brought out of the shadows, such as the Brazilian midfielder Fred, and youngster Tahith Chong, while Diogo Dalot was brought on as a winger. The Saints were game opposition and deserved something from the match, but Pereira's stunning equaliser and Lukaku's late winner sent United to France in good spirits. Solskjaer described the victory as 'just like the old days' and United had somehow clawed back their deficit to be in fourth place, ahead of Arsenal and Chelsea who still had games against Ole's team. With nine games left, Solskjaer could now feel it was reasonable to expect his team to make a good challenge of qualification for the Champions League. Certainly, that was the mood at the club; this writer was present at an event where one former player who had been in Solskjaer's company stated that Ed Woodward had reassured him that there was no expectation on United to finish in the top four due to the position they were in when he came in, and the success of the job he did would not be defined by a top-four finish. There was a growing clamour for Solskjaer to be given the job on a permanent basis because the results so far had been championship-contending form.

Solskjaer was missing a number of senior players but was hopeful of a miracle in Paris. 'We can't write games off, we've been fantastic away from home,' said Solskjaer. 'We're not going to go out without giving a fight. We're going to go out there and enjoy the game. We know it's a difficult place to come and they played really well at Old Trafford, so it's a great challenge for our players to go out there and show what they can do. We'd rather win 4-2 than try to get a 2-0. We've got to get to half-time better off than we are now. If you can get to 1-0 at half-time then anything can happen in the second half.'

In fact, United got to half-time with a 2-1 lead. Romelu Lukaku scored a brace either side of Bernat's equaliser to give the travelling support a sudden belief in the unbelievable. Whilst nobody would ever want to see a player injured, the erratic Bailly's withdrawal in the 35th minute proved a pivotal moment. The Ivorian had struggled hugely with Angel Di Maria so a change in shape and the introduction of Diogo Dalot provided balance, potency and a reason for the former United winger to look backwards.

In the 80th minute, Solskjaer withdrew Pereira — who had done a commendable job — for Chong, and in the 87th, Young was replaced by teenager Mason Greenwood. It was an ambitious attempt to unsettle a fairly nervous but not exactly rocking home team. In injury time, Dalot won a corner when his shot was deflected behind by Kimpembe. Or so it seemed. The referee checked the VAR system and changed the decision to a penalty kick for handball.

At 2-1, with such a weakened team, Solskjaer was already on the brink of a famous and highly commendable result. Marcus Rashford — who had grown into the star player in this interim run so far — showed nerves of steel to step up and take the penalty. The Manchester-born forward smashed the ball past legendary goalkeeper Gianluigi Buffon to put this game down in the history books as one of the greatest European nights for Manchester United.

Solskjaer was clearly delighted. 'It's this club. It's what we do, that's Man United,' he said. 'It's a typical Manchester United night. We had a game plan and the belief in the boys was what we hoped for. Everyone shares the huge pride. The players were really great. They were focussed, they listened to all the instructions like in training, and on the pitch they knew that we had to defend well. There was a lot of quality.'

Ole's former team-mate Rio Ferdinand led the chorus of the voices demanding that the interim appointment should be made permanent. 'I didn't have the confidence in these boys to do it, ten boys out, I didn't see this result coming with the way PSG played in the first leg,' Ferdinand said on BT Sport. 'Ole Gunnar Solskjaer was brave with his team selection, he had three teenagers on the pitch, the character of these players after the starvation of moments like this. The confidence this will give them. Ole has brought belief back to this team. People were doubting Lukaku — he's one of many who has been given a new lease of life.'

There was no doubting that Lukaku had been in good form of late, but it remained to be seen how Solskjaer would approach matters once players were available again. The Paris game was followed by a defeat at Arsenal in a blow to those Champions League hopes (it also ended a club record of consecutive away wins, with nine being accomplished since Solskjaer took over) but United fans, with their tempered and revised expectations, were generally more hopeful of a win in their next game against Wolves in the FA Cup. Knocking out Arsenal and Chelsea along the way made it feel as if United could be headed for glory and the team was boosted by the return of a number of players — Herrera, Matic and Pogba in midfield and Lingard and Martial up front.

Unfortunately it was a tremendously flat performance and Wolves found themselves 2-0 up, deservedly so. Rashford's late consolation came from their only real opening of the game and the exit at the quarter-final stage summed up a poor few days. Remote hopes of a Champions League and FA Cup double had been dashed by this exit and the quarter-final draw in Europe, which pitted United against Barcelona.

The international break came at a convenient time for all at Old Trafford to take stock. With just a creak in the form, the hint of bad habits creeping back in, United made the decision to appoint Solskjaer on a permanent basis in the hope that they might generate the same sort of bounce in form to see out the season.

The announcement was made public two days before United were due to face Watford at Old Trafford. 'This is the job that I always dreamed of doing and I'm beyond excited to have the chance to lead the club long term,' Solskjaer said, as it was confirmed he would be given a three-year contract. 'From the first day I arrived, I felt at home at this special club. It was an honour to be a Manchester United player, and then to start my coaching career here. The last few months have been a fantastic experience.'

Executive vice-chairman Ed Woodward also spoke, declaring Solskjaer's appointment 'richly deserved'. 'Since coming in as caretaker manager in December, the results Ole has delivered speak for themselves,' Woodward said. 'More than just performances and results, Ole brings a wealth of experience, both as a player and as a coach, coupled with a desire to give young players their chance and a deep understanding of the culture of the club.'

Also in the international break, David Moyes spoke to beIN SPORTS about his time at United, insisting events since his sacking proved the issues with the post-Ferguson transition were deeper than most realised. Moyes claimed that he had been involved in serious talks to try and sign Gareth Bale in 2013 and even confirmed that he and Woodward had a helicopter on standby if Bale changed his mind about going to Madrid. He said Cesc Fabregas was 'very close' to signing and that Toni Kroos had agreed to sign for the club. This came after Peter Schmeichel, the legendary goalkeeper, had told the same television network that he believed Moyes should have been given more time.

There were plenty with concerns still about Solskjaer — one being his capability to attract big names, just as Moyes had failed to do so, particularly if the club were unable to qualify for the Champions League. The concerns were more deeply founded for some. Whilst most observers would agree that Solskjaer had enjoyed a brilliant start, breaking and setting some club records along the way, the truth is that after those first three games the quality of performances had dropped off.

As early as January, Solskjaer had identified the fitness levels within the squad as a potential reason for their underperformance. 'We can get fitter and we have to do that through the training sessions here, but Dubai is a good chance because now is the first time we get a week of work together,' Solskjaer said ahead of a spell of warm-weather training. 'The ones who have not been in the squad have worked on their fitness.'

This feeling was borne out by the positive starts United would make in matches only to fade away; something that would certainly be a prominent issue in the run-in. United were able to squeeze a 2-1 win from a poor performance at home to Watford but a bright start at Molineux, which saw Scott McTominay score a fine goal — his first for the club — quickly fell away and Wolves got their second win in just a couple of weeks against United. It was hardly ideal preparation for the runaround Solskjaer's team were likely to get against Barcelona, and the Spaniards exerted their experience and dominance well, winning comfortably over both legs to end hopes of a miracle. The 3-0 defeat at the Nou Camp was seen as humbling but it was nothing compared to what followed in the next game at Goodison Park, where United were crushed 4-0 in arguably their worst performance in the post-Ferguson era.

Suddenly, the wisdom of appointing Solskjaer before the summer was called into question. 'From the first whistle, everything went wrong,' Solskjaer told Sky Sports. 'I just want to apologise to the fans. They're the only people with the badge on today who can hold their head high, because we can't. We just didn't perform. That was not worthy of a Manchester United team. That performance is not good enough for a Manchester United team, from me to players, we let the fans down, we let the club down. That performance is difficult to describe because it is so bad. They beat us on all the basics. We were beaten on all the ingredients you need, added to the talent. There is no place you can hide on the pitch. We hold our hands up and apologise to everyone associated with the club. We have a perfect chance to make amends on Wednesday.'

Solskjaer — who later repeated the point about poor fitness levels — had made changes from the tired team that lost to Barcelona, but in both games he had played Victor Lindelof (the best defender) at right-back, whilst persisting with Smalling and Jones in defence. The English pair had emerged as reliable alternatives to United's foreign options (aside from Lindelof) but their poor performances at Goodison Park came as no surprise. Furthermore, after initially finding systems that worked, it was fair to question Solskjaer for returning to use the same players who had proven themselves to not be at the standard United required them to be moving forward. The Norwegian had the benefit of the doubt of this being a squad he inherited and one he was stuck with until the summer but, nonetheless, playing Lindelof wide to accommodate weaker defenders was a black mark against the manager.

As usual in these dark days, though, the problems did not start and end with the defenders. United did not create a chance of note despite starting with Pogba, Matic, Fred, Rashford, Lukaku and Martial.

Martial in particular had concerned supporters with his downturn in form; having been a name 'at risk' under Mourinho, and a player that supporters backed in the row between squad and manager, the Frenchman penned a new contract in January to signal that he would now be happy to remain and play his best football. It hadn't quite worked out like that. But even Martial's poor showing wasn't enough to take the spotlight away from Paul Pogba, whose performance was probably his worst for the club.

Not for the first time this season, Pogba put it down to attitude. 'The way we played and the performance of myself, of the team, of everyone is disrespectful,' the midfielder told Sky Sports. 'Everything went wrong, but the mentality on the pitch has to change. The fans want a reaction from the players and the only way to apologise to them is to give everything on the pitch. That's how we should apologise to the fans, just to give everything for the club, for the shirt, for the team-mates and for ourselves because we can't perform like we did. We can lose games, but with a good performance and pride. When you wear this shirt, you have to work and respect the culture, the history of this club and give everything. We didn't respect ourselves, the club or the fans. What we did on the pitch is not respectful for the team-mates, for the staff, for the people, for the kit man, for everyone.'

United were marginally better in their following game, against Manchester City, but it spoke volumes about the regression in just one year that they were so far behind on the night. The match was preceded by footage of a leak in the Old Trafford roof allowing rain to cascade on to the stand. The comparisons about investment in the respective clubs ran deep into the very core.

It had been an odd game where supporters resented the situation they were in; victory would keep their hopes of a top-four finish alive but would hand Liverpool a huge advantage in the title race. Defeat and City would have an advantage and would close in on becoming the first team to win the domestic treble. Some United fans confessed to being happy if City won, but they wouldn't have left Old Trafford pleased to see their team outclassed by two clear goals.

Still, the bumpy form of the other contenders for the top four meant United welcomed Chelsea to Old Trafford knowing a win would put them in control of their own destiny with favourable games against Huddersfield and Cardiff, both relegated, to close the season. It was a familiar story as United started well and scored through Juan Mata before a David de Gea error allowed Chelsea to equalise; 1-1, and those Champions League hopes all but over.

Another 1-1 draw followed at Huddersfield with another dismal performance; United supporters could not wait for the season to end and it spoke volumes that the 2-0 defeat to Cardiff on the final day was as expected as it was humiliating. United ended the season in sixth. 'Today was not the problem,' Solskjaer said after the last game. 'You can have all the possession and chances you want but we concede easy goals and don't score at the other end. We have a long and hard way to be where we want to be. It will take some time to close in on the top, we finished five or six points behind third, fourth, fifth and that has to be our aim. The top two teams have set a standard higher than before and we have to take up the next challenge. The work starts now. Everyone has the summer off but we have to come back with a different mentality and different attitude of being a Man United team. The ones who played did well but it was not good enough.'

Later in May, Jose Mourinho spoke to *L'Equipe*, telling the French publication that he believed more strongly now than ever in his statement that his second-place achievement with United had been his 'greatest'. He said that people now understood, having witnessed what had happened to the club.

'I don't want to be the nice guy,' he said. 'Because the nice guy, after three months, is a puppet and that doesn't end well. When you are almost alone, in that you don't have the support of the club close to you, while certain players go somewhat against the coach, who is the nice guy? When I say that the second season was fantastic, I say it because the potential and the objectives were met. I really squeezed, like an orange, to achieve them.'

Mourinho was asked directly if he was referring to Paul Pogba when he said 'certain players', but he said that he meant others as well as Pogba. It was a blistering interview from Mourinho and it did have some uncomfortable truths within.

Was Solskjaer the 'nice guy'? Certainly in Mourinho's eyes, but in the scenario with United's issues? Well, it could be argued to be the case, as this was an individual who would not only curry favour with supporters but also be one that would be so grateful for the opportunity that he would not be as resentful of Ed Woodward's influence and suggestions as Mourinho clearly had been. The talk of a director of football, or sporting director, or some other person acting in some other role which would effectively be an intermediary between Woodward and the manager, continued. Names like Rio Ferdinand and Darren Fletcher were mentioned. Names like Gary Neville and Paul Scholes, who have been critical of the way the club is run, were not. Solskjaer, a modern coach, did not seem averse to this talk. Cynics wonder if it would be a case of too many cooks, another cog in a network where ultimately one man — Woodward — retains full responsibility.

While it remains a reasonable conclusion to say Solskjaer would not contest certain decisions with Woodward because of the opportunity he had been given, it is also true enough to say that supporters, as they have been for the last few years, are acutely aware of the decisions made in terms of hierarchy. They may have been divided over Jose Mourinho but are united (pardon the pun) enough to know the issues caused by the running of the club in the post-Ferguson era.

There was concern expressed over Solskjaer's inexperience and the timing of his permanent appointment, but the club legend had served an interim period and had demonstrated a capability to improve the standard of play, and also a tactical nous to achieve wonderful results. There was little else he could have done; and, once the problems that everyone was aware of anyway began to resurface, the logical thing to do from that point is to give him the chance to identify and resolve them.

Was Mourinho right about the players? Again, you can't dispute some of what appears to be the truth — Solskjaer had expressed frustration on numerous occasions, but had used poor fitness as a reason for more than one performance. Paul Pogba had, however, confessed that attitude played a major part in poor performances at the start and end of the season. Even the best managers can only be partly responsible for the attitude and ability of their players, and if neither attribute is positive for the squad then it becomes time for those players to leave. Some would argue that United have so many players who fit in that category that it is unreasonable for the issue to be fixed in a single transfer window and maybe that is a fair evaluation.

In early June 2019, Louis van Gaal gave an interview to *The Guardian* where he openly discussed his issues with the club, admitting he felt 'betrayed' by the way he was sacked, and suggesting that he was not given the backing he needed to succeed. The Dutch coach claimed that Wayne Rooney was 'over the hill' and that the issue of United's style of play was never discussed with him when he took the job.

'I didn't always get the players that I want,' he said. 'That's the problem. There is Woodward and his right hand is [head of corporate development] Matt Judge. Judge I met once in a while but not too much. And there was the head of scouting. That was the structure but you are always dependent on Woodward and Judge … I thought always Manchester United can buy every player because they have a lot of power. Seemingly a few players were not reachable for Manchester United. I cannot understand but it was like that.'

Van Gaal claimed that Angel Di Maria, for example, was not a player he had identified for the club to sign : 'I was satisfied, because he was a creative player, but I had other players on the list. Di María had a problem with the English football culture and the climate. You cannot buy players and know, for sure, that they can deliver. You cannot know because football is a team sport.'

One could reason that a major issue still facing the club is the apparent lack of a transfer strategy. The club's issues going forward are compounded by the status of the big contracts some of their more well-paid players have been on. The time of writing and the time of print (just before the end of the transfer deadline) means some change will happen but the scale of it is unpredictable and influenced heavily by the contract Alexis Sanchez is on. United are keen to offload the former Arsenal man in order to make their negotiations easier but, however it affects transfers moving forward, it has also had an impact on existing negotiations.

Sanchez's peripheral contribution means that United's star names demanded parity or huge increases in their own salary. Ander Herrera left the club, Martial's increase was from a reported £150,000 a week to £250,000 a week, whilst the biggest issue the club have had is in trying to convince David de Gea to sign a new deal. The Spaniard reportedly wanted the same contract as Sanchez, his position undeterred by the club's insistence that they were moving Sanchez on.

United had allegedly offered De Gea a world-record salary for a goalkeeper but this had not encouraged him to sign an extension. With his contract due to expire in 2020, the crossroads of a decision to cash in or risk losing him for nothing loomed large. Marcus Rashford, whose early form under Solskjaer had tapered off with the forward certainly looking tired at the end of the campaign, was reportedly asking for a contract similar to Martial's. Some supporters were agitated by this — even De Gea's own form towards the end of the season left some wondering why he felt justified in demanding such a high salary, but the prevailing feeling was one of concern that United had to address their own top players' futures before knowing what they were dealing with in terms of incomings.

'After a turbulent season, everyone at Manchester United is focussed on building towards the success that this great club expects and our fans deserve,' Ed Woodward said in May 2019, as the club announced an increase in revenue on a conference call to investors. 'Preparations for the new season are underway and the underlying strength of our business will allow us to support the manager and his team as we look to the future. The season clearly didn't end as we hoped, and with a disruptive managerial change midway through. The last few weeks were disappointing, but we are delighted to appoint Ole, Mike, Michael and Kieran. We look to continue to improve staff both on and off the pitch.'

The 2018/19 campaign ended with Woodward's own reputation on the line; he was, after all, the man with the track record of making these managerial appointments. However convenient Solskjaer may or may not have been in terms of an appointment, should it go wrong then supporters will be quicker to point the finger at the running of the club than they will a legend of it.

The truth is that there is no obvious sign of the direction Manchester United are heading in, and if pushed, even if they felt strongly enough to feel positive about Solskjaer, supporters are more inclined to be pessimistic due to the ownership of the club. Rumours of a Saudi takeover do not bring optimism; the political controversy surrounding the Manchester City owners is one headache United supporters do not wish to entertain, and consequently they feel stuck between a rock and a hard place.

Early rumours of young British talent being brought in seem encouraging, as did those early performances where commitment, energy, speed and aggression all seemed to be on show. The manager seemed as furious as the supporters were at Everton in April 2019, which was just about the nadir of this post-May 2013 journey where all of those listed attributes were missing; but even if it was the sort of performance that wouldn't be tolerated, it was the sort United fans had almost become used to, and the sort which you couldn't rule out happening again.

A writer must attempt to find some tone in a conclusion and so let us wish for a positive outcome, whilst stopping short of making a positive prediction, for Ole Gunnar Solskjaer's Manchester United. Certainly, on the criteria of 'getting' the club, there are few better qualified candidates for the job, and one cannot simply discount the importance of this attribute as it has emerged as the most important of all to supporters throughout the last few years.

United have gone through a number of coaches of different profiles; the hungry, homegrown coach, the experienced continental legend, and the best available (open to interpretation, of course). The club has undergone attempts to change style, though the 'total football' approach is perhaps a little closer to the identity of Manchester United than people give credit (Rinus Michels was a 'student' of Jimmy Hogan, as was Jimmy Murphy, as was Tommy Docherty, as was Ron Atkinson, as was Louis van Gaal). That style is open to interpretation and of course there has always been some compromise with it when it has been successful at Old Trafford.

In a book that took six years to write in the hope of arriving at a conclusion, it is a sign of the times that there is instead a question which remains as prominent as ever. It remains to be seen what long-term plans Solskjaer has and how closely they resemble the glorious tradition of the past, but he is, at least, more in tune with what that tradition is than his post-Ferguson predecessors were. He is, if you like, 'cut from the same cloth' as the club. Will that be the factor which finally makes the difference in re-establishing Manchester United as the force they once were?

Acknowledgements

Thanks first to Dave Murphy, you are less a friend and more a brother. Your support has meant everything to me.

Thanks to Dan Burdett for always being there at a moment's notice to check or verify something.

Thanks to all the people who have been supportive, in no particular order : Kim Burdett, the Winstons, Nipun Chopra, Matt Galea, Tyler Dunne, Michael Pieri, Stel Stylianou, Michael Garvey, Jon Wilson, Richard Fenton, Oyvind Enger, Tom Warren (Tam), Eifion Evans. Thanks to Gordon Hill and Paul Parker who have indulged me for the duration of this period.

Thanks to Paul Camillin and Jane Camillin for their faith in this book. Thanks to Duncan Olner, and to Cal Gildart.

Special thanks as always to my incredible wife, whose support I could not live without. Thank you to my family. To Freddy and Noah, who are our everything.

Thanks to you for reading!